THE LETTERS

OF

RICHARD HENRY LEE

VOLUME I

1762–1778

A Da Capo Press Reprint Series

THE ERA OF THE AMERICAN REVOLUTION

GENERAL EDITOR: LEONARD W. LEVY

Brandeis University

THE LETTERS

OF

RICHARD HENRY LEE

COLLECTED AND EDITED BY
JAMES CURTIS BALLAGH

VOLUME I
1762–1778

DA CAPO PRESS · NEW YORK · 1970

A Da Capo Press Reprint Edition

This Da Capo Press edition of *The Letters of Richard Henry Lee*
is an unabridged republication of the first edition published in
New York in 1911 and 1914.

Library of Congress Catalog Card Number 79-107678

SBN 306-71894-4

Published by Da Capo Press
A Division of Plenum Publishing Corporation
227 West 17th Street, New York, N.Y. 10011

Manufactured in the United States of America

THE LETTERS

OF

RICHARD HENRY LEE

VOLUME I

1762–1778

RICHARD HENRY LEE

THE LETTERS

OF

RICHARD HENRY LEE

COLLECTED AND EDITED BY

JAMES CURTIS BALLAGH, Ph.D., LL.D.

ASSOCIATE PROFESSOR OF AMERICAN HISTORY IN THE
JOHNS HOPKINS UNIVERSITY

VOLUME I

1762–1778

New York

THE MACMILLAN COMPANY

1911

Published under the Auspices of the National Society
of the Colonial Dames of America

Norwood Press
J. S. Cushing Co. — Berwick & Smith Co.
Norwood, Mass., U.S.A.

To

MY WIFE

WHOSE AID AND SYMPATHY HAVE LIGHTENED

MY TASK

AND MADE THIS WORK

POSSIBLE

PREFACE

RICHARD HENRY LEE, sometime President of the Continental Congress and mover of the resolutions for a Declaration of Independence, Foreign Alliances, and a Plan of Confederation, exerted a profound influence upon political and constitutional movements in his State and in America from the beginning of the Stamp Act agitation to the close of his public career in 1792. His life was devoted to the service of the public and to preserving and developing political liberty as he and Patrick Henry and Samuel Adams understood it. His constant and arduous labor as an active patriot leader in his county of Westmoreland, as a Virginia Burgess and Assemblyman, and as a member of the Continental Congress and of the United States Senate throughout an entire generation of unselfish public service finally destroyed his health and led to the ultimate sacrifice of his life in 1794, at the comparatively early age of sixty-two years; a debt paid to his tireless loyalty to his country's good. Probably no member of Congress, unless it be John Adams, served in a more important capacity and on so many and such effective committees of Congress, and at the same time maintained such literary activity as is shown in his extensive correspondence. Despite these facts and his contemporary fame as an orator and statesman and the interest and value of the letters written by him during this critical period of American affairs, no attempt at anything like a comprehensive collection of these letters appears to have been hitherto made, and his services and name have been almost forgotten by the public.

PREFACE

It has been the editor's agreeable task to discover, during a search covering a period of several years, and bring together for preservation in these volumes reliable texts, in most cases taken from original manuscripts or transcripts, of as many letters of historical importance as possible that are of the indisputable authorship of Richard Henry Lee. Of about 500 letters here collected the majority have never been printed, and the larger portion of those that have previously appeared in print have for half a century been practically inaccessible to the public. The *Memoir of the Life of Richard Henry Lee, and his Correspondence* by his grandson, Richard H. Lee, in two volumes, published in 1825, contains only some 70 letters written by Richard Henry Lee mingled in chronological disorder with more than twice this number written to him, and was intended more as a biography than as an edition of his letters. A still smaller number of the letters now long out of print in the *Southern Literary Messenger*, *The Virginia Historical Register*, and half a dozen other publications, when compared with the original manuscripts, have been found to be so inaccurate in text, that, like many of those of the "*Memoir*," they are unsafe for the student to use. Printed letters with a trustworthy text are so few or so scattered amongst publications like W. W. Henry's *Patrick Henry*, *The* [*Charles*] *Lee Papers*, and *The Deane Papers* as to be practically useless. In these cases where the manuscript was discovered and permission to consult it was granted, the letter has been reprinted from the manuscript in order to preserve any variations that the text contains.

Though a small portion of what was apparently his letter book survives, Lee seems either not to have made or not to have kept together a very large collection of his papers. He unfortunately had neither Franklin's genius for hoarding, nor his brother Arthur's faculty for

PREFACE

preserving, data of a personal character. Much that survives was kept by his correspondents and is widely scattered. However, two aggregations of miscellaneous Lee-family papers existed which contained a number of Richard Henry's letters. The first of these, made generally known by his grandson and biographer, was dispersed by him and deposited in the libraries of Harvard College, the American Philosophical Society, and the University of Virginia. Through the courtesy of the authorities of these institutions, in the order named, free access for purposes of transcription and comparison was readily granted to these "Lee Papers" and to other manuscript collections, such as those of Jared Sparks at Harvard and the Franklin Papers at the American Philosophical Society; and for personal attentions and aid the writer is particularly indebted to Professor Albert Bushnell Hart, and Mr. William Coolidge Lane, the Librarian, of Harvard University; Dr. I. Minis Hays, the Librarian of the American Philosophical Society; and Mr. Armistead C. Gordon, the Rector, Professors Richard Heath Dabney and Charles W. Kent, and Mr. John S. Patton, the Librarian, of the University of Virginia.

A second aggregation of "Lee Papers" of equal importance, including "Lee Transcripts," some of them of manuscripts lost in the fire at the University of Virginia that consumed its library building, was the gift of Mr. Cassius F. Lee of Alexandria to the Virginia Historical Society. These manuscripts were generously opened to my use by the Executive Committee of the Society, and it is a pleasure here to express my many obligations for kindnesses and valuable assistance rendered by the efficient Secretary, Mr. W. G. Stanard, and the Assistant Secretary, Mrs. Sally Nelson Robins, of that Society.

Professor William Shippen, Jr., M.D., of Philadelphia,

PREFACE

preserved, as did Samuel Adams, much of his correspondence with Lee, and a large number of Lee's letters, illustrating the personal as well as the political side of his life, have been found among the valuable papers of the Shippen family inherited and owned by the great-great-grandson of Professor Shippen and his wife Alice, a sister of Richard Henry Lee, Dr. Lloyd Parker Shippen of the United States Navy, and in the possession of his mother, Mrs. Edward Shippen of Baltimore. By their kind liberality, and the active aid of Mrs. Shippen in the search through her collections, these letters were made available to the editor, who, together with Dr. and Mrs. Shippen, examined in their original folders more than one thousand manuscript letters of the Shippen and Lee families.

A yet larger number of letters in the aggregate than those obtained from these three sources were, by a further personal search, found scattered through various manuscript collections in national and state archives, public and private libraries, state historical societies, and in individual ownership. For the courtesy and efficient help of their custodians and owners the editor owes a debt he can scarcely hope to pay by his grateful acknowledgments.

His greatest debt, however, is to Dr. J. Franklin Jameson, Director of the Department of Historical Research of the Carnegie Institution of Washington, without whose interest, encouragement, and valuable advice this collection would probably never have been completed or presented to the public. He not only supplied the funds from his Department for a search and collection of the letters found in Washington, but presented copies of important letters from time to time, called attention to the existence of others, and, through the kind offices of Mr. Waldo G. Leland, secured accurate copies of letters that the editor desired from the archives in Paris. At almost every stage of this work his kind and practical help has been of inestimable value.

Similarly Mr. Worthington C. Ford, while Chief of the Division of Manuscripts in the Library of Congress, and later as Editor of Publications of the Massachusetts Historical Society, has been unfailing in his kindnesses and aid by gifts of several transcripts of his own, by securing copies of other letters, and by suggesting possible and valuable sources of letters besides making available the manuscripts under his charge. From those in the Library of Congress, especially from the manuscript papers of Washington, Jefferson, Madison, and Monroe, and those of the Continental Congress, was obtained a large number of important texts.

A like search among the archives of the Department of State was most kindly permitted and facilitated in every way possible by Mr. William McNeir, and Mr. John A. Tonner of the Bureau of Rolls and Library. Though many letters were there found, signed by Lee's name, as well as by those of one or more other members of the Committee of Secret Correspondence or of the Committee of Foreign Affairs, they were either original clerical drafts or not in Lee's handwriting, and therefore could not be included among a collection of papers of his undoubted authorship. As most of them have been printed by Francis Wharton in his *Diplomatic Correspondence of the American Revolution*, their omission here seems abundantly justified.

Dr. John S. Billings, Director of the "New York Public Library, Astor, Lenox, and Tilden Foundations," most courteously permitted the use of the rich and varied collections in his charge, and every facility for the prosecution of the work was rendered by Mr. Wilberforce Eames, Librarian of the Lenox branch, and his experienced assistants, Mr. Victor H. Paltsits, now

PREFACE

State Historian, and Mr. Curtis. The Bancroft, Ford, Emmet, and Myers collections yielded a large number of valuable letters of Lee, none being more valuable than those among the "Samuel Adams Papers."

Another important source of Lee's letters was found in the Henry Laurens manuscript papers in the Long Island Historical Society, and these were kindly made available through the courtesy of Mr. Bryan H. Smith, Chairman of the Executive Committee, and Miss Emma Toedteberg, Librarian of the Society. By a like kindness of the authorities and the Librarian, Mr. Robert H. Kelby, of the New York Historical Society, a still further addition, greatly appreciated, was made to the collection.

Mr. Charles Francis Adams most generously had copies made of the letters of Lee found in the valuable papers of the Adams family, and presented them to the editor. Through the kindness of Dr. Samuel Abbott Green, permission was given to make copies of several letters found in the rare manuscript collections of the Massachusetts Historical Society under his charge. From the Mellen Chamberlain collection of manuscripts in the Boston Public Library the texts of several letters were obtained through the suggestions of Mr. Lindsay Swift and the kindness of the official custodians. Appreciative thanks are also due to the Secretary of the Commonwealth of Massachusetts for permission to search the Massachusetts Archives and to copy valuable letters found there. Mr. Albert C. Bates, Librarian of the Connecticut Historical Society, allowed a prolonged search through the numerous manuscripts in the Roger Wolcott, Oliver Wolcott, Jeremiah Wadsworth, Silas and Simeon Deane and other collections under his charge, and though the result was meager as to letters of Lee, the editor's appreciation of this personal courtesy is none the less great.

PREFACE

Dr. John W. Jordan, Librarian of the Pennsylvania Historical Society, made available the rich collections under his charge, and the great obligations of the editor to him for access to the manuscripts in the Dreer, Sprague, Etting, Conarroe, McKean, and Society Collections are gladly acknowledged. From the transcripts of the Langdon Papers, also in that society, important letters were obtained. In the Ridgway Branch of the Library Company of Philadelphia through the good offices of Mr. Bunford Samuel, the Librarian, several interesting letters here included were found. Through the courtesy of Mr. J. G. Rosengarten and the kindness of the Librarian of the University of Pennsylvania, permission was given to search the Franklin manuscripts in that library, but no letter of Lee's certain authorship was found. Through the kind suggestion of Dr. Edmund C. Burnett, of the Carnegie Institution of Washington, some important letters were located in the valuable Charles Roberts Autograph collection of Haverford College, Pennsylvania, and accurate copies of these were furnished through the courteous Librarian of the College, Professor Allen C. Thomas.

To Mr. Richard H. Spencer, the Corresponding Secretary and Librarian, and to the other officers of the Maryland Historical Society, the editor is indebted for several letters from the Samuel Purviance Papers, and his especial thanks are also due to Dr. H. R. McIlwaine, Librarian, and Dr. H. J. Eckenrode, Archivist, of the Virginia State Library, for the willingness with which they made accessible the Executive Communications and other manuscripts under their care, and for the verification by Dr. Eckenrode of the text of several letters elsewhere that the editor could not personally compare. From the Henry Laurens collection in the South Carolina Historical Society was obtained a single letter to Laurens through the kindness of Miss Mabel

PREFACE

L. Webber, the Secretary of the Society. Through the good offices of Mr. Nathan Goold, the Librarian of the Maine Historical Society, came several valuable letters contained in the Fogg collection. In the John Carter Brown Library the editor was kindly permitted by the Librarian, Mr. George Parker Winship, to transcribe several letters from Lee. Through the kindness of Professor Charles M. Andrews of the Johns Hopkins University, a valuable letter was obtained from the manuscripts of the Marquis of Lansdowne, and the editor is further indebted to him for his constant interest and fruitful suggestions at various stages of this work. The Proprietor of the "Sun Inn" of Bethlehem, Pennsylvania, generously contributed a facsimile of an interesting letter written by Lee.

To Mrs. A. Morris Tyson and to her father, Mr. Joseph Packard of Baltimore, a great-great-grandson of Richard Henry Lee, the editor is under especial obligations for some rare and important Lee letters.

Grateful acknowledgment is also made to the Officials and Librarians of the following institutions where a fruitless personal search was allowed through valuable manuscript collections: the Library of the Boston Athenæum; of the Essex Institute at Salem, by the courtesy of the Secretary, Mr. George Francis Dow; of the American Antiquarian Society at Worcester, Massachusetts, through the kindness of Mr. Edmund M. Barton; of the Historical Society and of the State of Rhode Island, through the kindness of Mr. Clarence S. Brigham and of Mr. Herbert Brigham; and of the State of Connecticut. Mr. Victor H. Paltsits, State Historian of New York, besides his many helpful suggestions, kindly had a search made for possible Lee letters at Albany, and Dr. Reuben Gold Thwaites courteously rendered a similar service as to the collections at Madison, Wisconsin. Mr. William Nelson kindly furnished

PREFACE

the editor information for the New Jersey Historical Society and Dr. Edmund C. Burnett generously gave him the benefit of his researches for the Carnegie Institution of Washington in North Carolina, South Carolina, and other places, and presented him with several letters of value. Mr. Clarence S. Brigham, besides his attentions at the Rhode Island Historical Society, kindly made inquiry into a valuable autograph collection existing in Providence. A personal examination was made without further result in several public and private libraries, such as those of Chicago and New York, and inquiry for possible letters in autograph collections in the hands of individuals. To many other persons who have taken valuable time to answer inquiries or letters, personal appreciation is gladly expressed.

Particularly is the editor indebted to Professor Charles M. Andrews, to Dr. J. Franklin Jameson, of the Carnegie Institution of Washington, and to Mrs. Albert Sioussat of Maryland, the Chairman, and the Publication Committee of the National Society of the Colonial Dames of America for securing an agency for the publication of these letters, and to Mrs. William Ruffin Cox, President, and the other Officers and Members of that Society for the generous liberality by means of which these volumes are offered to the public.

In all cases where the original manuscripts or faithful transcripts exist, and access to them was granted, the texts of the letters have been carefully collated with the originals by the editor. Though these originals were often found in a damaged condition or in the form of much-corrected drafts, it has been possible to preserve not only most of the original text but even the scarcely legible erasures. It has seemed well, however, to preserve here, in appended printed notes, only those erasures of some possible significance, omitting all mere variations of phrase or words which the author himself had discarded and which did not modify his thought. The texts are thus given *verbatim et literatim*, and not only is the author's spelling and capitalization, but also his punctuation and paragraphing, preserved. His division into paragraphs was infrequent and original, though his spelling is fairly good for his time. The salutation is given in the place and form in which it appeared in the manuscript, and it has seemed well to preserve also the formal ending, as it is varied and often characteristic; but the signature, which was usually the author's full name, is omitted. The postscripts were usually signed R. H. Lee, or R. H. L.

Though it can scarcely be hoped that all the letters of Lee have been found, it has been necessary to omit wholly or in part comparatively few of those that have been found, and any omitted passages are indicated by dots or by a note. Lee was a singularly chaste and careful writer and most of his letters have historical value, and with the exceptions specifically noted their texts are printed in full. A few relatively unimportant letters, particularly of his earlier years, are included, because of their personal bearing and the fact that we have no other view of the man at that time. Letters signed by Lee with other members of committees have been excluded when not in his handwriting or otherwise clearly of his authorship.

More than 250 letters of Lee are printed in the present volume, and the character of each manuscript — whether an autograph letter signed (A. L. S.), autograph letter (A. L.), autograph draft of a letter signed (A. dr. L. S.), autograph draft of a letter (A. dr. L.), autograph copy of a letter signed (A. copy L. S.), autograph copy of a letter (A. copy L.), letter signed (L. S.), transcript, or other copy — and the place where it was consulted and may be found are stated at the bottom of the page, in the first note to the heading of

PREFACE

the letter. In case the text is derived from a printed source, that fact with the source is specifically stated in the first note. For the purpose of clarifying the text little annotation has been needed, and it has been thought well to err on the side of too little comment rather than of too much, as space has thus been saved for letters that otherwise might necessarily have been omitted.

The limitations of space as well as of title have also made it necessary to exclude speeches, memorials, petitions, addresses, motions, and resolutions, etc., of Lee's authorship, though a collection of such interesting documents has been made which may subsequently be published.

The printed headings of the letters preserve the personal form of the address given in the originals or in reliable transcripts. Square brackets indicate the portions supplied from safe endorsements or other certain means of information.

As Lee generally wrote the salutation on the same line as the place and date in his manuscript this form has been followed in texts taken from printed letters where a different and varying style had apparently been adopted solely for editorial reasons.

JAMES CURTIS BALLAGH.

JOHNS HOPKINS UNIVERSITY,
BALTIMORE, December 12, 1909.

CONTENTS OF VOLUME I

1762

CONTENTS OF VOLUME I

1768

CONTENTS OF VOLUME I

CONTENTS OF VOLUME I

CONTENTS OF VOLUME I

CONTENTS OF VOLUME I

xxiv

CONTENTS OF VOLUME I

CONTENTS OF VOLUME I

CONTENTS OF VOLUME I

THE LETTERS OF RICHARD HENRY LEE

TO JAMES ABERCROMBIE[1]

SIR,   WESTMORELAND, VA. August, 27, 1762.

The acquaintance, I had the honour, to form with you when I was in London, in the year '51, will, I hope excuse me to you, for the freedom of this letter. When I consider the weight you deservedly possess, in affairs relative to this colony, I know not any person to whom I can, with more propriety, apply for an application in my behalf, that I may be appointed to fill the next vacancy in his majesty's council. I am the more induced to an application, at this time, as I am informed, that an address is preparing by the council, to his majesty, to remove Mr. —— from their board, on account of his extreme incapacity, to discharge the important duties of that station. If that address succeed, as I should imagine it would, from the weighty reasons assigned in it, then sir, I would lay myself under the great obligation that will arise from your interposition in my behalf: an obligation which will ever influence me, to consider you as my great benefactor, and particular friend. The desire I have to do my country

---

[1] From R. H. Lee, *Memoir of the Life of Richard Henry Lee and his Correspondence*, I. 13. Probably General James Abercrombie who succeeded Loudoun as Commander of the British forces in America in 1758, and was superseded by Amherst in 1759.

service, is my only motive for this solicitation; and governed by the same reason, my attention has been, for some time turned to public business, both as a member of the legislature, and of our inferior courts of justice. This experience supported by a laudable ambition, will, I hope, render me an object not altogether unworthy of your patronage.

I have the honour to be, with great respect and esteem, your obedient servant.

To JAMES ABERCROMBIE, Esq. In Craven street, London.

TO THOMAS CUMMINGS[1]

DEAR SIR,   WESTMORELAND, VA. August, 27, 1762.

I wrote to you a few days ago, that the council of this colony, had unanimously addressed his majesty to remove from their board Mr. ——, the last appointed counsellor, on account of his incapacity. If this address succeed, I entreat the favour of you, to exert your friendship that I might be appointed in Mr. ——'s place. If an ardent desire to serve my country, added to considerable time and application, already employed in the service of the public, are to be considered in this appointment, you may safely declare yourself my friend. I shall say nothing of the abilities of the gentleman, who, I understand, has a probability of filling the next vacancy, from the chance he stood last; because, as you know him, this would be unnecessary; and because I think it not proper, to establish my success, by making invidious observations on another. But in his favour, it is urged, that his contiguity to the seat of government, renders his appointment proper, as on government contingencies, his attendance in council could be presently obtained. If this argu-

[1] From R. H. Lee, *Memoir of Richard Henry Lee*, I. 14.

ment, independent of any auxiliary one, was to be admitted, might not *a cobbler in the city dispute the point
with him?* Less weight will be found in this reason,
when you consider that those who compose our council,
meet four times a year of course, to constitute the general
and oyer courts; when they sit, on the whole, more than
two months, besides the frequent meetings of the general assembly. At these times it is, that council business is chiefly discussed. If, in the intermediate time,
any contingency render a council necessary, there are
always six or seven of the board, whose situation admits
of a very speedy meeting. But in a variety of instances,
it may happen, that a dispersion of the councillors
through the several parts of the colony, will be attended
with advantageous consequences, by their having a more
minute and particular acquaintance with the circumstances of the country.

Against my success, I hear it is urged that I have a
brother already in the council. This is true; but can
any solid reason be assigned, why this friendly connexion
should banish virtue and morality from the breasts of
brothers? or does it follow, of course, that those thus
allied, should, to promote any views they may be supposed to have, unite to injure their country, and so
found their brotherly union on the destruction of
honour, duty, and public good? For my part, I think
the objection does not hold in theory; and, exclusive of
the many historic proofs that might be adduced to
confute it, we have a familiar experience here, of two
brothers having long sat together in the council, to the
honour of his majesty, and to the interests of the colony.

To whom, my dear sir, can you apply with so much
effect, as to your noble friend Lord Halifax, since a word
from him would accomplish the object; and then the
honour of the appointment would be enhanced, by its
being the direction of a person so universally admired

for the honesty of his heart and the ability of his head. I know you will excuse the length of this letter. With great sincerity, I assure you of the unabated esteem of your affectionate friend.

To THOMAS CUMMINGS, Esq. in London.

TO —— ——[1]

[—— — 1762.]

I hear it is objected to me that I have a brother already in the council. It is very true, I have; but candidly considered, how unimportant is this objection, nay, how invidious is it, since the only force it can possibly have, must be derived from a previously established want of virtue in the brothers, which may lead them to coalesce in schemes destructive of their country. For if honesty mark their character, no leagues of vice will ever be entered on, and an union in virtue can never be improper. But a vicious person should never be preferred, whatever may be his relation to, or disunion with the rest of his companions in office. If this strange objection should be urged, how easily could your genius and penetration thoroughly overcome it.   *   *   *

TO —— ——[2]

DEAR SIR,   [January 14, 1764.]

By the Governor's Speech, which you have inclosed, you may perceive, that considerable business was marked out for us. But our glorious resolution of yesterday, to be defended by Militia, to have no further concern with Regulars, will put a short period to the Session, which now we expect will rise by Wednesday

---

[1] From R. H. Lee, *Memoir of Richard Henry Lee*, I. 15.

[2] Typewritten copy. Virginia Historical Society, Lee Transcripts, V. 56.

next. Two addresses that are ordered by the House have not yet been presented.

I am with much regard, dear Sir, your most affectionate friend.

WILLIAMSBURG. January 14, 1764.

TO —— ——[1]

MY DEAR SIR,   CHANTILLY, VA. May 31, 1764.

At a time when universal selfishness prevails, and when (did not a very few instances evince the contrary) one would be apt to conclude that friendship, with Astrea, had fled this degenerate world, how greatly happy must be the man who can boast of having a friend. That this happiness is mine, the whole tenor of my life's correspondence with you proves most clearly.

Many late determinations of the great, on your side of the water, seem to prove a resolution, to oppress North America with the iron hand of power, unrestrained by any sentiment, drawn from reason, the liberty of mankind, or the genius of their own government. 'Tis said the House of Commons readily resolved, that it had "a right to tax the subject here, without the consent of his representative;" and that, in consequence of this, they had proceeded to levy on us a considerable annual sum, for the support of a body of troops to be kept up in this quarter. Can it be supposed that those brave adventurous Britons, who originally conquered and settled these countries, through great dangers to themselves and benefit to the mother country, meant thereby to deprive themselves of the blessings of that free government of which they were

---

[1] From R. H. Lee, *Memoir of Richard Henry Lee*, I. 27. Written to a gentleman in London. Cf. *Ibid.*, I. 26.

members, and to which they had an unquestionable right? or can it be imagined that those they left behind them in Britain, regarded those worthy adventurers, by whose distress and enterprise they saw their country so much enlarged in territory, and increased in wealth, as aliens to their society, and meriting to be enslaved by their superior power? No, my dear sir, neither one nor the other of these can be true, because reason, justice, and the particular nature of the British constitution, nay, of all government, cry out against such opinions! Surely no reasonable being would, at the apparent hazard of his life, quit liberty for slavery; nor could it be just in the benefited, to repay their benefactors with chains instead of the most grateful acknowledgments. And as certain it is, that "the free possession of property, the right to be governed by laws made by our representatives, and the illegality of taxation without consent," are such essential principles of the British constitution, that it is a matter of wonder how men, who have almost imbibed them in their mother's milk, whose very atmosphere is charged with them, should be of opinion that the people of America were to be taxed without consulting their representatives! It will not avail to say that these restrictions on the right of taxation, are meant to restrain only the sovereign, and not Parliament. The intention of the constitution is apparent, to prevent unreasonable impositions on the people; and no method is so likely to do that, as making their own consent necessary, for the establishment of such impositions. But if no such consent is allowed in our case, it will still be an aggravation of our misfortune to be the slaves of five hundred masters instead of one. It would seem, indeed, to be unquestionably true, that before a part of any community can be justly deprived of the rights and privileges, to which they are entitled by the constitution and laws, there must have been some great and palpable injury offered by them to the society of which they are a part. But did this happen in the case of the first settlers of America? or did they, by any treasonable combination against, or by any violation offered to, the laws of their country, make it proper, in their country, to deprive them of their birth right? It remains, therefore, that we cannot be deprived of English liberty, though it may appear expedient that we should be despoiled of it. But after all, my dear friend, the ways of Heaven are inscrutable; and frequently, the most unlooked-for events have arisen from seemingly the most inadequate causes. Possibly this step of the mother country, though intended to oppress and keep us low, in order to secure our dependence, may be subversive of this end. Poverty and oppression, among those whose minds are filled with ideas of British liberty, may introduce a virtuous industry, with a train of generous and manly sentiments, which, when in future they become supported by numbers, may produce a fatal resentment of parental care being converted into tyrannical usurpation. I hope you will pardon so much on this subject. My mind has been warmed, and I hardly know where to stop.* *

TO [LANDON CARTER][1]

CHANTILLY. June the 22$^{\underline{d}}$ 1765

DEAR SIR,

Is it true that one of the best friends, as well as one of the most able of the community, intends to quit the

[1] A. L. S. Virginia Historical Society, Lee Papers, IV. 278. Of "Sabine Hall," Richmond County, Virginia, Son of Robert ("King") Carter. A text of this letter with several unimportant omissions, additions, and changes in punctuation and capitalization is printed under the date "22 June 1766" in Edmund J. Lee, *Lee of Virginia*, 191.

service of his Country at this most important crisis; when every mental, every corporeal faculty that America possesses, should be strained to support its falling rights, against tyrannic power in opposition to the most palpable privileges of human nature, the legal rights of America, and the constitutional freedom of British Subjects?

I yet hope my friend, that you have only thought, not determined on declining to take a poll at the ensuing election. When the cause of our dissolution is known, will Ministerial cunning fail to suggest, that the people of Virginia disavow their Burgesses claim to freedom, if a considerable change is made by them, in their choice of new Representatives? Let us remove from despotism every shew of argument, and let us endeavor to convince the world that we are as firm and unanimous in the cause of Liberty, as so noble and exalted a principle demands. — The enclosed pamphlet is said to be written by the first Minister of Britain — If no better reasons can be assigned to support the measure he contends for, a strong proof is to be drawn from thence of its intrinsic vileness. It shews indeed, that systems calculated to destroy Human Liberty, can only be maintained by vain sophistry. and an idle affectation of wit, without one single ray of wisdom; and that such doctrines are[1] as far remote from true policy, as they are closely connected with the futile genius of a Dealer in Expedients, who never is able, and seldom willing, to draw the necessary supplies of Government from such sources only, as are consistent with the end of all Governments,[2] the safety, ease, and happiness of the people.

I would recommend the pamphlet to your attention,[3] not for its merit, but that it may receive a proper answer.

[1] The four words preceding are written above the line.
[2] The letter " s " appears to be erased.
[3] Substituted for " perusal " erased.

THE LETTERS OF RICHARD HENRY LEE

And such an one, it easily admits of as would make its Author blush, if it be possible for a Minister to blush. But though an answer might fail to do this, it will certainly have weight with the cool and sensible part of Mankind, and thereby perhaps, prevent the future extention of arbitrary unconstitutional power.

I am, with the most perfect esteem, dear Sir, your ever affectionate friend.

TO —— ——[1]

My Dearest Sir,   Chantilly, Va. July 4, 1765.

By Captain Talman, I was favoured with your obliging letter of April last, before the receipt of which, I had been informed of the fatal blow given to American liberty, by the ever to be detested stamp act. I am greatly obliged to you, my best friend, for your design of helping me to that collection;[2] but it is very well that the appointment has passed me, since, by the unanimous suffrage of his countrymen ...... is regarded as an execrable monster, who with parricidal heart and hands, hath concern in the ruin of his native country. The light in which our Assembly viewed that act, may be collected from their resolves at the last meeting, which occasioned their dissolution. I would have sent you a copy, had I not been persuaded that some of your numerous friends had done so already.

Have you read a pamphlet said to be written by

[1] From R. H. Lee, *Memoir of Richard Henry Lee*, I. 31.

[2] Lee had applied, in 1764, for appointment as a collector under the proposed Stamp Act, but as soon as he considered the bearing of the act, he became a vigorous opponent of it. See for his vindication, his letter of July 25, 1766, p. 16; and for James Mercer's controversy with him, the *Virginia Gazette*, October 3, 1766, and W. G. Stanard in the *Virginia Magazine of History and Biography*, X. 1–8.

George Grenville, in which he has, in vain, laboured to prove the legislative right of Britain to tax America? If no better arguments can be produced in support of the measures he contends for, it proves the intrinsic vileness of his scheme; and shows indeed, that systems calculated to destroy public liberty, can be maintained only by idle sophistry and a poor affectation of wit. It is most clear, that such doctrines are as far remote from true policy as they are apparently the production of a futile dealer in expedients, who understands not to draw the necessary supplies of government from such sources only as are consistent with the end of all government, the safety, ease, and happiness of the people.

Yours affectionately.

TO [ARTHUR LEE][1]

[July 4, 1765.]

* * * Every man in America hath much reason to lament with you, the loss of American liberty. As bad indeed as Egyptian bondage, is now become the fate of every inhabitant of America, by the mother country being converted into an arbitrary, cruel, and oppressive step-dame. But this most unjust proceeding (the stamp act) against us, should instruct every American, that as liberty can never be supported without arts and learn-ing, a diligent attention to those should be the ruling object, with every thinking man. But then, my brother, when these, or either of these are acquired, should not their possessor import them into his native country; [2] which, if forsaken by the best of her sons,

[1] From R. H. Lee, *Memoir of Richard Henry Lee*, I. 32. His brother, who had gone to Edinburgh for his medical education.

[2] Dr. Arthur Lee assigned his objection to the institution of slavery as one of his reasons for preferring England to Virginia as a home.

must fall into barbarous ignorance, and of course, become a fit subject for tyrannical natures to impose arbitrary and injurious acts upon. Should America make the same progress in the arts and sciences, as she infallibly must do in numbers of people, despotism will quickly learn, that her friendship is on no other terms to be obtained than by a free intercourse and equal participation of good offices, liberty and free constitution of government.

America, then, has a parent's claim to her descendants, and a right to insist that they shall not fix in any place, where, by so doing, they may add strength to cruel and tyrannical oppression.

I am, my dear brother, ever your affectionate, faithful friend.

TO LANDON CARTER [1]

DEAR SIR,   CHANTILLY August 15. 1765

I accidentally met with your favor the other day, and have now sent the book you were pleased to lend me in Town. 'Tis well written, and should be well studied in these times, when the true nature of that Liberty should be understood, which our Enemies beyond the water, are so unjustly depriving us of.

I am told that a Gentleman in the North has so effectually and forcibly answered G. Grenville's pamphlet, that even the Minister himself, supported by his infernal Crew of hireling Miscreants, dares not attempt a reply.

In time to come, it may be known and sensibly felt I hope, that America can find Arms as well as Arts, to remove the Demon Slavery far from its borders. If I should live to see that day, I shall be happy; and

[1] A. L. S. Virginia Historical Society, Lee Papers, IV. 282.

pleased to say with Sydney, "Lord now lettest thou thy servant depart in peace." Farewell. that you may be happy as you can wish, is the earnest desire of your affectionate friend.

TO [LANDON CARTER][1]

DEAR SIR   CHANTILLY September the 20. 1765
I shall not fail to send your packet to Jonas Green by the first favorable opportunity.

I have perused it, and am well pleased with your manner of defending us, as well as with the justness of your reasoning.

I heartily wish you a recovery of firm health, which will give the greatest pleasure to dear Sir your truly affectionate friend.

TO [LANDON CARTER][2]

DEAR SIR,   CHANTILLY February the 2ᵈ 1766
Tired at length with vain expectation, I have determined to make that opportunity I have so long waited for, to answer your obliging favor of Novʳ last. I am not surprised that your good sense should lead you to disapprove the proceedings that gave rise to the Gazette extraordinary. Absurdities are there too plain to be missed, nor do I hesitate to agree entirely with you in sentiment on that affair. — But, what my friend, is to be the issue of all this? Are we really to be en-

---

[1] A. L. S. Virginia Historical Society, Lee Papers, IV. 276. The copies of letters to Landon Carter in the Virginia Historical Society contain a transcript of this letter. See letter of February 2, 1766.

[2] A. L. S. Virginia Historical Society, Lee Papers, IV. 270.

slaved by part of our own Community, as a grateful return for the benefits they have derived from the danger and enterprise of our Fathers? And have we hitherto been suffered to drink from the cup of Liberty, that She may be more sensibly punished by its being withdrawn, and the bitter dregs of Servility forced on us in its place? This truly will be adding wanton cruelty to excessive injustice. Indeed every account seems to confirm their intention of abolishing our Liberty, by the establishment of these most oppressive Acts, for Laws I cannot call them, as I agree altogether with their own Maxim, — Nihil quod est contra Rationem est Licitum, quia Ratio Legis, est Anima Legis — This rule of judging the Law should be applied to the making it also — Unhappily for us, Fortune, or whatever Being presides in such cases, seems to favor these detestable designs! — Else why are Devonshire, Cumberland. and Churchill numbered with the dead, whilst Bute, Greenville, and Townshend (I mean Charles) not only live, but live in power? You may judge what profit we can propose to receive from Memorials, however fraught with reason, or filled with justice; When a Gentleman well informed, writes me from London in October last — "That every argument which Zeal and Reason could suggest was urged in vain to oppose the S. Act whilst it was under consideration, and that one of the Ministry being much dissuaded from specifying the mode of Taxation — the Minister replied passionately— G—d d—n them, we will shew them that we have power to tax them, and will tax them." — I think this is more the breath of brutality. than it is the [1] voice [1] of Reason, and when Brutes are allowed to govern Men, deplorable no doubt must be the consequence. — I want greatly to see you, that we may converse seriously on this greatly important busi-

[1] Inserted above the line.

ness, and I think of waiting on you as soon as my Shoulder (lately hurt by a Gun) permits me to travel.

I sent your packet for M.r Green by a safe hand, with charge not to let it contribute to establish despotism by going into the P. Office.

The Bearer brings a Letter for your Son, which please deliver him with my compliments — The family of Sabine Hall have always my best wishes —

I am dear Sir, your ever affectionate friend.

P.S. Can you spare me for a short time, Churchill's prophecy of famine, and his poem on retirement.

TO LANDON CARTER[1]

Dear Sir,   Chantilly February the 24.th 1766

As I was greatly surprised, and equally disturbed at M.r Ritchies declaration at Richmond Court, so am I now pleased to hear from you, that he repents of that dangerous step. I make no doubt, but the great resentment of the people will be appeased, when M.r Ritchie shall shew them in public his real sorrow for having offered so great an injury to the community, and convince them of his determination not to make use of that detestable paper, unless authorized by public consent. I most heartily rejoice with you dear Sir, at every favorable prospect for the restoration of Liberty.

I hope indeed, that the present great Men in power, are friends to the rights of human nature, and that their policy, founded on wisdom and virtue, will produce the entire subversion of Greenvilles corrupt and foolish system.

[1] A. L. S. Virginia Historical Society, Lee Papers, IV. 267.

I have read with pleasure your justification of, and advice to this Country [1] in the affair of not holding Courts. — But tho' I am most clearly of your opinion, that sound policy will direct us to shut up the Courts of Justice for a time, yet I fear the reason for so doing, being publickly communicated, may defeat the end thereby intended — Indeed I could wish some method were fallen upon, to inform the Northern Colonys, that our not following their example, proceeds from no regard for the Stamp Act,[2] but the very different[3] situation of our affairs from theirs with respect to Great Britain — And that our shutting here, whilst they open there the Courts of Justice, both contribute to the same end (defeating the S. Act) although by different means. Perhaps it might be better to mention it in this short way, than to proceed publickly to mention the manner how; which as I said before, may defeat the end proposed —

However I propose to see you, before I shall probably[4] have an opportunity to [go to] Maryland, and then we may converse more fully on the subject. I am with perfect esteem dear Sir your affectionate friend.

[1] The Ms. is torn and this word, supplied from a transcript, is missing.

[2] Lee drafted the famous "Articles of Association by the Citizens of Westmoreland," binding themselves "at every hazard and paying no regard to danger or death" to prevent the execution of the Stamp Act, in any instance, in Virginia, and to punish any person favoring the act in Virginia. He signed it, first on the list of one hundred and fifteen names, Feb. 27, 1766.

[3] Inserted above the line.

[4] Inserted above the line.

THE LETTERS OF RICHARD HENRY LEE

TO THE EDITOR OF THE VIRGINIA GAZETTE[1]

WESTMORELAND   July the 25. 1766

SIR,

To remove the painful consideration, that one worthy person should be induced by misrepresentation to think ill of me, is the reason that prevails with me to desire you will be pleased to insert what follows in your next Gazette.

I am your most humble Servant.

Early in November 1764, I was for the first time informed by a Gentleman, of the intention of Parliament to lay a Stamp duty in America, with a friendly proposition on his part, to use his interest for procuring me the office of Collector,[2] I call it friendly, because I believe the Gentleman, no more than myself, nor perhaps a single person in this Country, had at that time reflected in the least on the nature and tendency of such an Act. Considering this only in the light of a beneficial employment, I agreed the Gentleman should write, and did also write myself, inclosing my letter to a Gentleman now in the Country. It was but a few days after my letters were sent away, that reflecting seriously on the

[1] A. L. S. American Philosophical Society, Lee Papers, I. 11, No. 4. A text of this letter with variations is printed in R. H. Lee, *Memoir of Richard Henry Lee*, I. 40. This was a reply to Mercer's charge as to Lee's application for service under the Stamp Act. James Mercer replied in the *Virginia Gazette* of October 3, under date of September 14, 1766, quoting an extract of this letter.

The Ms. is endorsed, "Richard Henry Lee/letter 25ᵗʰ July 1766/ Very int. papers R. H. L's/vind. agt. being friendly/to the Stamp Act — his/ — vs Ritchie — Letter/to Mʳ Wythe resᵍ charges/vs him — Letter from/McDougal and reply — respg/non importation — &c 1775–6 — &c./: " and endorsed also, " R. H. Lees Ansʳ·/to Mercer's Charge/about Stamp Act/application."

[2] This word is substituted by the author for "Distributor" erased.

16

nature of the application I had made; the impropriety of an American being concerned in such an[1] affair[1] struck me in the strongest manner, and produced a fixt determination to exert every faculty I possessed both in public and private life, to prevent the success of a measure I now discovered to be in the highest degree pernicious to my Country. I considered, that to err is certainly the portion of humanity, but that it was the business of an honest Man to recede from error as soon as he discovered it, and that the strongest principle of duty called upon every Citizen to prevent the ruin of his Country, without being restrained by any consideration that should interrupt this primary obligation. But it did not appear to me, that a promulgation of my application was necessary, as I conceived that my actions would be the clearest proof of the rectitude of my intentions. That such was the conduct held by me in public, I desire not to be credited on my bare assertion, but with confidence appeal to the many worthy Gentlemen with whom I had the honor to serve in General Assembly. They know who first moved in the House of Burgesses for the address to his Majesty, for the memorial to the Lords, and the remonstrance to the house of Commons. They also know, what part I took in preparing these. For my uniform opinion and conduct in private life, I safely refer to all those with whom I have the pleasure of an acquaintance. Such being my principles, and such my actions, long, very long before my application could possibly reach Great Britain, before the Act passed, and therefore the appointment of any Distributor[2]; I leave the impartial Reader to determine, with what truth and propriety it has been asserted, that my sentiments of the Act were not discovered, until I was certain of having been

[1] Inserted above " business " erased.
[2] Written above " Collector " erased.

disappointed. But as a further confirmation, if a further is necessary, of my early formed determination to depart from the application I had made; no duplicates of my letters were ever sent, and by their not arriving until many months after the appointment of a Distributor [1] was made, and the execution of the Stamp Act prevented in America: no measures were taken by my friends in consequence of anything I had written. From this state of the case, as exactly related as my memory can serve to recollect the circumstances of a transaction, now above twenty months standing; it will appear to every considerate and candid person, that my proceeding amounts to nothing more, than the making a hasty application, the impropriety of which was presently discovered, and a constant tenor of conduct pursued, that operated (as far as my powers could make it) to prevent my success, in a point I am very untruly supposed to have wished for, until I found myself disappointed. Thus much I have judged it necessary to say in justice to my character and to say more would be trifling with the Public.

TO ARTHUR LEE [2]

DEAR BROTHER,   CHANTILLY Dec. 20. 1766.

It is at all times with great pleasure that I oblige you, and therefore, notwithstanding the request you have now made me, will be attended with many inconveniences, I shall endeavor to give you a just idea of our policy, the state of our Trade, the nature and amount of our Revenue, with an estimate of our military strength. These subjects, if I mistake not, will com-

---

[1] Substituted by Lee for another word erased, probably "Collector."
[2] A. L. S. University of Virginia, Lee Papers, No. 37.

prehend within them the information you desired re-
[ceive]. Tis no less to [you(?)] evident, that our Fore-
fathers in framing the Constitution of this Coun[tr]y,
had in view the excellent pattern furnished by the
Mother Country; But unhappily for us my brother,
it is an exterior semblance only, when you examine
seperately the parts that compose this government;
essential variations appear between it, and the happily
poised english constitution. Let us place the two in
comparative points of view, and then the difference will
be stricking. In Britain the three simple forms of
Monarchy, Aristocracy, and Democracy, are so finely
blended; that the advantages resulting from each species
separately, flow jointly from their admirable union.
The King tho' possessing the executive power of government, with the third of the legislative, and the House
of Commons representing the democratic interest, are
each prevented from extending improperly prerogative
or popular claims, by a powerful body of Nobles, independent in the material circumstances of hereditary
succession to their titles and seats in the second bench
of the Legislature. Thus you see of what essential
importance is the House of Lords in the British constitution, and how happily their independence is secured.
With us, the legislative power is lodged in a Governor,
Council, and House of Burgesses. The two first appointed by the crown, and their places held by the
precarious tenure of pleasure only. That security
therefore which the constitution derives in Britain from
the House of Lords, is here entirely wanting, and the
just equilibrium totally destroyed by two parts out of
three of the Legislature being in the same hands. It
happens also unfortunately that the same persons who
compose our Council during pleasure, with the Governor, at their head, are the Judges of our General
Courts (and only so long as they continue of the Council)

where all causes ecclesiastical and civil, both common law and Chancery business is determined. By this injudicious combination, all the executive, two thirds of the legislative, and the whole judiciary powers are in the same body of Magistracy. How severly, but how justly has the accurate Montesquieu determined against so impolitic a union — "Lorsque dans la même personne ou dans le même corps de Magistrature, la puissance legislative est réunie a la puissance executrice, il n'y a point de liberté; parce qu'on peut craindre que le même Monarque ou le même Sénat ne pass [1] des Loix tyranniques, pour les exécuter tyranniquement. Il n'y a point encore de lib[erté] [2] si la puissance [de] [2] juger n'est pas sé [3] parée [3] de la puissance légis[la] [2] tive et de l'exécutrice; si elle etoit jointe a la puissance legislative, le pouvoir sur la vie et la liberté des Citoyens seroit arbitraire; car la Juge seroit Legislateur. Si elle étoit jointe a la puissance exécutrice la Juge pourra [4] it avoir la force d'un oppresseur. Tout seroit perdu si le même hom meou le même Corps des Principaux, ou des Nobles, ou du Peuple exerçoient ces trois pouvoirs, celui de faire des Loix, celui d.exécuter les résolutions publiques, et celui de juger les crimes ou les différends des perticuliers" [5] —

But how must your surprise increase, when you are informed that even the third or democratic part of our legislature is totally in the power of the Crown! Tis by usage only that elections are directed and Assembly's called; in our code of laws not one is to be found that directs the calling of new Assembly's, or that appoints any time for the meeting of the representative body when chosen. To remedy this fundamental error, and to

---

[1] Author's error, for " fasse." [2] Almost illegible.
[3] Author's error for " séparée." [4] Should be " o."
[5] See *Esprit de Lois*, B. XI. ch. 6. Accent, punctuation, capitalization, etc., follow Lee's copy.

place the liberty of the Subject on a more secure footing, an Act of Assembly was passed upon the principles of the Act of Parliament adopted in England after the Revolution, directing that a new assembly should be called once in seven years at the least, and that the Represent[a][1]tives when chosen should be convened, at least, once in three years. The more frequent calling of new Assembly's and the more frequent meeting of them when chosen, was left; as of right it ought, a Prerogative possessions. This Act passed with a suspending clause, but tho it is now 4 Years since its passage, we have never had the royal approbation. May we not hope my brother; that this security to liberty will now be granted, when those great and good men preside who so lately evinced their generous and noble attachment to American Freedom, by opposing with matchless eloquence the Parliamentary right of imposing internal taxes on America. May we not also hope that when these great Personages have leisure from other weighty concerns, that a thorough reform in the faulty parts of our constitution will be directed. It may reasonably be enquired, how it happened, that with so ~ good a pattern as the English constitution, ours should be so exceptionally contrived? The answer is to be found in the arbitrary reign of James [the][1] first, and the subsequent confusion that happened in that of his Son. The first ocassioned the violent dissolutions of the Company to whom letters Patent were originally granted for this Colony, and the rebellion in the reign of Charles the first, with the consequent disorders in Government, prevented any kind of regularity from taking place in our affairs.

I am happy in being able to say with truth of our Countrymen that they have ever been remarkable for loyalty and firm attachment to their Sovereign. A

[1] Almost illegible.

celebrated instance of this they gave, in refusing as they always did to pay any obedience to the usurped power of Oliver Cromwell, and at the two last wars, no applications from our late or present King were ever made in vain — I have now accomplished the first part of my engagement by giving as accurate an idea of the constitution of this Country as I am able, and that I may not tire you with the length of this letter, I shall defer writing on the three remaining subjects, until some future opportunity.

I remain with truth and sincerity your ever affectionate brother and faithful friend.

To Doctor Lee.

TO LORD CAMDEN[1]

My Lord.   Chantilly in Virginia.   1 June 1767
Wonder not my Lord that the people in this remote part of his Majestie's dominions revere your Lordships character, since there is no part of the British Empire but feels the influence of Lord Camdens virtue. America in particular must ever regard your Lordship

[1] A. copy L. S. Virginia Historical Society, Lee Papers, IV. 288. A printed text with changes appears in R. H. Lee, *Memoir of Richard Henry Lee*, I. 48. Lee had secured a public meeting in Westmoreland County to thank Lord Camden for his opposition to the Stamp Act, and raised a subscription to pay for his portrait. See *Idem*. The following subscription paper is from an autograph copy signed by Richard Henry Lee in the Virginia Historical Society, Lee Papers, IV. 288:

" We who subscribe this paper highly venerating the character of the right honorable Charles Pratt Lord Camden Chief Justice of the Court of Common Pleas in Great Britain for his virtuous attachment to the cause of justice and public liberty and being particularly affected with gratitude for the noble and disinterested firmness with which this great Man supported America's just rights in the house of Lords against the Act for imposing Stamp duties here and from the wish we entertain that all future Judges may be induced from a

as the Patron of its liberty, the best possession of human nature. Prompted by gratitude they entreat your Lordship will condescend to accept their humble thanks, and favor them with permitting your picture to be taken, that it may remain a memorial to posterity of their veneration, and of the inestimable benefit derived to British America from your Lordships protection. I have the honor to be with the most profound respect My Lord &ᶜ

To the right Honorable CHARLES PRATT LORD CAMDEN, Lord high Chancellor of G. Britain.

contemplation of this worthy Judges picture to recollect those virtues the possession of which procures Lord Camden the love of his Country Do oblige ourselves to pay on demand into the hands of Richard Henry Lee esquire one of our representatives in General Assembly the sum of money by each of us subscribed in order that the said Lee may be enabled to employ the most excellent Portrait Painter of Great Britain to take a picture of Lord Camden to be placed in the most conspicuous part of the Court house of Westmoreland County. And we the Subscribers do also desire that the said Lee may by letter present the thanks of the Subscribers to his Lordship for his protection of their just rights and to entreat that his Lordship will be pleased to permit his picture to be taken for the purposes aforesaid Given under our hands in Westmoreland Country Virginia this 20ᵗʰ day of June 1766.

	£	s	d
William Lee	5.	— .	—
Richard H. Lee	5.	— .	—
Revᵈ Thoˢ Smith	5.	— .	—
F. Ligᵗ Lee	5.	— .	—
James Davenport	5.	— .	—
Richard Buckner	5.	— .	—
Geo. Turberville	5.	— .	—
Richard Lee	5.	— .	—
Jos. Lane	2.	— .	—
Willᵐ Newton	5.	— .	—
Thoˢ Chilton	2.	— .	—
Jnᵒ A. Washington	5.	— .	—
Wᵐ Peirce	1.	— .	—
Wᵐ Booth	1.	— .	—
Edwᵈ Ransdell	1.	— .	—

THE LETTERS OF RICHARD HENRY LEE

TO EDMUND JENINGS [1]

D.ʳ Sɪʀ   Cʜᴀɴᴛɪʟʟʏ ɪɴ Vɪʀɢ.ᴬ 1.ˢᵗ June 1767

I hope your goodness will pardon me for the trouble I am going to give you. The Gentlemen in this County having great veneration for the character of Lord Camden, particularly for his noble support of America's

	£	s	d
[Will ?] Spark	1.	—.	—
Edw.ᵈ Sanford	1.	—.	—
Jos. Peirce	0.10.	—	
Eliz. Steptoe	2.	—.	—
Dan. McCarty	5.	—.	—
J. Monroe	2.	—.	— Never paid
James Blair	1.	—.	—
Richard Parker	3.	—.	—
Gerard Kutt	1.	—.	—
Hannah Corbin	5.	—.	—
R. L. Hall	3.	—.	—
Arthur Lee	5.	—.	—
W.ᵐ Berryman	1.	—.	— Never paid
Ben. Weeks	1.	—.	—
John Newton	1.	—.	—
Anne Washington	2.	—.	—
	£96.10		

Ninety six pounds ten shillings currency at 25 p.ʳ Cent the exchange at which the business was negotiated is Sterling £77.4. Now it appears by my letter to M.ʳ Jenings June 1.ˢᵗ 1767 that the sum remitted him was only £76.8 which is /₁₆ sterling short of the subscription money, the reason of which is this : When the subscribed money came to be remitted all the Subscribers had not paid and some of them never did pay, but desiring not to stop the business for a trifle, I remitted M.ʳ Jenings a bill drawn by Capt. Johnstoun on James Russell for £52. sterling and my own bill on the same Gentleman for £24.8 sterling making in the whole £76.8 Sterling which M.ʳ Jenings received and has since Sept.ʳ 1772 paid to M.ʳ William Lee in London by my [   ]"

[1] A. copy L. S. Virginia Historical Society, Lee Papers, IV. 288.

liberty against the Stamp Act, wish much to have his Lordships picture to grace their Court house. For this purpose they have paid into my hands the sum of £76.8. sterling, which I inclose you two bills of exchange for, and beg the favor of you to wait on L.ᵈ Camden with the inclosed letter which entreats his Lordships permission to the taking his picture. This being obtained I must leave to yʳ judgment the choice of a Limner, observing only that the Gentleman would prefer Reynolds, unless you should think his difference of price may be more than his superiority in painting. Indeed I cannot help thinking, for my own part, that Mʳ West, being an American, deserves the preference in this business, if his skill should approach near to that of the best Limners, as I am informed it does. As £76.8. is the whole sum subscribed, out of this must come the charge for the frame of the picture (which let be a plain gilt one) with the case, and the shipping charges. The balance will be the neat sum for the Painters fee, to be applied, if it will be sufficient, to draw his Lordship at full length in Judges robes — But if it will not be enough for this, then he is to be drawn as far [   ] as the money will permit. I have been told there is a method of placing strong Canvass at the back of the picture so as to secure it greatly from the injuries of time & moisture. Be pleased to consult the Painter on this head, and let it be done, if he thinks proper, under his direction. The place where the picture is to be put renders it necessary also, that a rod should be fixed for hanging a Curtain before it, which curtain may be sent with the picture. Capt. Johnstoun who delivers you this, will receive and take proper care of the picture when it is finished and carefully put up for the voyage. I must once more entreat your forgiveness for troubling you in this affair. I thought you would not be displeased at this testimony of our esteem for the Patriot whose virtue has saved our common Country. I am with esteem &c

To EDMUND JENINGS Esq.ʳ at his Chambers in Lincoln Inn — London

By these Copies it appears that Mʳ Campbels name is not to the.[1]

TO —— ——[2]

MY DEAR SIR,   CHANTILLY, VA. March 27, 1768.

'Tis a pleasing reflection to one who loves his country, that some few, at least, are to be found, who watch over the public good, and having wisdom to discern with spirit to promote, the general good, will not silently suffer encroachments to be made on the rights and liberty, of the community. My long acquaintance with you, my friend, gives me a right to number you, among such worthy citizens. It being a common observation, does not lesson the value of it, that a prudent man should lend his assistance to extinguish the flames, which had invaded the house of his next door neighbour, and not coldly wait, until the flame had reached his own. History does not more clearly point out, any fact than this, that nations which have lapsed from liberty, to a state of slavish subjection, have been brought to this unhappy condition, by gradual paces. Great Britain, it seems, having discovered the error of attempting our ruin, by one bold and general stroke, has, at length, fallen on a method of singly attacking the colonies, hoping that the others will quietly behold the

[1] Lee's Ms. here ends incomplete. It appears from Jenings' letters that though Lord Camden consented to sit for West his promise was afterwards forgotten. R. H. Lee, *Memoir of Richard Henry Lee*, I. 50.

[2] "A gentleman, of influence in England." Text from R. H. Lee, *Memoir of Richard Henry Lee*, I. 53.

destruction of one, not immediately and sensibly, connected with the rest. But, though, the billeting act is not yet enforced upon *us*, we are equally with New York in the view of that oppressive measure, *for I cannot agree to call it law*. An act for suspending the legislature of that province, *hangs, like a flaming sword*, over our heads, and requires, *by all means, to be removed*. The late duties on paints and glass, though not perhaps, literally, a violation of our rights, yet as the connection between us and the mother country, renders it necessary that we should, excluding all other nations, take manufactures, only from her, in this light, the imposition becomes arbitrary, unjust, and destructive of that mutually beneficial connection, which every good subject would wish to see preserved. To obtain redress, sir, on these points, and to inform posterity what were our sentiments on them, it seems indispensably necessary, that a dutiful, decent, but firm address, should be presented to his majesty, by the Assembly, requesting his royal interposition, for the repeal of these acts. This method, you know, my friend, is constitutional. The subject, when aggrieved, has a right to appeal to the sovereign, for redress; and we have his royal word for it, (in a late speech to Parliament,) that he will equally protect the rights of all his people.

The unhappy wound,[1] which I received in my hand, will not yet permit me to travel, and indeed, I am sorry for it, as it would give me great pleasure to add, on this occasion, my poor assistance, to the friends of liberty, contending for their country's rights.

I am, yours with esteem, &c.

---

[1] Lee's wound was caused by the bursting of a gun while he was shooting swans. " By this accident, he lost all the fingers of one hand. He was, however, able to go to Williamsburg, to the meeting of the House of Burgesses." R. H. Lee, *Memoir of Richard Henry Lee*, I. 54, note.

THE LETTERS OF RICHARD HENRY LEE

TO ———[1]

[After June 27, 1768.]

*   *   *   *   *   *   *

I have been concerned to find, that your friends here are much surprised and displeased at the charge you have made of the parliamentary duty on tea. I confess it is extremely disagreeable to me, and I earnestly entreat that you, sir, whom we esteem here as our very good friend, would not lend a helping hand to deprive us of the most valuable of all possessions, our liberty. But certainly an arbitrary ministry will for ever proceed to tax and distress us, if they find the merchants will condescend to become their collectors, and so make the collection of a duty easy, which otherwise they never can get in. And I am very sure, that nothing can prevent the people here from regarding the trade as their most deadly foe, if they join in making easy of execution those oppressive acts. This act, levying a duty on paper, glass, *tea*, &c. is so unjust, and so badly contrived, that it never can be executed; and you run no risk here, however the collectors may bully and make a noise; for it is certain they do not know what to demand, *and dare not detain a ship on account of these duties.*

---

[1] A London merchant, "J. R." Text from R. H. Lee, *Memoir of Richard Henry Lee*, I. 55. Enclosed with a copy of a subscription paper, the original by Richard Henry Lee concluding as follows: "We, who subscribe this paper, do oblige ourselves to pay to J. R. Esq. Merchant, in London, or his order, on demand, for the quantity of *tea* by each of us subscribed for. But it is on this express condition that we desire the tea to be sent, that Mr. R. does not make the charge of the late parliamentary duty on tea, as we prefer our liberty to the gratification of our palates, and do not choose to drink our destruction in a cup of tea. Given under our hands and seals, this 27th June, 1768." The copy of subscription followed the text above.

THE LETTERS OF RICHARD HENRY LEE

TO JOHN DICKINSON[1]

Sir,   Chantilly, Va. July 25, 1768.

As a friend to the just and proper rights of human nature, but particularly as an American, I acknowledge great obligation to you, for the wise and well-timed care, you have taken of our common liberty.

Whilst men in general, are thoughtless and indolent, spirit and wisdom are necessary to rouse and inform minds, that incline to what is right, and wish happiness. You, sir, on this occasion, have the honour of giving a just alarm, and of demonstrating the late measures to be, at once, destructive of public liberty, and in violation of those rights which God and nature have given us.

To prevent the success of this unjust system, an union of counsel and action among all the colonies, is undoubtedly necessary. The politician of Italy delivered the result of reason and experience, when he proposed the way *to conquest, by division.* How to effect this union, in the wisest and firmest manner, perhaps, time and much reflection, only, can show. But well to understand each other, and timely to be informed of what passes, both here and in Great Britain, it would seem that not only select committees should be appointed by all the colonies, but that a private correspondence should be conducted between the lovers of liberty in every province.

From my brother, Dr. Lee, I have been informed of the kindness, with which you have expressed your willingness to begin a correspondence with me. To effectuate this good purpose, sir, I have taken the earliest opportunity of informing you, that when you are pleased to write, your letter to me by post, directed

[1] R. H. Lee, *Memoir of Richard Henry Lee*, I. 65.

to the care of Dr. Mortimer, Hobb's Hole, Virginia, will meet with a safe conveyance.

I am, sir, with singular esteem, your most obedient and humble servant.

To JOHN DICKINSON. Philadelphia.

TO JOHN DICKINSON[1]

SIR,   CHANTILLY IN VIRGINIA Novr 26th 1768

That I might not be troublesome is the only reason that has hitherto prevented me from answering your agreeable favour of the 10th of August. It is greatly to be lamented that any consideration, should prevail with so potent and so flourishing a people as those of Pennsylvania to be silent, when the Liberty of America is thus dangerously invaded, when her sister Colonies are generously contending against oppression, and when a Union of the whole must infallibly establish the public freedom and security. To what purpose do her merchants toil, her people labor for wealth, if Arbitrary Will, uninfluenced by reason, and urged by interest, shall reap the Harvest of their diligence and industry ! — I wish these people may not discover when it is too late, that the blessings of Liberty flow not from timid and selfish policy — I do not observe that your Assembly have even expressed the least dislike to the late duty Act, although all England now agrees its principal intention to be the establishment of a Precedent for American taxation by the British Parliament. Our long expected Governor[2] at length arrived, his lordship's good sense, affability, and politeness give general pleasure, but how far his political opinions may agree with those of

[1] American Philosophical Society, Lee Papers, I. 37, 38, 34; No. 13. Autograph letter-book copy. A text with many variations is in R. H. Lee, *Memoir of Richard Henry Lee*, I. 66.
[2] Lord Botetourt.

Virginia remains yet to be known. The late Assembly is dissolved, and writs have been issued for the choice of a new one, to meet, tis said, in May next — at which meeting; tis reported, we are to be informed, that his Majesty having seen, disapproves our objections to the duty Act, is determined to support the authority of the British Parliamt, and directs the Act of the 6th of his reign (commonly called the Bill of Right) to be laid before the assembly. It is supposed that the silence of the House would on this occasion be highly acceptable to Government, but the propriety of being so, is a question much agitated here. Say the time-serving Men, " As the Assembly have denied, and the King has asserted those rights, the matter ought to lie without their taking the least notice of it " — And this on a supposition, that the principle admitted, will never again be carried into execution. — On the other hand, it is contended, that silence in this case, must by all the world, be deemed a tacit giving up our Rights, and an acknowledgement that the British Parliament may at pleasure tax the unrepresented Americans. That every kind of reason makes it probable destructive execution will soon follow so dangerous an admission. The facts it seems are these. On the late Stamp Act being known here, the Assembly asserted their right to exemption from British Taxes. Since that, the Parliament by an Act declare the binding force of their Legislature over America in every instance. But this Act having never been laid before the Assembly by authority, and the Stamp Act being repealed, the Bill of Right passed off unnoticed. However, the world soon saw an intention to avail themselves of this declared right by the passage of the ill judged duty bill.

To this act the Assembly again object, and by petition entreat his Majesty's interposition for the security of their Rights against the principles of that act — should

a new Assembly be told that these objections are dis-
approved, that the authority of Parliament must be
supported, and the Bill of Right be laid before them by
the highest Authority — How Sir must silence in this
case, be construed ? The reception of the Act will be
registered, but no objection will follow — The poison,
unattended by its antidote, may be used for the destruction of the Body Politick — I confess, I cannot readily
go along with those who would derive our security from
our submission. Is it reasonable to suppose that so
sensible a people as the English, would disturb the peace
of all North America, and endanger their most valuable
trade here, for the poor purpose of establishing a principle they never meant to execute ! This it seems to
me would be sottishness not wisdom — When opportunity Permits, I should be extremely glad to know your
sentiments on this important point, for indeed I am
never so wedded to any opinion, but that I can readily
yield to clear and superior reason. I am, with very
particular esteem Sir &: &:

To JOHN DICKINSON, Esq: Philadelphia.

TO LANDON CARTER[1]

DEAR SIR,   CHANTILLY 8 Dec: 1768
Ever since I left M: Parker I have been in the most
unhappy condition — Poor M:s Lee and my two
sons laboring under a severe Pleurisy and now so ill
that I know not what may be the issue of this night —
Worn out as I am with fatigue and anxiety I must attend
the election tomorrow but I am not able to inform you
any thing about the opposition —

[1] A. L. S. Virginia Historical Society, Lee Papers, IV. 262.
Mrs. Lee died December 12, 1768, aged thirty years.

The boy brings a bottle of the best Madeira I have, and I wish it may be of service to you —
I am with infinite regard dear Sir your affectionate friend.

TO [RICHARD?] PARKER[1]

MY DEAR FRIEND — [January —, 1769]

I am infinitely obliged to Colonel Carter for the kind concern he is pleased to express for my unhappy situation, and I very well know that his goodness will excuse my attendance at Sabine Hall on this occasion. It is true indeed, that the company of a few sensible friends is very agreeable to me; but I should now be highly distressed in a crowd, especially in a gay Crowd.

I shall hope to see you at the time you mention, but in the mean while take this short account from D.̲ Lee— " In American affairs L.̲ᵈ Hillsborough is the absolute and responsible Minister, nor is any change expected — The sense of the people here seems to have changed in favor of America partly thro' conviction, but more thro' fear of the dangerous consequences which they apprehend will follow from an attempt to fix the yoke with which they wish to oppress America. Hudibrass (continues the Doctor) is of opinion, "He that's convinced against his will, Is of the same opinion still " —

This is truly the state of people here respecting the Colonies, and this should suggest the policy to us of watching over them, least they should accomplish that by guile, which they despair of enforcing — The Lords Chatham & Shelburne have resigned. L.̲ᵈ Rochfort has succeeded the latter, no one the former; but it is thought the Bedford Party will take the lead &.̲ᶜ "

The rest of the Doctors letter (which is too long to

[1] A. L. S. Virginia Historical Society, Lee Papers, IV. 258. Addressed, "To/M.̲ʳ Parker." Endorsed, " Jany 1769."

33

transcribe) you shall see when I have I have the pleasure of your company here — I am sorry for my good old friend M⸢ Beales indisposition — He knows that patience and exercise are the best remedies for his complaint —

I am with unfeigned regard dear Sir your affectionate friend.

P.S. The Doctor desires his particular compliments to you.

TO [ARTHUR LEE][1]

My Dear Brother,   WILLIAMSBURG 19ᵗʰ May 1769.

Yours 22ᵈ of Feb⸢ last I have just now received, and I thank you, as well for the political intelligence it contains, as for the papers that accompanied it.

We were called here in General Assembly on the 8ᵗʰ of this month, and we were dissolved suddenly on the 17ᵗʰ following, for reasons which the inclosed papers will suggest to you. The dissolution was immediately followed by an Association against the importation of goods, which the Members universally signed, and will undoubtedly be assented to by the whole Colony.

The flame of liberty burns bright and clear, nor can its light and luster be impair'd by any Ministerial art or delusion. The Americans, from one end of the Continent to the other, appear too wise, too brave, and much too honest, to be either talked, terrified, or bribed from the assertion of just, equitable, and long possessed rights — It is clear beyond question, that nothing but just honest, and friendly measures, can secure to Great Britain, the obedience and love of America. But such

[1] England, Mss. of the Marquis of Lansdowne, Vol. 67. fo. 73. Enclosure in Arthur Lee's letter to Shelburne of July 3; "inclosed papers" mentioned are not now with the letter. Copy secured through the courtesy of Professor Charles M. Andrews.

measures will undoubtedly restore us to the former unity and respect that bound the Parent state and her Colonies together. I cannot by this opportunity get a well bound Almanac for Lord Shelburne, but the next conveyance shall bring one. It is the duty of every American to exert all their powers to serve that excellent Lord, whose just and generous principles have so often shone forth in vindication of the violated rights of America. His Lordship is adored in this Country, and surely the good and great must feel inward satisfaction at the applause of thousands, who feel and acknowledge their virtue and goodness.

I have been so coverd with affliction this past winter, that I have thought but little of any thing except my own unhappiness, and am therefore unprovided with birds: but I will take proper care the next season: M! Cox has promised to ship a small cask of his best Virginia wine to D! Fothergill in Cap! Johnstown, and I expect you will get a Rattle Snake by the same opportunity. Continue my dear brother to love me, and to believe that I am and ever shall be your most affectionate brother.

TO DOCTOR FOTHERGILL[1]

SIR,   CHANTILLY, VA. May, 1769.

Your general humanity deserves the esteem of all; but permit me to say, sir, that *your particular kindness to Americans* claims their reverence and gratitude. When, therefore, my brother, Dr. Lee, informed me

[1] From R. H. Lee, *Memoir of Richard Henry Lee*, I. 80. Dr. John Fothergill (1712–1780), who was an eminent London physician. He was the author of a pamphlet in 1765, "Considerations relative to the North American Colonies," advocating repeal of the Stamp Act. In 1774 he was engaged in drawing up with Franklin a scheme for reconciliation between the Colonies and Great Britain.

that you wished to have some wine from our native grape, I lost no time in procuring the best for you. Captain Johnson will deliver you a small cask, together with a few bottles of older wine. The first is of last year's vintage, and that in bottles is several years old. This wine is, at present, of the true flavour of our grape, and is very gently acid, a quality natural to this fruit. I wish the season, and the heat of the tobacco load, may not injure it.

I am, with very singular esteem, sir, your most humble and obedient servant.

DR. FOTHERGILL, London.

TO [EDMUND JENINGS][1]

DEAR SIR,   CHANTILLY, VA. May 31, 1769.

The gentlemen of Westmoreland, desire me to return their hearty thanks to you, for your very genteel present of Lord Chatham's picture. It arrived in fine order, and is very much admired. They propose to place it in the court house, thinking the assembly may furnish themselves, with his lordship's picture.

The gentlemen are not without hopes, that they may yet obtain Lord Camden's portrait, as they seem very unwilling to believe, that that great man can so apostatize from a virtuous cause, so ably and invincibly defended by himself, as to put it out, even, of his own power, to make the American so much, as doubtful. Dr. Lee, my brother, can show you the proceedings of our last Assembly, by which, you may judge, how bright the flame of liberty burns here, and may surely convince a tyrannous administration, that honesty and equity alone, can secure the cordiality and affection of Virginia.

I am, dear sir, your affectionate friend.

[1] From R. H. Lee, *Memoir of Richard Henry Lee*, I. 51.

THE LETTERS OF RICHARD HENRY LEE

TO LORD SHELBURNE[1]

My Lord,   Chantilly, Va.   May, 31, 1769.

The wisdom and goodness, with which your lordship has patronised America, claims the reverence of all its inhabitants. As an individual of this country I am greatly honoured by any service that will be acceptable to your lordship; and now take the liberty to send you a Virginia almanac, and the last Virginia Gazette, containing the proceedings of our late Assembly. These proceedings my lord, may, to some, appear the over-flowings of a seditious and disloyal madness: but your lordship's just and generous attachment to the proper rights and liberty of mankind, will discover in them, nothing more than a necessary and manly assertion, of social privileges founded in reason, guaranteed by the English constitution, and rendered sacred by a pos-session of near two hundred years, that is, my lord, from the first settlement of North America, until a late period. When your lordship afforded the Americans your protection, it was given to a people, who are certainly loyal, very warmly attached to their mother country, and who wish its prosperity, with unfeigned heartiness.

I have the honour to be, your lordship's
most obedient and humble servant.

The Right Honourable the Earl of Shelburne. in London.

TO [WILLIAM] RIND[2]

Mr. Rind,   Westmoreland, Sept. 28, 1769.

I never yet have seen, nor till lately ever knew of your publication, concerning the picture of Lord Chatham

[1] From R. H. Lee, *Memoir of Richard Henry Lee*, I. 71.
[2] Reprinted from the *Virginia Gazette* of Thursday, Oct. 19, 1769,

37

presented to the Gentlemen of this county by EDMUND
JENNINGS, Esq., of London. I understand you mention this picture as obtained by subscription, when the
truth is, that the generous attachment of Mr. JENNINGS
to liberty, his native country, and their great defender,
influenced him, at his private expense, to present this
picture of Lord Chatham to the Gentlemen of Westmoreland. Your misfortune has arisen, I conjecture,
from a subscribed sum of money having been sent to
London for Lord CAMDEN's portrait, which gratitude,
and a just sense of the great support the American
cause received from that noble Lord, made the Gentlemen here wish to obtain.

TO [WILLIAM LEE][1]

DEAR BROTHER,   WILLIAMSBURG Decr 17. 1769

At this place we have been confined since the 7th of
last month attending on the assembly, and here I have
received your favors by Capt. Johnstoun and M.^r
Adams. The business of the Country, not having
been for three years considered, has occasioned this to
be a meeting of so much business and great perplexity,
that an adjournment to the middle of May will certainly take place. We hope by that time to know the
determination of Parliament on our affairs and would
therefore wish to have the most early authentic intelligence on this subject. And as scruples have arisen about
the authenticity of pr[ivate][2] letters, it may be well to

in the *Virginia Historical Register*, I. 70. William Rind started a
Virginia Gazette in 1766, Parks began his *Gazette* in 1736, and Pur-
die his in 1775.
[1] A. L. S. Virginia Historical Society, Lee Papers, IV. 246.
Endorsed, " R. H. Lee Esq. Virg.^a/Decr 17 & 20–1769/Rec.^d March
30. 1770/ Answ.^d April 4th/Post. 1/6. Ent. P. B. 3."
[2] This word is not clear in the Ms.; possibly it is " sev[eral]."

send the printed votes that relate to us. When I came here in November, I found no paces had been taken to effect a division between you and M.ʳ Paradise, and it being determined by the Trustees, that a Survey of all sh.ᵈ be made, together with a renewal appraisement of the personal estate, I have used every moment that attendance [1] in Assembly would permit, to be with Cary Wilkison, and urge him to push on the business with the greatest dispatch. that a division might be made before we adjourned. He has accordingly been very industrious, and now, tho' this is done, some other difficulties are started, that has occasioned the business to be defferred until our meeting in May. M.ʳ Nicholas & Col.º Corbin have shewn much willingness to have this affair finished, but I can say nothing of the others. Things being thus circumstanced, I had nothing left but to have every thing so exactly prepared against the May meeting that no plausibility may then be urged to prevent a final division and conveyance. This state of affairs makes it necessary, that things should remain (with regard to crops) as they were for another year, and the profits of the estate, be as usual divided between you and your Sister in law. I have done every thing in my power on this occasion, but you will discover, on reflection, that here was no room for force, nor would any undue pressing have been proper. When the division takes place, I will examine accurately into your part, and give you the most precise answers to all your inquiries that I shall then be able to do. You know my dear brother [tha][2]t in consequence of my having granted all my estate above [I][3] am quite out of the way of doing any thing in the [improve ?]-ment way, making little Tob.º where I live, having a

---

[1] Substituted above the line for " business " erased.
[2] Ms. torn.   [3] Covered by the binding.

heavy rent, and large public levies to pay. I can only say, and so thinks Loudon, that the dreadful gust in August, having lessened the crops so greatly below, might render precarious the getting a Ship loaded this year, unless a small Vessel, taking on liberty also might answer. But whether this method, or getting what could be got, and looking out here for liberty Vessels to take it for you, would best answer, must be left I think to the encouragement your other relations & friends transmit to you. Cary Wilkison tells me that the gust has prevented him from making a better crop this year than he has for many years last past had a chance of doing. He talks of 50 hhds Tob? to be made in the whole, half of which is I believe already sent to M! Cary for M! Paradise, and the other half will remain a little longer till it is certain whether or not you will send a Ship. Our good friend Col? Presley Thornton died a few days ago — If you and the Doctor should think it will be more in my power to serve my country in his place than in the one I hold, I doubt not, but you will exert yourselves to get me appointed, if not to this, to the next vacancy, another being likely soon to happen, from the uncommon age, and increasing debility of the old P—d. Indeed I find the attendance on Assemblies so expensive, and the power of doing good so rarely occuring, that I am determined to quit that employment.

I suppose you have before now heard of my marriage with Mrs Pinchard — I have the very great happiness to find in her a most tender attentive and fond mother to my dear little girls. I would not have you by any means give up the thoughts of engaging in the Tob? business, because I am well convinced, that in common years, it will be easy enough to get a small ship loaded, and that may prepare the way to more expensive business. I have exhorted Cary Wilkison to the greatest diligence, and he assures me, nothing in his power shall be omitted to push your interest, under his management to the utmost.

You may observe, that I write on association paper, and that principle admits not of copying my letter. I heartily wish you and my good Sister may enjoy uninterupted health and happiness. For my own part, I have been so long familiar with misfortune, that I have learned to look upon adversity with an undisturbed mind, and a steady countenance.

Farewell.

Dec.ʳ 20. 1769 WILLIAMSBURG.

TO ARTHUR LEE[1]

DEAR BROTHER, CHANTILLY IN VIRGINIA April 5, 1770

I wrote you last from Williamsburg by Capt. Nicks, since which I have been favored with two letters from you, the one by Somerville, the other by Page. I am much obliged to you for the political intelligence they contain. It is some comfort to have the virtuous on our side, altho, we are unsuccessful. I am therefore much pleased to hear these great and good men Lords Shelburne, Chatham, and Camden are with us. But alas I fear, the cause of public liberty, like the setting sun, is going to disappear. I mean from Britain, but I hope America will insist on being free. We are however a good deal disturbed here at the K——s speech — We cannot make it square with the promises (authorised by the highest authority) made to all the Assemblies by the several Governors. Time must develope this mystery. 'Tis some state trick, that plain honesty cannot easily penetrate. Our Assembly meets at its adjourned day in May next, when such measures

[1] A. L. S. University of Virginia, Lee Papers, No. 8. Addressed, " To/Doctor Arthur Lee/in/London. "

will be adopted, as our intelligence from London, shall render wise and necessary. Inclosed you have the certificates of your appointment that you desired. One of them is signed by M.ʳ Parker and myself, the other is an exact copy from the books, which it is proper M.ʳ W.ᵐ Lee should sign as he was then Treasurer. We expect you will resume our business when a favorable prospect opens, and I beg leave to refer you to my letter by Capt. Nicks on that subject. I do not know how you came to suppose our edition of the Farmers & Monitors letters to have been contrived by our friend M.ʳ Parker. It was the benefit of my Country that suggested the measure to me and I accordingly wrote the preface, and the terms, negotiated the whole matter with Rind, and got several hundred subscribers for the pamphlets — Rind thanked me for the great profit he had made, and indeed, in the hands of a diligent printer, a very considerable benefit would have arisen as the books were called for faster than he could finish them. Of these pamphlets I have sent one for Lord Shelburne, for Col.º Barre, M.ʳˢ Ma.ᶜCauley, M.ʳ Jenings, the Rev.ᵈ M.ʳ Porteus, M.ʳ John Stewart my friend. Yourself and M.ʳ W.ᵐ Lee. These, with letters for them in in a box directed to you, which I have desired M.ʳ Lee to open if you are not in Town, and deliver M.ʳ Jenings. M.ʳ Porteus, and M.ʳ Stewart their pamphlets. Those for Lord Shelburne M.ʳˢ MaCauley, Col.º Barre, I have requested M.ʳ Lee to get neatly bound in London before they are presented — The letters for them are left open for your perusal, which you will afterwards please to seal with your arms and deliver.

Capt. Johnstoun has bought your horse young Dabster for thirteen guineas I inclose you an order on him for. I have done everything in my power to sell the two Dabsters, and the chair, in vain — I sent them to the Fredericksburg fair, and then Col? Thomas our brother attended with them, and could get but £22. offered for them both — The times are greatly altered here, — Carriages do not sell, nor are high priced horses in demand. As quickly as I can get old Dabster and the chair off, you shall have the money — You have also a bill inclosed for £ 13. sterling, part of Will Brents protest. This bill came to my hands yesterday, with the ballance £ 3.8.6 in paper currency. If I can possibly, before Johnstoun sails, get a bill for this, and as much of my own money as will make up £20. sterling I will not fail to send it. It gives me concern, that I cannot remit all. I owe you for the two horses I bought, but I have been cruelly disappointed in not getting my cash up the country, where I have £ 200. now due me. I am going there in a few days, and I think you may depend on it by Greigs ship, that will sail I suppose next month. I am the more affected on this ocassion, because I know you want the money. Col? Phil, assures me that Molleson has orders to pay you the interest of your fortune immediately, and he is determined to pay up your interest annually, in consideration of which he requests that you will not send in any power of Attorney against him — He is now much distressed by a judgment that he was surprized with of one Bromn's Assigneés against him for £600. He is however going directly to sell off all his detached pieces of land, which with his income from Semple will discharge all demands against him soon. Semple I believe owes him largely now, and he intends (as his Mortgage warrants him) for the future to insist on the most punctual payments, or convey the works to one who will pay. I apprehend that Molleson supresses orders that he receives to pay you money from Col? Phil — Therefore I would enquire of him if he had not received directions to pay you so much money Annually.

In the box you will see the Virginia Gazette 15 Feb.[y] and you may observe the insolent letter from London 10 Nov.[r] 1769. I was resolved not to let insolence and falsehood go unpunished and therefore I sent the press and an animadversion on him as well as the other Adressers — This Gazette has not yet come to hand, but I will send it by next opportunity. Col.[o] Harry Lee tells me that he ordered M.[r] Molleson to pay you the seven pistoles for which you left me an order on him. Let me know if you have got this money, or if not, what is Molleson's reason for not paying it. Our relation Capt. John Lee of Essex request that you will write to Dr. Hamilton of Edenburg to get him a Tutor, and in doing this, the following method is to be observed. Capt. Lee has already written to one M.[r] Robert Fergusson Merchant at Sand gate in the shire of Air to procure him a Tutor; but fearing this gentleman might not be acquainted with such business and therefore fail to furnish him, he judged it prudent, by you, to apply to Dr. Hamilton — This M.[r] Fergusson is acquainted with M.[r] Lee's terms, which makes it necessary, that he should be applied to, before an engagement is made with a Tutor, and likewise to prevent an accident of two Tutors being sent over. I am acquainted with no part of the terms, but, that M.[r] Lee offers £30 a year salary. I have not yet got M.[rs] MaCauley's history — Will you be pleased to purchase it for me, and any other of her works that may be published — Apply to M.[r] Lee for cash to pay for these — You have never informed me, if the wine was received by Do[ctor][1] Fothergill, or how the old gentleman liked it. The storm in Sep[t][1] last, by distroying the grapes, prevented any wine from being made in these parts. I have been constantly on the look out for a rattle snake and am now promised by a gentleman above that he

[1] The Ms. is here damaged.

44

will exert himself to get one against Capt. Grieg's ship sails, or Walker's at furthest. Let me know if you please whether it will be agreeable to Lord Shelburne, that I send him a cask of our finest spirit made from the peach. It is so highly flavorous, and partakes so much of the fruit, that I really think 'tis much preferable to the finest Arrack —

I am my dear brothers most affectionate faithful friend.

Since writing this letter, I have inclosed your bills, one for £13 — the other for £20. and an order on Capt. Johnstoun for thirteen guineas by the Lord Camden in another Letter. Since writing the above I have thought it expedient to put in this letter duplicates of the bills and orders.[1]

TO [WILLIAM LEE][2]

DEAR BROTHER,   CHANTILLY IN VIRG^A. 7th July 1770.

This day Capt. Walker was here and gave me notice of his intention to sail in a few days, which sets me immediately to writing. — I wrote you hastily by Capt. Esten from Williamsburg, by which you will find I had then some doubt of our Countrymen, with respect to the liberty dispute — Since that the association, of which I now inclose you a copy, was unanimously agreed to, and is agreeable to the trade in general here. You will observe some clauses therein, calculated to produce the observation of this scheme, which, by being omitted before occasioned the shameful neglect of the former association among the Merchants here. Our Assembly have again petitioned the King for a complete redress of American grievances. The late repeal is so evidently

---

[1] The preceding paragraph is written on the back of the Ms. by R. H. Lee and signed by him.
[2] A. L. S. Virginia Historical Society, Lee Papers, IV. 149.

contrived to abuse [1] America, that instead of appeasing, it has inflamed all N. America; and produced a general determination to be most firm in opposition, until the slavish system is absolutely at an end. Vain, weak Ministers, to think that a sensible, brave people, can for a moment be imposed upon by their shallow, impotent plans of tyranny! I came a week ago from Williamsburg, about 5 days before the Assembly was prorogued, and I was present, when the division was made between you and M.ʳ Paradise. The conveyances were not made, but Col.º Corbin promised they should immediately be set about by an able Conveyancer, and the whole recorded at the next General Court. The houses in Williamsburg were divided by lot (having been first all valued by an experienced workman) and the large brick house that Rind lives in; the Mansion as it is called where my Uncles family lived in Town; with the blew Bell, a large house just behind the Capitol, fell to your share; and you were charged in account with their valuation. The first rents for £60. a year, the other 2 rent for £20. each, making £100. p.ʳ Ann in the whole. With respect to them, I think fortune favored you, they being to be chosen in preference to the rest. The Green spring lands, Govenors lands excluded, were valued at 20.ˢ/ p.ʳ acre, The Surry land at 40.ˢ/, and some of the land in Miss Fanny's part, that was, at £3. — The whole land west of Powhatan, M.ʳˢ Lee's by will, and so allotted her now, together with 164 Slaves, 217 head of Cattle, 190 head of Sheep, with 17 horses, 1 improved, and 1 unimproved Lot in James Town, and the above lots in Williamsburg were valued at £14997.6. When this was compared with the valuation of the Surry land, and other estate there, the disproportion was so great in favor of G. Spring, that it made necessary almost the whole of

[1] Substituted above the line for " ruin " erased.

what was willed Miss Fanny, to make the Sisters equal. I would willingly have given up all the houses in Town, and some Negroes from Green Spring, in exchange for lands near the Town. At length however, they determined to take a few Negroes from G. S. (your number remaining now as above, it being greater before) which added to the ballance that would have been due you, if M: Paradise had been appointed to the whole of Miss Fanny's part, except Town houses; accomplished the purpose of having M: Lee assigned 1000 Acres of land, about the head of Rich Neck mill, I think it is called; convenient for furnishing wood to the Town, and on which a quarter has long been, and we still think of continuing, as the land is good, and the Teams will be there ready to supply wood in the winter for the Town. In this valuation they have reckoned the Powhatan Mill worth £300. as the dam was lately extended by my Uncle, which extension begets the expense of £30. immediately to be paid M: Turner for former damage, and £7. p: An. for future injuries. Major Taliaferro's demand is not adjusted, but his will be much more. M: Paradise is to pay his part of former injuries as well as future demands for annual rent. But upon the whole, I submitted it to Loudoun and the Treasurer, whether it would not be better to let the Mill sink entirely, and build another small one, upon another stream belonging to the estate, sufficient to supply its own people, and convert your part of the land now in Pond, into Timothy meadow? My reasons were, that the gross profit of the mill is but £75. p: An. the annual repair as I was informed about £25. and you pay M: Paradise in valuation £200. more in the opinion of the Valuers for the mill as the dam is now extended, than it would be worth if reduced to its former bounds; the interest of this money is £10. yearly which with Turners and Taliaferro's allowances, would sink the greatest part of the mills profits, besides the risk of loosing the dam now and then. Whereas if the whole Mill was sunk, Mr Paradise must allow you from the present settlement £200. A fine meadow might be made and I suppose, from the expense of £50 or £60. upon the whole, a new Mill might be erected to furnish the plantation with meal. The remaining furniture at G. Spring, with the books, are to be sold for common benefit, and the money divided. I desired Wilkison to buy two of the beds, and some chairs on your account to be in the house when we went down to visit the estate. This is the most perfect account I can give you from the notes I took at the division. But very shortly, either from the Treasurer or myself, you will receive a precise copy of the whole. Your fee simple lands, west of Powhatan swamp amount to 6078 acres, to which is added of Governors land (leased I think for 99 years in Governor Dinwiddie's time at a very low rent) 925 Acres, making in the whole 7003 acres. This land is in general well timber'd and water'd, it is level, good corn land, but not very fit for tobacco unless manufactured in which case it brings very fine. If it were not for the amazing growth of the wild onion, or garlic as they call it in England, it would be very proper land for wheat, being a stiff soil. Upon this tract, there are six plantations properly furnished for cropping, including G. Spring, with 3 orchards. The gardens and orchards at G. S. are extensive, and furnished with variety of good fruit. Out of the 164 slaves, mentioned above, but 59 are crop negroes, I mean exclusive of boys, — 12 are house servants, 4 Carpenters 1 Wheel wright, 2 Shoe makers, 3 gardeners and Ostlers. The horses are realy useless, and consume a vast deal of corn, the plantation business is done with oxen — May these horses not be sold ? The plantation near Town, upon the 1100 acres assigned you is now worked by Mr Paradise's people, when they move at the years end, you must furnish a fresh set, and may not some be found among the numerous band of house servants, gardeners, ostlers &c. The gardens are indeed in tolerable good order, but I should think, less force might do. The G. S. improvements were all of them valued at £700 and the Valuers thought they guided themselves by the Will in not valuing them too scrupulously. The house at G. S. wants repair much. I fear that the long gallery will fall in despite of props, having already quitted the house a little. The walls appear good, and I believe the timbers are likewise so. I am informed that Major Taliaffero says he will make a thorough repair £500. —

Each of your parts is valued at more than £15,000. The woolens sent in for your people last year, are though[t] slight and insufficient. Good Welch cotton seems upon the whole to answer best. The weeding hoes, Wilkison says are good for nothing. Indeed I have found from experience, that the best hoes I can get sent me are useless, but as you are upon the spot, and a judge of such things, you might, I suppose have proper ones sent. I assure you, much loss is sustained from not having proper instruments of husbandry, one hand being able to do twice as much work in a day, with a good ax or hoe, as he can with a bad one. The profits of the estate this year are to be divided as usual. Capt. Walker brings you 24 ħħds. of your own Tob? being the half made on the estate, levies &c. deducted. The Captain brings you also 4 ħħds. from me. I had ordered 6 to be purchased above the best Tob?, but it seems my Collector fell short in his collection, and therefore got only 4. These I hope will be sufficient to pay you the ballance I owe you, and also furnish the few things included in the invoice now sent. Capt. Walker has an old shoe of Mrs. Lee's, which we have sent to direct the size of the new ones. You will please let these be as neat as the association price will admit, 5.^{s} / sterling a pair.

I beg your attention to the following affair. You know I have got the entail of my estate from my father dockt by writ of ad quod damnum, but not knowing how future judges and lawyers may explain away things I remain uneasy about my younger children, and wish securely to provide for my poor little helpless girls in the following manner. I understand there is in London an office, where any sum of money being put, draws 10 or more per cent annually. that at the end of every year the interest is engrafted into the principal and both draw interest. That this contin[u]es as long as the putter in chooses, always observing that if death interposes, the whole becomes office property. Now I would choose to place £100. sterling, for each of my girls there, and let it continue until they were either of age or married, and then, let them or their husbands do with it as they pleased. Now what I would request of you, is, to make accurate enquiry into the validity of this office (with respect to the security of the property I mean) and an exact account of the whole scheme that I may loose no time in sending my cash; for you know the little girls are coming on fast, and therefore, the earlier this plan is adopted, the better. I had almost forgot to mention that Cary Wilkison suggested to me in Town, his intention to quit yours, and adhere to Mr Paradise's business. I wanted him to remain, that we might have time to look out for a proper manager. He said he would consider of it. Our brother Loudon, who remained in Town after me, was to get a premptory answer, before he quitted it, that we might provide the best we could get during the course of this summer. Wilkeson pretended that Mr Paradise had, but that you had not offered him to stay. This by the by was nothing, because Col.^{o} Loudon and myself both offered him to remain last winter. But he seems to think the whole too much (perhaps he is right) and says, as he has no children, and a pretty good living, he rather inclines to be at home. I shall tire you as I have done myself, and therefore conclude (after presenting our best love to our Sister, and the children's duty to you both) with assuring you that I am your ever affectionate brother and faithful friend

July 9.

Would it not be proper to return the Liberty here as quickly as possible to prevent preengagements, and can she not, with good management, lay as cheap in Yeocomoco, as in the Thames? However, if she should be detained a little, in order to bring good accounts of sale, I think it would be wise — There are some capital Shippers here, that it might be prudent to take much pains by writing and other effectual methods to engage. Old Col? Loudon I hear is out with Molleson about his refusing to pay a Tradesman a small order of the Colonels — You know the old Gentleman — A little well applied flattery, contrition for not having corresponded with your God father before, and strong assurances of application to his interest in future may do great things in your favor. Counsellor Carter may by proper address be made a large Shipper. M? Carter of Corotoman: has purchased to oblige you. He is a person of much consideration. Counsellor Nelson had engaged to ship in the Craft that went for your own Tobacco, but she did not call on him. Suppose you were to thank him for his kind intentions — Both Col? R. Corbin & the Treasurer talk of shipping you a good deal next year. Ply them up. You know of what weight Col? Tayloe M? Loyd, & the Squire our Squire I mean are — M? Sam. Washington is much your friend, he will probably make large crops in Frederick and he may be persuaded to bring his Cousin M.ʳ Warner Washington to be your correspondent.   T. A. Washington likes flattery, try him.

I have many reasons that are absolutely decisive against continuing a popular Candidate any longer.   They are numerous as well as weighty, and I am certain would thoroughly convince you if I had time now to recapitulate them.   If therefore I am to continue in the public service, it must be in the Council.   I own the force of your general maxim, but I think in this Country the case is something different.   The power of checking ill, and the means of doing good occurring oftener in our upper than in our lower house.   This I believe is not a proper season for one of our family to expect favor.   I should be sorry it were.   But virtue must shortly drive vice & folly off the ground.

Our old President is now so entirely in his dotage that his opinion is not asked either in Court or Council, his exit may be daily expected.   On a change, may it not be so settled [1] as that I may be fixed on to fill the next vacancy, and the probability of a speedy one urged from the present condition of the President?

I fear you are too right with respect to your opinion of the Glass house business — I shall however converse with our monied men touching the Irish Gentleman you mention — I like much his character, and wish you to push your enquiries concerning him.

Yours for ever.

TO WILLIAM LEE [2]

DEAR BROTHER,   CHANTILLY   8ᵗʰ January 1771

An opportunity is presented from N. Potomack and I embrace it to answer your favor by D.ʳ Jones.   Loudon

---

[1] Substituted above the line for "found" erased.

[2] A. L. S.   Virginia Historical Society, Lee Papers, IV. 242.   Addressed, "William Lee Esquire/Merchant in/London."   Endorsed as received March 11 and answered the 19th.

and myself were lately at Green Spring, where we called in our way from Williamsburg, whither we were carried to defeat a North British scheme for the abolition of the Association. We effected our purpose, and now, this matter is not again to be considered until next June Oyer court. Wilkison remains at Green Spring another year, and he intends to settle the Quarter/now vacated by the withdrawing Mr Paradises people/with six hands, the best to be spared from among the house servants who are very numerous. We have directed the sale of the horses, and fixed upon the entire dropping of Powhatan mill. But a mill being exceedingly necessary to supply such numbers as belong to the estate, we desired Wilkison to get about building a new one upon a stream strongly recommended by him as sufficient for the purpose, and liable to none of the many objections which attend the Powhatan Mill. I have applied to the Treasurer to have this matter considered by the Trustees, and a proper allowance made, before they finally quit their administration of the personals yet remaining in their hands to be divided. You have now settled five plantations including G. Spring, and they are work'd with 57 Slaves.[1] The whole number of the grown people being 80, and the number of both old and young 153. The land, as I wrote you before, is generally good for corn, but with out dung, will not much of it produce Tobacco; and from the best information I can get, I suppose, that not more than a seventh part of the whole land is cleared. One of the old arguments prevails again this year, and as I find you are to get not more than 27 ħħds of Tob? from so many Workers. As the Adventurer John Ballandine used to say I fear they will not "clear their teeth." The crop of corn is middling. Our brother Frank and myself have considered your objections, and remain unshaken in our opinion

[1] In the Ms. this word resembles " Sharers."

touching the propriety of selling. Meeting with a purchaser for the land would undoubtedly be the most
difficult part of the business. But we would not propose hurrying that matter, resting contended with
renting contended with renting out the cleared plantations, which would do more than defray every expence
that the whole gives rise to. And let it be of standing
publication, that you will sell to any person, both lands,
and houses in Williamsburg, in the whole, or by parcels,
whensoever Purchasers offer for the whole a reasonable
price. It remains only to be considered, how the sale
of the Negroes may answer. Estimating the sum they
would produce at £6000. is far from being unreasonable,
which with the Stocks and Utensils, would raise the
whole to a principal, that by its interests alone, will
be found upon a fair average calculation of 6 or 7 years
to exceed the present profits. The experience of many
late Sales do not shew the objections you urge. It
having been proved from these, that Negroes, above any
other thing sold, draws forth the Planters cash, with
which they abound at present from the late high price of
Tob? Punctuality would perhaps be recommended
by this means — Let the sale be for 12 months credit, 5
p: cent discount be allowed for ready money, and if the
purchasers fail to pay at the end of the 12 months, then
such as fail, to pay interest from the time of purchasing.
Now if many should fail, yet they at length pay 5 p:
cent. from the time of the sale, which I am persuaded is
more than you at present receive from the estate. I
can not help thinking, that when once it was known that
you were inclined to sell, altho not urged by any necessity
to do so, that reasonable offers would e'er long be made,
and in the mean time, the land would, by renting the
clear ground only m[ore][1] t[han][1] defray its own expence. The Governor's land would in this case I think

[1] Ms. torn.

be all rented for w[hat]¹ it will bring, that the rent you are to pay for [it]¹ may at least be obtained. But it will do much more than this. At present, I think of going up with your Captain to Frederick when he arrives, the great crops made there by some lowland Gentlemen promising considerable consignments. Give my love to the Doctor, and say I will write him largely by Capt. Blackwell, who sails hence some time next month, in the mean time, I send him a bill of exchange for what his Chair sold — it being the utmost farthing I could obtain for it — I have got three fine Summer ducks for Lady Shelburne, which Capt. Blackwell will bring — I am sure if no accident happens to them they will please the two Drakes being exceedingly beautiful.

Our best love attends our Sister

Your ever affectionate brother and faithful friend.

TO LANDON CARTER²

DEAR SIR,   CHANTILLY 17ᵗʰ Janʸ 1771

It must be a very extraordinary cause that will prevent me from waiting on you Monday next — At present I resolve to give you the meeting at church, where I have no manner of doubt, but that we shall have a very good sermon, a thing quite usual with the revᵈ Mʳ Giberne.

My idea of coolness, is explained by a wise and well judged formation of the plan we have in view; foreseeing that it will be attended with extensive and very beneficial consequences.

Our best wishes are for the * * * at Sabine Hall.

Your affectiona[te].

¹ Ms. torn.
² A. L. S. Virginia Historical Society, Lee Papers, IV. 254. Addressed, "To/Landon Carter Esqʳ of/Sabine Hall." A copy of

THE LETTERS OF RICHARD HENRY LEE

TO LANDON CARTER[1]

CHANTILLY the 18th of April 1771

DEAR SIR,

I have met with the same difficulty in my attempts for the Patriotic store that you mention. All approve, but none have the money. For as yet, I have met with no one person hardy enough to condemn, occasioned I suppose, by my having never conversed with a B——d on the subject.

He is one of those who are born "to make absurdity fashionable." But let us go on my friend, and by persevering in a good cause, deserve that success which we may fail to meet with. If the people will submit to abuse, let them do it with their eyes open; if they will pursue the wrong, after having been shown the right way, they will then have themselves only to blame. With respect to the other subject of your letter, I agree entirely. I thought so from the beginning, nor did the application to me a whit alter the plan I have now pursued for more than six years. If I mistake not, the patriot Romans thought that every good Citizen should serve his Country seven years — I have done so twelve. And if in that time I have found it an hard[2] service, why should I press for it with an earnest solicitude.

I am with much regard, dear Sir, your affectionate and obedient Servant.

this original appears among the copies of letters to Landon Carter, Virginia Historical Society.

[1] A. L. S. Virginia Historical Society, Lee Papers, IV. 240. Addressed to him at Sabine Hall, and sent by Mr. Parker. A copy is found among the copies of letters to Landon Carter, Virginia Historical Society.

[2] Substituted above the line for "oppressive" erased.

THE LETTERS OF RICHARD HENRY LEE

TO WILLIAM LEE[1]

DEAR BROTHER   PECATONE 17 June 1771

Our friend and Kinsman John Turberville Esq.[r] has committed to your care a very important concern, the direction of his Sons education. He relys greatly on your sensible and tender attention to this business — The first object in view being a complete education, to have that purpose effectually answered, he chooses his Son to be placed either at Eton, at Winchester, or at Westminster; proposing that one of the three of the best present reputation shall be fixed on. Altho M.[r] Turberville does not mean so far to attend to frugal principles as to neglect by any means the great business of learning, yet every thing else being equal, he would prefer that one of the three where the greatest moderation in the article of expence prevails. I refer you to my many letters by this opportunity, wishing that you may have patience to go thro them all.

Our love to our dear Sister.

Your affectionate brother —

P.S. Walker is now at Essex Court so that I can get no fresh information touching him, but I believe Craft is out for Load.

Indolent as he is perhaps it may be after the close of this month before he sails.

[1] A. L. S. Virginia Historical Society, Lee Papers, IV. 131. Addressed, "William Lee esquire/merchant in/London.//By favor of/Master Turberville." Endorsed, " Recd 1st Aug. Ans 9 Oct[r]."

THE LETTERS OF RICHARD HENRY LEE

TO WILLIAM LEE[1]

June the 19. 1771

A fourth letter by the same Ship! The duce take this Man he will plague me to death with reading letters. Stop a little, 'tis only a newspaper I want you to read now—And that you may not discover an absurdity in presentin[g][2] a Londoner with a Virginia newspap[er] observe, 'tis only that you may see the most accurate account of the ravages made by the fresh.* If you have time, you may read of Tryons prowess, and learn from him/if it be worth knowing, but in fact such knowledge fits only the Servants of Carlton house/how to set one part of the community to murdering the rest. This Gentleman is surely recommending himself to the Dowager, and I doubt not but we shall shortly hear of him and his Cannon figuring in S.[t] Georges fields[.] In truth [the] whole of this business was dirty work in the mildest view of it. For you may know, that the Lawyers, *bad every where*, (don't let the Doctor see this)[3] but in Carolina worse than bad, having long abused the people in the most infamous manner, at length brought things to such a pass, that a bond of £500. was taken for a single fee in trifling causes, and this bond put in suit and recovered before the business was done for

---

[1] A. L. S. in initials. Original in the possession of Mrs. A. Morris Tyson of Baltimore, Maryland, who kindly permitted it to be transcribed. The letter is addressed, "William Lee Esq.[r] / Merchant in / London//By favor of / Cap.[t] M.[c] Gachen / Q.D.C." It is marked "N.[o] 5." and endorsed, "Virginia 1771/Rich.[d] Hen: Lee 15.th June /Rec.[d] . . . 1.st Aug.[t] Answ.[d] . . . 9/D.[o]. / Tryon's Massacre." It was probably enclosed with other letters.

[2] The Ms. is damaged by rents and portions are torn away, so this and all enclosures in square brackets are missing and here supplied.

* The mark, ⊢⊣ , in darker ink is here written in the Ms.

[3] This phrase is inserted above the line.

which the fee was paid. Grieved in this manner without being able to obtain redress, the people were at length driven by repeated injuries to do what otherwise they would never have thought of. The governor himself, in his speech to the Assembly acknowledges the grievances and recommends enquiry & redress, but instead of accompanying the redress with an Act of Amnesty, the constant political remedy [am]ong wise and humane Statesmen in like cases, [he] proceeds to murder with fire and sword the [p]oor abused injured people. But the story goes, that when the Parties met, after some small intercourse, it was at length agreed by the Governor to allow a certain space of time for the Insurgents to consider about laying down their Arms, and that before the allowed time was elapsed, he fell upon the unsuspecting multitude, and made great slaughter with his Cannon. One would think that a just Government should [1] oblige this Man [kil?]ler to produce the clearest exculpation [of?] his conduct on this occasion, after giving the injured the fairest opportunity of acquitting themselves and impeaching him. By this time I suppose you are tyred of M:̅ Tryon — For truth I did not intend when I set down to trouble either you o[r] myself so much about him. But whenever I reflect on this transaction, I feel the common cause of Mankind hurt by his procedure.*

You may see in this paper a very sensible protest [from? ve]ry sensible Men. For peace sake let us ** [2] Bishop. Neither Tythes nor Ecclesiastical courts will do in America Our law Courts can never have weight or strength sufficient to encounter the latter.

On second thoughts, you may show the Doctor this letter, with my own correction of the sentiment touching

[1] Substituted for "would" erased.
* The mark, ⊢, in darker ink is here written in the Ms.
[2] Probably "have no" are the words here torn away.

59

Lawyers — I never meant to include such as Sommers, Hawles, Camden, the late[1] Secretary to the Bill of Rights, or such as I doubt not Doctor Lee will be But . . . .[2] Wedderburn &.ᶜ &.ᶜ &.ᶜ &ᶜ almost wit[hout ?] number —
I am, as you would have me, your affectionate

Make insurance of 15 ħħds of Col.º G. Lee's Tob.º in the Liberty — Col.º Martins Tob.º in Fa[l]mouth, except 10 ħħds is lost —

TO WILLIAM LEE[3]

Dear Brother   Chantilly 3.ᵈ July. 1771

I have informed Mr Stephen Chilton of your good intentions with regard to him, that you were inclined to furnish him a Mates birth. In consequence of this, he now goes home in the Liberty. Added to Mr Chilton's being our Countryman, he understands Navigation well, and has the reputation of being an exceeding good Seaman. He certainly deserves encouragement, and I know that Merit will always meet with your countenance.

Your affectionate brother.

Virginia

[1] The partial word "Chair" is here erased.
[2] Illegible word, possibly "this." Only a portion of the first two letters remain.
[3] A. L. S. Lenox Library, Ford Collection. Addressed to him in London, and sent by Mr. Stephen Chilton. Endorsed as received "24 Sept."

THE LETTERS OF RICHARD HENRY LEE

TO WILLIAM LEE[1]

DEAR BROTHER   NOMINY IN VIRGINIA 23ᵈ De[c. 1771][2]

By meer accident, at Mᵣ Blains store I met with this
opportunity by Mᵣ Adams, and being taken by surprise,
I cannot so fully as I wish answer your letter lately
received. If you had recollected, when Montgomerie
sailed hence in July, both Loudon and myself were on
the Assembly at Williamsburg, (to which place) when
we set out, we expected Walker would have sailed in
four days, and in consequence of which, I had left my
dispatches with the Naval Office for the Liberty. The
cause of her not sailing sooner than she did, you certainly know before this time. We are however happy
to hear that the ship is arrived at London, and we are
now in expectation of her, or the return of another
from you in a short time. I think our crops are pretty
good, and therefore I hope your ship will[3] get reasonable dispatch. I have promised a young Gentleman
of worth in Frederick to import for him a sett of Sur-
veying Instruments, and therefore you will be pleased to
send consigned to me and at my expense by the first
opportunity to this or Rappahanock river a Surveyors
Compass with Ball and Socket, a Surveyors Chain,
with a case of Plotting Instruments to contain a paralell
ruler — The whole to be of the best kind that can be
got for six or 7 pounds sterling — Observe that the
Chain is for service in a stony country and therefore
must be unusually strong. [Ou]r[4] Assembly is called

[1] A. L. S. Virginia Historical Society, Lee Papers, IV. 99. Addressed to him in London. Endorsed, " Recᵈ, 14 Feb., 1772/Ansᵈ 16
Dᵒ & 25/Orders goods & will/write fully soon — "
[2] Margin torn.
[3] Following this word " now " ? is erased.
[4] Margin of the Ms. torn.

the 6th of February next when I shall have an opportunity of considering your affairs on that quarter, and will give you then my sentiments on the paragraph of Mr Treasurers letter as you desire.

In much haste I can only add my love for Mrs Lee and the Doctor

Your affectionate friend.

TO LANDON CARTER [1]

DEAR SIR,   WILLIAMSBURG, 7th March 1772

I am your debtor for two very obliging letters which I should have answered sooner if an oportunity had presented.   I admit your criticism on the expression we convened about, and then objected to a seeming contrariety in the words themselves.   I regret your losses much, and sincerely wish that fitter laws were provided to remedy the evil you very justly complain of.   But on this subject, the old sentiments prevail, and no alteration would be admitted.   I will not trouble you with the variety of undetermined business that is now before the house, because, the greater part will never go thro the Legislature.   Again the Agency bill has been warmly contended for, and rejected nevertheless.   The lower house has passed a bill to repeal that part of our law which forbids fine and recovery in this Colony, and they will pass an Act for rendering the choice of Vessels septennial.

When we shall get up Heaven knows, little being get done.

I am dear Sir Your affectionate and obliged friend.

[1] A. L. S.   Virginia Historical Society, Lee Papers, IV. 234.   Addressed, " To/Landon Carter Esqr./of/Sabine Hall." Endorsed, "Col. Lee's Sam is to be at/Mount Airy on Friday on his/way to Williamsburgh;/50 bushels."

THE LETTERS OF RICHARD HENRY LEE

TO LANDON CARTER [1]

DEAR SIR   MOUNT AIRY 31ˢᵗ March 1772

The Bearer will deliver you two letters that were put into my hands by your Son just as I left Williamsburg. I suppose these letters will inform you when your Son proposes to return. The Assembly is not yet up, nor will be so for ten or twelve days to come, there being abundance of small business before the house. I cannot give you a better account of this Session than by saying it began idly, proceeded busily, and is likely to end with having done nothing. The great bills were all drop't, either by the Council or in our house. The necessity of being at Westmoreland Court this day prevents me the pleasure of waiting on you. Your Godson's ship is arrived in Yeocomico, and we hope for your kind assistance in forwarding her load.

I am with great respect and esteem, dear Sir Your affectionate friend and humble Servant.

TO WILLIAM LEE [2]

DEAR BROTHER,   CHANTILLY IN VIRGINIA 13ᵗʰ April 1772

After a tedious session of Assembly I returned here the 31ˢᵗ of last month, and found the Liberty had been arrived in Yeocomoco but a few days before. I have seen the Captain twice since, and he informs me by letter two days ago, that he had engaged 200 hhds. Many unlucky causes have concurred to confine me closely at home since my return from Williamsburg,

[1] A. L. S. Virginia Historical Society, Lee Papers, IV. 236. Addressed as the preceding letter, p. 62.

[2] A. L. S. Virginia Historical Society, Lee Papers, IV. 228. Addressed to him in London, and sent by Capt. Greig, "Q.D.C."

but I have given Capt. Rayson warm letters of recommendation to my friends in the part of the country he has been visiting. I believe he has nearly delivered all his goods, and waits only for his iron, which is every hour expected, to begin stowing Tobacco. We had provided iron for him, ready landed at D.ʳ Floods, but Page coming in first, in our absence Lawson ordered that iron for him. This is Northumberland court day, after which, I expect Rayson to call here in his way up to Stafford, Prince William, Fauquier and Frederick. The Tobacco already engaged, being to be getting on board whilst he is on this trip. I cannot possibly form a judgment yet whether he can get his load entire from Potomac, but at all events some Tob? from rappahanock must be taken. Col? Martin's and Col? Carter's, with young M.ʳ Corbin's. Col? Martin desires you will insure twenty hhds of Tobacco for him in the Liberty. He does not mention the rate of insurance, and so I am inclined to think he means as much p.ʳ hhd as was insured last year. This gentleman writes me to inform you, that his convenience and interest are so considerable by carrying his Tob? to Falmouth, that he must continue to do so, and hopes for this reason, you will not be dissatisfied with his conduct in this respect. I shall observe what you write in respect to the loading of the Liberty. If it is possible, she will sail in all May. But I am inclined to think we may reckon the 10ʰ or 15 of June. The Planters are sanguine enough here to expect from 20 to 25 Shillings a hundred all cash, and so long as these expectations are entertained they will not be very much disposed to ship. Our exchange is at 20, and if 20.ˢ/ cash can be got here, no price now given in Britain will warrant shipping. Add to this difficulty, that you are not inclined to have your Tob? from York put in the Liberty, which, with most of the rappahanock Tob? being reserved for another purpose, seems to throw difficulties in the way of this Ship's quick dispatch. We shall however do the best. Young M.ʳ Peter Presley Thorton desires me to acquaint you, that for this year, his not receiving the advantage of his estate prevents his assistance to your Ship, but that the next year she shall have the greatest part, if not the whole. It will be very proper to return him thanks for this his good intention. This Gentlemen, S. M. Ball, R. Skinner, young Garvin Corbin, M.ʳ John Turberville, Col.º Martin, Lord Fairfax, Col.º Tayloe, S. Washington, and M.ʳ John Alexander of Stafford deserve to be carefully cultivated. This last Gentleman has promised me to ship this year, he is powerful in the Tobacco way, quite disengaged, and being governed by interest and vanity as his Master passions, he may, without much difficulty be secured by you. The Liberty will bring you 20 hhds from Col.º George Lee's estate and five from me. All these please to insure to recover £8. sterl[ing]¹ in case of loss. So much for the commercial affairs. Capt. Greig brings your accounts from Cary Wilkison. He tells me you will get only 24 hhds this year again. I believe he suffered greatly by the torrents of rain that fell in July last, as did most others in this country. The Treasurer declares he has taken no offence at all, that he is pleased with doing you offices of friendship whenever 'tis in his power, and that he in writing to you, alluded only to the pressure of public business on him. He is to make all possible enquiry touching the scheme of renting your estate below. If it can be well done, I think it will be greatly to your advantage. But what is to be done with the Gallery at Green Spring? It will absolutely tumble down presently if 'tis not thoroughly and speedily repaired. We have desired Cary to get some bricks ready, and sustain it as well as

¹ Hole in the Ms.

possible, so soon as he has done with the new Mill, which will be the case in a short time now. My goods p^r Liberty came well except the Cask N° 5 Nails & hoes not yet come to hand, and unhappily the Carboy of Vinegar is broke to pieces and that all lost, a very unlucky circumstance to our family. My boys will come home in the Liberty, and I am fixed that they go either to St. Bees, or to the Gentleman of [* * *]¹ near Bristol mentioned to me by Dr Lee. I understand from the [* * *]¹t this gentleman near Bristol; boards, educates &^c tolerably well [* * *]¹ more than £20 Sterling a year. Now £30. Sterling a piece for [b] ¹oardi[ng c] ¹lothing and education is all that for some years I can afford them apiece. If a thorough knowledge of english and the classics can with writing and arithmetic be obtained for this, I shall be happy, and the one will be then fitted to engage at the Temple, and with a little more, the eldest may be conditioned for the Church here, where we are determined to have no Bishops. If the Gentleman near Bristol is fixed on by you and the Doctor, it may be proper to write to him in time that he may not be too full, and thereby prevented from taking my Sons. I suppose you have received my former letter desiring a sett of Surveyors instruments for a Gentleman up the country might be sent me. Compass with Ball [* * *] ²ing chain, and case of plotting instruments with a [* * *] ² case. If these are not already sent, let them come [* * *] ² cannot imagine how much I am hurt for want of a good Ship ³ Joiner who understands something of the House Joiners business — I therefore entreat you will not cease trying until you furnish me with such a person. I will send you the ages of the young Lees and our G. Grandfather's will by next opportunity.

¹ Margin torn off.   ² Letters missing, Ms. torn.
³ Illegible word, "Stop"? "Shop"?

Our best love to our dear Sister.   Your ever affectionate friend and brother.

TO [WILLIAM LEE][1]

DEAR BROTHER   CHANTILLY the 12th June 1772
I was just writing in my letter book a long letter to you by Capt. Page who sails, he says, in a few days from this time.   But apprehending that Anderson will go first, I take the opportunity by Mr Wilson (who is just come here for a letter to you and the Doctor as he goes home in Anderson for orders) to inform you that Rayson had last friday 123 ħħds on board stowed. That he had Craft gone for 100 More and had in all 340 engaged.   But Rayson says he can store 380 at least this year, so that I fear it will be 10th or 15th of July before he sails.   But you may depend it will be as quickly as possible.   The York Charter has distressed us, because it required both Potomac & Rappahanock to load Rayson, as no liberty could be had in either River so soon as we wanted it, and the Norfolk business of Staves liable to such sure and certain imposition if not guarded against by the personal presence and knowledge of the purchaser.   Rayson seems willing to overlook a few days for the advantage of a Tob? frieght.   We have been at last obliged to take all the Tob? yet to be gotten from both Rivers to dispatch Rayson, as Outram appears inclined to give up 100 ħħds of his Charter.   Between 30 & 40 consigned are expected from York and I expect the rest will be purchased.   But this you will be fully informed of by our brother Loudon — Mr Wilson is in great haste, so

---

[1] A. L. S.   Lenox Library, T. B. Myers Collection, No. 827.

that I must have done. Shall write largely in a few days by Page.

Yours.

Col! Martin 18

M! Washington $\dfrac{8}{26}$ All from Frederick

This a great disappointment. —

TO JAMES STEPTOE [1]

DEAR SIR,   CHANTILLY the 4$\underline{^{th}}$ of July 1772

By the joint advice of my friends, confirmed by my particular situation, I had taken a resolution to apply to M! Secretary for a Clerkship when one in these parts should fall vacant. My two Sons going this summer to England, added to the heavy charge of supporting so many more here, made an aid of this kind extremely necessary for me. I have been allways determined however, that if Prince William should fall, not to accept it, if I found it in my power, provided you retained your desire of coming this way. But I considered, that provided as you are, with a Clerkship inferior very little, if any, to the best in the Colony; that it was more than probable you would not wish any delay to my success in the present precarious state of things. I wish, with all my heart, that I could have personal conversation with you about this business, but as that I fear is not likely soon to happen, I should be glad to have your sentiments candidly and fully on this subject. Your inclinations you may be assured shall be conclusive with me. As I would wish this to be

[1] A. L. S. Virginia Historical Society, Loose Mss., File 8. Addressed, "To / M! James Steptoe / clerk of Bedford / Court in / Bedford County."

secret, it will be necessary to trust your answer only to a person who will deliver it with his own hand to our brother William at the College in Williamsburg.

I very sincerely wish you health and happiness, being your affectionate brother and friend.

TO [WILLIAM LEE][1]

DEAR BROTHER,   [July —, 1772?]

I wrote you lately & fully by the Justicia Capt. Gray whom I expected would sail before Dobby, but now I learn that Dobby will first sail — This therefore is to inform that Capt. Rayson will (barring most extraordinary accident, sail hence by the middle of this month of July, he has now 260 ħħds on board & 3 Craft some time out for the rest of his Cargo. Capt. Rayson desires me to request you, that if a prospect of war takes place whilst he may be supposed on his Voyage, that you insure three hundred pounds sterling worth of property for him in the Liberty

Your affec[tionate].[2]

TO WILLIAM LEE[3]

DEAR BROTHER,   CHANTILLY IN VIRGINIA the 12ᵗʰ July 1772

Inclosed you have a letter open for Mr. Jenings, which when you have read, be so kind as seal with your arms and deliver. You will see by it, that the Gentlemen Subscribers to Lord Camdens picture here, have,

[1] A. L. S. Virginia Historical Society, Lee Papers, IV. 108.
[2] Ms. torn.
[3] A. L. S. Virginia Historical Society, Lee Papers, IV. 218. Addressed to him in London, and endorsed as received September 21.

at the repeated request of M⸱ Jenings, determined to withdraw their money. He is desired to pay it into your hands, and so soon as you receive it, let £4. sterling be taken to yourself, and the same sum paid to our brother D⸱ Lee, for your several subscriptions of £5. — currency which being reduced into sterling as it was, at the exchange of that time, brought it down to £4. — Sterl⸱ You will please loose no time in communicating to me the reception of this money, and the sum received, that I may immediately restore their several quotas to the Subscribers. The whole sum in the hands of M⸱ Jenings is £76.8. sterl⸱, from which deducting £8. for yours and the Doctors subscriptions, the balance of £68.8. sterling you will put to my credit. The very unexpected disappointment I have met with in getting my cash from above, compels me just now, to give M⸱ Balmain a bill on you for £25. sterl⸱, which I beg the favor of you to pay him on demand, because it will be quite necessary for him in London, where he is not willing to make any longer stay than the nature of his business renders absolutely necessary. He comes home for orders, and as he has lately taken much care of my boys, I must entreat you to give him all the assistance in your power towards forwarding his ordina-tion. Introduce him, if necessary, to D⸱ Porteus, who I know can aid him essentially in his affair with the Bishop. He will require assistance in readily getting Queen Annes bounty to Clergymen coming to America. Permit me now to engage your attention about a very tender concern. 'Tis the care of my dear Boys that I recommend to you with true parental warmth. Their welfare you may be sure is deeply at my heart. Great reflection, aided by observation, and my own experience, sufficiently convince me, that education is much cheaper obtained in England, than in any part of America, our College excepted. But there, so little attention is paid

either to the learning, or the morals of boys that I never
could bring myself to think of William & Mary.

In either of the Northern Colonies, the avowed charge
with their various items will be more than an hundred
sterling p̲ annum. The sum beyond which I cannot
afford now to go, is £30. sterling apiece for Board clothing, and education. This sum either at S̲ Bees, at
Warrington in Lancashire, or with the Gentleman near
Bristol will certainly do, as well from the accounts you
have given me as from the information [I have.?]
Whichever of these will best answer the purpose of
education, there I would have them sent without delay,
because, at their time of life, they forget very quickly,
and now, they are good Scholars so far as they have gone.
I propose Thomas for the Church, and Ludwell for
the Bar. A tolerable share of learning is requisite for
either of these professions. About 15 years old Ludwell
may be entered of one of the Inns of Court, and actually
come there to study law at 18. So that he may return
with the Gown at 21. We shall hereafter consider the
cheapest, and fittest place for the eldest, until the time
comes that he can be ordained. He is 14 years old next
October, and Ludwell 12 the same month. I am sorry
the schools mentioned are so far removed from you,
because I well know how apt they are to neglect boys
at a distance. You will infinitely oblige me, by falling
on the best possible plan to remedy this too common
and pernicious evil. If some Gentleman living near the
place, could be persuaded to observe how they proceed,
or when any of your acquaintance may be passing by
the place, to call and enquire. But above all, frequently
to remind the Master of his duty, and know often from
the Boys themselves (for they can write well) how they
go on, and what books they are reading. They have
never yet learned Arithmetic, it may be proper soon to
have them entered in this branch. I hope you will

make the passage as light as possible, for in fact they have their own bed, and as much provision as they will or can eat during the voyage, so that their water, and the room they take up in the Ship is all the expence they create. Pardon me for not now making you a better remittance. My intention was to have sent a £60. bill of exchange with the boys, and to have paid M! Balmain his last years salary here, but M! Blackwell writes me, he cannot send my money yet, but expects every day to do it. I shall before the close of this year send you an hundred pounds, and for the future, I will have more punctuality above. You will readily see that my boys must be very frugally clothed. The plainest, to be decent, will please me much the best. They will want a plain cheap furbishing up on their arrival. With 5 children and another it may be, two, on the Stocks, a small estate must part with nothing unnecessary. I take all possible care, but I assure you, if the varying state of politics on your side, would enable my brother to fix the profit of some place with me, it would remove many difficulties. Have an eye to the deputy Secretarys place. I suppose more than £ 1000. p! annum is not paid the principal, and I really believe 'tis worth £3000. p! An. this currency. Suppose then £1000 ster. was paid the principal, this at 25 difference of exchange, would leave £1750 currency for the Deputy. One half of this, I would undertake most readily to do the business for, and remit the rest. In this view, it might be well to give a pretty good sum for the Deputyship, besides the annual composition. M! Treasurer promised me on the Assembly, to consider and make enquiry touching the renting of your estate here, and communicate the result to me. I inclose you his letter on the subject. Wilk[ison's] profit may influence his opinion. I own, I do not feel the force of the Treasurers reasons so fully as he seems to do. Perhaps there may be difficulties in renting properly, as well as in selling. But I have no remaining doubt, that if either could be done in any near proportion to the value of the estate, it would be far more profitable than the present system I hope Wilkison will better his crop this year, as his hands are more divided and this has hitherto been a much better year than the last. Capt. Rayson [send]¹s two bottles of damask rose water for our Sister. The crop of roses was [s]¹mall this Spring, which prevented us from repeating the distillation so frequently as we would have chosen. For Col? Barré. a dozen bottles [o]¹f peach brandy are sent. 'Tis of my old stock. The last year very little [b]¹ut bad brandy was made in this Country. The wet weather causing the peaches to rot and fall before they were ripe. You have our G. Grandfathers Will as you desired. I beg leave to refer to so much of my letter by Capt. Page as relates to Master Geo: Lee, and again repeat my wish, that, advised by D. Porteus you provide him with a good Tutor at Cambridge, and pay this Gentleman Yourself. M. Russell pays his other charges at the University. I fancy much pains will be taken in London to draw this young Gentleman entirely from your interest when he comes to this Country, and therefore it will be proper to counter act all such evil machinations with all possible care. You have several bills of loading inclosed together with my invoice, which is long but not to very great amount. Old Capt. John Lee is now here using your Wilkes & Liberty pipes, He thinks they smoke better for the inscription, and he desires to be remember'd to you and the Doctor. The Alpine Strawberry roots were all dead a second time — If the roots were put into a basket of earth when first the Ship arrived, and be in a growing state before they left England, by being kept

¹ Torn off.

73

in Captains Cabbin they w.? be certain to reach in safety and I should be obliged to you for having some so managed. Neither the Cauliflower seed or any of the flower seeds ever vegitated. The Seedsman used us ill[.] Capt. Chilton has been told here since Walker arrived, that [he re]¹ fused to pay his brother Stephen wages that he (Walker) had agreed with him for, until Walker introduced him to you, that you offered him only to be Steward of Raysons Ship, and treated the young Man ill in every respect. I believe the Capt. is by this time satisfied that the whole is a Lye, and as the Man with whom Stephen was first ill, has sent here a very unreasonable account comprehending as Rayson says, funeral charges that you have paid, I wish you would see this matter properly settled for Capt. Chilton and send him a State of it —

I am my dear brothers ever affectionate faithful friend.

Our best love to our dear Sister.

P.S. I have no manner of reason to suppose that Capt. Rayson will not continue in your business, but it may be necessary to inform you of a dispute concerning damaged Tobacco which it may be proper to consider when a final settlement is come to with him. It seems the Capt. employed M.? Kenners Schooner to bring Tob.? from Rappahanock, and going over by land, he found the Schooner at the mouth of Rappahanock creek unprovided with a Tender to get the Tob.? down from Beckwiths. To give dispatch, the Capt. as a friend, hired a small Flat with one Hand to help them get the Tob.? down. The Skipper with his own people took the Flat and in bringing down a load damaged 4 ħħds. One of these has been since recovered — Three others are greatly hurt. The Inspectors think 15 or

¹ Torn and almost illegible.

74

16 hundred will be totally lost. Kenner (I think unjustly) refuses to pay for this, but has agreed with the Capt. to leave it to arbitration. If it sh⁴ be determined in Kenners favor, the Ship must pay it, and this I judged you should know, that if the Captain is answerable for any part, it might be detained. This is the 22ᵈ of July, the Ship now cleared, but Rayson says he cannot sail until tomorrow or the next day. I do not suppose there will be a word of dispute about Laydays, but this is a fact unquestioned, that the same quantity of Tob? now on board, might have been so before the Laydays were expired. And if it be necessary, ample proof may be had, that the fault was not on your part, that the Ship went not within her lay days. But I suppose this point will not come in controversy. My old acquaintance Mʳ Downman of Lancaster has by my persuasion sent his son to your care for education — He has become a Shipper, and having a good estate both here and in England he may be a good Correspondent in time. I do not doubt but that you will take proper care of the Young Gentleman.

Farewell.

P.S. Capt. Rayson has received from Col. Francis Thorton One hundred and thirty pounds current money for the ballance of his debt to you. And the Captain has also receiv'd an hundred pounds which this moment I got from our brother Col? Francis Ligᵗ Lee making in the whole £230.—.— Currency besides some Cash formerly received by him from Manokin, which I suppose our brother will acquaint you with. Our exchange since the Captain has been here, has been uniformly 20 pʳ cent. I have just seen yours to the Squire about Negro consignments. 8 pʳ Cent with 2 or 2½ deducted and the remittance insisted on makes it an object by no means desirable. The risk, the expence of attending Sales, advertising &ᶜ

will hardly leave Porters wages for the Consignees —
If the old plan could be obtained, 10 p! Cent with a
faithful remittance of all that could be got without too
much injuring the Sale, by the Ship, and the ballance
as fast afterwards as the utmost diligence could collect
it — Then the 2 or 2½ per Cent might be allowed for
the Security. 'Tis impossible to suppose that any
business of this kind can be transacted in a proper
manner where the Agreement is ruinous to one of the
Contracting parties. As the Planters are nearly out
of debt and Negroes are become valuable here, I should
be extremely glad to be employed [1] on reasonable terms,
but those you have mentioned are really too hard.

Yours.

TO LANDON CARTER [2]

DEAR SIR,   STRATFORD the 9ᵗʰ of Oct. 1772

I am just now favored with yours covering a letter
for M! Peele. For the following reason I have returned
the letter to you. So far as I am able to judge, I think
M! Peele has much merit in his profession, but in the
article of mixing colors for duration, he would seem to be
deficient, by the picture he has drawn of Lord Chatham now at Chantilly. The colors of that piece have
greatly faded in the short time since it was drawn. I observe in your letter to M! Peele that this is one of
your capital objections to the copies that have been
already taken of your mothers picture. This Gentleman may possibly have by experience improved in this
material branch of his art, but this circumstance I am
not acquainted with, and therefore concluded it the

---

[1] Compare the *Virginia Magazine of History and Biography*, XVI.
87.

[2] A. L. S. Virginia Historical Society, Lee Papers, IV. 250. Addressed to him at Sabine Hall and sent by " the hon. Col? Lee. "

better way to submit the matter to your own determination. If in this respect he would answer, I think he would in every other, and perhaps there is much propriety in encouraging American Artists in America. I would beg leave to refer you to my brother Frank on his return from Annapolis, where he will have many opportunities of seeing Mr Peels performances, and knowing the opinion entertained of him there by the best Judges. I assure you that I regret extremely being detained so long from Sabine Hill, and I am determined now, when the evenings grow long, and admit of the sociable pipe, that I will not fail to be happy with your agreeable conversation. Mrs Lee is not here, but I will inform her of your civility when I return to Chantilly.

My best compliments, if you please, to Sabine Hall

I am dear Sir Your affectionate friend and obedient Servant.

TO WILLIAM LEE[1]

DEAR BROTHER,   LEE HALL the 23.^d of October 1772

Yesterday at Nomony ferry, in my way with Mrs Lee to Northumberland, I received your several favors by our Cousin Lancelot, and just catch a moment here to answer them by Capt. New who is expected every hour to clear. In consequence of yours by Steel, I sent immediately for A. Moxley, who came, and received your proposition in his favor. He declines it how ever, with many professions of zeal for your interest, and thanks for your kindness. The truth is, that he is immediately to be married to the young widow.

[1] A. L. S. Virginia Historical Society, Lee Papers, IV. 206. Addressed, " William Lee esquire/Merchant in/London//By favor of/ Capt. New/Q. D. C." Endorsed, in autograph of William Lee, " Rec.^d 20 Ap.^l 1773."

Hoe[.]..... At present I do not know of any person fit for your business, but, I will shortly consult with Loudon, and you shall have immediate intelligence when we have fixt upon, and agreed with a proper person. I am greatly obliged to you for your kind intentions respecting me. A profitable employment would certainly be very convenient for me, oppressed as I am with a numerous family. Five — children already, another far advanced on the stocks, with a teaming little Wife, are circumstances sufficiently alarming. But I confess, that having never hitherto been favored by fortune, I incline to doubt her future benevolence. I have not time now to overlook your observations on Wilkisons accounts, but I shall attend most exactly to what you write concerning him. It is, as you rightly apprehend, a difficult affair to manage on account of the Treasurer who strongly supports and recommends him. Both M⠟ Nicholas and myself had heared the same that you have done concerning the inequality of the division. He wrote to me on the subject, and solemnly declared that he had enquired again and again, but could not, if it were again to do, fix on a more equitable division. It was admitted then, that the immediate profits of M⠟ Paradise's part would exceed yours on account of the wood, his land being so contiguous to the Town, and by reason of the great number of young Negroes that fell in your division. When they were making partition, so far as I knew, I could only object to the very great disp[r]oportion of Negroes they were going to appoint for you, and so far prevailed as to have a larger part of the more permanent estate (the land) alloted you, by taking away some Slaves, and adding that plantation which you now hold near Town, and is the only place from whence you carry any wood to Williamsburg. I should think that greater crops of Tobacco might be made, but then it is to be considered that the land with out dung will not do, and that fatal disease among the Cattle absolutely prevents the keeping a sufficient Stock of them. Sheep appear to me a very precarious Stock in this country. Wheat might well be raised on your land, if the wild Onion did not so capitally injure its sale. Indian Corn I fancy would be the most profitable cultivation, and I believe pretty good crops of that are made.

I am very glad to hear that Master Turberville is likely to mend, and I hope for his thorough alteration. I have not told his father the whole, but I have informed him that George has been wild and negligent; have recommended it to him to insist on peremtory and implicit obedience to D: Lee and D: Wharton, and by all means to withhold money from him, which the youth it seems has been strongly soliciting. All this he promises punctually to perform.

So far as I know, I believe you will not be much oppressed with bills this year. Yesterday I understood from M: John Turberville that he had drawn on you for an hundred and odd pounds in consequence of a demand, for which Col: Tayloe was his security, he has drawn much more largely on M: Russell, and it is not quite certain that these bills will go, but if they do, and you can pay the draft on you, I advise you by all means to do it, because it will contribute much to your future advantage.

I am in a great hurry and I have a bad headach so that I can write no more, but beg my love to M: Lee and the Doctor. Tell the latter how I am circumstanced and that I will write him by the next Ship.

Your Ship should by all means be here in all January and I think one in Potomac for this & Rappahannock will do for the present.

Your ever affectionate brother and friend.

Rayson cleared at this Office the 22ᵈ of July. I hope long e'er now he is arrived.

THE LETTERS OF RICHARD HENRY LEE

TO —— ——[1]

DEAR SIR, · BELLE VIEW the 18 Dec.[r] 1772.

You will receive with this a letter for M[r] Grayson open for your inspection. If on conversation with him you find him disengaged, seal and deliver it. My brother Thomas and myself conversing on the subject, think it will be quite prudent to get the Attornment of those Tenants on Col[o] Geo. Lee's land claimed by Grymes, as soon as possible; even before a survey can be made, that we may proceed after that to publicly counteract M[r] Grymes's advertisement, thereby to prevent that title which an innocent Purchaser from Grymes without notice might set up against us. You may therefore my dear Sir most essentially serve the son of your deceased friend by the following method. When visiting your plantations soon, go to the several Tenants placed on the land, let them Know the land belongs to us, and get their obligations to pay annually a very small rent, assuring them that the Executors have empoyered you to say that they will not remove them whilst the Heir is under age, and he is young, but that we expect the Heir may give them Leases when he comes of age. Those who refuse will certainly be Ejected when we survey the land as we intend to do in a short time. I leave to you the fixing the rent, which should be low in order to engage the submission and friendship of the Tenants. This is a point of much consequence to the Child, and therefore let me entreat you to get it done as soon as possible, and this

[1] Ms. copy. From a transcript from the original A. L. S. made by Mr. Joseph Packard, and kindly lent by him. Not superscribed, but endorsed, " Dec.[r] [tear]/Rich[d] Henry Lee's/Letr & M[r] Masons/ Opinion about/Lancelot Lees Land/Claimed by Philip/Ludwell Grymes/Esq[re]."

I hope may be effected without much trouble to you as the land in dispute joins your Salisbury plain Quarters.

Our best regards to Mr.ˢ Lee & the children.   I am dear Sir your affectionate friend and Kinsman.

P.S.   It may not be amiss to sound the Tenants and get as good rents in the meantime as they will willingly pay.

TO WILLIAM LEE[1]

DEAR BROTHER   LEE HALL   15ᵗʰ Janʸ 1773

I am here with a housefull assembled at the Squire's anniversary feast.   Hearing that a Ship is soon to clear for Glasgow I inclose the second of a bill, the first of which went about a week ago from Rappahanock. With this bill you have also an order on yourself in my favor from Mr. Thoˢ Washington for a small ballance which he says you owe him.   Let them be both put to my credit.   I received yours — and the Doctors favors by Page.   I am glad my little boys are safe and that they please you.   I hope they will continue to deserve your affectionate care of them.   We expect your ship here next month, and I speak to all I see to have Tobacco ready for her.

Your affectionate brother.

[1] A. L. S.   Virginia Historical Society, Lee Papers, IV. 210.   Addressed to him in London, and endorsed as received March 1 and answered March 4.

THE LETTERS OF RICHARD HENRY LEE

TO SAMUEL ADAMS[1]

SIR,   CHANTILLY, VA. February 4, 1773.

From a person quite unknown to you, some apology
may be necessary for this letter. The name of my
brother, Dr. Arthur Lee, of London, may perhaps,
furnish me with this apology. To be firmly attached to
the cause of liberty on virtuous principles, is a powerful cause of union, and renders proper, the most easy
communication of sentiment, however artfully disunion
may be promoted and encouraged by tyrants, and their
abettors. If this be true in general, how more certainly
is it so, in that particular state of affairs, in which every
scheme that cunning can form, or power execute, is
practised to reduce to slavery, so considerable a portion
of the human species, as North America does, and may
contain. Every day's experience proves this, to an attentive observer. Among other instances in proof, if I
mistake not, the manner of resenting the loss of the
Gaspie, is one. At this distance, and through the uncertain medium of newspapers, we may never, perhaps,
have received a just account of this affair. I should be
extremely glad, sir, when your leisure permits, to have as
true a state of the matter, as the public with you, has
been furnished with. At all events, this military parade
appears extraordinary, unless the intention be, to violate
all law and legal forms, in order to establish the ministerial favourite, but fatal precedent, of removing Americans beyond the water, to be tried for supposed offences
committed here. This is so unreasonable, and so unconstitutional a stretch of power, that I hope it will never
be permitted to take place, while a spark of virtue, or

[1] R. H. Lee, *Memoir of Richard Henry Lee*, I. 86. See *Ibid.*, I. 87,
for Adams' reply beginning their correspondence to protect American
liberties.

one manly sentiment remains in America. The primary end of government seems to be, the security of life and property; but this ministerial law, would, if acquiesced in, totally defeat every idea of social security and happiness. You may easily, sir, perceive, that I understand myself, writing to a firm and worthy friend of the just rights and liberty of America, by the freedom with which this letter is penned. Captain Snow, of your town, who comes frequently here, and who takes care of this, will bring me any letter you may be pleased to favour me with.

I am, sir, with singular esteem, yours, &c.

To SAMUEL ADAMS, Esq., Boston.

TO JOHN DICKINSON [1]

SIR/   CHANTILLY IN VIRG⁴ the 4ᵗʰ of April 1773

I should not have been silent so long if any important consideration had made writing necessary. On this quarter, much alarm has been create[d] [2] by a new court of criminal jurisdiction, it is said, havᵍ been lately opened in Rhode Island. Neither the power, nor the object of this Court, has been perfectly understood here; but in general we have been informed that it was designed to put in execution the dangrous advice of the two houses of Parliament in 1769 to seize obnoxious Americans and convey them to Britain for trial. When our Assembly met lately, they were unfurnished with Proper documents touching this business. But they have now adopted a measure which from the beginning

---

[1] A. L. S. American Philosophical Society, Lee Papers, I. 29, 36, No. 10. See R. H. Lee, *Memoir of Richard Henry Lee*, I. 90, for a much altered text. See *Ibid.*, I. 91, for the answer.

[2] Ms. damaged.

of the present dispute they should have fixed on, as leading to that union, and perfect understanding of each other, on which the political salvation of America so eminently depends. I have inclosed you that part of our Journal which relates to this matter. You will observe Sir, that altho full scope is given to a large[1] and thorough union counsels, yet our language is so contrived as to prevent the Enemies of America from hurrying this transaction into that vortex of treason, whither they have carried every honest attempt to defend ourselves from their tyrranous designs for distroying our constitutional liberty. I sincerely hope that every Colony on the Continent will adopt these Committees of correspondence and enquiry. I should be much obliged with your sentiments concerning this Rhode Island Court, and with the knowledge you have of its powers and object.

I am with singular esteem sir
    Your most obedient humble servant.

To JOHN DICKENSON, Esq.ᵣ in Philadelphia —

TO WILLIAM LEE[2]

DEAR BROTHER.   MANOKIN 7ᵗʰ June 1773

Early tomorrow morning this letter goes to a Glasgow Ship now ready to sail from Yeocomoco, and being in great haste you are not to expect such exactness as otherwise you would meet with. The Liberty has now 96 ħħds on board. A Craft is at Coan for 33, another up Rappahanock for 40, and one dispatched up to the Falls of Potomac and Colchester for 54, making in the

[1] Written over "long" erased.
[2] A. L. S. Lenox Library, Ford Collection. Addressed, "To/William Lee esquire/Merchant in/London//By favor of/Capt. Park/Q. D. C." Endorsed as received July 17, and answered July 31.

whole 223 ħħds. The ballance of her load 149 ħħds (for Rayson says he cannot engage to take more than 372 his last years quantity) is engaged on Potomac and Rappahanock, and will be taken on board as quickly as by any means Craft can be got to bring it in. The Cap.ᵗ is now here, and he things [*sic*] sure, (no unforseen accident happening) that he will sail by the 5ᵗʰ of July. The list on the other side will shew you how his load is made up, and this is as certain as any thing of this kind can be. You will see that Col.º Harry Lee has 20 ħħds, certainly they will be in, and weighing about 1400 neat a piece, I have agreed that he shall draw on you the 25ᵗʰ of July next for £90 ster.ᵍ and in Oct.ʳ following for £100. more   This is large drawing, but his Tob.º is good & heavy, and I agreed before I was sure of the ships load other ways. You will pay these drafts. But the Col.º says he will draw for £100 instead of £90. the first draft. At this rate there can be not much ballance against him I think.

But now comes the principal point — there are about 220 or 30 ħħds more than Rayson can carry and among these are 80 of M.ʳ Merriweather Smiths 120 of Hudson Muses, (besides his 30 in Rayson) with 10 of M.ʳ Edmunsons and some others. Our brother has by this Ship informed you on what terms M.ʳ Smiths Tobacco would be shipt, but the Liberty being full cannot take it, and now, we have this day sent to M.ʳ Smith desiring he will come here in the morning that we may consult about going to Piscataway in Maryland where Capt. Eden from London we hear will take on liberty.

If we can agree with him, it is proposed that he shall get the before mentioned 220 ħħds, and in that case Hudson Muses 120 go on the following terms. His 30 in Rayson are to be applied to the discharge of his last ballance with you. For this years Cargo to himself and brother, he proposed to remit in due time ; but these 120 ħħds, he is to apply to the payment of another Creditor thus — He will draw on you 25 of next July for £5. a ħħd. bill payable at 120 days. He says the Tob° shall be so weighty as that his draft will not exceed £4. the thousand. And he has such confidence in you, that he will run the risk of your paying his bills rather than submit to what his Creditor proposed of Shipping it on consignment to Glasgow. In short, on this plan you will get the commission on 120 ħħds and most probably the Tob° will be sold before the money is payable. Col° Loudon and myself are clearly of opinion that both this and M: Smiths desire are worthy your attention and we warmly recommend them to your complyance, if it will be possible. Should this plan of sending on Liberty take place, you will have ample notice and circumstantial by more opportunities than one in 10 or 12 days from hence. You will have in Rayson 15 ħħds. of Tob° for Servants sold, so you may insure if you please. Capt. Rayson desires you will take care of his Law [ing? or suit ?]. Capt Markham has not got a Craft yet & I fear 'twill be some time before he does. Your G. Spring Tob° is already in Outram, the Blacksmith is gone and is at Work.

My love to the Doctor & my Sister.

Farewell.[1]

[1] The following list is given on the final page of the manuscript of this letter.

	hhds	
" G. Lees estate	14 I.	[" I " red ink]
R. H. Lee	6 I.	[" I " red ink]
F. L. Lee	22	
Doct:· Thomson	1	
Capt Chilton	2	
Leroy Griffen	4	
Capt. Belfield	1	
M: Parker	1	
Mol. Ball	16	

THE LETTERS OF RICHARD HENRY LEE

T. A. Washington	4	
Col? Martin	18	on board. I ["I" red ink]
Col? Henry Lee	20	√[" √ " red ink]
Mʳ Carr	4	
Capt. Oldham	2	
Jos. Lane	1	
Col? Gaskins	2	
Mʳ Giberne	10	
Jn/Turberville	16.20	I. [red ink, all but "6"]
Triplet & Thornton	48	√[" √ " red ink]
Col? Hull	2	
Reub Jorden	1	
Charles Lee	1	
Mʳ Booker	2	
John Graham	4	
Col? Tarpley	2	
Warren Washington Junʳ	8	
Wᵐ Gerrard	2	
G. Waugh	1	
Mʳ Ransdell	1	
Rho. Kenner	8	
Mʳˢ A Washington	4	
Mʳ Spotswood	20	
Richᵈ Lee Esqʳ	30	
Col? Champe	4	
Mʳ Alexander	4	
Mʳ Hudson Muse	30	
	321	
Hon. Cul. Tayloe	8	
Hon. R. Carter	4	
John Craul	1	
For Servants	15	I. ["I" red ink]
Col? F. Thornton	2	
Capt. John Hull	1	
Mʳ Cox	1	
Mʳ James Edmunson	10	
Mʳ Butler	4	
	375	

N.B. This List may be regarded as right most generally but as there is much more Tob? than the Ship can carry, if any in this list should fail their gross [?] weight [?] will be supplied by others."

87

THE LETTERS OF RICHARD HENRY LEE

TO WILLIAM LEE [1]

DEAR BROTHER   CHANTILLY IN VIRGINIA   28$\underline{th}$ June 1773
After referring you to my letters by Page and Glasgow,
I must observe that the above list of Raysons Load is as
exact as can possibly be now made out. Indeed I do
not believe it will vary 6 from what he clears with.
Three days ago the Ship had 168 hhds on board, and
four Craft had been out some time with Notes and orders
for all his load but about 30 hhds, for which the Captain
had orders & notes, and for which a Craft was immediately to be dispatched. The Captain thinks he will clear
out in a fortnight from this time, but if he is allowed
to the 15th or 16th of July, it will in all probability, be
nearer his time of sailing. Rayson arrived in Yeocomico
the 28 April, so that he will be greatly within his Lay days.
He has known all and more than his Load a fortnight
since, so that it is his own look out if he does not get away
sooner than I have above allotted for him. But I have
supposed the usual delays. The 20 hhds shipt by Col?
Henry Lee are about 1400 neat on an average, and his
Tob? is generally of a superior quality. Knowing
this, I agreed he should draw at the next meeting of
Merchants 25th July coming for £90. sterling and next
Oct? for £100 more. So that I think you can be very
little in advance by paying his bills to that amount,
which I hope you will do. We find nigh 300 hhds more
than the Liberty can carry offered to us, and hitherto we
have in vain sought for a charter, or liberty of consignment. Yesterday we dispatched an Express to Maryland, where we were informed a Vessel of 250 hhds
might be chartered, we shall take her if we can get her,

---

[1] A. L. S. Virginia Historical Society, Lee Papers, IV. 202. Addressed to him in London and sent by Capt. Gray. Endorsed as
received August 30 and answered August 31.

and then I suppose you will get Merrywether Smiths and Hudson Muses Tobacco on the terms formerly mentioned to you by Loudon and myself. But, if a charter cannot be had, you will probably get no Tobº. from the former now, and only 30 from Muse by Rayson which are to be applied I understand, to the discharge of his last years ballance. Your Smith is fixt at work at G. Spring, with two apprentices under him. Credit me 12ˢ/currency paid the Squires Sam when he went down with the Smith for their expence Exch. 30 pͬ Cent. Edwards has met with an offer that he prefers to yours, and so has declined your Stewardship. My brother Frank has in view one Fontleroy, son of the Colonel at Naylors hole, of whose industry, skill and honesty, he has a good opinion. Your G. Spring Crop is in Outram, I think 30 ħħds. Mͬ Russell arrived in a short passage to Maryland, and George Lee has been some time with us, the former not yet come here. I have spoke with young Mͬ Lee about Dͬ Shepard's demand and he says it is rightly due, he thinks about £120, but says he has the Notes in his Trunk, together with the letter you wrote by the Ship he came in, but his Trunk is not yet sent from Patuxent. You will be pleased to pay Doctͬ Shepard the money due him immediately on receipt of this letter, and let me annually have your account current with Colº G. Lees estate. I observe what you say about R —s attempt with the young Gentleman, but I trust it will all be in vain. Insure the estates 14 ħħds and my 6 now in Rayson. I must entreat you to be more exact and punctual in getting my Boys account from Sͭ [Bees ?] completely made up every year, and annually send me them with the discharges from the proper persons. I mean by this, to preclude all possibility of after charges, which often happens I know from the English schools. Pray do not omit this. More than £30. apiece they cannot annually be, and

I am not without hope that £28. will be found sufficient. The £80. Ster§ bill that I sent you on Cuninghome & C? of Glasgow I hope is paid, because you do not mention it in yours 20ᵗʰ of April last. Give my love to the Doctor and deliver him the inclosed piece of our Journal which contains the proceedings of Assembly at their last meeting in March about the Rhode Island business. The information which this will procure must in all probability occasion strong resolves at next meeting. Nothing else, but the private business of the Colony, was done last session, and an account of this was sent by first opportunity after I came from the Assembly. I desired Mʳ Potts of Barbados to send me a barl of rum & one of sugar for which he is to draw on you, pay his draft. Send me by first Ship to Potomac or Rappahanock next Fall 100 yᵈˢ Mendal Cotton and 100 Ells of German Oznaburgs for my Negroes winter clothing. Our best love attends Mʳˢ Lee —

Farewell — The next by Rayson —

TO [WILLIAM LEE][1]

DEAR BROTHER[1]   CHANTILLY 4ᵗʰ of Jully 1773

I begin this early before Rayson sails that I may have opportunity to be more full and particular, intending still to add as new occurances shall render it necessary to do so, between this time and the departure of the Liberty. I must again refer you to my letters by Page, Glasgow, Dobby and Gray, and again I repeat my request that you will once in every year, with out fail, let me have a particular and full account of every fathing that my

[1] A. L. Virginia Historical Society, Lee Papers, IV. 198. The early portion of this letter, though varying from his usual handwriting, is in Richard Henry Lee's autograph, as is clearly the remainder of it.

Boys expenses at S! Bees amount to for every purpose. and if you have not done it before this comes to hand send me by the first opportunity to Potomac or Rappahanock 100 y^{ds} of Mendal Cotton & 100 Ells of German Ozna-burgs, observing if they are sent to the latter River to put in the bill of Loading to land them at Manorkin, the house of F. L. Lee Esq! Rayson brings you 6 hhds of Tob? from me & 14 from Col? G. Lee's estate. My Tob? is of much better quality than any I have made for some years past and has therefore, admitted of heavier prising; the 6 hhds weigh! neat 8074. I wish they may produce enough to furnish the invoice I have enclosed. But at all events I must remit you a bill when my rents came in at the Fall. I hope you have either received Cash for Robinsons bill to me, or if protested, that you loose no time in returning it. I have put in my invoice a Water proof close bodied Great Coat. Let Scots' sucessor be told that the Clothes he sent me this spring are much too short in the sleeves & do not reach down above half way of my thighs. He must allow accordingly in the Great Coat. It must be larger and longer in the body, and have longer sleeves. Loudon & myself have ceased to look out for an Agent to do your business here until we know your determination about M! Nash his proposals sent you by Cap! Page, because, if you agree with him great part of the business of an Agent will be transacted by him. I wonder much to see you give so largely into the business of sending out Cargoes of goods, because it seems to me as if this very plan had been one of the most powerful causes that has contributed to ruin so many as have given way in London in the Tob? Trade. You will be the best able to judge by the fidelity with which those you have already supplied in this way make their remittances, whither 'tis worth your while or not, to continue sending them Cargoes — For it signifies little what their fortunes may be here, if by wanting punctuality, they distress you in your London engagements on their accounts. I believe indeed, that George Thornton and his brother, who are Securities for Tripletts & Thornton[s] Cargo this spring, are good men for, perhaps, 5 or 6 thousand sterling. And I suppose, in the cautious manner that M.ʳ Mer. Smith proposes to carry on his future business, that moderate supplies would be safely ventured to him, but after all, it appears to me, that allowing drafts from the Gentlemen for a moderate sum on each ħħd consigned, after the Ship sails, is the most prudent and most effectual way of loading a Ship. Between these two methods, or a mixture of both, you will determine for yourself, which is best. It is clear to me however beyond a doubt, that a too exclusive concern in the Cargo way is highly injurious. You have inclosed a fair copy of the terms of Copartnership proposed for yourself and M.ʳ Nash to enter business on. It is proper that your answer to this should be sent by the first opportunity that occurs as Mr Nash is waiting. I have conversed with M.ʳ George Lee about D.ʳ Shepards demand. He says 'tis due, and he thinks the sum is about £120. ster.ᵍ You will please pay the Doctor this money as quickly as possible. Be not surprised at finding inclosed the subscription paper & letters relative to Lord Camden's picture. My design is, to enable you to remove any bad impressions that may take place on your side the water, by Countroller Campbell applying for money which he says that he furnished to this scheme. You will see by these papers, that he was not a Subscriber, and that no money of his enters at all into the sum of £76 sterling which M.ʳ Jenings received from me, and which he paid you in consequence of my letter. The real Subscribers are paid, but as M.ʳ Jenings may not know who they are, he might suppose M.ʳ Campbell one, and wonder that I had withheld the money from him.

The very great regard I have for the good opinion of M.
Jenings made it necessary that I should guard against
any misunderstanding in this business. With my
other goods you will please send me, carefully pact up,
a Groce of best Red Port Wine, and for part payment of
this, you will be desired by our brother Loudon to
charge £7.13.10 Sterl.ᵍ to his account, and the ballance
of the Groce I pay you for. Both Loudon and myself
think that there will be a considerable part of the present crop left after all the Ships are loaded, and therefore,
that a small Ship from you to Rappahanock early in the
Fall would probably meet with dispatch, especially as it
will afford your Debtors in the cargo way; an opportunity of making you more speedy remittances than I
fear they will otherwise do. A larger Ship than the
Liberty may still, at the usual time, about February,
come to Potomac as your annual constant ship. I
mention being here in Feb.ʸ because our lower Tob.º
is by that time ready, and whilst that is getting on
board, the upper Tob.º may be inspected. At all events,
being here early, will prevent preengagements. I much
fear that Col.º Phil being greatly pressed with the payment of Hanbury's judgment, may fail in his usual
remittance to our brother Doctor Lee. If so, and the
Doctors calls should make it necessary, he will apply to
you for £100. sterling on my account. The payment
of a ballance to M.ʳ Russell pushes me at present, but if
you advance this money on my account, I will exert myself to refund it as quickly as possible. July 12ᵗʰ 1773.
Since writing the above M.ʳ Russell has been here, and
we have settled. By this settlement it appears that his
charge of interest of the respective ballances due him
from time to time, amounted to rather more than 10 p.ʳ
Cent on the several sums I had remitted him in the course
of business, so we amicably agreed that the commission
should ballance the interest, and thereby left a ballance

due him £388.12.4 Sterling. To discharge this, I have given him a bill of exchange on you for £200. Sterling payable in four months after sight, and he has promised me on his honor that he will not send, but carry the bill with him when he goes himself, and that it will be at the soonest, the first of February 1774 before it can be payable. Before that time, I must be very ill used indeed if I do not lodge that sum at least in your hands by bills remitted you. But you are to remember, that I do not desire you to incur any risk, or danger, by accepting the bill, or by paying it, but either one or the other, or both you will do, as your perfect conveniency, or my remittances may enable you. You may be sure that I would wish to avoid 10 p! Cent, and as I have now, and shall have due to me by Christmas, more than £600. it will be very hard if I cannot get a sufficiency in time to place the money with you before the first of next February. The remaining sum of £188.12.4 is to be paid him 1ˢᵗ Feb⁷ 1775 without interest in the mean time, in consideration of my settling Col. H. Lee's, John Lees estates, and Mer. Smiths accounts with¦ charging commission for doing them. You will wonder no doubt that you hear'd not from me by Greig. You will find a letter inclosed which was intended to go by him but he slipt me by accident.[1] You desired I would have no account of the Liberty's left unsettled this voyage, but it has been impossible so to do. The dispute about damaged Tob⁹ last voyage with Mʳ Kenner is not settled nor has been in my power by every effort to get it yet referred to arbitration. There are three hogsheads disputed about and the Proprietors look to the Ship, so that it is absolutely necessary that in settling with Capt. Rayson you make a reserve for this purpose. One Read has now sued the

---

[1] Inserted here are these words erased, "I again confirm the contents of that letter and press your [*two words illegible*] of it."

Captain for one of these damaged hhds.[1] and I am his appearance Bail. The Servants you will see are[2] all sold, but[3] some not paid for. So that in your settlement with Capt. Rayson consideration should be had of these unavoidable things. You will please send by return of your Ship a plain Gold watch for Mr Geo. Lee made by Ellicot with a neat steel chain and charge it to his father's estate. The things you furnished M̲ṛ Geo. Lee with in London must be charged in the same manner. 16 July, just rec̲d̲ your letters by Geo. Lee, they having been detained in Maryland with his baggage—The dispatches by Page will, I suppose, show how your part of the estate comes to be less than M̲ṛ Paradise's, so to them I refer. We have not yet agreed with a manager to succeed Cary Wilkeson, but we shall do so in proper time. I cannot imagine that M̲ṛ Nicholas can be displeased with your letter, there being nothing in it capable of giving just offence.

19͟t͟h͟ July. The Liberty clears this day, and the Capt. proposes to sail day after tomorrow. He cannot I suppose talk of demurrage now, but the inclosed from him to me will at all events prevent it. You have inclosed Capt. Raysons draft on yourself in my favor for £33.13 Sterl̲g̲ which you will please put to the credit of my bill on you to James Rusell. You have also Rayson's receipt for £71.10. paid him here on account of money rec̲d̲ for Servants, and in the same receipt for £6. Cur̲ỵ which I rec̲d̲ of your money from Col̲ọ Fran. Lig̲t̲ Lee and delivered to Capt. Rayson. The whole remittance by this Ship for the Servants is £109.10 including the price of the Squires Servant and mine, with 16249 lb̲ṣ of Tob̲ọ as the Acco̲t̲ Sales and bill of Loading directed to you

---

[1] The preceding five words are substituted above the line for, "a Craftage account of last year" erased.

[2] A word, "not," is here erased.

[3] Substituted above the line for "and" erased.

and Capt. Rayson will shew. It was impossible to make a more full remittance now, but we shall be careful to collect the —[1] The most accurate list that can be made out of the Libertys Load 28th June 73—G. Lee's estate 14 hhds. R. H. Lee. 6. F. L. Lee, 22. Doc: Thomson, 1. Capt. Chilton 2. Leroy Griffen 4. Capt. Belfield 1. Parker 1. Mol. Ball 16. T. A. Washington 3. Sam Washington 6. Col. Martin 18. Harry Lee 20. W. Carr 4. Cap. Oldham 2, Lane Joseph 1. Col. Gaskins 2. Col. Peacly 2. M: Giberne 9. John Turberville 13. Triplet & Thornton 50. Col. Hull 2. R. Jorden 1. Charles Lee 1. M: Booker 2. Col Tarpley 2. Warner Washington Jun: 8. W. Gerrard 4. Ed. Ransdell 1. Rhod Kenner 8. Anne Washington 4. Spotswood 14. Richd Lee 30. Hudson Muse 30. Col? Champe 4. Hon. Tayloe 6. P. P. Thornton 8. Hon. Carter 4. F. Thornton 2. Captn Hull 1. M: Cox 1. B. Butler 4. Moore Fauntleroy 4. M: Booth 2. Mr Buckner 1. Revd Smith 1. John Gordon 4. Inspector, not James, Edmunson 1. For Servants sold 15. M: Ross 2. John Eustice 6. James Gordon 2. Making in all 372 hhds, from the large size of which, the Captain doubts whither he shall be able to take them all.[2]

TO WILLIAM LEE [3]

DEAR BROTHER,   CHANTILLY IN VIRG^a Sept 27. 1773

I must beg leave to refer you to my last letters 9th Aug. 26th July & by Rayson, where you will find many of my opinions and desires both with respect to your own business and mine. Since writing the last I have

---

[1] A new page begins here, as if there were a break in the writing and the Ms. incomplete.

[2] For an earlier list with variations see note, pages 86, 87.

[3] A. L. S. Virginia Historical Society, Lee Papers, IV. 194. Addressed to him in London and sent by Capt. Robinson. Endorsed as received December 1773, and answered "fully" December 24, 1773.

received yours by Mitchell, and shall give your new Steward the direction you desire with respect to the kind and
the prizing your Tob? About 6 weeks ago, Cary Wilkeson told me that M! Treasurer intended to quit all conon-
cern [sic] with your business, but the inclosed seems
to imply the contrary. This letter I received and answer'd the other day at York Court. Twice I have been
obliged to attend that distant Court, to compel justice
from the brother and heir of Will Templeman for
Doct. Lee. The last time, judgement in favor of the
latter was obtained for £16.18 Sterl. being principal,
interest, and the cost of suit in P. Court, where the suit
was brought previous to W. Templeman's death, &
which I paid. Give my love to the Doctor and tell him
this, and that the money shall be forwarded as soon as
I receive it, tho' I yet expect all the delay that knavery
can procure, or the law warrant. We have never been
able to get a Charter, or liberty that would by any
means suit. Capt. Robinson is full and wants liberty
for 2 or 300 hhds more to his Owner. Capt. Dutchman
cannot carry on liberty to you, because M! Watson, Bells
Agen[t][1] says, you are not an *Acquaintance* of M! Bells.
At this late Season we are unwilling to part with what
Tob? we have or could get, because we expect a small
Ship from you into Rappahanock this Fall according to
our former desire. M! Nash got your letter immediately
M! Mer. Smith agrees to your terms of sending goods
with this alteration only, that he be at liberty to make
his remittances in the time stipulated, either in good
bills of exchange or Tob?, which he choses. This seems
reasonable. But before he writes for his Cargo, he says
he must settle his affairs with Perkins & Brown. I
have not been able since my last to get any further authentic intelligence about the Trents company. Loudon
will attend at the Merchants meeting in Oct!, and inform

[1] Ms. torn.

you fully of that. In general I learn they have got largely dipped with former connections. Cary, & Perkins in London, besides their Liverpool concerns. I believe M: Edward Carters estate is not entailed, and it is considerable in Lands & Slaves. One of the Trents I understand has a large landed estate. But again I repeat it, that how large soever their possessions here may be, a want of punctuality may ruin and disgrace you, and leave you to seek redress in our tediously dilatory Courts of law here. As they have I believe, sound bottom and your terms oblige to punctualy under forfeiture of heavy penalties, if the wealthy Tradesmen, who can afford to lay out of their money some time, for the great advantages offered, would run the venture, it would in that case be a very eligible plan, as you might without risk, gain the comission on the consigned Tob? To conclude this subject, on which I have written so often and so much, Your own experience of the punctuality with which those that have been supplied by you make remittances may determine you about shipping them future Cargoes. They surely can have no pretence to future supplies, if they comply not with their first promises. I do not know how it may seem to you, but it appears to me much the better scheme to take bonds from Gentlemen of good fortune here, and advance moderately on their Tob? shipt, by which method a large consignment may be procured without a very great advance, and with no final risk. The inclosed for you came to hand two days ago, with a request for me to enforce its contents, but I can not do it, if they are as I am informed. That Adam Mitchel of London has shipt you in the Hibernia 6 ħħd Tob? weigh near 8000, and draws for £90 Sterl with a promise of his next years Crop which may be perhaps, as much more. The terms are so inadequate to the advance considering the low price of Tob?, that I cant pretend to recommend them. You know the Man as well as I do. Indeed, I think, I should only pay so much as the real value of his Tob?, and apologize for protesting the rest.

I congratulate my dear Brother on the good opinions entertained of him by his fellow Citizens, expressed by their choice of him to the important Office of Sheriff of London. I wish the expence may not injure, and the business interfere with your Mercantile plan. Much good advice, and singular circumspection are necessary to carry you with honor thro this arduous Office, rendered much more difficult by the particular character of the times. The eyes of multitudes are upon you, which makes it necessary that every the most minute action should be well considered, and when a wise and proper resolution is taken, let it be executed with firmness and Manly strength. The Law is the grand and glorious Lum[inar]¹y that will, closely attended to guide you with honor and applause to the end of your office.

I go up the Country in a few days to meet my Collector and to be furnished with the means of filling your hands, against my bill in favor of M⁻ Russell comes due. You may be assured no care on my part shall be wanting for this. We expect your annual Ship here at the time recommended in my former letter, about the first of February

Pray do not forget my Gardener. Our best love to our Sister and the Doctor.

Your ever affectionate brother.

¹ Blurred by seal.

99

THE LETTERS OF RICHARD HENRY LEE

TO WILLIAM LEE [1]

DEAR BROTHER, CHANTILLY IN VIRGINIA 15 December 1773
Your favors by the Eliza and M̲ᵣ Wigginton have come safely to hand. That by Capt. Curtis I have not received, altho he sailed with Greig, who arrived here four days ago. As I expected would be the case, the James river company declare off from assisting the Eliza in any manner, and she was yesterday expected hourly at her moorings at Hobb's Hole, to load in Rappahanock. Col̲? Loudon & myself have agreed to push this Ships load with the united efforts of both rivers Potomac & Rappahanock in order to get her her away without demurrage, which we expect to do. When the Potomac ship arrives, we also agreed to forward her from both rivers likewise. The Rappahanock ship could easily have been dispatched in time without aid from Potomac, if her late coming, her size, and our earnestness lately, to make remittances quickly as possible, had not occasioned our urging into Mitchell & the Noble Bounty, all the Tob? we could get, before Capt. Brown arrived. However I hope she will not be detained. I think the two Ships above named will have about 200 h̅h̅ds of Tob? for you, among which number, in Mitchell are three h̅h̅ds shipt by Lee & Rayson, which are to be put to credit of the servants consignment in the Liberty last spring. I suppose our brother Loudon has written you fully about the James river bussiness. I do not like it, and I wish you fairly disengaged. When I drew that bill on you in favor of M̲ᵣ Russell, I never meant the least possible distress to you, or one uneasy moment, and I shall be perfectly

[1] A. L. S. Virginia Historical Society, Lee Papers, IV. 190. Addressed to him in London and sent by Capt. Mitchell of the *Argo*. Endorsed as received February 22 and answered February 23, 1774.

satisfied with its fate. The Treasurer writes, that he has got bills and remitted you all your money in his hands, so that he could not supply Loudon with an hundred pounds sterling which the latter had agreed you should advance for Thomas Turner esq[r] on his consignment of 40 hhds Tob[o] to you in Mitchell. To prevent M[r] Turner drawing on you, he gets that money from me, and has already received £ 100 currency, the bal. he is to have in a few days. In the payment made Turner there were 329 dollars, which to avoid the high exchange, I was going to ship to you in Mitchell, when we fell on the above plan, agreeing that you should allow me, what that number of dollars may be worth in London when Mitchell arrives, which from what I have heard, I hope may be 4[s] 10[d] sterling apiece. Added to what these 329 dollars may be so worth, you are to credit me also for the further difference between such value and £100. Sterl[g] and this whole sum, if you please, is to go to credit of my bill on you to Russell. Notwithstanding the large sums. I have due to me, and in good hands, I have not been able to make a better remittance before now. — But I shall still continue pressing and remitting, until we are upon the square. M[r] Turner may be a very valuable correspondent, and I recommend him strongly to your attention. I have not yet heard of our exchange being higher than 30. As I shall soon write again no more business now. Give my love to the Doctor and say I shall write him soon, and that I hope to hear of his being in the H. of Commons for the City of London next Parl[t][1] I do not know how the Livery may determine, but I [trust] ch[oo][2]se Wilkes & Bull in the contest for Mayoralty. [O][2]ur best love to M[rs] Lee — My little Woman has brought me another

---

[1] Seal.　　　　　[2] Ms. damaged.

daughter. M.ʳˢ Washington of Wakefield & M.ʳˢ
Ha[rr]ᵗison of Eagle'snest are both dead.

Farewell, Yours forever.

P.S. In your last Account current you omit by mistake to credit me with Tho.ˢ Montgomeries bill of exchange remitted you 8 June 1771 for £ 9 — sterling.
It went at the time I finished with Bently by a small
bill on you.

TO LANDON CARTER [2]

MANOKIN   6 Feb. 1774

DEAR SIR,   Quarter before 5

I am greatly obliged to you for the assistance I have
received from Nassau. He has performed two operations from which relief is already discernible — But
my dear Sir, I beg you will not be so hard of belief, as
to suppose my attendance at Sabine Hall far off for I
assure you, that notwithstanding my powerful avoca-
tions have so long prevented me from being there, it
has always been with regret. — And my settled determination is to see you very soon after my present
painful visitation will permit me.

I am, with much regard dear Sir

Your affectionate friend.

To LANDON CARTER, esquire of Sabine Hall.

[1] Ms. damaged.
[2] Ms. copy. Virginia Historical Society, Lee Transcripts, II.
"Copies of Letters to Landon Carter."

THE LETTERS OF RICHARD HENRY LEE

TO [WILLIAM LEE]¹

DEAR BROTHER   CHANTILLY, IN VIRG.ᴬ 2.ᵈ March 1774

Inclosed I send you an order on yourself in my favor for £16.10. Sterlᵍ drawn by Mᵣ Charles Bell of Fauquier. This Gentleman is a Tenant to [* * *]² in that County, and has good possessions in Slaves [* *]² &ᶜ He makes good Crops, but money being scarce here, I have persuaded him to Ship [* * *]² and give me an order, which he has done. Capt. Brown has four heavy hogsheads of his made on very rich fresh Fauquier land. He proposes to be an annual Shipper to you for this purpose and to get his goods on the best terms. Mᵣ Bell has forgot to order insurance, but I advise you to make it. I have proposed the same thing to several of my Tenants. Since my draft on you in favor of Mᵣ. Russell, the matter stands thus, remitted Charles Raysons Bill on your Self for £33.13 Sterlᵍ Capt. Parks Ship bill for £57.1 Sterlᵍ and Mᵣ Bells order for £16.10 Sterlᵍ Cash furnished Col.ᵒ Francis Lighᵗ Lee here for your use 429 dollars and £1.6 paper currency. The paper at 30 pᵣ Cent & These dollars I am to be credited for at their sterling value when Capt. Mitchel of the Argo arrives in London, because if they had not been wanted here for your use, they were to have been remitted you in that Ship. That agreement we formerly acquainted you with.

During the whole Winter, until this fortnight [,]³ the Waters have been all bound up in Frost [so]³ that Capt. Brown has not been able to do any [thing?]³ in the way of getting Tob.ᵒ on board. Now I hope he will go on quickly, and altho by this unlucky & un-

---

¹ A. L. S. Virginia Historical Society, Lee Papers, IV. 181.
² Ms. torn, and missing.   ³ Ms. defective.

usual hard frost he will probably be after his lye days, yet not so long I trust as to make any difference with the Charter parties.

Russels Ship Caroline is arrived, no letters from you nor account of your Potomac Ship.

Our love to Mrs Lee and the Doctor, not forgetting our little new Cousin. Farewell.

Your affectionate brother.

P.S. Mr Ponsonby has never sent me my Sons accounts. I insist on his doing this.

TO WILLIAM LEE[1]

DEAR BROTHER,   CHANTILLY IN VIRG.^A 15th April 1774.

I beg leave to refer you to my last by the Nelly Frigate in which among other things I inform you that Capt Roman and myself were just setting out for Frederick. From that journey we returned last night, and this day send my letter over to Manokin in great haste for fear of missing Capt Brown. The inclosed list of Shippers in the Friendship will shew you our success above, and by it you will see there is little danger of Capt Romans getting his load; as plenty of room is given for some of the list failing. In general I think it may be relied on. The last of this month we go to the Assembly which meets on the 4th of May, but before we do go, proper measures will be taken for the Friendship's load, and I will come up about the time of her sailing to attend her clearing. You will please insure Six hhds for me in Roman, 'tis the best I have shipt for many years. As Col.^o Lee's estate

[1] A. L. S. Virginia Historical Society, Lee Papers, IV. 175. Sent by Captain Brown of the *Eliza*. Endorsed as received June 10 and answered September 3.

sends you 29 hhds this year, whatever of that number, the Eliza does not bring you, will come in the Friendship and must be insured; this you will know when Brown arrives, but which I cannot at present know, because I gave an order for Brown to take it all if he wanted it, before I went up the Country. I was with your friend Col? Henry Fitzhugh, he had ordered all his Tob? to Campbell, but says he does not know what he may do next year. I find Col? F Thornton is persuadeding him to send you 100 hhds, do you press him by your next Pot? Ship. M: M: Carty begins with you this year and he is well worth Cultivating. You see how steady Col? Martin is, but as for the Hites & other consignments there which Rayson mentioned to you, 'tis all a fable. I shall surely continue remitting you as quickly as the scarcity of Cash in this Country will allow my debtors to pay me, for it is by no means my desire to put you in advance. M: Potts is desired to furnish me a few things and to value on you. There is all imaginable reason to suppose that the Crop of Tob? of 1773 will be greatly short of the year before, occasioned by the long continued wet & hot weather in the time of housing, which moulded and rotted abundant and has occasioned great distruction at the Warehouses. At Dumfries, Colchester and Falmouth they had not taken 10 days ago, much above one third of their usual quantity. I know some Planters have kept back their Tob? and others have been stayed by bad Roads, but both these causes are not sufficient to account for the great falling short that I have mentioned and which you may depend is certain, at the Warehouses I have mentioned. How it is in other parts of the Country I do not know certainly, but I hear generally that the Crop proves Short — I am greatly obliged to you & our kind Sister for agreeing we shall have the Crop — But as it was never my desire to remove her against her own consent, so I fear her connection below will prevent her coming here — This place it is true is not the most healthy, but the difference of numbers being allowed, I will venture to affirm, that you have a very great superiority of Sick & deaths at Green Spring over [1] us [1] here. In fact, I have lost but very few Since I lived at this place. Give my love to the Doctor & tell him that His money from Templeman is in the Sheriffs hands from whence it shall be removed & remitted with all possible expedition. Tell him also, that when a favorable opportunity offers, the Mississippi Company hope that he will push their petition with all possible Vigor — There is plenty of room yet for us on the North side of Ohio between that & [2] Illinois, on the Wabash, the Miamis, and other waters between Illinois and Ohio. 'Tis a much finer Country than any on this side Ohio. I hope soon to hear from you on the subject of M͞r Lawsons Agency. Begging your attention to my former letters & our love to our Sister

Farewell.

TO [SAMUEL ADAMS][3]

SIR,   CHANTILLY IN VIRGINIA April 24. 1774

Since my letter to you of December the last, I have not been favored with any from you, and now, in a few days, I shall go to Williamsburg, where our Assembly will be convened on the 4͟t͟h͟ of next month. There we shall remain I expect, until the last of June, during which time, should any material information concerning the American cause reach Boston from Parliament or Administration, I should be glad to have particular intelligence from you. At the same time, it

---

[1] Substituted above the line for "than we have" erased.
[2] "Niagara" is here written and erased.
[3] A. L. S. Lenox Library, Samuel Adams Papers.

will be highly conducive to the general good, that your Corresponding Committee write a public letter to Ours on any such occasion. Its reception whilst the Assembly is sitting will be the most fit time for information coming to hand. I am led to suppose that something material may happen, in consequence of the well deserved fate which befel the Tea on your quarter, and which I see has so mooved the Spleen of some ill judging Writer in the Public Advertiser, as to induce him to persuade the adoption of harsh measures against America. However consonant this advice may be the opinion of our Tory Ministers, yet I think two considerations will secure the quiet of the British Empire against the effects of their despotism.

The extreme difficulty of fixing on any plausible mode of of resentment and the approaching General Election in England. The wise and good in Britain are too well convinced of the unmerited abuse we have received for 10 or 12 years past not to produce consequences from a dispute with America, fatal to the views of Ministry at a general election. — A few days since came to my hands a letter from London dated January 29$\underline{^{th}}$ 1774 in which the Gentleman says "I have just come from the Privy Council, where the petition from the house of Representatives in Massachusetts Bay praying for the removal of Gov! Hutchinson & Lieu! Gov! Oliver was enforced by M! Duning and Councillor John Lee. The Govrs were vindicated by Wedderburne who was exceedingly abusive of the New England & Rhode Islanders, calling them factious, seditious, disaffected, and even rebellious. In short, I never hear'd a man speak for two hours so very little to the purpose respecting the case before the Council, or more insolently abusive of every person whom he thought of different sentiments from himself. Duning was very unwell, however, in his reply, he gave the

N. Briton some smart wipes. The Board was very full, and the Room exceedingly crowded. I do not yet know the Councils report." He concludes however With fearing that it will be unfavorable to America ! The truth is Sir, that we have only to be cool, firm, and united, to secure as well ourselves, as our fellow Subjects beyond the Water, from a Systematic plan of despotism, that has already fallen with a heavy hand on every part of the Empire. Unless N. Britain may be excepted, the Inhabitants of which Country are much favored indeed, altho the most accurate Searchers into their history, can find no peculiar merits they have with the present reigning family.

I am, with very particular esteem, Sir Your most humble and obedient Servant.

TO [LANDON CARTER][1]

DEAR SIR,   CHANTILLY 25$\underline{th}$ April 1774

I have often heared it said, but never until now felt the force of the observation, that the truth is not at all times to be spoken. So frequently has the necessity of my affairs opposed my warmest wishes, and compelled me to assign this as the true reason for being prevented from paying my respects to you, that it would seem to be no longer admissible. And yet it remains still the truth. The time I had devoted to Sabine Hall, I have since found myself obliged to employ in journeying to Frederick; and now my good friend will excuse me for discharging the duty I owe my Country in Assembly. Thither I go in a few days, and when there, nothing will give me greater pleasure

[1] A. L. S. Virginia Historical Society, Lee Papers, IV. 161.

Endorsed, "Richd H. Lee, Esqr/Ap^l 25. 1774 an excuse/for not calling to see me/and a dun for £35 due for two Servts; to be pd/him in W^{am}burgh//Bundle N° 4/Listed by R. W. Carter."

than to be aided to your good advice in any important questions that may be under consideration, where your leisure and other opportunities admit. I am told from London the 29 of Jan.ʸ thus, " Just returned from the Privy Council where the petition from the house of Representatives in Massachusets Bay praying for the removal of Gov.ʳ Hutchinson & L.ᵗ Gov.ʳ Oliver was enforced by M.ʳ Duning & Councillor John Lee. The Gov.ʳˢ were vindicated by Wedderburne who was exceedingly abusive of the N. England & Rhode Islanders, calling them factious, seditious, disaffected & even rebellious. In short I never heared a Man speak for two hours, so very little to the purpose respecting the case before the Council, or more insolently abusive of every person whom he thought of different sentiments from himself. Duning was very unwell, however in his reply he gave the N. Briton some smart wipes. The Board was very full and the room exceedingly crowded. I do not yet know the Councils report but if I have any judgment in Physiognomy, the Members all came to their Seats with one opinion — Instead of displacing the Governors, highly to honor & recommend them to further favor. The Tea Ship is returned from Philadelphia & I hope every port of America will follow the wise example of [1] Pennsylvania. Tis not yet known what steps will be taken in consequence of the destruction of the Tea at Boston. Some folks here are strongly inclined to violent measures, but fear restrains them, and I am well convinced if the Colonies are all united they will never [venture ?] even in any instance to do a material injury to one. Let every American remember the Liberty song.

> By uniting we stand
> By dividing we fall
> Then Steady Boys &c &c"

[1] " Philadelphia " is here erased.

The impracticability of seeing you before Capt Roman sails, and the necessity of closing the Servant consignment of last year, obliges me to beg the favor of you to send me a bill or order to Williamsburg for the value of the two Servants you purchased from the Liberty last year that I may thence transmit it to Mr Lee. The Servants and their prices were, Joseph Gunnall £15. Peter Vassey £20. — The two £35.—.— My best wishes are always for Sabine Hall, and I am truly dear Sir Your affectionate and obedient Servant.

TO SAMUEL ADAMS[1]

SIR,   WILLIAMSBURG the 8th of May 1774

Nothing material has occurred since I wrote you last, except that we have seen here the Nefarious proceedings of the Privy Council, in the case of your petition against the infamous Hutchinson and Oliver. The determination is viewed here with horror and astonishment! We are likely to have a long Session, and before we part, I hope we shall declare our strong approbation of our Sister colonies repelling the revenue act with the Tea ships, and animadvert on some other tyrannic proceedings of Administration. I take pleasure in introducing to your acquaintance General Lee, a most true and worthy friend to the rights of human nature in general, and a warm, spirited Foe to American oppression. This Gentlemans principles do him honor, and I am sure his acquaintance will give you much pleasure.

I am, with singular regard. Sir your most obedient humble Servant.

[1] A. L. S. Lenox Library, Samuel Adams Papers. Addressed to Adams in Boston, and sent by General Lee.

THE LETTERS OF RICHARD HENRY LEE

TO SAMUEL ADAMS[1]

SIR,   CHANTILLY IN VIRGINIA   23ᵈ June 1774

I did myself the pleasure of writing to you from this place before my departure for our Assembly in May last and again from Williamsburg immediately after our dissolution, inclosing the order for fast, which produced that event, and the subsequent conduct of the Members after this political death had been inflicted on them. The day before we were dissolved, I had prepared a sett of resolves, the last two of which were thus expressed. Resolved that the blocking up, or attempting to block up the Harbour of Boston, until the people there shall submit to the payment of taxes imposed on them without the consent of their Representatives, is a most violent and dangerous attempt to destroy the constitutional liberty of and rights of all North America. Resolved that   be appointed Deputies from this House to meet at   such Deputies from the other Colonies as they shall appoint, there to consider and determine on ways the most effectual to stop the exports from North America, and for the adoption of such other methods as shall be most decisive for securing the constitutional rights of America against the systematic plan formed for their destruction. I have not a remaining doubt but that these resolves would by a very great majority, have been agreed to, had they been proposed. However I was prevented from offering them by many worthy Members who wished to have the public business first finished,

[1] A. L. S. Lenox Library, Samuel Adams Papers. A much altered text is printed in R. H. Lee, *Memoir of Richard Henry Lee*, I. 97. For Adams' reply see H. A. Cushing, *The Writings of Samuel Adams*, III. 136.

III

and who were induced to believe, from many conversations they had heared, that there was no danger of a dissolution before that had happened. It seems that government was very much alarmed at that spirit which the order for Fast denoted, and fearing its consequences interposed a dissolution. The subsequent conduct of the Members was surely much too feeble an opposition to the dangerous and alarming state to which despotism had rapidly advanced. So thinking, I did propose to the dissolved Members the plan of a Congress, but a distinction was sett up between their then state, and when they were a house of Burgesses. Most of the Members, with myself among the rest, had quitted Williamsburg before your message from Boston arrived. Twenty five of them were however assembled to consider of that message, and they determined to invite a meeting of the whole body on the 1st of August next, to consider of stopping the exports and imports. Since that, an Indian invasion of our Frontiers has compelled the calling a new Assembly, for which purpose writs are now issued returnable the 11th of August, at which time, it is thought, the house will meet; when, I think there is no manner of doubt but they will directly adopt the most effectual means in their power for obtaining redress of American grievances. In the mean time, the sense of the Counties is taking, and two have already declared their desires to stop their exports and imports. It seems very clear to me that this will be the general agreement. 'Tis apprehended here, that if the grain were allowed to be exported to the south of Europe, that bad men would, tempted by the high price in the W. Indies, supply them fully under pretences of distress of weather, and many other false and delusive pleas. Do you not think Sir, that the first most essential step for our Assembly to take, will be an invitation to a general congress as speedily as the nature of the thing will admit, in order that our plan may be unanimous, and therefore effectual? I shall be in Williamsburg on the first of August, and continue there until the meeting of the Assembly on the 11th, and it will be exceedingly agreeable to me to know your sentiments fully on this most important subject. And I am sure it will be of great consequence to the common cause that your corresponding Committee write fully, their opinions to ours, at the same time. It will be well, so to time the matter, as that your letters may be in Wiliamsburg before the 1st of August, at which time and place a meeting of the late Representatives, I expect will take place, notwithstanding the return of our election writs to the 11th Please direct your letter for me to the care of Robert Carter Nicholas Esqr in Williamsburg. I hope the good people of Boston will not be dispirited under their present heavy oppressions, for they will most certainly be supported by the other Colonies, their cause being rightly and universally considered as the common cause of British America. So glorious a one it is, and so deeply interesting to the present and future generations, that all America will owe their political salvation, in great measure, to the present virtue of Massachusetts Bay.

I am, with singular esteem and regard, Sir your most obedient and most humble Servant

P.S. My best respects, if you please, to all the friends of liberty, particularly to Mr Hancock, Mr Cushing & Mr Otis.

THE LETTERS OF RICHARD HENRY LEE

TO [ARTHUR LEE][1]

My dear Brother.   Chantilly 26th June 1774

I am extremely obliged to you for your favor of the 18th of March, which, with our brother Williams 26th of same month are the only letters I have receiv'd from either of you lately. And I am the more concerned at this, as Ships from London, late in April, have arrived in Potomac, Rappahanock, and the Southern rivers. At this time of immense danger to America, when the dirty Ministerial Stomach is daily ejecting its foul contents [2] upon us, it is quite necessary that the friendly streams of information and advice should be frequently applied to wash away the impurity. We had been sitting in Assembly near three weeks, when a quick arrival from London brought us the Tyrannic Boston Port Bill, no shock of Electricity could more suddenly and universally move — Astonishment, indignation, and concern seized on all. The shallow Ministerial device was seen thro instantly, and every one declared it the commencement of a most wicked System for destroying the liberty of America, and that it demanded a firm and determined union of all the Colonies to repel the common danger. The first step taken by our Assembly was to appoint the 1st of June, the day on which hostility began against America, to be observed as fast. The spirit that this denoted was not liked by Government and we were dissolved in two days afterwards, the Country business unfinished, no fee bill passed, and the Courts of Justice consequently stopt. The day after our dissolution, the late Members assembled and sent the inclosed advice to the people — The day before we were dismissed, I had prepared a

[1] A. copy L. S. Virginia Historical Society, Lee Papers, I. 42.
[2] The words " on America " are here erased.

sett of Resolves [1] the two last of which were thus expressed. Resolved that the blocking up or attempting to block up the Harbor of Boston until the people there

[1] The full set of resolutions from a copy by " Squire " Lee is as follows:
  " [1774, June]   Resolves by Richard Henry Lee.
  [1] Resolved that the Disposal of their own Property is the inherent Right of Freemen; that there can be no property in that which another may of Right take from us without our Consent, that $^{the}_{\wedge}$ claim of Parliament to tax America is, in other Words, a claim of Right to levy Contributions on us at Pleasure.
  [2] Resolved that the Duty imposed by Parliament [Ms. torn] upon Tea landed in America is a Tax on the Americans, or levying Contributions on them without our Consent.
  3 Resolved That the express Purpose for which the Tax is levied on the Americans, Namely for the Support of Government, Administration of Justice, and Defense of his Majestys Dominions in America, has a direct Tendency to render Assemblies Useless and to introduce Arbitrary Government [and Slavery]?
  4 Resolved
    That a Virtuous and steady opposition to this Mini[ste]rial Plan of governing America is Absolutely — necessary to preserve even the Shadow of Liberty, and is a Duty which every Freeman in America owes to his Country, to himself, and to his Posterity
  5 Resolved
    That it is the opinion of this Committee that East India Tea be not Used in this Colony so lon[g] as a duty remains on it for raising a Revenu[e] in America, and that whoever does Use it is an Enemy to the Rights and libertys of America
  6 Resolved that the blocking up, or attempting to block up the Harbor of Boston, until the people there shall submit to the payment of Taxes imposed on them without the Consent of their representatives, is a most Violent and dangerous Attem[pt] to destroy the constitutional liberty and rights of all British America
  7. Resolved that   be appointed Deputies from this House to meet at,   such Deputies from the other Colonies, as they shall appoint there to consider and determine on ways the Most effectual to Stop the Exports from North America and for the adoption of of [sic] such other Methods as shall be most decisive for securing the Constitutional rights of America against the Systimatic plan formed for their destruction."

shall submit to the payment of Taxes imposed on them without the consent of their Representatives, is a most violent and dangerous attempt to destroy the constitutional liberty and rights of all British America. Resolved that   be appointed Deputies from this House to meet at   such Deputies from the other Colonies, as they shall appoint there to consider and determine on ways the most effectual to stop the exports from N. America, and for the adoption of such other methods as shall be most decisive for securing the Constitutional rights of America against the Systematic plan formed for their destruction.

It is beyond doubt that these would have been assented to by a majority of an hundred to one, and I was prevented from offering them by a great many worthy Members wishing to have the public business first done, as they were persuaded, from many conversations they had hear'd, that a dissolution would not take place until the Country business was finished. It was not until most of the late Members had quitted Town, that an Express arrived with the Resolve of Boston and the determinations of Maryland, Pennsylvania, and some other northern Colonies. This occasioned a meeting of 25 late Burgesses who sent letters of invitation to all the late Members to meet in Williamsburg on the 1st of August next to consid[er][1] of stopping the Exports and Imports from this Colony. So the matter stands at present, and in the meantime the sense of the Counties is taking both in Maryland and Virginia. Many Counties in the two Provinces, all that have hitherto met, have resolved on the propriety of [2] stopping Exports, Imports, and Courts of Justice until Boston is redressed, and American grievances removed. An Indian invasion of this Colony having lately happened [has com-

[1] Ms. damaged.
[2] The three preceding words are inserted above the line.

pelled the] [1] calling of [a new] [2] Assembly, and writs are now out returnable the 11th of Aug^t

It has excited much curiosity and conversation in the Country, how the meeting of Assembly comes to be put off to the 11th when all the late Members were publickly invited to meet on the 1st, especially as it is pretty certain that almost every Man of the late Assembly will be chosen again into the New one, and as the calling an Assembly was determined in Council on the 17th or 18th of Julye,[3] which admitted of making the writs returnable to the 27th or 28th of July. This County have already, (and I suppose the rest will follow) directed their Representatives not to fail being in Williamsburg on the first, in order to prevent a prorogation which may happen from having the power of preventing the advice and assistance of this Colony from reaching the rest.

I suppose when we meet, the first thing done, will be to invite an immediate Congress of Deputies from all the Colonies, when no doubt his Majesty will receive the united supplication of his truly loyal American Subjects for the removal of their great grievances, and the Merchants and Manufacturers of G. B.[4] will receive the American Apology for stopping their exports and imports, it being most repugnant to their inclinations to do injury to them their innocent fellow subjects, if invincible necessity did not compel the adoption of this, the only method that Heaven has left us for the preservation of our most dear, most antient and constitutional exemption from Taxes imposed on us not by the consent of our Representatives, hoping they will pity, forgive, and assist us in procuring redress. Thus

[1] These words are supplied from a letter of June 23, 1774, p. 112.
[2] Words are here missing, but see letter of June 23, 1774.
[3] " June " evidently was written and erased.
[4] A lengthy address to them, explaining conditions, was drafted by Richard Henry Lee.

I think I have given you as just an account of our present unhappy political state as I am able, and will now proceed to private affairs! From the Knave Templemans estate I have recovered for you the £14. Sterᵍ for which your horse was sold to him, which with the interest amounted to £16.8. Sterᵍ & the money Capᵗ Roman has had for the Ships use. I shall inclose you his bill for it on our brother William.

I shall also inclose Lord Shelburnes Almanac to you — I observe that worthy Lord still continues his friendship for the distressed Americans. You will much oblige me by writing as often as you can to my little Boys, advising a close attention to the business that carried them to England. The present Mʳˢ Lee has furnished me with two daughters, Nancy & Henrietta, who are fine thriving girls — These make my number 6, our brother Thom has 7, Phil 2, Loudon 0 —

Farewell my dear brother

I have written our brother W. solely on business referring him for politics to You.

TO [WILLIAM LEE][1]

DEAR BROTHER,   CHANTILLY IN VIRGᵃ 29ᵗʰ June 1774

I wrote you so fully by way of Glasgow lately touching the most uncommon and unpardonable neglect of Capᵗ Roman in not attending his Craft to quicken them, and in not waiting on the Gentlemen according to my directions, that he might in time inform me who failed that had promised, in order that I might in time have provided other Tobacco for him, all which, in the constant never failing custom of Captˢ in the consignment business to do. I say, having written you fully

[1] A. L. S. Virginia Historical Society, Lee Papers, IV. 149.

on these points before, it is the less necessary to say much now, however it is proper to make some observations.

I had great reason when at Williamsburg to suppose from the inclosed letter, that there was no doubt of the Friendship being soon filled by means of the orders and directions that I had left with the Captain. But you may judge my surprise, when after a month's absence, returning the 8$\underline{th}$ of June to find that he had only 101 ħħds. on board, and finding by enquiry in the Ship and from himself together, that in a month he had only been twice or so, in the neighborhood of his Ship, under pretence of having been sick, altho he had one Craft up Potomac and another up Rappahanock that had been gone between 3 and 4 weeks when less than a fortnight was fully sufficient. And being informed by his Son that he had no person who understood how to stow the Ship but himself, I concluded his illness to be pretence, in order to cover his not being provided, as surely he ought to have been, with a proper Stower. Finding things going on in this abominable manner, and that he proposed to profit from a charge of demurrage occasioned absolutely by his own fault, by his own inex[cu]sable neglect; I did on the 13$\underline{th}$ of June give him notes and orders for what he said was as much as he could carry, and immediately after that, the next day he got 10 or 12 ħħds more than what I had given him on the 13$\underline{th}$. He assured me then that he would sail in 10 or 12 days; this being the 3rd of July (my letter not being finished the day I began it) is 19 days ago and he is not ready yet. The [cause?][1] of this is owing clearly to his total neglect of his Craft, and not following them up as is the constant custom of every consignment Captain in this Trade. All this, which can be most amply and fully proved by Squire Lee, myself, and

[1] Illegible word.

many others whenever it shall be necessary, would now have been stated in a protest from me, if he had protested when his lye days were out. But I have omitted it as he did not protest, but assured me, that as you had by Charter many more days for discharging the Ship at the Port of London than are necessary; if you would allow out of them in propotion for his extra stay here, that there should be no word of difference between you. As I think it always better to avoid disputes where it can be done reasonably, I have not yet protested against him. His being late with Tob? this year will rather be of advantage, as the Market must sure be rising, and in a short time will probably¹ be very high, as well from political as natural causes. The Crop likely to be made this year I am very certain will not exceed half a Crop, and the report of 74 will be considerably short of last year. I must refer you to Capt. Blackwell, and his mate Capt. Dennis for information, whether Roman had either water, fuel, or Mess sufficient for sailing when his lye days were out. And to them also, for the truth of accounts I have received of Roman talking much to your discredit in public company here, saying you had cheated and imposed on him about his Charter and other [things?]² injurious to y[our Ch]¹aracter. Whether, what [he d]²id will be found actionable, or not, I can't tell. But I am sure it was very Rascal like, to abuse behind his back, a Gentleman, whose interest he had undertaken to promote and advance to the utmost of his power. You may be sure I heard him not, but I am told that Capt⁵ Blackwell and Dennis did. As this Creature can never come again in your business, I would recommend Capt Blackwell, who has a good personal interest in Northumb⁴ & and Lancaster, and is well acquainted

¹ The two words preceding are substituted for "must sure" erased.
² Ms. torn.

with, and much esteemed by all the Gentlemen in these parts. But if you cannot get him, there is one Capt. Cockeril, who has loaded a Ship in Corotoman last winter, and having sent her home remains here to load another. I forget whose business he is in, but I understand he is not well fixed in his present employ, and he has universally established the first reputation in his way where he is known. We have really had most oppressive work with Walker, Rayson, and Roman. Upon my word I believe such another Triumvirate cannot be matched on this side the river Styx. You must not imagine that this arises from any difficulty of pleasing us, no, every body here agrees, that they are not to be equalled. I make no doubt but you have, or will soon, inform me touching your intention to employ Cap.t John Lawson for your Agent. I still think he will answer your purpose extremely well. In the present political state of America, when there appears so universal a determination in all the Colonies to stop exports and imports, especially in Virginia & Maryland, I cannot venture to advise your sending another Ship until this unhappy dispute is ended. A meeting of all the late Members of Assembly, is called by the Moderator & 24 other G[entlemen to m]'eet at Williamsburg on the 1.st of August next [* * *]¹ king exports & imports. The sense of the Coun[* * *² th]e in the meantime, and those, already met are c[l * * *]². The determination of the [Augus]'t meeting y[ou shall hear .the ?]¹ first opportunity afterwards. When you can send Ships, Loudon and myself agree, that the Potomac Ship should be the earliest, sometime in January we think, and the Rappahanock Ship about May; because no rival ships appear in Rappahanock before then, but many in Potomac. A Ship of between 3 and 4 hundred hhds for Potomac & about 400 for

¹ Ms. torn.　　　　　² Words missing.

Rappahanock. But as the larger sized Ships sail much the cheapest, if a plan were settled either to draw moderately or to purchase in case of Accidents, then Ships of between 4 and 5 hundreds hhds had best be sent. It is indispensably necessary that you send immediat-[ely][1] in, y̅ proved account against the Trents to Col. F. L. Lee, that no time may be lost in the settling their business after the Courts are opened (for they are now Shut up) unless they have made you payment. And such account should always be sent where you intend the Debtor may be sued. But it is of the last consequence that you request them all to make their remittances thro the hands of Loudon, to avoid this signal inconvenience. When he, or I, apply, they say remittances have been already made you, and we not knowing but it may be true, are oblidge to acquiesce. There is no point that Loudon & myself are clearer about, than that it is essentially necessary for your interest and the right adjustment of your affairs that you visit Virginia for a few months. You have many debts that none so well as yourself can settle, and besides, a fine growing interest, which your personal application to would benefit exceedingly. For my part, I would not wish you to come away before the next election in England, but as that is in Apri[l * * *][1] be here with your Rappahanock Ship in [* * *][1] be a very good time for that river. I pray [* * *]t[1] this, if by any means you can effect [* * *][1] Fairfax's lately I was told that you proposed [* * *][1] loss Trade[2]) and the j[udgmen]t

[1] Ms. torn.   [2] Written above the line.

THE LETTERS OF RICHARD HENRY LEE

TO WILLIAM LEE[1]

DEAR BROTHER,   HOMONY[2] HALL   13$\underline{^{th}}$ July 177[4]

Capt. Blackwell clears today, & so does Roman, but for fear of accidents, please be informed that Roman has of your own Tobacco Forty eight h̄h̄ds, vid! 40, purchased from Hudson Muse, 6 from Daniel Muse, 1 h̄h̄d Servants [Tob? ?][3] & one saved from the damaged Tob? of Cap! Rayson last year, about which you are inform[ed][3] in my letter from Chantilly. The N! weight of 6 h[hds][3] bot of Dan Muse is 5939^{lbs} at 10^s/D? of 40 h̄h̄ds purchased of Hudson Muse 40950 at 10/sterling as per Manifest which see — The weight of Raysons damaged h̄h̄d 991. & of the Ser[vants][3] Tob? [?] 972. The Friendship has 2 h̄h̄ds shipt by Jno. [?][4] Kinner [?][4] as Ex! of Catherine Monroe which [   ][3] may be insured at £5.—.— Sterling p! h̄h̄d
    Farewell
            Your affectionate broth[er][3]
VIRGINIA.

TO WILLIAM LEE[5]

DEAR BROTHER,   PHILADELPHIA. 20$\underline{^{th}}$ Sept! 1774

We have been here in full Congress of Deputies from the Principal Colonies near three weeks proceeding slowly but with great unanimity on the important business that brought us to this Town. The proceedings are yet on

---

[1] A. L. S. Virginia Historical Society, Lee Papers, IV. 123. Addressed to Lee, "Merchant in London;" and sent by Captain Blackwell of the *Caroline.* Endorsed as received August 30 and answered September 3, 1774.

[2] Lee's error for "Nomony."   [3] Ms. torn.   [4] Illegible.

[5] A. L. S. Lenox Library, Emmet Collection, 414. Addressed to him,"Merchant in/London." Endorsed as received, "9 Jany 1775."

honor to be kept secret, but we have great hopes that their vigor and unanimity will prove the ruin of our Ministerial Enemies and the salvation of American Liberty. About a fortnight more will produce a publication of our plan, after which, you shall have it by the first opportunity. Since we came to this place, a universal alarm has been occasioned by a report that Boston had just been Cannonaded. This proves not true, and took its rise from a night manouvre of the Generals, to seize some Provincial Powder that had been stored by law for Militia uses. The report served however to show the spirit and situation of the people in that part of America, for we have good intelligence that 50,000 Men were in Arms in the Massachusetts Government and Connecticut, and that 30,000 were on march, well armed and provided, to Boston when they were informed all was peace at that place, on which they quietly returned home. Does not this shew that no small difficulty will attend forcing a submission from these people, and that they are most firmly resolved to dye rather than submit to the change of their Government. In this too they will have the concurring support of the other Colonies as the Congress have in fact already published their determination by approving in strong terms the resolves of the County of Suffolk as the inclosed Paper will shew you. It seems to me, that if Ministry have not their hearts hardened, as the Scripture has it, they will best consult the good of thei[r] Country and their own safety by a prudent and speedy reversal of their ill judged measures. For they may be certain of a full, complete and steady opposition from all North America — I mean every part of it that is worth regarding. Give my love to the Doctor and communicate this letter to him.

I heartily wish my Sister & yourself health and happiness. Farewell.

THE LETTERS OF RICHARD HENRY LEE

[LETTER OF CONGRESS TO COLONIAL AGENTS] [1]

PHILADELPHIA, October 26, 1774.

"GENTLEMEN,

"We give you the strongest proof of our reliance on your zeal and attachment to the happiness of America, & the cause of liberty, when we commit the enclosed papers to your care.

"We desire you will deliver the petition [2] into the hands of his Majesty, & after it has been presented, we wish it may be made public thro' the press, together with the list of grievances. And as we hope for great assistance from the spirit, virtue, and justice of the nation, it is our earnest desire, that the most effectual care be taken, as early as possible, to furnish the trading cities, & manufacturing towns, throughout the united Kingdom, with our memorial to the people of great Britain.

"We doubt not, but your good sense & discernment, will lead you to avail yourselves of every assistance, that may be derived from the advice & friendship of all great & good men who may incline to aid the cause of liberty and mankind.

"The gratitude of America, expressed in the enclosed vote of thanks, we desire may be conveyed to the deserving objects of it, in the manner you think will be most acceptable to them.

[1] Drafted by Richard Henry Lee. Printed in W. C. Ford, *Journals of Congress*, I. 104. Lee and John Jay were the committee appointed to prepare this letter to accompany the Address to the King, which was approved October 25, 1774. The letter was reported and adopted October 26. See *Idem*.

[2] Richard Henry Lee was chairman of the committee appointed October 1, 1774, to draft an address to the King, but the Petition adopted by Congress differs materially from an autograph draft found among Lee's manuscripts. See Ford, *Journals of Congress*, I. 53, 115.

THE LETTERS OF RICHARD HENRY LEE

"It is proposed, that another Congress be held on the tenth of May next, at this place, but in the mean time, we beg the favour of you, Gentlemen, to transmit to the Speakers of the several Assemblies, the earliest information of the most authentic accounts you can collect, of all such conduct & designs of ministry, or parliament, as it may concern America to know.

"We are, with unfeigned esteem and regard, Gentlemen, &c.

"By order and in behalf of the Congress,

"HENRY MIDDLETON, *President.*"

To PAUL WENTWORTH, DOCT.ᴿ FRANKLIN, Wᴹ BOLLAN, ARTHUR LEE, THO.ˢ LIFE, EDM.ᵈ BURKE, CHARLES GARTH.

TO LANDON CARTER [1]

DEAR SIR,   CHANTILLY december 20ᵗʰ 1774

I wish with all my heart you had found the Harlem oil as effecatious as Mʳ Allen supposed, but when I heard the old Gentlemen recommending it in such strong terms, it occurred to me, that like other Carmenatives it was palliative only, and that the cause must be removed by other medicines. I do not remember any further direction for its use than the number of drops for a dose, and a general reference to the paper of directions. You reason very well on the distemper, and I make no doubt but that a proper attention to food, keeping the body from costiveness, whilst a proper tone is restored to the Intestines, will at length produce a radical cure. In sudden fits of severe pain, the Oil may perhaps, like other Carminatives procure ease, but I am convinced

[1] A. L. S. Virginia Historical Society, Lee Papers, IV. 165. In answer to a letter of Carter's, of November 29, 1774, Lee had sent him, for flatulent colic, the only bottle of Harlem oil that he had brought from Philadelphia.

that a recurrence to other remedies is necessary to remove the cause. I have not any calcined Magnesia, but surely any common crucible would effect this purpose. My family are a little indisposed at present, but next week I did propose to visit Richmond, and whilst there, I will endeavor to persuade M.r Parker to join me in paying respects to Sabine Hall which always gives pleasure to your affectionate friend.

P.S. Nat brings you a small but well written Pamphlet on the American dispute. A native of Pennsylvania is the Author — But I fancy, by the arrival of 5 Ships of the Line at Boston with fresh Troops, the Ministry propose to try if we can fight as well as write.

TO SAMUEL ADAMS[1]

SIR,   VIRGINIA 4.th February 1775

I fear the friends of liberty and virtue may wonder at the few efforts that have been made by this Colony since the dissolution of the late patriotic Congress. But tho we have not yet had an opportunity of publickly expressing our sentiments, I think the general private conduct has not been exceptionable. Among all ranks and Classes of people (a very few interested foreign Traders excepted) there appears great unanimity, and firmness of zeal in support of the American cause.

A ship from London, owned by a much favored Merchant here, has been forced to return without being suffered to take a single hogshead of Tobacco, because she had brought a few chests of tea; and every measure is taking to enforce the Continental association. Hitherto we have had no Colony Congress, because our Assembly was to have met early in November, but Lord Dunmores excursions on our frontiers occasioned a prorogation

[1] A. L. S. in initials. Lenox Library, Samuel Adams Papers.

until the 2ᵈ instant, at which time many reasons concurred to induce a firm belief that a meeting would then take place. However a few days past, we have been surprised with a further prorogation to the first thursday in May next. This has been followed by a call from our late worthy President, Mᵣ Randolph, upon the several Counties to choose Deputies to a Colony Convention on the 20ᵗʰ of March. A compliance with this[1] now occupies our attention, and will certainly be unanimously obeyed. It seems that this latter prorogation is in consequence of a letter from Lᵈ Dartmouth forbidding the calling of any more Assemblies, unless the exegencies of an Indian war should render it necessary. How perfectly coincident is this, with the conduct of the Tyrant Stewart race, whose wicked and ruinous policy made them fear to meet their people, and rendered it necessary to deprive the community of the aid resulting from wise and collected councils. The event of their despotism is well known. — May we not hope that the same causes will produce similar effects and that ruin may recoil on the heads of the detestable contrivers of the present unjust and destructive system of Colony Administration? The cause of Liberty must be under the protection of Heaven, because the Creator surely wills the happiness of his Creatures; & having joined the faculty of reasoning with our natures, he has made us capable of discerning that the true dignity and happiness of human nature are only to be found in a state of freedom. You have no doubt seen the speech to Parliament, and from thence may judge what our Ministerial enemies propose for us.

A letter from London 6ᵗʰ of december says "the present intention of the Ministry is to declare all meetings and associations in America illegal and treasonable — To guard the Coast against all Traffic and Communication with Holland, France, and Spain. To corrupt

---

[1] The two words preceding are inserted above the line.

N. York, and to employ a military force, chiefly from Canada if necessary. Having their designs before you, your attention will be bent to defeat them with all earnestness which the greatest question in the world demands "

Added to this, I understand they propose to forfiet and confiscate all the estates of all those who meet, associate, or combine against the Commerce of G! Britain! Should such Acts pass, will it not be proper for all America to declare them essentially vile and void, and that whoever takes or claims any Estate so said to be forfieted, shall be deemed a public Enemy and that it shall be meretorious in any person to put such Claimant to death? This would probably deter, and defeat the wicked design. I find the Ministerial Manoeuver of dissolving the Parliament, has, notwithstanding the timely warning of Junius, answered their purpose so far as to rest the matter now on the firmness of our own virtue, or on the general exertion of the people of England. Tho' the latter should fail us, I hope the former will be immovable.

The opportunity that conveys this, brings a small testimony of our esteem, in this County, for the patriotic virtues of Boston, and we shall be glad to hear by return of this Vessel that the contribution has been duly received. If any late intelligence from G. B. has reached you, be so kind as favor me with it by Capt. Layton who returns immediately here. Is the fortification on the Neck compleated, how many Ships & of what size in your Harbor, and how many Soldiers in Town? Are your people in good Spirits, and does the business of discipline go on well? I think a certain M! Ruggles with you, whose Body itches so much for the stroke of Knighthood, should be first stricken with rods, and then find his fate on that Tree where Traitors to their Country should all hang.

I am with very singular esteem Sir Your most affectionate friend and Countryman.

TO ARTHUR LEE [1]

D.B.[2]   [Feb. 24, 1775].

All America has received with astonishment and concern the Speech to Parliament. The wicked violence of Ministry is so clearly expressed, as to leave no doubt of their fatal determination to ruin both Countries, unless a powerful and timely check is interposed by the Body of the people. A very small corrupted Junto in New York excepted, all N. America is now most firmly united and as firmly resolved to defend their liberties ad infinitum against every power on Earth that may attempt to take them away. The most effectual measures are everywhere taking to secure a sacred observance of the Association — Manufactures go rapidly on, and the means of repelling force by force are universally adopting. The inclosed Address to the Virginia Delegates published a few days since in the Gazette will shew you the spirit of the Frontier Men — This one County of Fincastle can furnish 1000 Rifle Men that for their number make most formidable light Infantry in the World. The six frontier Counties can produce 6000 of these Men who from their amazing hardihood, their method of living so long in the woods without carrying provisions with them, the exceeding quickness with which they can march to distant parts, and above all, the dexterity to which they have arrived in the use

---

[1] A. L. S. University of Virginia, Lee Papers, No. 16. Addressed to Lee at The Temple, London. On the back of the letter under the address is the following autograph note by William Lee signed with his initials: "I will meet you at 7 o'clock tomor/row even.[g] at the George & Vulture/in Cornhill."

[2] Dear Brother.   W. L. Sunday./

of the Rifle Gun. Their is not one of these Men who wish a distance less than 200 yards or a larger object than an Orange — Every shot is fatal. The Virginia Colony Congress meets the 20th of next month for the appointment of Delegates to the Continental Congress in May next, and for other purposes of public security. The Ministry who are both foolish and wicked, think by depriving us of Assemblies, to take away the advantage that results from united and collected counsels. But they are grievously mistaken. In despight of all their machinations, public Councils will be held and public measures adopted for general security. Still we hope that the proceedings of the last Continental Congress when communicated to the people of England will rouse a spirit that proving fatal to an abandoned Ministry may save the whole Empire from impending destruction. The honorable Col? Lee of Stratford was buried this day, he died the 21st ultimo after a months painful illness. He is a public loss, and if the Ministry go on filling up these vacancies in the Council with raw boys and hotheaded senseless people, that affairs of Virginia must be in perpetual confusion, altho the present dispute should be accommodated. It is absolutely necessary that some grave sensible Men should now be placed there in order to temper the present body.

The pamphlet entitled an Appeal &c is, I think, the best I have read on the subject amidst such a variety of finely reasoned ones.

Farewell.——

P.S. By authentic accounts just come to hand, all the Ministerial efforts with New York and the Jersey Governments have failed, both Assemblies have highly approved the proceedings of the Continental Congress, thank their Delegates — and appointed them to represent their respective Colonies in the next May Congress.

From N. York we have lately sent back a Ship from Glasgow with goods that arrived after 1.ˢᵗ of Feb.ʸ scarcely allowing the Vessel time to get fresh provisions. It is now therefore certain that without a redress of Grievances, G. Britain must prepare to do entirely without the N. American trade, nor will the British Isles in the W. Indies get their usual necessary supplies from the Continent. Georgia has acceded to the Continental Association, and we understand Canada will have Delegates in the next Congress. You will oblige me greatly by giving my boys advice and pressing to diligent application as often as you have leisure to do so. You never say whether or when you take the Gown, and where you propose to practice.

Farewell.

TO LANDON CARTER [1]

DEAR SIR, CHANTILLY 24ᵗʰ April 1775

We had hear'd of the Lords flight before your letter came, and we apprehend it to be for fear of reprisal, as we suppose one part of the Ministerial plan has been already executed in Boston. by seizing the Massachusetts

[1] A. L. S. Virginia Historical Society, Lee Papers, IV. 137. Endorsed on fold of the enclosing sheet below the address [by L. Carter?]: "Rich [tear in Ms.]
April 1775 [in pencil.]
Containing the Vigilance of frien/ship in London wch has at last/ got into the Cabinet held agst Ame/rica, and often for a disguise in a/certain [St]ableyard, where Vigilance/had at last got intelligence, and by/their own modes I do suppose a bribery/got into [their] Secrets One of wch is a/Black list of Proscribed Americans/ 32 in Number and as, Some of them/are Virginians, the reason for his/Ldshps flight is plain The Continental/Congress had on an application from/Suffolk County Convention Massachu/setts Governmt resolvd that in any case of a [r]emoval of one man of note/reprisals would be Justifiable. But/yet from Ld Dunmores

proportion of the proscribed Americans, of which there are 32. Some Virginians are in the black list. Manuscript intelligence from London 11 Feb.y from our most vigilant sensible & well informed friends, put the determined hostility of Ministry beyond doubt — They have to a Man both publickly & privately, solemnly avowed it. The notorious practise of this profligate Administration being to deceive with lies and flattering appearances in the very moment of determined vengeance would render belief in any thing they say or do, sottish in the extreme — When they offer any thing favorable, a wise American should say with the cautious Trojan 'Timeo Donaos et dona ferentes" — Unluckily for the Liverpool news, that Greenwood who conveys it, is a Ministerial Agent, and his name is here among those Villains who were Securities for the safety of the Ministerial Tea sent to S. Carolina. You may be assured Sir that the Ministry and all their Agents will lie, deceive, and blind by all manner of means; well knowing they have no chance for success but by such infamous ways, and by putting their Adversaries off their Guard. We propose sending a Pilot boat immediately for Gun Powdr and she can bring the Richmond quantity[1] if their Cash is quickly collected — But of this no mention should be made but to the most trusty and secret Gentlemen for fear that some Capt. Collins may be waiting to intercept it. You may be assured that the plan of Ministry is fixed to Compel immediate submission by force of Arms, well knowing that if our Association has time to work, that their ruin is infallible.

letters sent/into Virg of a Malicious nature I do con/clude the [e]ra of harmony is near at hand/or North who refusd it in Parliamt wod/not have [*illegible word*] the Author of those letters/wch he laid on the table only in theire/extracts —"

[1] Word erased and Ms. torn.

THE LETTERS OF RICHARD HENRY LEE

God put us into the hands of better men and better times, which will surely be the case if we provide ourselves immediately with Arms & Ammunition, learn the discipline, behave like Men, and stick close, religiously close to the Association. I am dear Sir Y.ʳ Affect friend.

TO [WILLIAM LEE][1]

PHILADELPHIA 10 May 1775

DEAR BROTHER,

I am exceedingly pressed with business and therefore must be short, and for this time mix politics with business of a private nature. The Virg.ᵃ Delegates arrived here yesterday, where they find all those from the Southward of this, with Deputies from N. Hampshire — In an hour all from the Colonies north of this will be here and then the Congress will be opened. There never appeared more perfect unanimity among any sett of Men than among the Delegates, and indeed all the old Provinces, not one excepted are directed by the same firmness of union, and determination to resist by all ways and to every extremity. The Province of N. York is at last alarmed, the Tory Ministerial faction are driven from their influence and virtuous patriotism taken place. The shameful defeat of General Gage's Troops near Boston (after a wanton and cruel Attack on unarmed people, after they had brutally killed old Men, Women, & children) has revitted such union, roused such an universal Military Spirit throut all the Colonies, and excited such universal resentment against this Savage Ministry and their detestable Agents, that now no doubt remains of their destruction with the establishment of American Rights. 800 of the Regulars commanded by a Col.º Smith was defeated by 600 pro-

[1] A. L. S. Virginia Historical Society, Lee Papers, IV. 133.

134

vincials hastily[1] gathered[1] together[1]—Altho' tis' agreed
the Col° personally behaved with the true spirit of a good
Soldier. These 800 were afterwards supported by 1200
under command of Ld Piercy but the whole were compelled (upon reenforcement coming up to the Provincials) to retreat to Boston having had several men
killed, wounded, and taken prisoners. The Provincials
are since increased to 20.000 and lay now encamped
before Boston. All communication is cut off between
Town & Country. The Troops, by way of insult
marched first out of Town to the tune of Yankee
doodle, and sometime after fired unprovoked[1] upon
some people who were exercising, as they told the Regulars for amusement without having any amunition
with them. This is the most authentic account we have
here of this business. The Connecticut people with the
N. Yorkers are preparing to prevent any bad designs
of the Troops coming to the latter place. I expect
Capt Brown will soon be loaded, as he had Tob° enough
ready—You will please insure for Col° George Mason
one hundred hogsheads in the Adventure to recover £10.
sterling in case of loss. 22 hhds of Col° P. L. Lee's estate
& 5 of mine at what you judge proper. The proceeds of
these 22 hhds are to be applied to the use of our brother,
Doctor Lee. 15 of them are Top stem'd heavy hhds.
So that you may advance the Doctor at least
200 Guineas on the whole. Mr. Willing's Tobaccos'
were all engaged another way before your application.
Loudoun & Mr. Brown will take care of y^r Virg^a business. The Doctor's family here send their love.
farewell.

[1] These words are inserted above the line.

THE LETTERS OF RICHARD HENRY LEE

TO [FRANCIS LIGHTFOOT LEE][1]

DEAR BROTHER,   PHILADELPHIA 21st. May 1775.

An Express just arrived here from Williamsburg informing of the Assembly being called to the 1st. of June, which carries our Spea[ker] away. We supose the design is chiefly to lay Ld. North's conciliatory plan before the house. 'Tis most [sure?] that if this is done, you should, after making . . . proper spirited observations on the folly, inju[ry] and insidiousness of the proposition; refer him to the united opinion of N. America in Congress. Many and powerful are the reasons that render it necessary you should fully approve in Gen. Assembly of the proceedings of last Continentl. Congress, of this present appointment and of your Delegates. Ministry and their Tools have constantly informed the Nation that the Provincial Conventions were factious meetings, that their proceedings were not the sense of the people, and that the Constitutional Assemblies (as they contrast the two) would not be of such opinion. To prevent a contradiction of this they have prevented the meeting of Assemblies, unless when they had some special wicked purpose to answer. The Assemblies that have been allowed to meet, all except New York, have reprobated this Ministerial lye, and have resolved as above mentioned. For heavens sake avoid compliments (except to the Soldiery, [)]] on the Indian expedition last summer. Nothing has given more concern and disgust to these northern Colonies than our unhappy vote of that sort in last Convention. Yesterday one of the first Men on the Continent for wisdom, sound judgment, good information, and integrity said to me "I

[1] A. L. S. Harvard University Library, Lee Mss., II. 53. Endorsed, in Arthur Lee's autograph, across the last page at the end: "Liberty Quos nolumus Arthur Lee."

was much grieved, and concerned for the honor and good sense of Virginia, when I saw that ill founded illjudged Compliment" Perhaps the scheme is to get another invasion Law and your approbation of another ruinously expensive excursion on the frontiers. A few scatter loping Indians will never be wanting to commit irregularities for the encouragement of these Land exploring schemes. But the Land hunter ought to accomplish his purpose upon terms less destructive than £100,000 charge to the public annually. Never encourage by complimenting the last, a second tour among the Indians and Frontier men. The Continent looks with jealous eyes on the visits of Governors to such places at this crisis." We know the plan of Ministry is to bring Canadians and Indians down upon us. For this reason the Provincial Troops of Connecticut & Massachusetts have wisely taken by a brave coup de Main, possession of the Forts at Ticonderoga & Crown Point. In the former they got 200 pieces of of large Cannon, some field pieces, Swivels, Powder &c. The Congress have directed N. York, Connecticut & Massachusetts to remove these stores &c. to the South end of Lake George and take strong post there to intercept the communication and march of Cannadian & Indian forces into those colonies. The taking of Ticonderoga last year cost G. Britain many thousand lives and a great expense, but now it has been taken from them, tho strong & well garrisoned, by the bravery and enterprise of a few Provincials and at a very small expence. There never was a more total revolution at any place than at New York. The Tory's have been obliged to fly, the Province is arming, and the Governor dares not call his prostituted Assembly to receive Ld. Norths foolish plan. The Delances, Watts, Cooper, Rivington, Colo. Philips & the rest of the Tory Leaders are fled some to England, and some to private places in the Country where they are not known. The Congress have advised the Yorkers to make provision for carrying their Women & Children into the Country, and to remove their warlike stores before the arrival of Troops there, whom they are not to suffer to encamp, or commit with impunity any hostilities against the people. The latest and best accounts from Boston make the loss of Regulars in killed, wounded, & missing 1000 men. The Provincial loss was trifling. 10,000 men are now encamped before the Town between which and the country there is no intercourse. G. Gage refuses to let the people out in consequence of which their distress must presently must be grievous indeed. The Beseiging Army keep the one Beseiged in constant alarm, so that 'tis said they rest neither Night nor day. Every day is expected to bring 2000 Men more from Ireland, and seven Regiments to N. York where the Torys had informed Ministers they would be well received, but now behold they come to a Country universally hostile, and in Arms to receive them. Connecticut has 12000 Men in Arms, the Jerseys a good many, and the Province at least 8000, — There are 2000 in this City well armed and disciplined Men. In short every Colony this way is well prepared for War and appear to be secure against any Force likley to be sent against them. It would seem as if the Southern Colonies were alone vulnerable at present, and this should be remedied as soon as possible." We are just informed that the Dutch have imported a large quantity of powder into Statia,[1] and that two English Men of War are laying off the Island to prevent its exportation to N. America—That a large quantity is also landed at Cape Francois where no guard is yet placed. The Treasurer should be prevailed with to employ a Mr. Goodrich in in Norfolk, a famous Con-

[1] St. Eustatius.

traband Man, to send immediately some swift sailing Pilot Boats for 20 or 30000 weight to supply the Counties whose money will no doubt be collected before the powder arives. I hope Capt. Brown is near full by this time, and I suppose Mr. Lees charter'd Ship as well as Outram is arrived in York River — You will have time to load these Vessels as it is not now probable that the Congress will stop the exports sooner than the 10th of September, except provision to the British fishery on the Banks of Newfoundland." It seems the bill for restraining the trade of the Colonies is not to have force until a certain time after its arrival in N. America. So that in this instance the whole power of Legislature is given to Ministry, for it will depend on them when the Act shall arrive here since they may send it when, or never, as they please." Mr. Brown should be immediately informed that there is no prospect of the exportation being stopt, that he may act on full knowledge, about buying or not Tobacco. "We find by the late accounts that Ministry will be more puzzled than they imagine to accomplish their detestable purposes against us Mr./Lee/writes the 26 March that the embarquement from England has been delayed by the impossibility of getting Seamen for the Ships, but he adds let not this delay your vigorous efforts for defence. From Ireland we learn, that the people there have interposed to prevent, the embarquement, and that a contest has happened in which several lives were lost on both sides. The other day G. Gage (hearing that all the provincial Troops, except 1500 were retired to sign an association prepared for them at some distance from the Encampment,) marched with his whole force out of Boston, but seeing the 1500 Provincials drawn up in order of Battle, and disliking their Countenance, he returned within his Lines.

A Man of Wars Tender at Rhode Island lately Seized

a vessel loaded with provisions for the Army at Boston and the Country People in Boats attacked and took both the provision Vessel and the Tender, having wounded the Lieutenant of the M. of War and taken his men prisoners whom they conveyed Captives into the Country.

Thus you see our infant struggles on the water are not unsuccessful." You have all the news of this place — I am hurried, as I suppose you will be tired, with the length of this Letter — Let me know by every Post how you go on at Williamsburg & the objects of your deliberations — Remember me to all friends and particularly to Mr. Treasurer. farewell.

TO GOUVERNEUR MORRIS[1]

Dʳ Sɪʀ,   Pʜɪʟᴀᴅᴇʟᴘʜɪᴀ 28 May. 75

The friends of virtuous liberty in New York have certainly effected a most important change in the political system of that flourishing City. I congratulate you Sir and your worthy Associates in this happy revolution. It is most certain that a profligate Ministry have greatly relied on the assistance of your fine fertile province for carrying into execution their cruel System. A System by which existing millions, and Millions yet unborn are to be plunged into the abyss of slavery, and[2] of consequence deprived of every[3] glorious distinction that marks the Man from the Brute. But happily for the

[1] A. L. S. American Philosophical Society, Lee Papers, I. 141, No. 42. A text with changes is found in R. H. Lee, *Memoir of Richard Henry Lee*, II. 155. Endorsed, in Lee's autograph, "to be copied by/M Hamilton "

[2] The following words are here erased, " for ever deprived of from [*words illegible*] which no day of "

[3] The following words are here erased, " light, would pierce to "

140

cause of humanity, the Colonies are now united, and may bid defiance to tyranny and its infamous Abettors. You will see that M[r] Rivingtons case is involved in all of a similar motive, which are to be determined on by the Colony Conventions where the offence is committed. I am sorry, for the honor of human Nature, that this Man should have so prostituted himself, in support of a cause the most detestable that ever disgraced Mankind. But he repents and should be forgiven. It is not yet too late to exert his powers in defense of the liberty and just rights of a much injured Country. I wish you happy Sir and assure You that I am, with singular esteem, your friend and Countryman.

[LETTER OF CONGRESS TO THE LORD MAYOR OF LONDON][1]

MY LORLD,   [July 8, 1775].

Permit the Delegates of the people of twelve Antient Colonies, to pay your Lordship and the August body of

[1] A. dr. L. American Philosophical Society, Lee Papers, I. 139, No. 41. Drafted by Richard Henry Lee and endorsed, "Letter to the/ Lord Mayor/from Congress/May 1775." This letter was ordered by Congress, July 6, 1775, to be prepared by the committee appointed to draft "a Letter to the people of G[reat]-B[ritain]," of which Lee was chairman; and both letters were reported and approved July 8, 1775. See Ford, *Journals of Congress*, II. 80, 157, 163, 170. The text of the former was first printed in the *Pennsylvania Packet*, December 11, 1775. *Ibid.*, II. 171, note. A text with variations is found in R. H. Lee, *Memoir of Richard Henry Lee*, I. 153. See Ford, *Journals of Congress*, II. 170, for another text, with slight variations. Several other endorsements appear on folds of the Ms., such as: "Fasher's Legacy to/his/Daughter/by D[r] Gregory," "Robt Eden/ Dan[l] Dulaney/Robert Eden Gov[r]/of Maryland/Dan[l] Dulaney." The following misleading heading has been written by some one on

141

which you are head a[1] just tribute of gratitude and thanks for the virtuous and unsolicited resentment [2] you have shown to[3] the violated rights of a free people. The City of London my Lord, having[4] in all ages approved itself [5] the patron of liberty, and the support of just government, against lawless tyranny & usurpation; cannot fail to make us deeply sensible of the mighty aid our cause receives from such[6] advocation. A cause my Lord worthy the support of the first[7] City in the world, as it involves[8] the fate of a great Continent, and bids fair to shake the foundations of a flourishing, and until lately, a happy empire.

North America My Lord wishes most ardently for a lasting connection with G. Britain on terms of just and equal liberty[9] less than which[10] generous minds would not offer,[11] nor brave and free ones be willing to receive.

A cruel war has at length been opened against us, and whilst we prepare to defend ourselves like the Descendants of Britons, we still hope that the mediation of wise and good Citizens, will at length prevail over[12] despotism and restore peace & harmony on per-

the Ms. at the beginning of the letter: " 1775.—May. Letter written by R. H. Lee on behalf of the Delegates of the City of London to the Lord Mayor."

[1] Substituted above the line for " the " erased.
[2] Substituted above the line for " regard " erased.
[3] Written above the line and substituted for " for " erased.
[4] Substituted above the line for " hath " erased.
[5] Preceding this word on the line " themselves " is erased.
[6] Written above the line and substituted for " their " erased.
[7] Substituted above the line for " greatest " erased.
[8] Following this word " in it " is erased, and before the word " fate," an " f " is erased.
[9] The words " We think a generous mind " are here erased on the line.
[10] " a " is here erased on the line.
[11] The word " and " here on the line is erased.
[12] The word " vicious," following here upon the line, is erased.

manent principles, to to an oppressed and divided Empire.

We have the honor to be

[*The remainder of the page is covered with figures.*]

TO ALEXANDER McDOUGAL [1]

PHILADELPHIA 24 July 1775.

SIR,

Attention to the public business, and an immediate answer to your letter not being necessary, will, I hope be my excuse for not sooner acknowleding the receipt of your favor of June the 5$\underline{th}$. The case you mention has not yet come under consideration of the Congress. It is a hard one no doubt, but how to give relief, without again introducing that Commodity to public use, is a question of much difficulty. New York is not a singular instance of such suffering, they [2] are plentifully [3] scattered thro all the existing Colonies. Should Congress determine to admit the sale and the use of what tea is on hand, may not bad men take the advantage of the impossibility of distinguishing this from newly imported Tea & exerting their wits conceal the importation, and thus render abortive [4] our Association against this article, the hateful cause of the present disagreeable situation of N. America. I fear this case, is among the number of those unavoidable evils introduced into

[1] A. dr. L. S. University of Virginia, Lee Papers, reverse of Ms. No. 76. Answer to McDougal's letter of June 5, 1775. McDougal, Merchant of New York, presided in 1774 at the meeting preliminary to the election of delegates to the Continental Congress. He was Colonel of the 1st New York Regiment in 1776, and was made Brigadier-General in August, 1776, and Major-General October, 1777.

[2] Substituted for "the equal instances" erased.

[3] Substituted for "to be found" erased.

[4] The words "the whole of" are here erased.

143

Society, by the want of public virtue. I am acquainted with very many instances of large quantities of stopt Teas in Virginia, but I am happy to find that the Sufferers bear their misfortune with much patience in consideration of the public good resulting therefrom. It is more than a year now, since the use of Tea has been totally banished from Virginia. Do you not think Sir, that Gen. Gage will turn his eyes to N. York for winter quarters for part of his Army, and [1] may it not be wise to be prepared for resisting a plan caculated to afford shelter in [2] cold weather to Men who will certainly enter upon our destruction when the Season changes?

I am, with much regard, Sir your most obedient humble Servant.

ALEX. M^c DOUGAL Esq. N. York.

TO [GEORGE WASHINGTON] [3]

DEAR SIR,   PHILADELPHIA 26 July 1775

With most cordial warmth we recommend our Countryman Mr Edmund Randolph to your patronage and favor.

This young Gentlemans abilities, natural and acquired, his extensive connections, and above all, his desire to serve his Country in this arduous struggle, are circumstances that cannot fail to gain him your countenance and protection.

---

[1] The words "if so" above the line are erased.

[2] The word "the" above the line is erased.

[3] A. L. S. by Lee. Library of Congress, Letters to Washington, VI. 157. Signed in autograph also by Patrick Henry and Thomas Jefferson. A printed text is in Sparks, *Correspondence of the Revolution*, I. 24.

You will readily discern Sir, how important a consideration it is, that our Country should be furnished with the security and strength derived from our young Gentry being possessed of military knowledge, so necessary in these times of turbulence and danger.

Encouraged by your friendship, and instructed by your example, we hope M.ʳ Randolph will become useful to his Country and profitable to himself.

We most heartily wish you health and success, with a happy return to your family and Country, being with great sincerity dear Sir Your affectionate friends and obedient Servants.

TO [GEORGE WASHINGTON][1]

DEAR SIR,   PHILADELPHIA. 1ˢᵗ August 1775

After the fatigue of many days, and of this in particular, I should not sit down at eleven o Clock at night to write to a Gentleman of whose goodness of heart I have less doubt than I have of yours. But well knowing that you will pardon what flows from good intentions, I venture to say that my hopes are, you will find from what Congress has already done, and from what I hope they will do tomorrow, that it has been a capital object with us to make your arduous business as easy to you as the nature of things will admit. The business immediately before us being finished, the approaching sickly season here, and the great importance of our presence

[1] A. L. S. Library of Congress, Letters to Washington, VI. 175. A text with alterations is printed in Sparks, *Correspondence of the Revolution*, I. 11. Lee voted for Washington as general and commander-in-chief and was chairman of the committee appointed, June 15, 1775, to draft his commission and instructions as General. See Ford, *Journals of Congress*, II. 91, 93, 96. Lee's letters of this period show an affectionate regard for Washington.

in the Virg.ª Convention, have determined a recess of a Month, it standing now, that the Congress shall meet here again on the 5ᵗʰ of September. The capital object of powder we have attended to as far as we could by sending you the other day six Tons, and tomorrow we shall propose sending six or eight Tons more, which, with the supplies you may get from Connecticut, and such further ones from here, as future expected importations may furnish, will I hope enable you to do all that this powerful article can in good hands accomplish. We understand here, that Batteries may be constructed at the entrance of the Bay of Boston so as to prevent the egress & regress of any Ships whatever. If this be fact, would it not Sir be a signal stroke to secure the Fleet & Army in and before Boston so as to compel a surrender at discretion. While I write this, I assure you my heart is elated with the contemplation of so great an event. A decisive thing, that would at once end the War, and vindicate the injured liberties of America. But your judgment and that of your brave Associates, will best determine the practicability of this business. I think we have taken the most effectual measures to secure the friendship of the Indians all along our extensive frontiers, and by what we learn of the Spirit of our Convention, now sitting at Richmond, a spirit prevails there very sufficient to secure us on that quarter — The particulars of their conduct I refer you to Mr. Frauer [?] [* * *]¹ for, who comes fresh from thence, & who goes to the Camp a Soldier of fortune — You know him better than I do, and I am sure you will provide for him as he deserves.

We are here as much in the dark about news from England as you are, the London Ships having been detained long beyond the time they were expected.

---

¹ Illegible omission.

The indistinct accounts we have, tell us of great confusion all over England, and a prodigious fall of the
Stocks. I heartily wish it may be true, but if it is not
so now, I have no doubt of its shortly being the case.
I will not detain you longer from more important
affairs, than to beg the favor of you, when your leisure
permits, to oblige me with a line by Post, to let us know
how you go on —
There is nothing I wish so much as your success, happiness, and safe return to your family and Country,
because I am with perfect sincerity dear Sir Your
Affectionate friend and countryman.

TO [WILLIAM LEE][1]

DEAR BROTHER,   CHANTILLY 5ᵗʰ Sept.ʳ 1775.

M.ʳ Browne having promised me a few days ago to
see me here before he sailed, I had not began a letter to
you expecting first to converse with him. But I have
this moment at 6 °Clock in the evening, received a line
from him, informing me that he must leave Hobbe's
Hole early tomorrow morning for York, to sail immediately for England. You must in this hurried state
expect a letter of much confusion, and many things
omitted that I should have written, and which you perhaps might expect. From the 10ᵗʰ of May to the 4ᵗʰ
of August I was confined at Philadelphia, and as the
Congress adjourned to this day, I seized the opportunity of visiting my family. And since my return to
this Colony, great part of my time has been spent at our
Convention in Richmond Town where I was obliged
to go. You can therefore expect little from me on the

[1] A. L. S.   Lenox Library, Ford Collection.

subject of your business. I suppose the Squire has written you concerning the Servants ballance but at all events, I will take care to have this business settled.

Upon the whole as things were circumstanced, your two Ships have come pretty well off — The 100 hhds that I luckily engaged from Col? Geo. Mason put Capt. Brown finely forward. You no doubt will have a Ship here as early as any other when we are so fortunate as to have peace again restored. At present, you may depend that a most faithful adherence to our Non-Export will be observed. This takes place now in 5 days. All who have seen M? Edw. Browne like him much, he is very clever, and I approve most heartily of your union with him. Capt. Browne tho, like another North Briton, got himself into a fray up Rappahanock, calling some people Rebels and asking the Negroes if they w? not fight for the King against such Rebels, and actually fired his Gun on the people — He got rufly handled and his conduct gave much Offence — I dont think he will do. This story our brother Thomas & several Gentlemen in Fredericksburg affirmed to me was true. I observe you are satisfied that I ought to have credit for the £9. bill — It was drawn by Thomas Montgomerie 8 June 1771 — I am contented to be credited an hundred Sterling for the dollars I paid to Col? Loudon. You have not credited me for £7.13.10 sterling. which our brother Frank wrote me in 1773 he would desire you to do on his Account. The exchange in Seldens bill for the Servant, was, I assure you on my honor, the established exchange of the Court but a few days before I settled with him, for I saw him on my way home from Williamsburg. I am very sorry that some of the Tob? for the Servants turned out so bad, but if Inspectors will be Villains, it is not easy to guard against them without previous reason to suspect them. Our Inspection Law is now expired, and will not be revived until peace takes place. This will be one effectual security for the Non-Exportation.

I thank you and the Doctor much for your letters, they have been of great use to me, tho some of them did not reach me until very lately. I have inclosed you a packet for my dear boys left open for your inspection — There are some politics for them — Please seal, pay the postage, and send the packet. On you and my brother I depend solely for the care and protection of my dear Boys in this tempestuous Season, when I can do little for them — I hope their gratitude and virtue will prevent your having much trouble with them — M⸢ Ponsonby has never sent me any of their Accounts. The Greenspring Tob? you complain of having been put up dirty, was done by Cary Wilkeson; for he insisted on finishing his own Crop. The Tob? that comes this year is the first of Fauntleroys. I had just sent an Express to him and expected a full account of all your affairs, but M⸢ Brownes sudden departure will prevent your getting it by this opportunity.

Our best love to M⸢⸢ Lee & kiss your little Patriot for me.

Your affectionate.

P.S. The Barrister has all my Politics & papers, refer to him.

TO [GEORGE WASHINGTON][1]

DEAR SIR,   PHILADELPHIA 26ᵗʰ Sept⸢ 1775

Two days ago I arrived here from Virginia, which the late short adjournment just allowed me time to visit and return from. I brought two letters from thence for you

[1] A. L. S. Library of Congress, Letters to Washington, VI. 357. Endorsed, "From/The Hon. R⸢ H⸢ Lee Esq⸢/26 Sep 1775/ Answered 13ʰ Oct⸢/1775."

which come with this. Having some business with Col? Mason, I travelled that road and having sent to your Lady to know if she had any commands this way, had the pleasure to learn that all were well at Mount Vernon. As I suppose it will be agreable to you to know what is passing in Virginia, I have inclosed you the proceedings of our last Convention, with two of Purdies Gazettes. I am greatly obliged to you for your favor of August the 29ᵗʰ, and you may be assured I shall pay great attention to it. When I mentioned securing the entrance of the harbour of Boston, it was more in the way of wishing it could be done, than as conceiving it very practicable. However the reasons you assign are most conclusive against the attempt. I assure you, that so far as I can judge from the conversation of Men, instead of their being any who think you have not done enough, the wonder seems to be that you have done so much. I believe there is not a Man of common sense and who is void of prejudice, in the world, but greatly approves the discipline you have introduced into the Camp; since reason and experience join in proving, that without discipline Armies are fit only for the contempt and slaughter of their Enemies. Your labors are no doubt great, both of mind and body, but if the praise of the present and future times can be of any compensation you will have a plentiful portion of that. Of one thing you may certainly rest assured, that the Congress will do every thing in their power to make your most weighty business easy to you. I think you could not possible have appointed a better Man to his present office than Mʳ Mifflin. He is a singular Man, and you certainly will meet with the applause and support of all good men by promoting and countenancing real merit and public virtue, in opposition to all private interests, and partial affections. You will see in the proceedings of our Convention, that they have agreed to raise the pay of our Rifle Officers & Men to the Virginia standard — It may perhaps encourage them to be told this.

We have no late accounts from England, but from what we have had that can be relied on, it seems almost certain, that our Enemies there must shortly meet with a total overthrow. The entire failure of all their schemes, and the rising spirit of the people strongly expressed by the remonstrance of the Livery of London to the King, clearly denote this. The Ministry had their sole reliance on the impossibility of the Americans finding money to support an army, on the great aid *their* cause would receive from Canada, and consequent triumph of their forces over the liberties and rights of America. The reverse of all this has happened, and very soon now, our Commercial resistance will begin sorely to distress the people at large. The Ministerial recruiting business in England has entirely failed them, the Shipbuilders in the royal yards have mutinied, and now they are driven as to their last resort to seek for Soldiers in the Highlands of Scotland. But it seems the greatest willingness of the people there cannot supply more than one or two thousand men, A number rather calculated to increase their disgrace, than to give success to their cause.

I beg your pardon for engaging your attention so long, and assure you that I am with unfeigned esteem dear Sir Your affectionate friend and Countryman.

TO [GEORGE WASHINGTON][1]

DEAR SIR, PHILADELPHIA 8th Octr 1775

A Ship in 7 weeks from London brings us pretty perfect intelligence of the infernal designs of our Minis-

[1] A. L. S. Library of Congress, Letters to Washington, VII. 16.

151

terial enemies, as you will see by the inclosures in D.[r] Shippens[1] letter. I believe they are the most perfect that could be obtained, and so may be much relied on. God grant that our successes at Boston and in Canada may disappoint, and thereby ruin these fatal foes to the liberty and happiness of the British empire.

My love, if you please, to Gen. Lee, Mifflin, Griffen, and my other friends with you.

May heaven preserve you, and give your Army success in the most glorious cause that was ever contended for by human nature.

I am dear Sir your affectionate friend and obedient Servant.

TO GENERAL [GEORGE] WASHINGTON [2]

DEAR SIR,   PHILADELPHIA 22.[d] October 1775

I thank you for your obliging favor of the 13th and I assure you that no Man living approves the vigorous measures you mention more than myself. Great bodies, you know, move slow; and it is as sure that the most palpable and glorious events may be delayed, and the best causes finally lost by slow, timid, and indecisive counsels. We must be content however to take human nature as we find it, and endeavor to draw good out of evil. You will, no doubt, have heared the disgraceful conduct of our Norfolk, in suffering Lord Dunmore, with a few men to take away their printing press! It happened when the good men of that place were all awy, and none but Tories & Negroes remained behind. Virginia is much incensed, and 500 are ordered im-

---

[1] Doctor William Shippen, Jr., of Philadelphia.
[2] A. L. S. Library of Congress, Letters to Washington, VII. 68. Addressed, "His excellency/General Washington/at the Camp at Cambridge &/near/Boston." Endorsed, "Answer'd 8.th Nov.[r]"

mediately down to Norfolk. I expect, by every Post, to hear of the demolition of that infamous nest of Tories. By a Vessel in 20 days from Quebec, which I believe brings us later intelligence than you had from thence when the last Express left Camp, we learn that the D. Governor had 12 Companies of Canadians in training and that they were generally on their guard. But the same acco[unt] says, the Government was so suspicious of the attachment of its Troops, that they were trusted with no more than 4 rounds of Cartridge. This still gives us some hopes of success on that quarter. Before this reaches, you will have heard of Col? Allens unlucky, and unwise attempt upon M! Real, nor have we, from the last accounts, much prospect of success from S! Johns. The Ministerial dependance on Canada is so great, that no object can be of greater importance to North America than to defeat them there. It appears to me, that we must have that Country with us this winter cost what it will. Col? Stephen writes me from Fort Pitt, that the Indians on that quarter come slowly in to the Commissioners, and that they evidently appear to be waiting the event of things in Canada, when they will surely according to custom join the strongest side. We have so many resources for powder, that I think we cannot fail of getting well supplied with that most necessary article.

Remember me, if you please, to Gen. Gates, and to all my acquaintances with you.

I am with great esteem and sincerity, dear Sir Your affectionate and obedient Servant.

P.S. Monday morning—'Tis with infinite concern I inform you that our good old Speaker Peyton Randolph Esq? went yesterday to dine with M! Harry Hill, was taken during the course of dinner with a dead palsey, and at 9 ?Clock at night died without a groan —

THE LETTERS OF RICHARD HENRY LEE

Thus has American liberty lost a powerful Advocate, and human nature a sincere friend.

To SILAS DEANE, ESQ.   [November 7, 1775.]

You are desired to repair immediately to the City of New York, and there purchase a Ship suitable for carrying 20 nine pounders upon one deck, if such a Ship can there be found. Also a Sloop, suitable to carry ten guns, which we would choose should be Bermudian built if such a one can be had. If you succeed in purchasing both, or either of these Vessels, you will use all possible expedition to procure them to be armed and equipped for the Sea. For this purpose you will apply to, and employ such persons as can carry this business into the most speedy execution. Should there be danger in fitting these Vessels at New York from the Kings ships; you may then send the Vessels eastward thro the Sound to New London or Norwich in order to be armed and fitted. Should this be the case you will repair immediately to the place where the Ships are to be fitted, and there use every means in your power to procure this to be done with the utmost expedition. In the Colony of Connecticut you are to procure powder for both these Vessels, and such other Military Stores as can there be had. You will procure the Cannon and other Stores at New York or any other place where it can be done in the best and most expeditious manner. You

[1] A. L. S. Connecticut Historical Society, Silas Deane's Accounts, No. 19. The body of the letter is in the autograph of Richard Henry Lee, but it is signed also in autograph by "Step. Hopkins, Christ. Gadsden, Joseph Hewes, John Adams, Jn? Langdon." Lee signs third. The postscript is in a different handwriting.

will also procure Officers and Men suitable for these Vessels.[1] As soon as these Vessels can possibly be fitted for the Sea, you will order them immediately in to Delaware Bay. You will by every opportunity give us the most exact intelligence of all your proceedings by conveyances the most safe and secure that can be obtained. You are empower'd to draw on Governor Hopkins for such sums of money as may be necessary for the above business.

PHILADELPHIA November the 7th 1775

P.S. In the course of your Journey at New York, or elsewhere you are to employ proper persons to engage experienced and able-bodied seamen to man the Ships now fitting out who must repair to Philadelphia with all possible dispatch.

TO GENERAL [GEORGE] WASHINGTON[2]

DEAR SIR,   PHILADELPHIA Novem^r 13th 1775

I must beg leave at the beginning of this letter to apologise for any incorrectness as I write in great haste —

---

[1] The words "except a Captain for the * * * Ship.," following "Vessels," are erased.

[2] A. L. S. Library of Congress, Letters to Washington, VII. 185. Addressed, "His Excellency/General Washington/at the Camp at Cambridge/near/Boston// Free/Richard Henry Lee." Encloses a copy of a page and a half of manuscript n.s. but addressed, "Dr Sir," and dated "Sept. 4th 1775," informing as to plans in Great Britain against New England, Virginia, and South Carolina, and that the Duke of Alva was condemned to death. Encloses also a clipping from Williamsburg, dated Oct. 28, concerning Dunmore and Hampton, a half-page of print signed, "By order of the Com. of Safety, John Pendleton, Jun. Clk." In volume VII. of Letters to Washington, page 187, is found the following note in Richard Henry Lee's autograph,

Indeed the hurry of business is such with many of us, that we have little time for the ordinary offices of life. You may be assured that I will do Col? Read all the service that I can in the way you desire. We have a Ship here in 6 weeks from London, that brought the original letter of which the inclosed is a copy. Tis from a wellinformed, sensible friend, and may be relyed on. All the other letters from London join in confirming it to be the fixt determination of K—— and Court to leave undone, nothing that they can do, to compell implicit obedience in America. One very sensible letter that I have seen, mentions that Gen. Amherst had recommended (& 'twas said it would be executed) to remove the Army this winter from Boston to Long Island, in order to get amply supplied by ravaging N. Jersey, N. York, and Rhode Island. Should this be attempted, I suppose you will be furnished with an opportunity of giving them a genteel parting salute.

And besides, I should suppose that a winter favorable for us, would expose them to ruin from a timely, strong attack, of superior numbers on that naked Island. It seems that immense stores of Indian goods are sent to Canada in order to bribe the Indians to an early and vigorous attack on all our frontiers next Spring. God grant that Col? Arnolds success and Montgomeries may frustrate this diabolical part of their infernal plan against the common natural rights of Mankind ! —

We hoped here, that the surrender of Chamblé, with the military stores there obtained, would speedily procure the reduction of S! Johns, but no accounts are yet

on the inside of an addressed sheet, " The Continental, and Virginia Commissioners, have just concluded a treaty of firm friendship with the Ohio Indians and those of the Six nations that inhabit near that Quarter. We have taken the most effectual measures, by sending Runners into the Indian Nations thro which he proposes to pass, to await and secure Ld Dunmores wicked Agent Conelly."

come of this wished event. After Lord Dunmore, supported by the North British Tories had long committed every outrage at Norfolk unapposed, our people not having Arms or amunition until lately; his Banditti at length attempted Hampton, where they met with the chastisement you will see described in the part of Dixons paper inclosed. The Lieutenant Wright there mentioned has been since found dead on the Shore, a bullet having been placed in his body before he jumpt over board. We have not yet heard the consequence of their next intended attack, but it seems a very heavy Cannonade was heard there the next day. If the Devil inspired them to come on shore, I make no doubt but we shall have a good account of them. I have a very particular reason for entreating that you will inform me by return of Post, what number, and what strength of Armed Vessels could possibly be procured from the ports where you are[1] to be in Delaware Bay, if Congress should desire it, by the middle or last of December at furthest. Two or 3 Vessels of tolerable force, issuing from hence, may effect a stroke or two of great consequence to us at that Season. We have certainly 4000 weight of powder, and a very considerable quantity of Oznaburgs arrived in Virginia from Statia for the use of our little Army consisting of about 2000 men now at Williamsburg & Hampton —

Be pleased to let Gen. Lee see the letter from England.

I heartily wish you every happiness, and all the success the goodness of your cause deserves & I am, with great esteem dear Sir Your affect friend and obedient servant.

Congress has ordered 500,000 to you soon as they can be signed.

[1] Written above "have" erased, and an illegible erasure follows on the line.

157

THE LETTERS OF RICHARD HENRY LEE

TO HENRY TUCKER [1]

SIR, PHILADELPHIA 24th of Nov? 1775.

As the contents of the enclosed paper concerns our common Countries, I have thought it my duty as a Delegate to Congress from Virginia to inclose it to you by the first opportunity. As Salt is now much wanted in Virginia and the Country has been favored with a plentiful crop the last season, it will be very convenient for both Countries that your Island furnish that article quickly as possible, and to the full amount permitted by the resolution of Congress. The restraining Act of Parliament of the last Session does not interfere with you in this business, yet it will be prudent to make use of quick sailing Vessels, and if a few guns & men are put on board to keep off the small Tenders in Chesapeak Bay, that are every now & then committing Acts of piracy, they might be of service. It will be the most safe to run immediately up York, Rappahanock, or Potomack, as the Men of war generally lye in Hampton road or about Norfolk. The Committee of Safety sits constantly, and means will be taken to give all possible dispatch to your business in Virginia.

I write in great haste, and [*The remainder of the Ms. is missing.*]

[1] A. L. University of Virginia, Lee Papers, No. 85. Tucker was chairman of the District Committee, Bermuda, and the letter is addressed to him there.

THE LETTERS OF RICHARD HENRY LEE

TO [GEORGE WASHINGTON] [1]

DEAR GENERAL.   PHILADELPHIA 26th Novr 1775

As Mr Custis can furnish you with an exact account of our affairs in Virginia, it will be unnecessary for me to say any thing on that subject. Proper persons will certainly and presently be appointed, under proper regulations, to determine on sea Captures. I heartily congratulate you on the surrender of St Johns. That of Montreal must, I think, quickly follow, because it is quite defenseless, and because the far greater part of the Canadians are surely on our side. If Colo Arnold meets with success at Quebec, we shall be in fine posture to receive our enemies next spring. I have been strongly inclined to think that the design of this last reenforcement to Boston, is intended for something decisive this fall. Their credit, their necessities, and many other considerations seem to render an attempt on yr lines probable. I make no doubt but the most effectual guard will be taken to render this attempt fatal to its Authors. It is impossible that vice can so triumph over virtue, as that the slaves of Tyranny should succeed against the brave and generous Assertors of Liberty, and the just rights of humanity.

We expect every day to hear from England, but no intelligence has come from thence since I wrote you last.

I heartily wish you a happy meeting with your Lady who leaves this place tomorrow for Cambridge.

I am with singular esteem, dear Sir Your most affectionate and obedient Servant.

P.S. We have sent a Committee to Canada to invite Delegates here and to settle the affairs of that Army.

[1] A. L. S. Library of Congress, Letters to Washington, VII. 233.

159

THE LETTERS OF RICHARD HENRY LEE

TO MRS. [CATHERINE] MACAULAY [1]

Philadelphia 29th Novr 1775.

Dear Madam,

As a good *Christian* properly attached to your native Country, I am sure you must be pleased to hear, that North America is not fallen, nor likely to fall down before the *Images* that the King hath set up. After more than ten years abuse and injury on one side, of modest representation on the other; Administration at length determine to try if the sword cannot effect, what threatening Acts of Parliament had in vain attempted; that is, the ruin of the just rights and liberty of this great Continent. Lexington, Concord, and Bunkers Hill opened the tragic scene; and clearly proved to the whole world that N. America had no reliance but on its own virtue in Arms. The battle of Bunkershill tho followed by strong reenforcements, has not enlarged the prison of the Ministerial Army many paces. After the clearest proofs that the Quebec Act was going to be carried into effect by marching an Army of Canadians &c into these Colonies, and when every attempt had been made to bring the Savages on the defenceless women and Children along our extensive frontiers; it became high time, on [pri]²nciples of self preservation, to avert the medita[ted.]² The war was therefore sent into their own Country having first, by proper Agents and Memorials, explained to the Inhabitants of Canada and to the Indians, the views and objects of the United Colonies. Success, equal to the justice of the cause,

---

[1] A. dr. L. University of Virginia, Lee Papers, No. 86. Mrs. Catherine Macaulay, historian of England and controversialist, wrote in 1775 an "Address to the People of England," etc., opposing the Quebec Act. Lecky calls her "the ablest writer of the radical school."
[2] Ms. torn.

has followed this undertaking. With indefatigable zeal 3000 Men crossed Lake Champlain and laid siege to Fort St. Johns which place, as the prey to Canada, had been made very strong by Govr Carlton, and garrisoned with 500 regular Troops and 100 Canadians. During this siege, a detachment from the Army pierced further into the Country, invested, and took Fort Chambly (between St. Johns and Montreal) that was garrison'd by, about 80 Regulars. Gen. Carleton having by this time collected about 800 Men, marched to the relief of St Johns, when 600 of of the Am. Troops and defeated him. This was presently followed by the surrender of St. Johns, with all the Garrison prisoners of war, and there they found a plentiful supply of military stores. A rapid march to Montreal was next made, and yesterd[ay] brought the account of the surrender of that Town. General Montgomerie on monday the 13th instan[t] upon condition that the people should quietly enjoy their religion and not be molested in their property. Gen. Carleton had escaped down the St. Laurence with 2 or 3 Vessels, but it was expected he would fall into the hands of Col^o Arnold, then at Quebec, to which place he had penetrated with 1000 men, by the rivers Kenebec and Chaudiere. No doubt is entertained here, but that this Congress will be shortly joined by Delegates from Canada, which will then complete the union of 14 provinces. Thus have the evil machinations of an unprincipled Administration been turned greatly to the honor and security of the people they meant to ruin. The proclamation that followed the receipt of so humble a petition has determined the Councils of America to prepare for defence with the utmost vigor both by Sea & Land. Altho' upon the former of these elements, America may not at first be in condition to meet the force of G. Britain, yet as Hercules was once in his Cradle, so, time and attention, will, under the fostering hand of Liberty, make great changes [in] this matter. The knowing Ones, are of opinion that by next Spring, so many Armed Vessels will be fitted out, as to annoy our enemies greatly, and to afford much protection to the Trade of North America. It is wonderful what great benefits have already been obtained by the infant efforts of some Colonies in this way. Whilst this Country abounds in Wood, iron and Artizans, whilst a soil and Climate fitted for the abundant production of Hemp is possessed by an industrious people, strength on the sea cannot long be wanting. The Congress has ordered a suspension of all exportation for a certain time. This looks like ruin to the West Indies. The almost infinite distress that these Islands will feel in a short time is really shocking to humany, but in this case, charity must begin at home, and the liberties of North America be at all events secured.

The animation and perseverance that the spirit of Liberty and resentment furnishes was well displayed in the siege of St. Johns. It was a wet and cold season and the Men thinly clothed, the ground so low & wet on which they were placed, that they were compelled to lay heaps of brush, and weeds on the Top of the brush, that they might sleep out of the water at night. In this horrid situation they vigorously pressed the siege for 47 days, when the Garrison surrendered prisoners of war.

Lord Dunmores unparalleled conduct in Virginia has, a few Scotch excepted; united every Man in that Colony. If Administration had searched thro the world for a person the best fetted to ruin their cause, and procure union and success for these Colonies, they could not have found a more complete Agent than Lord Dunmore—

We regret not having heared from England since early in September, but our Congress disregarding this, are proceeding with vigor, perseverance, and judgment in affecting the great purpose for which they were appointed.

You know the Writer of this letter and therefore it is as unnecessary to sign it, as it would be to assure you of his affection and esteem for your whole self, and all your connections. We hope all are well at St. Bees, and that proper care will be taken there in this tempestuous Season.

The last Post produces a proclamation from Ld Dunmore declaring Liberty to the Slaves and proclaiming the Law martial to be the only law in that Colony— And all this he says is done "in virtue of the power and authority to me given by his Majesty" Is it possible that his Majesty could authorize him thus to remedy evils which his Lordship himself had created? I would have inclosed you a copy of this curious proclamation, had I not feared it would too much increase the size of this packet—

The inhumanity with which this war (unprovoked as it has been on this side) is prosecuted, is really shocking.[1]—A few days since, in the midst of winters[2] that northern climate, did Gen Howe turn out of Boston between two & three hundred Women and Children without even the necessaries of life— Some of them died on the water side before their hospitable Countrymen could relieve them— This cruelty is the more unpardonable as these unhappy people have been by violence detained in Boston until now, contrary to the faith of a most positive agreement entered into between the Town and Gen. Gage—

The inclosed printed papers will shew you Madam how successful the cause of liberty has been in Canada. No doubt is entertained of Quebec and Govr Carleton having fallen into the hands of Gen. Montgomerie and Col^o Arnold. A Valuable Artillery Store Ship is just

[1] The words "to humanity" are here erased.   [2] Ms. torn.

fallen into our hands and the Stores now at our Camp at Cambridge

The Ships is the Nancy I think.

TO THE COMMITTEE OF NORTHAMPTON [1]

GENTLEMEN   PHILADELPHIA 5th Decr 1775

I have the honor to enclose you a resolve of Congress in answer to your application for assistance. The three companies therein ordered will march in a few days, and I hope will be sufficient, with the assistance of the good and virtuous Men of Northampton, to secure the peace of your county, and prevent any lapse from the great Continental system so well laid, and so necessary for securing the just constitutional rights and liberty of North America.

I have the honor to be Gentlemen Your most humble Servant.

TO [GEORGE WASHINGTON] [2]

DEAR SIR,   PHILADELPHIA 6th Decr 1775

The inclosed letter from Col? Pendleton came to hand two days ago, and as it will save a good deal of unnecessary writing, I send it to you. The proclamation there alluded to we have seen. It proclaims martial law thro Virginia and offers freedom to all the Slaves, calling their Masters rebels &^{c} — It seems this unlucky triumph over Hutchings with his less than half armed Militia, so dispirited the miserable wretches in that neighborhood, that many have taken an oath of Lord Dunmores prescribing, reprobating Congress Com-

---

[1] A. L. S.   Haverford College, Charles Roberts Autograph Collection, 932.   Addressed to the Chairman of the Committee.

[2] A. L. S.   Library of Congress, Letters to Washington, VII. 265.

mittees &ᶜ — Long before this Colᵒ Woodford with 800 good men, must be arrived in those parts, and I make no doubt has forced his Lordship on board his Ships again. All this would have been prevented, if our troops could have crossed James River in proper time, but they were obstructed & forced to march high up by the Men of War, and indeed, such is the nature of our water intersected Country, that a small number of men provided with Naval force, can harrass us extremely. I have good reason to hope, that in a few weeks, the state of things in Virginia will be greatly altered for the better. I thank you for your list of Armed Vessels, but at present no use can be made of them. I hope that some of them will be fortunate enough to meet with prizes eastward. I had not heared of your improvements on the Kanhawa being destroyed, and unless Mʳ Lund. Washington has received very accurate information on this head, I am yet inclined to doubt it; because I see in the treaty lately concluded with all the Ohio ¹ Indians they first inform the Commissioners of the Kanhawa fort being burnt by some of their rash young men, but they promise to punish the offenders and prevent repetition of the like offence. They are very precise in their information, and mention only the Fort, as well as I remember. I hope therefore that your property may yet be safe. This treaty with the Indians is the more likely to last, as Connelly, with his little Corps of Officers, are now in close custody in Maryland, having been arrested there, as they were stealing thro the Country to Pittsburg, from whence they were to proceed to Detroit, and with the Troops in those Western parts, Indians &ᶜ he was to have done wonders. This wonderful Man is now in close jail. I congratulate you on the surrender of Montreal, and from Gen. Montgomeries letter giving account of

¹ Substituted for "Western" erased.

that event, I think we have room to expect that Quebec is fallen before now. A Committee of Congress some time since sent to Canada, have direction to raise a Regiment in that Country[1] to invite Delegates to this Congress, and to give the strongest assurances of protection, to their Civil & religious rights. I am glad to hear of your getting Cobble hill & I hope it will prove useful to you. We are told that your enemy troops are very uneasy on Bunkers hill. God grant that their uneasiness may increase to their ruin. No accounts yet from England, but Ships are daily expected. I am, with much esteem, dear Sir Your affectionate and obedient Servant.

TO DOCTOR WILLIAM SHIPPEN, JR.[2]

My Dear Sir,   BALTIMORE 1ˢᵗ January 1776

A happy new year is my wish for you and your family, that it will be a year of freedom our brave troops appear determined on, and whilst they are so, the Instruments of tyranny, and the perpetrators of Devilish deeds will not, cannot face them. The removal from Philadelphia was not a measure of mine, but had my hearty disapprobation so long as disapproving availed anything; but when go they would, I endeavored to put the best face on it. The Congress have lately invested General Washington with complete powers to displace, place, and direct everything relative to the military Hospitals. To him therefore, let me advise you, to make your im-

[1] Substituted, with the preceding word, for " Canada " erased.
[2] A. L. S. Shippen Mss. Addressed to him at Bethlehem, Pa., and sent by Colonel Stewart. Doctor William Shippen, Jr., of Philadelphia, married Alice Lee, a sister of Richard Henry Lee. In July, 1776, he was appointed Physician-in-chief to the Flying Camp. He planned a hospital department, and from April, 1777, to January, 1781, was Director General of all military hospitals.

mediate application, lay your plan before him, and prove as you have done to me the propriety of adopting it. No doubt can remain but that it will meet with his approbation and support — As for Morgan, the very Air teams with complaints against him — If all charged against him be true, I would not have my conscience so burthened for Mountains of Gold — Reasons for expecting the strongest friendship from France & Spain multiply upon us every day — If they can be prevailed with to make war, farewell the glory of England, and it may then be said as formerly it was of Rome Sevior[1] Armis Luxuria incubuit, victumque ulciscitur orbem — Had it not been for the vile appendages of Luxury, we should not have been abused, nor Britain overwhelmed by France — It will give us great pleasure to hear from you often, but greater still to see you — I will endeavor, but I know not how to hear from my Cousin Thom[?][2] — But he is in a peaceful Country, and I make no doubt he is happy. Our best love attends

farewell

TO SAMUEL ADAMS[3]

Dear Sir,   Chantilly the 7th of February 1776

I very sincerely condole with you on our illfortune in Canada. I hope, however, that this will yet turn out well. Those who sail gently down the smooth stream of prosperity, are very apt to loose that energetic virtue so necessary to true happiness. It seems that discipline, and pretty severe discipline too, is necessary for the depraved heart of man, nor have we any right to expect security in the enjoyment of the greatest human blessings until we have learnt wisdom and moderation in the

---

[1] For "Saevior."   [2] Thomas Lee Shippen, probably.
[3] A. L. S. Lenox Library, Samuel Adams Papers. Addressed to him, "Member in Congress in/Philadelphia."

school of adversity. We must never forget tho, that God helps them that help themselves, and by straining every nerve for the purpose, cost what it may, let us pour into Canada Troops enough to reduce and fortify Quebec before the ice permits relief to come there from our enemies. The winter is the season for our surest and best exertions, and by wisely availing ourselves of this opportunity the most important points may be secured without much effusion of human blood. I pray you Sir to leave nothing undone that may secure Canada & New York this winter. These are the openings thro which America may, by able fencers, receive the worst wounds. I think our Canada Committee reported there were more important heights on Hudsons river than that which had been fixt on — Let all the very important heights have strong batteries with troops well commanded placed on them, and a strong Camp fixt either at Kings bridge or nearer the City Has not Tryon, that *great friend to America* something of much moment, as he thinks, in agitation; by his calling on Assembly. This man is one of those kind of *friends* that requires the most constant and unremitting watching — What means his agent in his public summons of the freeholders when he says "To be representatives of the said city and country to *assist* the *Captain General*, or Commanders in chief, in a general Assembly" This is new language I think, and wants explanation. Cant you furnish us with a good general officer or two from the northward to command the 9 battalions raised here? This will be quite necessary should 'any considerable force be sent [1] to this quarter. We have already done, with the enemy now here, all that can be expected from us — They are driven to seek shelter on board their Ships where they are not furnished with a single carrot, nor suffered to come on shore for water without chastise-

[1] A word, apparently "here," is erased.

ment. Would our fleet could come this way where a great prize is and I think attainable without much risk — We learn that the Tory property on float in a number of small Vessels amounts to more than £150,000. and it is protected by three ships of war only, the Liverpoole, Otter, & Kingfisher — As for the small Tenders, & Merchantmen badly manned and worse provided by Dunmore, they are of little consequence. Our Convention have not taken up government totidem verbis, but I think totis viribus, because Sheriffs & Judges are appointed by ordinance, and the Committee of Safety vested with all the Executive powers. This indeed has been indispensable in the present situation of things.

I hope to see you early in March, and in the mean time shall be extremely glad to hear from you —

I am dear Sir Your affectionate friend.

TO [GEORGE WASHINGTON][1]

Dear Sir,   Philadelphia 13 March 1776

I was in Virg[a], (from whence I am but just returned) when your favor of th 26th Dec[r] came here, and now I have but a moment before this Gentleman goes off to thank you for it, and to cover a letter from your brother, with the proceedings and ordinances of our last Convention — Gen. Clinton had left Virginia before I did, and was gone to one, but which we do not know, of the Carolinas — Gen. Lee is now here on his way to the Southward where he is to take the direction of our and the Carolina Troops — I shall write you more fully in a Post or two, in the mean time, beg my compl[s] to your Lady, M[r] & M[rs] Custis. I am dear Sir Your most affectionate friend.

[1] A. L. S. Library of Congress, Letters to Washington, VIII. 233.

THE LETTERS OF RICHARD HENRY LEE

TO SAMUEL PURVIANCE[1]

DEAR SIR,   PHILADELPHIA 17 March 1776

I received your account of the retaking Hudsons ship and the flight of the enemy with great pleasure — I hope you will make wise use of the opportunity to render the avenews to y? flourishing Town inaccessible to the enemy. I think you have the means of doing this most effectually, and sure it ought not to be neglected. I suppose the Defence and her Tender will now be employed in keeping your Bay Coast as far as Potomac clear of Sloops and Tenders from our Enemies — I am sure Capt. Squires will not interrupt your Trade so long as he knows Capt. Nicholson is with you, and as for larger Ships, if they should come, which is not very probable, it will be no difficult matter to get out of their way by returning to shallow waters — I expect this will be delivered you by General Lee who is on his way to his Southern command. I am in no doubt of the worthy General meeting with those civilities from you that prove so agreeable to everybody else. It is of great importance that Gen. Lee should quickly get to the place of his destination, and therefore, if he should want either horses or Guides for this purpose, I know your patriotic Committee will furnish them. I need not trouble you with news, as the General can give you any that prevails here.

I am, with much esteem, Sir your obliged and obedient Serv?

[1] A. L. S. Maryland Historical Society, P. F. No. 8 (1). The letter is addressed, " Samuel Purveyance Jun Esq'/Chairman of the Committee/of/Baltimore," and was sent by General Lee. Purviance was chairman of the Committee of Safety of Baltimore.

THE LETTERS OF RICHARD HENRY LEE

TO GENERAL [CHARLES] LEE[1]

My Dear Friend,   [PHILADELPHIA, March 25, 1776.]
I have just received your letter from Baltimore covering one for M! Hancock. My Brother who was
present in Congress when the Resolve you allude to
passed, says that every Gentleman acknowledged the
necessity under which you acted, and approved the
measure. The precedent alone they feared, when less
judgment was used. They endeavored therefore to
guard against pointing at you by directing their Resolve
to future occasions. As then there was no design to
reflect on you, so we have concluded that the better
way will be not to present the letter, but content ourselves with informing Congress of your having taken
the Engineers and getting their approbation. Gen.
Washington entered Boston this day sennight, the
Enemy having quitted it with some precipitation, and
apparent apprehension of being disturbed in their
retreat. To prevent this, they left their works unde-
molished, and placed images large as life representing
Soldiers on guard as usual on Bunker Hill — Our
friend Sullivan first discovered the cheat. They have
left 30 of their light Horse behind them almost famished,
and stores to the amount of 25 or 30,000 pounds.
Where they will go next, heaven knows, but we must
endeavour to be prepared at all points. I this day
moved in Congress and succeeded, to send an order for
four battalions to be detached for Canada from Gen.
Washington's Army.   I am afraid we shall loose poor
Gov! Ward, who now lies dangerously ill with the small
pox taken in the natural way. The Eastern Army will
all be at N. Y. presently.

[1] From a printed text in New York Historical Society *Collections*,
The Lee Papers, I. 362.

171

THE LETTERS OF RICHARD HENRY LEE

I sincerely wish you happy and successful because I am with great affection Yours.

GENERAL LEE, at Williamsburg, in Virginia.

TO GENERAL [CHARLES] LEE[1]

MY DEAR FRIEND —   PHILADELPHIA 28th March 1776

Give me leave to indroduce my friend and relation Colonel William Aylett to your acquaintance and friendship. You will find Col? Ayletts worth deserving your esteem, and his connection [2] with me, will, I am sure not lessen it.

No news since my last, we know not yet where the Boston fugitives are gone

farewell my dear Sir.

TO LANDON CARTER [3]

DEAR SIR   PHILADELPHIA 1st April 1776

It hurts me exceedingly that you should attribute to declining friendship what realy arose from the necessity of my situation. After an absence of many months, I had obtained leave to pay a short visit to my family, where I had been but a few days when the public business called me to Williamsburg and Mrs Lees illness occasioned a summons from thence. She was but just recovered before I was compelled to return to this place. This situation of my affairs will very sufficiently account

[1] A. L. S. John Carter Brown Library, Ms. collections. Addressed to General Lee in Virginia, and sent by Col. Aylett.
[2] Colonel Aylett married a sister of Richard Henry Lee.
[3] A. L. S. Maine Historical Society, Fogg Collection. Addressed to Carter at Sabine Hall, Richmond County, Virginia, and franked by Lee.

for my not gratifying myself by visiting Sabine Hall, without imputing it to want of regard. You will have heard no doubt of our enemies shameful flight from Boston, where they left behind them many marks of apprehention and hurry, altho they took time to remove with them all the American prisoners (they had made) in chains, while they left to the resentment of an injured country, many Tories to whom they had promised protection. Where these hostes humani generis will go next, we can only guess, and hav⁶ already strengthened N. York, we are preparing with 10.000 men well commanded, to meet them in Canada, the Capital of which Country still continues besieged by the Continental forces. It is curious to observe, that whilst people here are disputing and hesitating about independancy, the Court by one bold Act of Parliament, and by a conduct the most extensively hostile, have already put the two Countries asunder — They think forever and are therefore preparing the minds of the people / people of England for this event by having hired Dean Tucker to prove the measure an eligible one. As well, dear Sir, might a person expect to wash an Ethiopian white, as to remove the taint of despotism from the British Court — The vicious principle has pervaded every heart, perverted every head, and will govern every movement of that Body. The measure of British crimes is running over, and the barbarous spoliation of the East is crying to Heaven for vengeance against the Destroyers of the Human Race. Out of 8 Vessels from [1] Whitehaven with provisions for their army, 7 have been taken and the 8ᵗʰ driven on shore — They are disgraced in the East and the North, and their friends beaten in the South. Were it not for their present Marine superiority, I do verily believe that N. America could give law to that proud imperious Island. Be

[1] "Island" is here erased.

so kind as to give my compliments to your Son and inform him that I, as well as my brother, applied to Gen. Lee to receive Squire Landon as an Aid de Camp, but the General was already provided with two, M: Byrd & M: Morris, and two only were allowed by the Continent; but the General is willing to receive M: Carter into his family if he chooses to attend on his own expence as an Aid de Camp — I wish you healthy and happy dear Sir for I am sincerely your affectionate friend.

P.S. If M: Carter chooses to go as above mentioned I shall be ready to furnish him with a letter to General Lee.

TO GENERAL [CHARLES] LEE[1]

My Dear Friend,   Philadelphia, 1st April, 1776.

I hope my former reasons for not delivering your letter to the President will meet your approbation. Since I wrote you last, the Congress has appointed two Engineers for the Southern department, Mr John Stadler, now in Virginia, and the young German Massenbach whom you took with you from Baltimore. They have also appointed Monsr Dohicky Arundel (who I expect will deliver you this) a Captain of Artillery in the Continental service with the following resolve, "That General Lee be directed to set on foot the raising a Company of Artillery, and that it be recommended to the Convention or Committee of Safety of Virginia to appoint the other officers of said Company of Artillery." The better opinion now is, that Gen. Howe will rest awhile at Halifax, and embrace the first opportunity of pushing up to the relief of Quebec, and we are making ready to meet him there. I think the number of men

[1] From a printed text in New York Historical Society *Collections*, *The Lee Papers*, I. 367.

already ordered for that country amounts to more than 10,000. We are informed that General Howe carried off all his American prisoners with him in chains. The people of New-York have collected and burnt publickly every copy they could find of Plain Truth, and they have treated the Effigies of Tryon in the same manner. The arrival of 10 tons of powder and a considerable quantity of sail cloth to the Eastward, is all the news we have here. Farewell my dear friend, I wish you happy, healthy, and successful.

Cato still continues to write nonsense, and the other Tories to forge lies about the Commissioners.

GENERAL LEE, at Williamsburg, in Virginia.

TO GENERAL [CHARLES] LEE[1]

DEAR SIR,   PHILADELPHIA, 15th April, 1776.

I have but a moment to acknowledge your last favor which gave me the pleasure of knowing you were well arrived at Williamsburg. It would seem as if Gen. Howe was yet floating on the Ocean incertum quo fata ferant, because the greatest part of his fleet sailed southward from Boston, and because a sloop of war came into N. York and carried Tryon out to sea, to consult we suppose. The riflemen have had a fair engagement with a small man of war for the watering place at N. York, when the former drove the latter off, and have since fortified the spring, so that they must go some where else for water. If it be true as reported here that Sr Peter Parker is arrived in Virginia with Troops we must look to you for news in future, and I make no doubt but we shall have good news.

Our old Commodore Hopkins has actually beaten

¹ From a printed text in New York Historical Society *Collections*, *The Lee Papers*, I. 421.

the Glasgow in a fair fight, and Wallace with his Squadron have fled from the Rhode Island station. Capt. Barry in an armed Brig from hence has taken off the Capes of Virg^a and sent her in here, a cutter, with 8 carriage Guns belonging to the Liverpool, with one of that ships Lieutenants commanding her. He fought his tender well, not submitting until he was near sinking.

Farewell my dear friend. May you be healthy, happy, and successful.

Gen. Ward has resign'd his command in the Continental Army.

GENERAL LEE, at Head Quarters in Williamsburg, Virg^a.

TO [PATRICK HENRY][1]

DEAR SIR,   PHILADELPHIA 20th April 1776.

Having done myself the pleasure of writing to you by General Lee I must now refer you to that letter, and at present invite your attention to the most important concerns of our approaching convention. Ages yet unborn, and millions existing at present, must rue or bless that Assembley, on which their happiness or misery will so eminintly depend. Virginia has hitherto taken the lead in great affairs, and many now look to her with anxious expectation, hoping that the spirit, wisdom, and energy of her councils, will rouse America from the fatal lethargy into which the feebleness, folly, and interested views of the Proprietary governments, with the aid of Tory machinations, have thrown her most unhappily. The 12 years experience we have had of the perfidy and despotic intentions of the British

[1] This letter, as far as the asterisk on page 180, is printed in William Wirt Henry, *Patrick Henry*, I. 378. The remainder is from a text in the *Richmond Enquirer* of September 26, 1804, where the entire letter is printed with some variations.

Court is still further demonstrated by the King's speech, by the express declaration of every Ministerial Man in both houses of Parliament, by their infamous retrospective robbery Act, and by the intercepted letter from the Secretary of State to Governor Eden. All join in proving the design of the British Court to subdue at every event, and to enslave America after having destroyed its best Members. The act of Parliament has to every legal intent and purpose dissolved our government, uncommissioned every magistrate, and placed us in the high road to Anarchy. In Virginia we have certainly no Magistrate lawfully qualified to hang a murderer, or any other villain offending ever so atrociously against the state. We cannot be Rebels excluded from the King's protection and Magistrates acting under his authority at the same time. This proves the indispensable necessity of our taking up government immediately, for the preservation of Society, to effect the purpose of applying with vigor the strength of the country to its present critical state; and above all to set an example which N. Carolina, Maryland, Pennsylvania, and N. York will most assuredly, in my opinion, follow; and which will effectually remove the baneful influence of Proprietary interests from the councils of America. When this is done, give peremptory instructions to your Delegates to take every effectual step to secure America from the despotic aims of the British Court by Treaties of alliance with foreign States, or by any means that shall be thought most conducive to that end. A slight attention to the late proceedings of many European Courts will sufficiently evince the spirit of partition, and the assumed right of disposing of Men & Countries like live stock on a farm, that distinguishes this corrupt age. St. Domingo, Louisiana, Corsica, & Poland indisputably prove this. Now Sir, I leave it with you to judge, whether, whilst we are hesitating about forming alliance, Great Britain may not, and probably will not, seal our ruin by signing a Treaty of partition with two or three ambitious powers that may aid in conquering us — Upon principles of interest and revenge they surely will. When G. B. finds she cannot conquer us alone, and that the whole must be lost, will she not rather choose a part than have none? Certainly she will, and to gain the necessary aid give up a part, and thus involve us unaided, unassisted, in a very unequal destructive contest with three or 4 of the greatest states in Europe. Nothing in this world is more certain than that the present Court of London would rather rule despotically a single rod of earth, than govern the world under legal limitations. All this danger however may be prevented by a timely alliance with proper and willing powers in Europe — Indeed we are a singular instances in modern times of a people engaged in war with a powerful Nation, without taking steps to secure the friendship or even neutrality, of foreign states — leaving to our enemies the full opportunity of engaging all. And we know with certainty that every maritime state in Europe has been interceded with not to supply us with military stores, and many states have been applied to for troops to destroy us, as Russia, Hesse, Hanover and Holland. Is it not the most dreadful infatuation in us to remain quiet in this way and not stir until it is too late? But no State in Europe will either Treat or Trade with us so long as we consider ourselves Subjects of G. B. Honor, dignity, and the customs of states forbid them until we take rank as an independant people. The war cannot long be prosecuted without Trade, nor can Taxes be paid until we are enabled to sell our produce, which cannot be the case without the help of foreign ships, whilst our enemy's navy is so superior to ours. A contraband sloop or so may come from foreign parts, but no authorised, and consequently sufficiently extensive Trade will be carried on with us whilst we remain in our present undefined unmeaning condition. Our clearest interest therefore, our very existance as freemen, requires that we take decisive steps now, whilst we may, for the security of America. It is most fortunate for us that the present quit-rent revenue, with the impost on Tob° & Tonnage will do more than defray all our expences of Civil government without fresh Taxes on the people, and the unappropriated lands will pay the expences of the war.

The inclosed pamphlet on Government is the production of our friend John Adams. It is sensible and shows the virtue of the man, at the same time that it proves the business of framing government not to be so difficult a thing as most people imagine. The small scheme printed in hand bill I had written before I saw this work of Mr. Adams, and he agrees that the Council of State had better be a distinct body from the Upper house of Assembly, meaning the upper house; their duration indeed may be too long, but it should be for a longer term than the lower house, in order to answer the purpose of an independant middle power. The sheriffs had better I think be appointed as now in Virginia, or by choice of the free holders in each county.

The recommendation of congress about taking Government is, as you see, of old date, and therefore it is said during the continuance of the present disputes. But it matters not much, for the Government taken up ought to be the best, whether it be for this, that, or another term of years. This I take to be the time and thing meant by Shakespeare when he says,

"There is a Tide[1] in the Affairs of Men
Which taken at the Flood leads on to Fortune —
That omitted, we are ever after bound in Shallows,"[2] &c.

[1] In a text printed in the *Richmond Enquirer* this word is "time."
[2] In the text in the *Enquirer* " and miseries " follows here.

THE LETTERS OF RICHARD HENRY LEE

Let us therefore,[1] quitting every other consideration, heartily unite in leading[2] our countrymen to embrace the * present flowing tide, which promises fair to waft us into the harbor of safety, happiness, liberty and virtue.

Perhaps some may endeavor to injure you on account of your concurrence in opinion with Mr. Glyn and others, relative to the right derived to the company of Wharton and others from their Indian grant of lands within the colony; but as I consider it meant only to say, that unappropriated lands had better be purchased from the Indians or prime occupants, not denying the propriety of paying dues accustomed to the colony in which such lands lie, and complying with its laws: the objection against such an opinion loses its force.

I am well pleased to hear that you are going into Convention, and I hope your powers will be fully exerted in securing the peace and happiness of our country, by the adoption of a wise and free government. I shall be impatient to know your thoughts on these great subjects, and hope you will inform me as early as possible.

Excuse the length of this letter, And believe me sincerely Yours,.

His Excellency Patrick Henry.

[1] The words " then, sir," appear in the text in the *Enquirer*.
[2] This word is " persuading " in the text in the *Enquirer*.
* "The remainder is lost from the Ms.," says Mr. William Wirt Henry. The continuation is from the printed text in the *Richmond Enquirer*.

THE LETTERS OF RICHARD HENRY LEE

TO [GENERAL CHARLES LEE][1]

My Dear Friend,   Philadelphia, 22nd April, 1776.

I thank you heartily for your obliging favors by this and the last Post, they have made me very happy by the good opinion you have of our officers and troops. I have no doubt they will verify upon the Enemy, when they come, your opinion of them. It always gave me much pleasure to reflect on your appointment to the Southern Department, well knowing the signal benefit and security that would result to my country therefrom. Your measures are in my opinion extremely wise and well adapted to the ends you have in view. I am sure your water manœuvres will give great security to our rivers and confidence to the people thereon, at the same time that it will distress the enemy by preventing their getting provisions. The idea entertained by some that the battalions were to be stationed here and there to defend against Cutters was very absurd, and if executed would have rendered the Regiments useless for that and for every other purpose, unless we could have prevailed on the enemy to go there only to maraude where the troops were fixed. It was certainly the idea of Congress, and it is so expressed in their resolve, that you should raise a Company of Artillery for Monsr. Arundel, and the Convention or Committee of Safety to appoint the inferior Officers — Capt. Innis's company it was never proposed to affect in any degree by this new raised Company. You will hear more of this hereafter. Your desire is complied with by a Resolve of Congress directing letters to Generals commanding in separate detachments to go post free. The pay of an Engineer under the chief is no more than twenty

[1] From a printed text in New York Historical Society *Collections*, *The Lee Papers*, I. 440.

dollars a month, and as yet no rank is settled. Your letter to Congress concerning shoes and blankets has been considered, and a very good man is ordered to procure and forward immediately to Williamsburg 5000 blankets and as many shoes for the Troops in Virginia. Three tons of powder are likewise ordered. You may expect these ere long. The want of discipline among our Troops in Canada this winter has occasioned some disturbances in that country where a small engagement has actually happened between the country people and a party of our men in which the former were defeated. We are taking all the means in our power to compose these unhappy differences, and hope it will be effected by our Committee, better discipline, and the large body of troops going thither. We know not yet where the mercenaries from Boston are gone unless it be to Halifax. Manly has taken one of their Transports with two capital Tories and Tory goods imported from G. B. valued at £35,000. sterlg. 2 of their Transports with provisions from England for Boston have been lately taken. You have no doubt heard how Commodore Hopkins has drubbed the Glasgow and would certainly have taken her, if he had not been so heavy with Providence stores — A Bomb Brig & 3 Tenders he did take and carry into N. London — Wallace & his little Squardon have fled from the Rhode Island Station, and left it to our Fleet. The Commodore we expect is now out on another cruise. When Sir you find anything whatever deficient about the troops, a letter from you to Congress thro' the President will be the quickest and surest way to obtain it, as happened the other day when you applied for powder, blankets, and shoes. You ask me why we hesitate in Congress. I'll tell you my friend, because we are heavily clogged with instructions from these shamefully interested Proprietary people, and this will continue until Virgᵃ.

sets the example of taking up Government, and sending peremptory Orders to their delegates to pursue the most effectual measures for the Security of America. It is most certain that the people in these Proprietary Colonies will then force the same measure, after which Adieu to Proprietary influence and timid senseless politics. You have enclosed a sensible little pamphlet on government written by Mr John Adams. 'Tis well fitted for the times, shewing that to be easy and necessary, which the unthinking people have supposed to be unnecessary and difficult. We have an account in Town that the Court of London has demanded from that of Portugal all the American property in the Portugese dominions, and 'tis supposed this will be complied with. Every days experience still confirms the most diabolical wickedness and violence of that execrable Court. I do most heartily wish it were in my power to attend our Convention at their coming Session — But it is impossible to leave this place, and you would think it quite improper if you were here.

Your affectionate friend

I am so hurried that I scarcely know what I write.

TO ROBERT CARTER NICHOLAS [1]

PHILADELPHIA 30th April 1776

DEAR SIR,

I thank you for your kind favor by the last Post, and I am well pleased to hear that Gen. Lee is exerting himself for the security of our country. His military talents are considerable; and his zeal in the American cause equal to his martial accomplishments. His plan for securing our rivers with armed boats, from piratical

[1] A. L. S. Massachusetts Historical Society, Jefferson Papers, 1770–1826, 94. Nicholas was at this time Treasurer of Virginia, and the letter is addressed to him at Williamsburg, and franked by Lee.

ravage, is very wise, and I hope it will meet the countenance and support of our convention. The manner of making common salt, as practised in France, and well described in a pamphlet we sent the Committee of Safety, seems to deserve the most serious attention of the public. Our water is more salt & our Sun hotter than in France, nor are they much less subject to rains, but from this interruption we need not fear much inconvenience, where the evaporation from the suns heat is so great as in Virginia. I really think that revenue as well as supply of the commodity may be obtained from public works of this kind. Saltpetre too is an object of great consequence, but I incline to believe that bounties to encourage the making this in private families will more certainly produce it in large quantities than any other plan. We are told that Massachusetts Government alone will in this way furnish 100 Tons by midsummer. But Sir, do you not see the indispensable necessity of establishing a Government this Convention ? How long popular commotions may be suppressed without it, and anarchy be prevented, deserves intense consideration. A wise and free government may now be formed and the sensible advantages soon derived from it, will, added to the Magistrates authority, effectually prevent the numerous evils to be apprehended from popular rage & licence whenever they find the bonds of government removed, as is certainly the case, by the last wicked Act of Parliament. We cannot be in rebellion, and without the Kings protection; and Magistrates acting under his authority at the same time. Would not the President act as Governor, if chosen by the Convention ? I sent you a small pamphlet by Squire Lee, written here by a very sensible Gentleman on the subject of Government. His plan, with some variation, would in fact, be nearly the form we have been used to.

Our enemies are at this time holding a treaty with

the Indians at Detroit, and propose another at Niagara the 1st of May, to persuade these Savages to join them in the war against us. This mischief will forever attend us whilst one of the forts are suffered to remain in possession of the enemy in that Country. However I expect an expedition will soon be sett on foot that will effectually oust them. Gen Howe is certainly gone to Hallifax to refresh his dispirited, fugitive army, but his distress there must be considerable. We conclude here that Quebec and Hudsons river will be their great objects this Campaingn, and we are preparing to give them a proper reception both in Canada and New York. I think Ld. Germains intercepted letter shews us pretty clearly that the 7 regiments under Cornwallis are all that are intended for the Southern Colonies this year, and their insufficiency is very apparent, But this is one good consequence arising from Ld. Dunmores vain boasting of his own prowess, and what he could do in Virgᵃ· with a few troops, He has led his friends into another scrape. We have sent 8 Gallies & 2 Ships of war down after the Roebuck as she is reported to be on Shore near the Capes of Delaware. Should this prove true it will be a fine acquisition.

Colo. Harrison told me you desired the account of each Delegate to be sent you. I have accordingly inclosed you mine. The general Account of the disposition of the money obtained from the bills you have sent here, will likewise be transmitted. I had, in my last account sent you when in Virga., stated our allowance at half a joe pr. day because I was informed that was the sense of the Convention. But since the Ordinance mentions forty five shillings we must abide by the loss. The Congress has sent 250,000 dollars to the Paymaster in Virga. & 50,000 to the Committee of Safety to get changed for specie to support the Troops in Canada. From this quantity of Continental money in Virginia you will have no difficulty hereafter I suppose Sir [in] [p]rocuring as much as will pay our wages. [You]r goodness will, I am sure, pardon the length [of] this letter — I am dear Sir your affec[tionate] and obedient Servant.

Mr. Ro. Morris purchased the bills you sent by me and the exchange was 77s.

TO SAMUEL PURVIANCE[1]

DEAR SIR,   PHILADELPHIA 1ˢᵗ May 1776

I thank you for your favor of the 23ᵈ of April which I should have answered before now if I had not been prevented by much business. If zeal in a good cause may not cover small irregularities or deviations from the strict line of Office, and regard for the public safety be chained to the letter of business, I fear such pedantic politics will ruin America, as they must fatally injure every country where they prevail. The public of America is a generous public, and when appealed to will readily distinguish things dictated by the General good though [ir][2] regularly executed, from such as are evil in [the][2] ir nature and merely the suggestions o[f fo][2]lly [and w][2]ickedness. I am sure a generous

[1] A. L. S. Maryland Historical Society, P. F. No. 8 (1). The letter is addressed " Samuel Purveyance Junʳ Esqʳ/of Baltimore in/ Maryland," and was sent by Doctor Bankhead. Lee's frank is erased. A printed text is in Purviance's *Baltimore*. For report of the Committee to examine Purviance's papers see Force, *American Archives*, Ser. 4, V, 1581. The Ms. report, dated May 10, is among the University of Virginia Lee Papers. Purviance, at the urging of General Charles Lee, and supposing he had authority from Congress, April 16, had on the 18th of April ordered the seizure of Governor Eden and his papers, and was in consequence brought into conflict with the Council of Safety at Annapolis.   [2] Ms. torn.

Community will not suffer [a]¹ny person to be perse-cuted for the former, nor would I scruple in such a case to say as of old Provoco ad² Populum, and then look the proudest connections in the face, trusting to the wisdom of the Object, & the integrity of design, not-withstanding the manner might be something unusual.

I find Capt. Nicholsons merit is well understood here, and therefore I hope he will succeed in his desires.

You have my congratulations Sir on your marriage, for I am truly your friend and obliged humble Servant.

TO SAMUEL PURVIANCE³

DEAR SIR,   PHILADELPHIA May 6ᵗʰ 1776

I received yesterday your favor of the 2ᵈ instant, and in answer to that part of it desiring to know if Mʳ Hancock gave a copy of your letter to any person, I must say that I do not know whether or not, but I am inclined to think he has not. This business appears to me thus — When Mʳ Hancock received the dis-patches from Baltimore, he proceeded to read the whole in Congress, and among others, a letter containing ob-servations on the Council of Safety of Maryland, rela-tive to the timidity of their Councils; which it appears he had not previously read in private, because, when he came to that part of it which mentioned its being written in confidence, he stopt, and observed it was private, and proposed it should be so considered; but as he had read so much of it, he went on, but read no name at the bottom, & in the debate consequent upon it, 'twas supposed to be anonymous, and it was conjecture alone that fixed you as the Author. I should have certainly

---

¹ Ms. torn.   ² Written in the place of another word.
³ A. L. S. Maryland Historical Society, P. F. No. 8 (1) Ad-dressed to Purviance at Baltimore, and franked by Lee.

informed you of this, if I had then found myself at liberty to do it, and when I hear'd from you of your summons before the Council, it was too late for a letter to reach you before your appearance at that board. But the idea of drawing from the mouth of a person accused his own condemnation is reprobated by English jurisprudence, and is the practise only of inquisitorial or Star chamber Tyranny. I should incline to think that this persecution will be carried no further, at least I am sure the time is quickly coming when violence from without will render absolutely necessary a perfect union within. A late arrival from Port L'orient with 13 tons of powder & 30 of Salt petre brings us a Cork paper near the middle of March, by which we learn that more than 40,000 men would sail from Portsmouth & Grenoch about the 1st of April for N. America — They consist of Hessians Hannoverians, Mechlenburghers, Scotch Hollanders, & Scotch Highlanders, with some British Regiments. Their destination not certain, but said to be N. York. New, England; Canada, & 2 expeditions more South —

Should the persecution go on against you, I would advise answering no interrogation, but plainly detail my conduct, acknowledge such parts as were without the strict line of duty, and lay it to the account of my zeal for the cause of America, which I hoped a generous community would pardon and forget.

My time and attention is so taken up with public business, that I must now conclude with refering you to my letter by D.r Bankhead

I am, with regard, Sir your friend and obedient Servant.

THE LETTERS OF RICHARD HENRY LEE

TO GENERAL [CHARLES] LEE[1]

My dear Friend,   PHILADELPHIA 11th May 1776

Since I wrote you last nothing of consequence hath happened, unless it be, that the Roebuck & Liverpoole coming up the river Delaware, were met about Christeen, some miles above Newcastle, by the 13 Gondolas of this City, and after a cannonade of 3 hours each day for 2 successive days, the Ships returned down the river, and the Gallies to their old station, with out much hurt, I believe on either side. My friendship for you is so strong, and the sense I have of the obligations America is under to you so high, that I will ever pray the liberty of being full and free on every subject that may materially concern you. I find a spirit prevailing here, which leads its possessors to regard with a jealous eye, every instance of deviation (in a Military or Naval Commander) from the line of instructions, and also every undertaking productive of expence which is not warranted by express order of Congress. Thus animated I find some Gentlemen expressing dissatisfaction at your having promised forage to such Cavalry as might be assembled in Virginia, and likewise because of the Boats you had ordered to be built for the security of the rivers, You know my friend, that the spirit of Liberty is a jealous spirit, and that those appointed to guard it, are not always wise and candid Counsellors. Upon this consideration, will it not be prudent to put it out of the power of any person to complain with justice, by a timely representation of such things as are necessary, and unless in great and most urgent cases, not to let the adoption precede the Congressional order of any

[1] A. L. Virginia Historical Society, Lee Papers, I. 48. Addressed to him as, "Commander of the Continental/Armies in the Southern Department."

189

measure. I am very sufficiently conscious of the thousand occasions in which the service must suffer immensely if Commanders at a distance are not to accomodate conduct to circumstances — But I know also that all men are not candid, not wise; and that some are governed frequently by envy, by enmity, and by evil designs. I would therefore carefully avoid furnishing such men with the opportunity of cavil, by obtaining the proper sanction for all such things as were extraneous to the immediate line of duty, unless, as I have before mentioned, in cases where the Distance time and public good would not admit of delay.

TO [EDMUND PENDLETON ?][1]

DEAR SIR.   PHILADELPHIA, 12^{the} May 1776.

Before this reaches you I hope[2] much progress will have been made towards the establishment of a wise and free government, without which neith— public or private happness or security can be long expected. I make no doubt but you have seen a small pamphlet published here, with the Title of an "Address to the convention of the Colony and ancient Dominion of Virg^a on the Subject of Government &c." This Contemptible little Tract, betrays the little Knot or Junto from whence it proceeded. Confusion of ideas, aristocratic[3] pride,[3] contradictory[3] reasoning,[3] with evident ill design, put it out of danger of doing harm, and therefore I quit it. The difficulty we have to encounter in constructing this fabric from whence so great good or evil may result, consists certainly in a blending the three

[1] A. dr. L. University of Virginia, Lee Papers, No. III. A transcript with minor variations is in the Virginia Historical Society, Lee Transcripts, III. 65. Judge Pendleton was President of the Virginia Convention of 1776.   [2] Substituted for "fear" erased.
[3] Substituted for "vain display of reading" erased.

simple forms of Government in such manner as to prevent the inordinate views of either from unduly affecting the others, which has never been the case in Engl^d., altho' it was the professed aim of that System. But there, a fine design, was spoiled in the execution. The perogative of making Peers and Boroughs effectually destroyed the equipoise,[1] and prevented an opportunity of applying that corruption which has now swallowed up every thing but the forms of freedom in Great[2] Britain.[2] However imperfect the English plan was, yet our late Government in Virginia was infinitely worse. With us 2 thirds of the Legislature, and all the executive and judiciary Powers were in the same hands — In truth it was very near a Tyrany, altho' the mildness with which it was executed under Whig direction, made the evil little felt. Abridged duration, temperate revenue, and every unnecessary power withheld, are potent means of preserving integrity in public men and for securing the Community from the dangerous ambition of that too often governs the human mind. But why need I mention these things, to a gentleman who knows them so well — I have only to wish your health may enable you to attend to this arduous[3] business with the closeness it deserves.— If you consider the nature of the funds with which the War has been hitherto carried on, the great and growing expense of this contest, and the probable prospect of its continuing for some time longer, I suppose untill G[reat] B[ritain] has lost all hope of regaining us, it must be evident beyond a doubt that foreign Alliance is indispensable, and should be immediately sought — Our Trade must be opened, which cannot be done until we get protection for our property on the water, and can induce some competent

---

[1] The words "and made effectual" are here erased.
[2] Substituted above the line for " that country " erased.
[3] Written above "most important."

191

power to undertake to trade with us. About this no time is to be lost, and therefore I wish positive Instruction on this head may be sent your Servants in Congress soon as possible. Would it not be well to appoint M! President Nelson, the first Governor if he would accept, since he possesses knowledge, experience, and has already been in a dignified station? The Roebuck & Liverpoole, were lately met Coming up the Delaware, by thirteen Gondola's from this City, when after 2 engagements, on two following days, of 3 hours each time — The ships returned down the river well bored with large Cannon Shot — We have had upwards of 20 tons of powder and more salt-petre with several brass field pieces, arrived within the last 10 days, and we daily expect to hear of the arrival of the Hessian, Hanoverian & Higland Commissioners — I hope my countrymen will push the Articles of Common Salt, Salt-Petre & arms; and that all possible encouragement will be given to manufactures of every useful kind. Let a Wire Mill be set up for the purpose of making Wool and Cotton Cards. I am inclined to think there is no better way to produce a spirit of manufacture, than by offering very encouraging public rewards for the 1st & 2^{d}, and so on, largest quantity of Linnen or Woollen cloths.

TO GENERAL [CHARLES] LEE [1]

My Dear Friend,   Philadelphia, 21st May, 1776.

As I wrote you yesterday by your Express, I have now only to thank you for your favor by last post. If you discovered any languor in my letters it must have been merely corporeal, the mental powers having been just as vigorous as ever. Excessive writing and con-

[1] From a printed text in New York Historical Society *Collections*, *The Lee Papers*, II. 31.

stant attention to business afflicts me a good deal I own, but they are far from depressing my spirits in the great cause of America, and if you were to consult with our *moderate men* in and out of doors you would think me possessed of something else than languor. The mischievous instructions from some Colonies have indeed fettered Congressional Councils, but many of these are done away, and the rest will be so immediately The [late] Resolve of Congress respecting government hath wrought a great change hereabouts, and very soon the Public affairs will wear a different aspect, and be directed with better spirit. I expect an expedition to Detroit will be undertaken, Niagara will probably be suspended, as the Indians thereabout wish it to continue a place of trade yet awhile. A Gentleman just from N. York, tells us that 70 sail of Transports with 10,000 troops were arrived off the Hook; and that Gen. Washington was despatching an Express to Congress, a confirmation is hourly expected. They have made the works about N. York very strong, and tho' the detachment of 10 Battalions to Canada, has not left above 8,000 yet 10, or 12000 militia may be thrown in, so that we apprehend no danger from that quarter.

Farewell, my dear Sir.

Early in April I gave you an Account of the affair of the Annapolis Council.

GENERAL LEE, Commander of the Continental Forces in the Southern Department, at Williamsburg, Virginia.

TO GENERAL [CHARLES] LEE [1]

MY DEAR FRIEND,   PHILADELPHIA 27 May 1776.

The inclosed intelligence lately received from England, will give you a better idea of the designs of our

[1] From a printed text in New York Historical Society *Collections*, *The Lee Papers*, II. 45.

enemies than any we have before received. In a letter I have seen from London of unquestionable authority is the following paragraph — "A General of the first abilities and experience would come over if he could have any assurance from the Congress of keeping his rank, but that being very high, he would not submit to have any one but an American, his superior, and that only in consideration of the confidence due to an American in a question so peculiarly American." Let me have your opinion of this matter. Prince Ferdinand's recommendation of the General mentioned above is, in these words "Si l'on veut un Officier aprouvé, intelligent, et brave; je ne scai si on peut trouver un autre qui le vaille.".

There is no person in America can answer this paragraph so well as yourself. Our friend Gates, who with Generals Washington and Mifflin (the latter lately made a Brigadier, and M: Gates a Major General) are now here, is of opinion that the officer desiring to come to America is Major General Beckwith. But this is merely conjecture, founded on the mans political principles, and his abilities as a Soldier. The papers I formerly sent you, with the evening post now enclosed, will shew you the political convulsions of this Province, but I incline to think that this sensible spirited people, will not long be duped by Proprietary Machinations, whatever may be the fate of Maryland. Apropos, what do you think of the representative bodies of this latter Province? Of all the extraordinary Phenomena of this extraordinary age, these are the most extraordinary! Is the Convention of Maryland, a Conclave of Popes, a mutilated legislature, or an Assembly of wise Men? By the manner in which they dispense with Oaths, it w^d seem they conceived of themselves as the first of those, for surely a mutilated legislature, an unorganized government cannot do what these men by their Resolve of May the

15th have undertaken — Nor is their 2^d resolve of the 21st better founded, unless they can shew, which I believe is not in their power, that the people had in contemplation these things when they chose them, and elected them accordingly. What do these folks mean by a "Reunion with G. Britain *on constitutional principles?* I profess I do not understand them, nor do I believe the best among them have any sensible ideas annexed to these terms. But I have done with them being satisfied they will never figure in history among the Solons, Lycurgus's or Alfred's. Our Commissioners ·in Canada seem to be on the fright, but I hope Thomas, Sullivan, Thomson, &c will restore the spirits with our affairs in that Province. The disgrace apart, our late capture of the valuable Transport to the Eastward, much more than compensates for the loss before Quebec. The Continental armed Ship, Franklin has certainly taken & secured a most valuable Transport with 75 Tons of Gunpowder 1000 stand of arms, and a variety of other useful articles valued at £50,000, this money. The sensible and manly resolve of Virginia of the 15th instant has gladdened the hearts of all wise and worthy men here. It will powerfully contribute to sett things right in these Proprietary governments. We have here 4 Tribes of the Six Nation Indians, and yesterday we had between 2 & 3 thousand men paraded on the Common to their great astonishment and delight. We hope effectually to secure the friendship of these people.

Farewell dear Sir, and be assured you have my hearty wishes for success and happiness. Can't Clinton (if he is on shore) be disturbed before the rest of his Myrmidons join him?

My compliments to Gen. Howe.

GEN LEE. Commander of the Continental Armies in the Southern Department at Williamsburg, Virginia.

THE LETTERS OF RICHARD HENRY LEE

TO THOMAS LUD[WELL] LEE[1]

My Dear Brother,   Philadelphia, 28th May 1776.
This is Post morning and I am obliged on a Committee of conference with the Generals Washington, Gates, & Mifflin by 9 on the operations of this Campaign, so that I cannot possibly write to many of my friends and particularly Col°. Mason. Pray make my compliments to him, let him have the news sent, and apoligize for me. Col° Nelson is not arrived, but I suppose he will by this day sennight, about which time I shall sett out for Virginia, and after resting at home a day or two, will attend the Convention at Williamsburg. The sensible and spirited resolve of my Countrymen on the 15th has gladdened the heart of every friend to human nature in this place, and it will have a wonderful good effect on the misguided Councils of these Proprietary Colonies. What a scene of determined rapine and roguery do the German treaties present to us, and Ld Dartmouths answer to the Duke of Graftons motion, 16th March, has shut the mouths of all Gapers after Commissioners. The transport Prize taken to the Eastward is extremely apropos. The vessel and Cargo are valued at £50,000. We are not without hopes of getting some more of the same flock, if fortune should have separated them from the Shepherd, they will most probably fall. This is the Campaign that we shall be most tried in probably, and we should endeavour as far as human care can go to be more invulnerable than Achilles, not exposing even the heel, where the stake is so immense. We have not lately heard from Canada, but we hope for better news soon than our last. A

[1] From a printed text in New York Historical Society *Collections*, *The Lee Papers*, II. 47. Brother of Richard Henry Lee.

196

potent push will assuredly be made there this Summer by our enemies, and if we can prevent them from communicating with the Upper Country, and thereby debauching the Indians, we shall answer every good purpose there. The Roebuck is gone from here crippled, but the Liverpoole remains thinly manned and in want of provisions. It is to be hoped that the death of the King of Portugal will produce something in Europe favorable to us. Let no consideration interrupt your attention to the making of Common Salt, Salt Petre & Arms; and every kind of encouragement should be given to all sorts of useful manufacture.

Farewell my dear brother.

Our brothers in London were well, the 13. Febry. last. I write Gen. Lee by this post — do see that the letter is forwarded from Williamsburg.

Thomas Lud Lee, Esquire, at Williamsburg, in Virginia.

TO LANDON CARTER[1]

PHILADELPHIA 2ᵈ June 1776

DEAR SIR,

Since the establishment of our Westmoreland Rider, I conclude the papers come so regularly into your neighborhood from this City, as to render it the less necessary to repeat in letters what you will find exactly detailed in the Gazette. I cannot help congratulating you on * * * * Virginia has obtained by the resolve of Convention on the 15ᵗʰ of last month — A Gentleman of the first understanding here, and of very moderate passions said on reading the resolve, "Virginia has determined like a brave, sensible and injured people." Still the

[1] Ms. copy. Virginia Historical Society, Lee Transcripts, II. "Copies of Letters to Landon Carter." Addressed to him at Sabine Hall, and franked by Lee.

views of interested weak and wicked men, obstruct the public service in these proprietary governments —

The infamous treaties with Hesse Brunswick &c (of which we have authentic copies) and the Ministerial reply to Graftons motion leave not a doubt but that our enemies are determined upon the absolute conquest and subduction of N. America.

It is not choice then, but necessity that calls for Independence, as the only means by which foreign Alliance can be obtained and a proper confederation[1] by which internal peace and union may be secured. Contrary to our earnest, early and repeated petitions for peace, liberty and safety, our enemies press us with war, threaten us with danger and Slavery. And this, not with her single force, but with the aid of Foreigners. Now altho' we might safely venture our strength circumstanced as it is, against that of Great Britain only, yet we are certainly unequal to a Contest with her and her Allies, without any assistance from without, and this more especially, as we are incapable of profiting by our exports for want of Naval force — You seem to apprehend danger from our being aided by despotic States, but remember that France assisted Holland without injury to the

---

[1] Lee, on June 7, pursuant to the Virginia resolves of May 15, 1776, rose in Congress and moved the following: —

" Resolved/That ~~they will pass~~ [?]* these United Colonies are, and of right ought to be, free and independent States, that/they are absolved from all allegiance to the British/Crown, and that all political connection between them and the State of Great Britain is, and ought to be,/totally dissolved.

That it is expedient forthwith to take / the most effectual measures for forming foreign/Alliances.

That a plan of confederation be prepared / and transmitted to the respective Colonies for / their consideration and approbation."

* [In the autograph draft of these resolutions by Lee, Library of Congress, Papers of the Continental Congress; this erasure is almost indistinguishable, except the " they."]

latter — Will the help we desire put it by any means
in the power of France to hurt us tho' she were so
inclined —

Supplies of Military Stores and Soldiers clothing, Ships
of war to cover our Trade & open our Ports, which
would be an external assistance altogether, could never
endanger our freedom by putting it in the power of our
Ally to Master us, as has been the case where weak
States have admitted powerful Armies for their De-
fenders. When last we heard from Canada, our forces
that had retreated from Quebec, on the arrival of succors, had fixt at De Chambaud, or Falls of Richlieu,
about 30 miles above Quebec and were strongly fortify-
ing there — If they can maintain that Post, which commands 8 tenths of Canada, we shall do almost as well
as if we had Quebec, as we thereby effectually cut off
all communications with the upper Country, or Western
Indians, and prevent the West Indies receiving supplies
from that fertile Province. We are making the best
preparation to meet the numerous foreign Mercenaries
with which we are to be invaded this Campaign. The
expence of G. Britain this Summer is estimated at 10
millions, exclusive of the ordinary expenses.—

With half her Trade subducted, with a debt of 140
Millions, how can she go on?

The Dutch begin to fear for their money in English
funds, and say they w^d give 30 p^r cent discount to have
it withdrawn.

Franklin, the late Governor of New Jersey you will
see by the inclosed papers, is endeavoring to bring himself under the notice of Congress, and I believe he will
effect it now, as the plan of calling an Assembly by a
King's Governor, the resolve of the 15th cannot be
passed.

I hope to be in Virginia in 10 or 12 days, when I shall
endeavor to visit Sabine Hall.

THE LETTERS OF RICHARD HENRY LEE

I am with great esteem, dear Sir, your affectionate and obedient Servant.[1]

P.S. We have just seen a petition from London to the King * * * * in * * * * and moving language that he w^d let explicit terms of justice decide the operations of Arms in America. His * * * * that he is sorry for the rebellion, but that force on his part & submission (?) on ours is all he proposes. This is the substance of his Tyrannic answer to the most sensible & humble Address that Modern times has produced.

[1] The following note is added to the Ms. by Mr. Cassius F. Lee. " The letter is in poor condition & in places very difficult to decipher. Col. Carter endorsed the letter as follows, hand writing bad & ink much faded.

'Col° RICHARD H. LEE from Philadelphia June 2, 1776.

'This Gentleman is a correspondent, but so late in his reply that I almost forget what I wrote to him. I see he says I am apprehensive that by courting foreign assistance they who assist us will demand terms equally injurious: and puts me in mind of france who assisted Holland. But he should consider the claim of France on America wch was mostly taken from her. Now the case was different as to Holland. But he seems to think we dont want any internal assistance but only as to trade &ᶜ. If we dont I hold no argument. At least I see, though he does not care to own it, He agrees that our Independence is by Compulsion. If this is granted I hold no argument (then or there) neither. All that I urged was that the Pure British Constitution was not to be so reprobated as Common sense had done it: and he I know was a great Stickler for that Authority (so the word abbreviated seems to be). However, he is to call and see me as * * * to Convention from Philadelphia.' C. F. L."

THE LETTERS OF RICHARD HENRY LEE

TO GENERAL [GEORGE] WASHINGTON[1]

DEAR SIR, PHILADELPHIA 13<u>th</u> June 1776

I am informed that a certain Mr Eustace, now in New York, but some time ago with Lord Dunmore, is acquainted with a practise that prevailed of taking letters out of the Post Office in Virginia and carrying them to Dunmore for his perusal and then returning them to the Office again. As it is of the greatest consequence that this nefarious practise be stopt immediately, I shall be exceedingly obliged to you Sir for getting Mr Eustace to give in writing all that he knows about this business, and inclose the same to me at Williamsburg. I wish to know particularly, what Post Offices the letters were taken from, by whom, and who carried them to Lord Dunmore. This day I sett off for Virginia, where, if I can be of any service to you, it will oblige to command me. It is more than probable that Congress will order our friend Gates to Canada — His great abilities and virtue will be absolutely necessary to restore things there, and his recommendations will always be readily complied with. You will find that great powers are given to the Commander in that distant department. The system for Canada, adopted since the arrival of the Commissioners here, will, I hope, be of essential service to our affairs. All good Men pray most heartily for your health, happiness, and success, and none more than dear Sir Your affectionate friend and obedient Servant.

[1] A. L. S. Library of Congress, Letters to Washington, X. 13. Addressed, "His Excellency/General Washington/at Head Quarters/ New York."

THE LETTERS OF RICHARD HENRY LEE

TO [WILLIAM LEE][1]

PECATONE   17 June 1776

DEAR BROTHER

Our friend and Kinsman John Tuberville Esqr has committed to your care a very important concern, the direction of his Sons education. He relys greatly on your sensible and tender attention to this business — The first object in view being a complete education, to have that purpose effectually answered, he chooses his Son to be placed either at Eton, at Winchester, or at Westminster; proposing that one of the three of the best present reputation shall be fixed on. Altho Mr Tuberville does not mean so far to attend to frugal principles as to neglect by any means the great business of learning, yet every thing else being equal, he would prefer that one of the three where the greatest moderation in the article of expence prevails. I refer you to my many letters by this opportunity, wishing that you may have patience to go thro them all.

Our love to our dear Sister.

Your affectionate brother.

P.S. Walker is now at Essex Court so that I can get no fresh information touching him, but I believe Craft is out for all his load.[2]

Indolent as he is perhaps it may be after the close of this month before he sails.

[1] A. L. S. Virginia Historical Society, Lee Papers, IV. 132.
[2] Signed "R. H. Lee." The body of the letter is signed, as usual, in Lee's full name.

TO GENERAL [CHARLES] LEE[1]

My Dear Friend, Williamsb^g 29th June, 1776.

The desire of being here at the formation of our new Government brought me from Philadelphia the 13th of this month. I have been in this City a week where I have had the pleasure to see our new plan of Government go on well. This day will put a finishing hand to it. 'Tis very much of the democratic kind, altho' a Governor and second branch of legislation are admitted, for the former is not permitted voice in Legislation, he is in all things to be advised by his Privy Council, and both are by joint ballot of both houses to be chosen annually, altho' the Governor may be continued in Office 3 years, after which he is not eligible for 4 years. Both the Houses of the Legislature are chosen by the whole body of the people — Our former House of Burgesses, now called the House of Delegates to be chosen annually in the usual manner. The other House, now called the House of Senators is to be 24 in number and to be chosen from Districts into which the Country is to be laid off. One fourth of this Body go out annually by rotation, and the vacancy filled by the District whence they came. The Judges and other Great Officers of State are to be chosen by Joint ballot of both houses, and to hold their Offices during good behaviour. These are the outlines of our political machine, which I hope is sufficiently guarded against the Monster Tyranny. When I left Philadelphia the Military arrangement stood thus — For N. York 10,000 regular troops joined by 15,000 militia — For Canada 7,000 regulars joined by 6,000 militia and 2000 Indians, a Flying Camp of

---

[1] From a printed text in New York Historical Society *Collections*, *The Lee Papers*, II. 97.

10,000 in the middle Colonies — 11 Battalions in the eastern Colonies and 23 in the Southern. Gen. Wooster had so misconducted matters in Canada that with very little opposition our Troops were obliged to retreat to the mouth of Sorell, and a Regiment posted at the Cedars, 12 miles above Montreal was shamefully surrendered to a party of the Enemy coming from Niagara. The letters by this post from Phil[a] tell us that our affairs in that Country were recovering fast, and that Gen. Thompson, with 2000 men was gone down to Dechambeau or Falls of Richlieu, to dispossess 300 regular Troops there, and recover that important post. I incline to think our friend Genl. Gates will be sent to Canada as Chief Commander, poor Thomas having died at Chamblée of the small pox. We have already taken three transports with Highlanders — The 217 that have fallen to our share are distributed thro' this Colony, a few in each County, and permitted to hire themselves out to labour, thus to become the Citizens of America instead of its enemies. Great distress prevails in the British West Indies, and the French preparations in that part of the World, formidable. The news of Phil[a] when I came away was that the Court of France had stopt the Hessians &c from coming here. I have not the least doubt but that Independence will, in a few days, be publicly announced by the General Congress. All restraining instructions are now removed except from Maryland, and there, the people were up, and instructions sending from all parts to their Convention, which met 10 days ago, expressly directing to rescind their instructions and pursue a different line of political conduct. I incline to think therefore that Independence will carry it nem. con. and Foreign Alliance immediately sought. The business of Confederation will also then be set on foot.

I shall return to Chantilly in a few days and remain there until the last of August, when I go to Philadelphia.

It will give me a singular pleasure to hear from you when your leisure will permit, because there is nothing I more sincerely wish than to know that you are happy and successful.

Remember me to M: President Rutledge, and tell my friend, Gen. Gadsden, that I remember him with much affection.

Farewell my dear friend.

Col° Harrison and M: Braxton are left out of our delegation to Congress, the other 5 continued — This Convention voted 6 Troops of Horse.

Major General Lee,
 Commander of the Continental Armies in the Southern Department, at Charleston, South Carolina.

TO [GENERAL CHARLES LEE][1]

My Dear Friend,   WILLIAMSB^G 6th July, 1776.

The inclosed form of Government will shew you that this Country has in view a permanent system of Liberty. Mr Henry is chosen Governor, and a Privy Council is appointed to assist him in the discharge of his important duty — A new Great Seal, adapted to our State is ordered to be made, and now, we have in all respects a full and free Government which this day begins the exercise of its powers. The Convention of Maryland has rescinded the mischievious instructions with which they had bound their Delegates, empowered three of them to join the other Colonies in a vote of Independence, Foreign Alliance, Confederation, &^c By this time I expect the two former are settled in Congress —

[1] From a printed text in New York Historical Society *Collections*, *The Lee Papers*, II. 123.

Before this reaches you, no doubt you will have heared of our having taken in this Bay a Transport with 217 Highlanders, and by this Post we learn that 5 Transports more with the same kind of Cattle have been carried into the Eastern Ports — But this good news is allayed by more adverse fortune in Canada — Gen. Thomson with 2000 men went to dislodge 300 Regular Troops at the three Rivers whence he was met by Gen. Burgoyne with a considerable force — Thomson's forces were routed himself and Col. Irwin taken prisoners, with the loss of 150 men killed, wounded, & taken prisoners. The rest joined our Army at the mouth of Sorel. In short, our affairs in Canada, at present wear but an indifferent aspect. We learn by this post that a very extensive conspiracy (pushed on by British gold) has been detected at New-York — General Washington was to have been assassinated, the magazine blown up, and the cannon spiked — 'Tis said the Mayor of N. York was concerned in the Plot. Many are now in Jail for this nefarious business. Lord Dunmore still remains on Gwin's Island where Caterpillar like, we hear he has devoured everything in that place, so that it is probable force of some kind or other will shortly drive him thence but where he will fasten next we cannot guess. We are concerned here at not hearing from you, and are obliged to comfort ourselves with the consideration that no news is good news. I shall return to Congress about the last of August, and in the meantime nothing will more contribute to my happiness than to hear that you are healthy, happy, and successful. Our cause is the cause of Virtue and mankind, and well supported as it is, I have no doubt of its success. Farewell my dear Friend.

My direction is at Chantilly, Westmoreland County, Virginia.

THE LETTERS OF RICHARD HENRY LEE

TO [SAMUEL ADAMS][1]

My dear Friend,   Williamsburg   6 July 1776

A fortnights stay here has enabled me to assist my Countrymen in finishing our form of Government — The mighty work is now done as the enclosed papers will shew you — M.ʳ Henry chosen Governor, himself and his Privy Council qualify this day and take the Government upon them, the Committee of Safety being abolished. The Convention adjourned yesterday, and our new Legislature, under the name of General assembly, meets the 1.ˢᵗ Monday in October next. I hope the Congress will take early and effectual measures to reenlist the Continental Troops in every Colony. Already our 1.ˢᵗ & 2.ᵈ Batallions talk of going home when their time is up in Sept.ʳ — This will be a critical time,

[1] A. L. S.   Lenox Library, Samuel Adams Papers.   Lee evidently, from Adams' answer of July 15, 1776 (Ms., Samuel Adams Papers), inclosed in this letter his draft of the device on the Great Seal of Virginia which is described in his autograph as follows : —
"To be engraved on the great Seal/ Virtus the genius of the commonwealth/dressed like an amazen, resting on a spear/with one hand, and holding a sword in the/other, & treding on tyranny represented by/aman prostrate, a Crown fallen from his head/a broken Chain in his left Hand and a Scourge/in his right.   In the exergon the word Virginia/over the head of Virtus and underneath the words
sic semper tyrannis —
on the reverse a Group/ Libertas, with her wand and pileus — on one side of her Ceres with the Cornucopia/in one hand and anear of Wheat in the other
On the other side Æternitas with the/Globe and Pheenix —
In the exergon these words
Deus nobis haec Otia fecit"
Endorsed in the handwriting of Richard Henry Lee,
" Device on the New Great Seal of Virginia ordered by Convention July 1776."

and every previous wise measure should be taken to prevent such a weakening of our force when the enemy may be making their greatest push.

I am grieved that our affairs have so bad an aspect in Canada — If they can be retrieved, I hope it will be done cost what it may. Surely the great business of Independence and Foreign Alliance is rightly determined before now — I shall be rejoiced to hear it. You cannot oblige me dear Sir more than by often writing to me — You have my direction — I leave this place today for Chantilly, where I shall remain until the last of August when I sett out for Congress.

Our Devil Dunmore is as he was, but we expect shortly to make him move his quarters —

Remember me to all my Friends, particularly your Namesake whose promise of writing to me I remember with pleasure.

We have letters from Gen. Lee this moment received which are dated from George Town 9th June They say "We expect to be in Charles Town this night — The enemy with their whole force are laying off the Bar waiting, as 'tis supposed for a tide & wind to get up — We shall be there to receive them with all the warmth their merit deserves"

Farewell dear Sir.

TO LANDON CARTER [1]

Dear Sir,   Chantilly 21st July 1776

I cannot omit so good an opportunity as Mr Beale furnishes me with of thanking you for your favor whilst I was at Williamsburg which at that time I by no means

---

[1] A. L. S. Lenox Library, Emmet, 1629. Addressed to Carter at Sabine Hall.

had leisure to do. The experiments you have made are discouraging, but yet I am strongly inclined to think, from the experience of other countries, as well as from the trials made here, that we may yet succeed in the important business. Captain Chilton and myself, from the water of this creek, make 2 bushels a week of very fine blown salt.

I have received your summons, and shall obey it by meeting in district Committee, from whence I will do myself the pleasure of visiting Sabine Hall. The enemy of every thing good, has at length turned his wicked steps to this river, on the north side of which, we can every day see the smoke occasioned by his conflagrations. We learn that the people of Maryland are not quiet spectators of his proceedings, but that they have attacked and killed some of his people, and obliged the whole fleet to move its station. They are continually blasting away at each other. Last night I was engaged with a party of Militia expecting a visit from four of the enemies Ships and 3 Tenders that appeared off this house about sunset. They are gone up the river, upon what errand I know not, unless to get water where the river is fresh, or to burn Alexandria. We understand they are in great want both of water and provisions. I am, with very particular esteem dear Sir Yours entirely.

[*The following autograph note, signed in initials, is written on the back of the letter.*]

Gen. Howe has landed 10,000 Men on Staten Island near N. York —

Be pleased to send the Newspaper to your Neighbor Col? Tayloe when you have perused it — [*Signed here.*]

I congratulate my Friend on the Declaration he will find in the paper now sent

THE LETTERS OF RICHARD HENRY LEE

TO THOMAS JEFFERSON [1]

Dear Sir,   Chantilly 21ˢᵗ July 1776

I thank you much for your favor and its inclosures [2] by this post, and I wish sincerely, as well for the honor of Congress, as for that of the States, that the Manuscript had not been mangled as it is.

It is wonderful, and passing pitiful, that the rage of change should be so unhappily applied — However the *Thing* is in its nature so good, that no Cookery can spoil the Dish for the palates of Freemen.

I congratulate you on the great success in South Carolina, and we have no reason to be sorry for the disgrace of our African Hero at Lwins [Levins ?] Island — He is now disturbing us in Potomac, having attached himself to Sᵗ Georges Island on the North side. But it seems the brave spirit of the Marylanders will not permit these folks to remain long where they now are. Our friend Mʳ Wythe proposes to me by letter that I meet him at Hooes ferry the 3ᵈ of September, and I have agreed to do so, unless some pressing call takes me to Congress sooner. Can you have patience so long? It will always make me happy to hear from you because I am very sincerely your affectionate friend.

P.S. I will thank you for Dʳ Prices pamphlet by next post — How do you like our Government?

---

[1] A. L. S. Library of Congress, Jefferson Correspondence, Letters to Jefferson, Ser. 2, Vol. 51, No. 12. Addressed to him, "Member of Congress in / Philadelphia."

[2] Jefferson sent to Lee a copy of the Declaration of Independence, "as originally framed," in his letter of July 8. This copy of the draft inclosed has apparently been lost. See P. L. Ford, *Writings of Thomas Jefferson*, II. 59, and R. H. Lee, *Memoir of Richard Henry Lee*, I. 275.

THE LETTERS OF RICHARD HENRY LEE

TO [SAMUEL ADAMS][1]

My dear Sir,   Chantilly 29ᵗʰ July 1776

I am much obliged to you for your favor by last post,
and with you sincerely regret the unhappy state of our
affairs in Canada. It appears to me that the small
pox has hurt us more in that country than all our own
misconduct, considerable as that has been. But even
this, nor the pestilence itself, can be of greater injury
than the discord you suggest. Nothing can prevent,
as experience fully shews, the evils arising from the last,
but seperating the Commanders, and this I wish were
done let the consequence be what it may. The enemy,
are at length, strongly pursuing their best interest,
which is to secure Hudsons and S! Laurence rivers,
but from this they *must* be prevented at every hazard.
The union that has accompanied the declaration will
gladden the heart of every true friend to human liberty,
and when we have secured this, by a wise and *just*
confederation, the happiness of America will be secured,
at least as long as it continues virtuous, and when we
cease to be virtuous we shall not deserve to be happy.
I hope no time will be lost in dispatching Ambassadors
to foreign Courts, especially to France, whose interest
it so clearly is to support the new Confederacy. When
the Court of France has publicly received our Ambassadors as from Independent States, most of the other
European powers will, I apprehend, quickly follow the
example. I think that our want of commerce and a few
strong ships cannot much longer be dispensed with,
and therefore, no delay should be suffered to obstruct
this salutary measure. The Storm thickens at N. York,
may it burst with destructive powers on the guilty foes

[1] A. L. S. Lenox Library, Samuel Adams Papers.

of human rights — What mean the Jersey Convention by the last clause of their new Charter — Shall we never cease to be teazed with the Bugbear Reconciliation, or must we hang for ever on the 'haggard' breast of G. Britain"? This clause is realy detestable now that the declaration of Congress is published & the two ought not to appear together, lest the world sh^d think we have no consistency, no firmness in our Councils — You say we are forever parted, that we are independent, the Jerseymen are contemplating the former subjection, and seem to consider their present state as a transient thing!

I wish you happy dear Sir being affectionately yours.

P.S. Four ships of Dunmores fleet have been lately up for fresh water in this river (Potomac) & burnt a Gentlemans valuable seat near the Shore.

I hope to be with you soon after the middle of August.

adieu & remember me to all our friends —

TO [JOHN AUGUSTINE WASHINGTON][1]

Dear Sir,   Chantilly 12th August 1776

I inclose you the demand against the public from our Lookouts which much business prevented me from attending to when I was last at Williamsburg. I fancy the Governor & Council will order payment in demand. You have also the determination of the Court Martial in Mr Simpsons case — You know my sentiments touching how the Court ought to have proceeded — But as it is, I leave it intirely with you whether to summon a General Court Martial, or let the matter rest, —

[1] A. L. S. Lenox Library, Emmet, 5789. Brother of George Washington.

It is at best, a business that will create trouble in calling the Gentlemen from home, & whether any good effects will result I realy know not — I wish you and yours happy being sincerely dear Sir your affectionate friend.

TO THE GOVERNOR OF VIRGINIA [1]

(PATRICK HENRY)

DEAR SIR,   BELLE VIEW 20th August 1776

I am thus far on my way to Congress,[2] having been sometime detained by the slowness of the Workman that made my Carriage wheels, the old being quite shattered and useless.

I have learned with much pleasure that recovery of health promises your speedy return to public business, and I heartily wish the latter may be benefitted as it will be by your uninterrupted enjoyment of the former.

I have been informed of two things, which if true, I think we may benefit from — These are, that the ships of war have all left our Bay, and that plenty of Salt is stored in the Islands of Bermuda. Would it not be proper to fall upon some method of giving the Bermudians speedy notice how things are circumstanced here, that they may embrace the opportunity of supplying us with that useful article. The present rainy season, will I fear disappoint the wise measures of Convention for making salt — But at all events our manufactured salt will be too late for many purposes, which a quicker supply from Bermuda, would effectually save.

[1] A. L. S. Maine Historical Society, Fogg Collection. Addressed, "His Excellency/Patrick Henry Esq/Governor of/Virginia," and franked by Lee. Printed texts with variations are in the *Virginia Historical Register*, I. 172, and Henry's *Patrick Henry*, III. 8.

[2] Jefferson had written Lee, July 29, a most urgent letter for his return to Congress.

Among these, the curing of grass beef and early Pork for the Army, are important objects. But should our Works fail, I fear most extensive and powerful convulsions will arise from the want of Salt, to prevent which, no precautions, I think, should be omitted. Our enemies appear to be collecting their whole force at N. York (except what goes to Canada) with design, no doubt, to make a last and powerful effort there. Our numbers, it seems, increase with theirs, so that I hope we shall be able to parry every thrust the Tyrant can make.

I learn from Maryland that the Counties have excluded from their new Convention all those that have been famous for *Moderation* as it is strangely called, and under this idea, that Johnson, Gouldsborough, Stone and Tilghman are left out, with the new Delegates to Congress, Alexander & Rogers.

I hope to have the pleasure of hearing from you at Philadelphia — I mean, exclusive of public writing, and in the mean time assure you that I am with much esteem and regard dear Sir your affectionate friend and obedient servant.

P.S. Be so kind as to contrive the enclosed to our friend. I do not Know rightly where he is, so you will please finish the direction.

TO PATRICK HENRY[1]

DEAR SIR,   PHILADELPHIA, 15th Sept., 1776.

I am happy to hear of your returning health and hope you will long enjoy it. We still continue here in anxious suspense about the event of things at N. York.

[1] From a text in William Wirt Henry, *Patrick Henry*, III. 10.

214

Since the removal of our troops from Long Island nothing of consequence hath happened, but the enemy show by their motions a design to land their army above ours, on the tongue of land upon which stands the city of N. York. Their design being foreseen, I hope it may be prevented, if the large frequent desertions of the militia do not weaken us too much. The enemies' force is very considerable, it being by the best accounts about 24,000 men, besides their Canada army which is about 7,000, opposed by 13,000 of our people under the command of Gen. Gates, who with a superior marine force on lake Champlain, appears not to be apprehensive of injury from that quarter this campaign. Lord Howe's great powers to do us good have lately been bared to public view, as you will see by the Congress publication of a conversation between his Lordship and a committee of their body lately on Staten Island. The tories are almost driven out of their last holds, but still they say "Lord Howe could not be expected to produce his powers, when such strong independents as Franklin & Adams were sent to him." These men will not be right, tho' one should rise from the dead to set them so. The conduct of the militia has been so insufferably bad, that we find it impossible to support the war by their means, and therefore a powerful army of regular troops must be obtained, or all will be lost. It seems to be the opinion that each State should furnish a number of Batallions proportionate to its strength, appoint all the officers from the Colonel downwards, and the whole be paid by the Continent. Letters from Bourdeaux the last of June, inform us of the greatest preperation for war in France and Spain. From the French W. Indies we have the same accounts, and the strongest assurance and acts of friendship imaginable shown to N. America. I verily believe that all the submission, art and management of G. Britain cannot much longer prevent a war with France. When we consider the water accessibility of our country, it is most clear that no defence can avail us so much as a Marine one — and of all sea force practicable to us, that of Gallies is the cheapest and the best. I wish therefore most earnestly that my Countrymen, at their next meeting of General Assembly, may early direct the immediate building of 10 or 12 large sea Gallies, upon the plan of these large ones now building here by Congress, to carry two 32 pounders in the bow, two in the stern, and 10 six pounders on the sides, to row with 40 oars, and be manned with an hundred men. These placed between the Middle ground and Cape Charles, near to a fine harbour in the Eastern shore, will secure our Bay against everything but line of battle ships, keep open our trade, and secure our shores better than 50,000 men. An able Builder here advises them to be ship-rigged. Besides the great security these Vessels will yield, they will be a fine nursery for seamen so much wanted by us. If the forge and foundry on James River be well attended to, we may easily and quickly be furnished with plenty of Cannon. I pray you, sir, to consider this matter, for I am sure if it be viewed in the light that I think it may be seen in, the plan will be adopted, and pushed with vigor into execution. At present, two or three Sloops of war can stop up our Bay, harrass our shores, and greatly distress our country, when with the Gallies I have described, it would not be safe for twice as many line of battle ships to attempt it, and utterly impossible for smaller vessels to effect it.

The committee that waited on L. Howe have not returned their written report, and therefore it is not yet published, but the verbal report was, substantially, that his Lordship had no power at all but to grant pardon and prosecute the war.

I am with much esteem, dear Sir, your affectionate and obedient Servant.

His Excellency, PATRICK HENRY, JR.

TO SAMUEL PURVIANCE [1]

DEAR SIR,   PHILADELPHIA 16ᵗʰ Septʳ 1776

Since your brother left this City, Mʳ Nicholson has been confirmed first Lieutenant of the Washington, — and his worthy brother [2] may be assured that in settling the rank of the Captains his merit will not be forgotten. It is not probable that the Frigates will sail in fleets for some time; and therefore tis likely, that no higher appointment than that of Captain will soon take place. It will be highly proper for Captain Nicholson to hasten on the Virginia (for that is most certainly the name of the Baltimore Frigate) as [m][3] uch as possible. Her great obstruction, I fear, will be Anchors — However we hope that will be removed eer long, as measures have [be][3] en taken to procure them[.][3]

You will shortly see published the conference of our Members with Lord Howe on Staten Island, in which you will find that his Lordships much talked of powers, are no more than to *confer* & *converse* with Gentlemen of influence, and to prosecute the war! We anxiously expect here, the issue of a long Cannonade at York, and another lately on Lake Champlain —

I am Sir Your most humble Servant.

[1] A. L. S. Maryland Historical Society, P. F. No. 8 (1). Franked by Lee, and addressed on reverse of Ms., "Samuel Purviance junʳ Esqʳ Merchant in/Baltimore/Maryland."

[2] James Nicholson of Maryland, later Captain of the *Virginia*, and, in January, 1777, promoted to the command-in-chief of the Navy.

[3] Ms. torn.

THE LETTERS OF RICHARD HENRY LEE

TO [THOMAS JEFFERSON][1]

DEAR SIR,   PHILADELPHIA 27<u>th</u> Sept. 1776

I should have written to you before now if I had not been uncertain about finding you at home, as the distance was great, and the meeting of our Assembly approaching. All the material events that have happened since you left us are to be found related pretty faithfully in the public papers, which I suppose are regularly conveyed to you.

The plan of foreign treaty is just finished, and yourself, with Doctor Franklin, & M. Deane now in France, are the Trustees to execute this all important business. The great abilities and unshaken virtue, necessary for the execution of what the safety of America does so capitally rest upon, have directed the Congress in their choice; and tho ambition may have no influence in this case, yet that distinguished love for your country that has marked your life, will determine you here. In my judgement, the most eminent services that the greatest of her sons can do America, will not more essentially serve her and honor themselves, than a successful negotiation with France. With this country, every thing depends upon it, and if we may form a judgement of what is at a distance, the dispositions of that Court are friendly in a high degree, and want only to be properly acted upon, to be wrought into fixt attachment and essential good. We find ourselves greatly endangered by the Armament at present here, but what will be our situation the next campaign, when the present force shall be increased by the addition of 20 or 30 thousand Russians with a larg[e] body of British

[1] A. L. S.   Library of Congress, Jefferson Correspondence, Letters to Jefferson, Ser. 2, Vol. 51, No. 30.

218

and Irish troops? I fear the power of America will fail in the mighty struggle — And th[at] the barbarous hand of despotism will extirpate lib[erty] and virtue from this our native land; placing in th[eir] stead slavery, vice, ignorance, and ruin. Already these foes of human kind have opened their Courts of Justice (as they call them) on Long Island, and the first frui[ts] of their tender mercies, are confiscation of estates, and condemnation of Whigs to perpetual imprisonment.

The idea of Congress is, that yourself and Dr Franklin should go on different Ships — The Doctor, I suppose, will sail from hence, and if it is your pleasure, one of our Armed Vessels will meet you in any River in Virginia that you choose.

I am, with singular estteem, dear Sir your affectionate friend and obedient Servant.

TO SAMUEL PURVIANCE [1]

DEAR SIR,   PHILADELPHIA 11ᵗʰ October 1776

Among the inconveniences of this busy scene, I esteem it not the least, to be so often prevented from acknowledging the favors of my friends sooner than I do. It has been owing to much business that your letter of the 27ᵗʰ has not received an answer before now. I have the pleasure to acquaint you that in ranking the Captains of our Continental Ships, the Congress have placed Captain Nicholson at the head, he being the first Captain. I wish it were in my power to give you a satisfactory answer about the building another Frigate. Hitherto nothing has been determined on this subject, the Committee having been prevented by an infinite

[1] A. L. S. Maryland Historical Society, P. F. No. 8. (1). Addressed to him as " Merchant in Baltimore," and franked by Lee.

multiplicity of other business; and to the same cause has it been owing t[hat][1] no orders have been sent concerning the Frigate Virginia. I have no doubt but that another Frigate will soon be directed, and that the Builder of greatest merit will be prefer'd. It would give me the greatest pleasure to hear that the Virginia was ready for Sea, and I am happy in being satisfied that the Managers of this business in Baltimore will not loose a moment in effecting so salutary a work. I suppose a want of Anchors will be the greatest obstruction, as I take it for granted no time will be lost in getting the guns down from M͓ Hughes's works, and having the Carriages made. I shall be glad to have an exact state of the Frigate & what she wants to complete her. I refer you to the papers for news and am Sir Your most obedient Servant.

TO [GEORGE WASHINGTON][2]

DEAR SIR,   PHILADELPHIA 27ᵗʰ October 1776

I congratulate you sincerely on the several advantages your Troops have lately gained over the enemy, for tho' each has been but small, yet in the whole they are considerable, and will certainly have the effect of inspiring our army, whilst it wastes and discourages the other. May the great Dispenser of justi e to Mankind put it in your power, before this campaign ends, to give these foes to human kind, the stroke, their wicked intentions entitles them to. 'Tis amazing with what force, and infamous perseverance the Devils of despotism with their corrupted Agents pursue the purpose of enslaving

[1] Ms. torn.
[2] A. L. S. Library of Congress, Letters to Washington, XII. 122.

this great Continent! Their system of policy has been evident for some time past — They mean to keep their own people in G. B. quiet, and the other powers of Europe still for this campaign, by an infinite number of falsehoods touching the progress of their arms, and the consequent probable submission of the colonies; whilst they endeavor by an extraordinary exertion of force to put things realy into such a situation this year, as to terrify foreigners from interfering, and encourage with hope their own deluded people. Pursuing this idea, Europe will be made to ring with sounding accounts of their immense successes in Canada and at New York, when in fact, considering the greatness of their force both by sea and land, with the amazing expence these will create, what they have done is meer nothing. But should fortune favor us so, as that any considerable impression could be made on Gen. Howes army this Campaign, the high hopes they have raised, and the numberless lies they have told will disgrace and ruin them with the whole world.

I have the pleasure to assure you the train is so la[id] [1] that we have the fairest prospect of being soon suppli[ed,] [1] and copiously too, with military stores of all kind[s] [1] and with clothing fit for the soldiers. Immediately to be sure we are much pres ed for want of the latter but if we can brush through this crisis, we shall be secure. The French court has given us so many unequivocal proofs of their friendship, that I can entertain no doubt of their full exertions in our favor, and as little, that a war between them and G. B. is not far distant.

I sincerely wish you health sir, and that you may be happy in the success you are so eminently entitled to. I am with, with perfect esteem, dear Sir your most affectionate and obedient Servant.

[1] Ms. torn.

THE LETTERS OF RICHARD HENRY LEE

TO THOMAS JEFFERSON[1]

DEAR SIR, PHILADELPHIA 3ᵈ Novʳ 1776

As I have received no answer to the letter I wrote you by the Express from Congress, I conclude it has miscarried. I heard with much regret that you had declined both the voyage, and your seat in Congress. No Man feels more deeply than I do, the love of, and the loss of, private enjoyments; but let attention to these be universal, and we are gone, beyond redemption lost in the deep perdition of slavery. By every account from Lake Champlain whe [we] had reason to think ourselves in no danger on that water for this Campaign. Nor did Gen. Arnold seem to apprehend any until he was defeated by an enemy four times as strong as himself. This officer, fiery, hot, and impetuous, but without discretion, never thought of informing himself how the enemy went on, and he had no idea of retiring, when he saw them coming, tho so much superior to his force. Since his defeat our people evacuated Crown point, and joined their whole strength at Ticonderoga. We do not hear the enemy have thought proper to visit them there, and the Season must now stop operations on the Lake. on the borders of the Sound it has been a war of skirmishes, in which I think we have gained 5 or 6. Never was a Ship more mauled than a Frigate that lately attempted Fort Washington, she had 26 eighteen pounders thro her and most of the guns double shotted. At the same time an attack on the same place by land was repelled, but the day following the enemy gained an eminence from our people near the white

[1] A. L. S. Library of Congress, Jefferson Correspondence, Letters to Jefferson, Ser. 2, Vol. 51, No. 13. Addressed to him at Williamsburg, and franked by Lee.

222

plains, on the sound, about 10 miles above Kings bridge. The loss on our part in killed, wounded, and Missing, between 3 & 400, the enemies loss considerable but numbers not fixt — Our troops fought well and retired in order before a much superior force. This was McDougals brigade consisting of York, Maryland, & I believe some Eastern Troops. In a skirmish the next day We learn the enemy were defeated. By London papers middle of August it seems quite probable that the quarrel between Spain & Portugal with the manœuvres of the Russian fleet, will produce events in Europe of great importance to our cause.

I have been informed that very malignant and very scandalous hints and innuendo's concerning me have been uttered in the house. From the justice of the House I should expect they would not suffer the character of an absent person (and one in their service) to be reviled by any slander[ous] [1] tongue whatever — When I am present, I shall be perfectly satisfied with the justice I am able to do myself. From your candor Sir, and knowledge of my political movememts, I hope such mistatings as may happen in your presence will be rectified.

Among the various difficulties that press our Country, I know of none greater than the want of Ships and Seamen — Perhaps a good basis for remedying the latter might be an alteration of the Act of Assembly for binding out Orphan & poor Children, and direct that, for some time at least, the whole of such children should be bound to the Sea. Without safe Ports to build ships in, and give protection to foreign Vessels, our trade must long languish. Would it not we proper therefore, to make Portsmouth and Norfolk immediately as strong as Cannon can render them, by adding to the guns already there as many from York as will answer the pur-

[1] Ms. torn.

po[se] Gen. Stephen tells me that the works he laid out at Portsmouth will put (if properly gunned) that place in a state of security from any Sea force that can come against it. The Cannon are of no use at York, experience proving incontestibly, that Ships will pass any fort or Battery with ease, when favored by wind and tide. The quantity of seasoned timber said to be in the neighborhood of Norfolk would furnish a number of fine Vessels, whether for fighting or for commerce. I think the large Sea gallies that carry such a number of men for war and for the navigation part of the Vessel, are well contrived for the defence of our bay and for raising seamen quickly. I sent our Navy board a draught of the large gallies building here by order of Congress. It seems to me, that for the different purposes of battery and Ships our Country could well employ a thousand Cannon. How very important it is that the Cannon foundery on James river should be pushed on with all possible vigor and attention. I understand Mᵣ Ballantine manages some part of these works, if so, my fears are that very little may be expected. He will talk amazingly, promise most fairly, but do nothing to the purpose. This I fancy has been the case with a variety of that Gentlemans undertakings, but such conduct, in the Cannon business, will ruin us. I am very uneasy, I own, on this account. Let us have Cannon, Small Arms, gunpowder, and industry; we shall be secure — But it is in vain to have good systems of Government, and good laws, if we are exposed to the ravage of the Sword, without means of resisting — This winter will be an age to us if rightly employed. Let us get strong in Vessels, Troops, and proper fortification in proper places. Let us import plenty of military stores, soldiers cloathing, and Sail cloth for tents, shipping &c [?] — I do not think our armed Vessels can be so well employed in any other business as in [making ?] two or three trips to the French & Dutch Islands for these necessaries, carrying Tob? & fine flour to purchase them.

I am, with much esteem, dear Sir, affectionately yours.

P.S. Let every method be essayed to get the valuable old papers that Col? Richard Bland was possessed of.[1]

TO [SAMUEL PURVIANCE ?][2]

DEAR SIR,   PHILADELPHIA 24.[th][3] Nov.[r] 1776

You have imputed to the right cause my not answering your former letter sooner, it was indeed multiplicity of business.

Very long before your recommendation of M.[r] Plunket came to hand, a Capt. Disney had been appointed Capt. of Marines on board the Virginia, upon the recommendation of M.[r] Stone.

The Congress have determined to build in Maryland two Frigates of 36 guns each, and I make no doubt but that one at least of these will be built at Baltimore. I suppose, when the Committee meets on Tuesday next, that directions concerning the building the new ships will issue to the respective States. Not a word has been yet said in Congress touching a quarrel with Portugal, no[r] will any such thing happen, I imagine, unless they should confiscate any of our Vessels.

It will give us much pleasure to hear that Capt.

[1] The ink of the postscript is blacker than that of the body of the letter, but the postscript is signed " R. H. L."

[2] A. L. S. Maryland Historical Society, P. F. No. 8 (1). The letter is addressed on the back to General Stephen at Amboy in New Jersey, and franked by Lee; but lines of erasure have been drawn through this address. A text is printed in Purviance, *Baltimore*, 206.

[3] The "2" originally written has been changed to "4," making " 24.th"

Nicholson is ready for sea, and I think we can furnish him from hence with one such Anchor as you mention. Capt. Biddles frigate Randolph of 32 guns is now completely ready except that she wants Men, which want we hope to remedy when the Vessels, daily expected, arrive. The Virginia & the Randolph cruising together, might bring us in some of the enemies scattering frigates that now go about, very badly manned, injuring our trade extremely. I wish therefore, that every effort were strained to get the Virginia ready. Our enemies army has been pretty busy since they retreated from the White plains — Already they have got possession both of Mount Washington and Fort Lee, and they talk, or the Tories talk for them, strongly of their aiming at this City. I fancy they will find some difficulty, and not a little danger in the accomplishment of this part of their plan.

My compliments, if you please, to the reverend M⸳ Allison, and my other friends in Baltimore.

If the Tories do not mend their manners, be more modest, and less noisy, they will shortly be haled over the coals in such a manner as will make this country too hot to hold them.

I am Sir your most obedient humble Servant.

List of new Ships to be immediately undertaken

N. Hampshire	One Ship of 74	guns	
Massachusetts	1	d⸳	D⸳ & 1 of 36 guns
Pennsylvania	1	d⸳	d⸳ & 1 of 18 d⸳
Maryland	2	d⸳	36 guns each
Virginia	2	d⸳	d⸳ d⸳ d⸳

P.S.[1] Nov⸳ 25 1776. I thank you for your favor of the 22ᵈ with its inclosures, and will answ⸳ your letter

[1] Written on the back of the letter where the fold would cover it. The Ms. is endorsed, " Rᵈ Henry Lee/Nov⸳ 24ᵗʰ 1776 —/ "

226

by next post, not being able now to do it wth proper effect — I know we want Vessels both on Charter & to purchase in Virg^{a} & Maryland — But more of this hereafter — Gen. Howe seems intent on this City —

TO PATRICK HENRY [1]

DEAR SIR,   PHILADELPHIA 3rd Dec., 1776

The present moment is critical in the American war. The enemy have taken vigorous advantage of the space between the old and the new enlistments, and have rushed like a torrent through the Jersies, our little army of no more than 5,000 men under the command of Genl. Washington being compelled to retreat rapidly before them. The object is this city, and they were on sunday last at Brunswick, about 60 miles off in the Jersies. The Associators are at length alarmed and turning out to reinforce the General, but they move rather slower than the important stake demands. We hear that Gen. Lee has crossed North river and is following quickly after the enemy, but we are not sure, that his numbers are sufficient for any thing decisive. However, if the people here have any title to the freedom they claim, Mr. Howe will not be gratified with the possession of this city. And if he gained 20 such Cities, still he would be short of gaining the point meditated over America. You remember, Sir, we told them from the beginning that we looked on our Cities and Sea Coasts as devoted to destruction, but that ample resources were still left for a numerous, brave, and free people to be content with.

Our latest accounts from the French W. Indies tell

---

[1] From the text printed in William Wirt Henry, *Patrick Henry,* III. 31.

us that war between G. B. and France and Spain is inevitable, and must be immediate.

I hope our winter councils will be every where devoted solely to the purpose of carrying on a vigorous, active, and early campaign. For this purpose the recruiting officers in all quarters should be often called upon by the respective governments to know how they go on, and to urge them to quick and effectual execution of the business. Every thing, my dear Sir, depends upon the new levies being early ready. Col. Charles Harrison leaves this place to-day with 250,000 dollars under his care for the use of our forces in Virginia, and for paying the bounties. Your recommendation of this Gentleman, seconded by his real merit, has procured him the command of a regiment of artillery, to be raised in Virginia, Congress having resolved to keep the artillery and engineer's departments under immediate continental inspection. The other day we dispatched for the head of Elk to the care of Mr. Hollingsworth there, the arms taken from our soldiers here that better might be put in their hands. They are between 7 & 8 hundred in number, and may be had from thence when you are pleased to receive them. With some repair they will do tolerably for the new levies.

I am extremely pleased to hear that you have recovered your health, may it long continue good.

I am with great regard, dear Sir,
Your most affectionate and obedient.

Business and alarm press so constantly that we have scarce one moment to spare.

His Excellency, PATRICK HENRY, JR.

THE LETTERS OF RICHARD HENRY LEE

TO PATRICK HENRY [1]

BALTIMORE, December 18th, 1776.

The movements of the enemy's army in the Jerseys, by which the neighborhood of Philadelphia had become the seat of war, determined Congress to adjourn from thence to this town, where publick business will be entered on the 20 instant, unless a sufficient number of members should be assembled to begin sooner. At this place the publick business can be conducted with more deliberation and undisturbed attention, than could be the case in a city subject to perpetual alarm, and that had necessarily been made a place of arms. The propriety of this measure was strongly enforced by the continental Generals Putnam and Mifflin, who commanded in Philadelphia, and who gave it as their opinion, that, although they did not consider the town as liable to fall into the enemy's hands but by surprise, yet that possibility rendered it improper for Congress to continue there.

So long as the American Army kept together the enemy's progress was extremely limited, but they knew and seized the oportunity of coming forward, which was occasioned by the greater part of the army dispersing in consequence of short enlistments; and this indeed was a plan early founded on hopes of accommodation, and for the greater ease of the people.

When a new Army is assembled, the enemy must again narrow their bounds, and this demonstrates the necessity of every State exerting every means to bring the new levies into the field with all possible expedition.

[1] From the text printed in William Wirt Henry, *Patrick Henry*, III. 33.

It is the only sure means of placing America on the ground where every good man would wish to see it.

The British army is at present stationed along the Delaware from above Trenton, on the Jersey side, to Burlington, about 20 miles above Philadelphia. General Washington, with near 6000 men, is on the river side, opposite to Trenton; and the gondolas, with other armed vessels, are stationed from Philadelphia to Trenton, to prevent the passage of the Delaware. General Lee, with about 5000 men, remains on the enemy's rear, a little to the westward of their line of march through the Jerseys.

In this State, if the country associators of Pennsylvania, and from this neighborhood, reinforce the General with a few thousands, so as to enable him to press the enemy's front, it may turn out a happy circumstance that they have been encouraged to leave their ships so far behind.

We have good reason to expect a general war in Europe soon, and we have such proof of the friendship of France, as to leave little doubt of the willingness of that country to assist us.

The enclosed handbill will sufficiently instruct the Americans what treatment they are to expect from the cruel disturbers of their peace, and evince the necessity of the most speedy and manly exertions to drive these foes of the human race from this continent.

I am, &c.

His Excellency PATRICK HENRY, JR.

[COMMITTEE OF SECRET CORRESPONDENCE TO COMMISSIONERS IN FRANCE][1]

[B. FRANKLIN, S. DEANE, ARTHUR LEE]

HONORABLE GENTLEMEN,   BALTIMORE Dec.ʳ 21ˢᵗ 1776

After expressing our hopes that this will find you all three safely fixed at Paris, we proceed with pleasure to acknowledge the receipt of M.ʳ Deanes letter of the first of October — When we reflect on the character and views of the Court of London, it ceases to be a wonder that ₐ the British Ambassador and every other British
                    -will- employ every means
Agent, should -leave nothing- ₐ that tended to prevent -every- European powers, but France more especially, from giving America aid in this war. Prospects of
                it is
Accommodation, -they- well known, would effectually prevent foreign interference, and therefore, without one serious design of accommodating on any principles
            the
of but ₐ absolute submission -on the part- of America, the delusive idea hath been industriously suggested on. both sides the water, that under cover of this dividing
                prospect
and aid withholding -view- the vast British force sent. to America might have the fairest chance of succeeding.
And
This policy hath in fact done considerable injury to the United States as we shall presently shew by a just detail of this -present- Campaign, for it is not yet

[1] A. dr. L. by Richard Henry Lee. American Philosophical Society, Lee Papers, I. 263, 264, 260-262, No. 76. A text, with changes, from the clerical draft in the Department of State, signed by Harrison, Lee, Witherspoon, and Hooper, is in Wharton, *Diplomatic Correspondence*, II. 226. In this letter, and in like important drafts of public letters, insertions and erasures are retained in print as written by Lee.

ended. ~~Views of Accommodation~~ You know Gentlemen that at the moment a potent land and marine force was preparing to be sent here, an Act was passed ~~to~~ for appointing Commissioners whom too many ~~f~~ expected were to give peace to America — As therefore the war might be ~~sho~~ soon concluded, so ~~th~~ ^{were} our Military arrangements ~~were~~ accommodated, and ~~the last springs~~ the Troops ~~engaged~~ taken into service the last Spring, consisting of regular Corps and bodies of Militia, were ~~all~~ all engaged for short periods. With these the Campaign began in various parts of N. America — ~~In Canada, where distance, food, and water~~ [* * *][1] against Dr. Franklin is so well acquainted with the progress of the War in Canada previous to his departure, that we need only observe ~~that with conclusion~~ the Campaign has ended as favorably for us in that quarter as we could reasonably expect. ~~The very great superiority of Water force with which Gen. Carleton at length appeared on lake Champlain having given him a victory over our small fleet, occasioned the General Gates~~ ~~to collect all his force at Ticonderoga where having strongly posted himself — The enemy having — Generals Carleton & Burgoyne with.~~ The enemy having been able to pierce no further than Crown Point, ~~where,~~ after a short stay, and reconnoitrering Gen Gates's Army at Ticonderoga ~~they~~ thought proper to ~~return to Cro~~ recross the Lake and leave us in quiet possession ~~of~~ of those passes. ~~The~~ General ~~having left~~ Gates having left a proper force at Ticonderoga & on the communication retired with the rest of his Troops — New York & its neighborhood, not being defencible _∧ ^{by an army singly} against a strong land and sea force acting in conjunc-

[1] Words erased illegible.

tion, was of necessity yielded to the enemy after some contest, General Washington retiring until the situation of the Country above Kings bridge no longer enabled the enemy to receive aid from their Ships. Gen. Howe being stopt here, and Gen Carleton at Crown Point effectually disappointed the great object of joining the two Armies. The latter as we have said returning to Canada, and the ~~latter,~~ ^former^ ~~finding its [enemies?] about~~ retreating from the White plains towards N. York — ~~Their Army halted~~ gave us a favorable prospect of seeing a happy end put to this dangerous Campaign — However, ma^{n}y causes have concurred in producing an unlucky reverse of fortune. The nature of the Country, the uncommon fineness of weather even to this day, and above all, ^the^ short inlistmentments, which gave the Soldiery an[1] opportunity of going home, tired as they were with the operations of an acctive summer. ~~have conspired to produce the consequences that h[ave] followed~~. When Gen. Howe retreated from the White plains he halted his whole Army on the N. river between Dobbs ferry & Kings bridge where he remained for some time. Having effected so little of the great business that brought him here, and the season allowing time for it, most men were of opinion that the next attempt would be to get possession of Philadelphia, by a march thro the Jersies whilst a fleet should be sent up the Delaware to facilitate the enterprise. To guard against such a man[œ]²uvre, Gen. Washington crossed the N. River with all the Batallions that had been raised to the westward of it, leaving Gen. Lee with the Eastern Troops to guard the pass of the Highlands on Hudson river — In this situation ~~our~~ of things, Mr Howe made a sudden attack on Fort Washing-

[1] An illegible letter is erased.   ² Blotted.

ton with the greater part of his Army, and carried it with a considerable loss — Here he made near 3000 of our men prisoners — By this event, ~~the~~ it became unnecessary longer to hold Fort Lee, or Fort Constitution as it was

formerly called, which ~~was~~ ^{is} on the west side of N. River & nearly opposite to Fort Washington. It had been therefore determined to abandon Fort Lee, ~~which~~ but before the Stores could be all removed, the enemy came suddenly upon it, and the Garrison retreated, ~~with~~ leaving some of their baggage & stores behind. About this time Gen. Howe became possessed of a letter (by the Agency of some wicked person who contrived to get it from the Express) ~~and~~ written by Gener Washington to the Board of War, in which he had given an exact account of when the time of service of all our ~~def~~ Batallions would expire & his apprehention that ~~they~~ Men w^d not ~~continue~~ reenlist with¦ first going home to see their families & friends. Possessed of this intelligence, the ~~ti~~[?] opportunity was carefully watched, and a vigorous impression actually made at the very crisis when our Army

_{in the Jersies}
ᴀ was reduced to 3000 men by the ~~causes~~ retiring of numbers, and the sickness: of others, and before Militia could in this extensive Country be brought up to supply their places.

The enemy marched rapidly in thro the Jersies whilst our feebly Army was obliged to retreat from Post to Post until it crossed the Delaware at Trenton, where about 2,500 militia from Philadelphia joined the General. Since Gen. Howes arrival on the borders of Delaware, various manœuvres and stratagems have been

^{over}
practiced to effect a passage ~~of~~, the river but they have hitherto proved abortive. Gen. Washingtons ~~Troops~~ small Army is placed along the West side of Delaware

from ^above ^ Coryells ferry to within 14 miles of Philadelphia, which ~~with~~ ~~and~~ the Gondolas, with one frigate, and other armed Vessels, in the river above the Cheveaux de Frize, cover the passage of ~~the river.~~ ^it ~~This~~ Gen. Lee (,who had crossed the N. River with as many of the Eastern troops as could be spared from the defence of the Highlands, ~~and who had arriv~~ either to join Gen Washington, or to act on the Enemies rear as occasions might point out), was ^the other day ^ unfortunately surprised and made prisoner by a party of 70 light horse, who ~~surroun~~ found him in a house a few miles in the rear of his Army with his domesticks only. This loss tho great, will ~~be~~ in some degree be repaired for the present by Gen Gates, who we understand has joined the Army commanded by Gen. Lee and who we have reason to think has by this time effected a junction of. his force with that of Gen. Washington. As the Militia are now marching from various quarters to reenforce the General, if the enemy do not quickly accomplish their ~~plan~~ wishes of possessing Philadelphia, we hope not only to save that City, but to see Gen Howe ~~in his turn~~ obliged to ~~go back thro the Jerseys as fast as he~~ ~~return~~ retreat as fast as he advanced thro the Jersies. Gen. Clinton with a fleet in which 'tis said he carried 8000 men has gone ^from N. York ^ thro the Sound, some suppose for Rhode Island, but his destination, or its consequence we yet have no certainty of. Thus Gentlemen we have given you a true detail of the progress and present state of our affairs, which, altho not in so good as posture as they were two months ago, are by no means in so bad a way as the Emissaries

235

of the court of London will undoubtedly ~~endeavor persuade~~[?] represent them. ~~to have believed.~~ If the great ~~for~~ land & sea force with which we have been attacked, ~~and the~~ be compared with the feeble state in which ~~we have~~ the com- mencement of this war found us ~~with~~ in respect to Military Stores of all kinds, Soldiers cloathing, Navy, and regular force, the wonder will rather be that our enemies have made so little progress, not that they have made so much. All views of accommodation with G. B but on principles of peace as independent States, ~~[?]~~ & in a manner perfectly consistent with the Treaties our Com- missioners may make with foreign States, being ~~now~~ totally at an end, ~~Congress have~~ since the declaration of in- dependence and the embas[sy][1] to the Court of France, Congress have directed ~~th~~ the raising of[2] Infantry with Cavalry some ~~horse~~ and we hear the levies are going on well in the different States. Until they are collected, the Militia must curb the enemies progress. The very considerable force that G. B has already in N. A. the possibility of recruiting it here within their own Quarters, by force and fraud together, added to the reenforcements that may be sent from ~~G~~ Europe, and the difficulty of finding funds in the present depressed state of Ameri- can commerce, all conspire to prove incontestibly that if the France ~~mean~~ desires t[o]t[a]l[3] to preclude ~~all~~ possi-

---

[1] Ms. torn.
[2] Ms. torn. The text in Wharton has "ninety-four battalions."
[3] Illegible letters, " o " and " a "

bility of N. A. being ever reunited with Great Britain,
possess
~~and thereby to take~~[?] [* * *]¹ ~~and commercial~~
~~advantages that will be derived from~~ this² is the³
the
favorable moment for establishing ~~her~~ ₍ glory, strength
greatness of ~~France~~ the former kingdom
and comme[rcial]³ ~~advantages~~ ₍ by ~~a decisive~~ [* * *]₍
[* * * * * *]⁴ the ruin of her antient R[ival]³   A de-
the Court of Versailles,
cided part now taken by ~~France~~, and a vigorous entry
[into?]³ the War in Union with N. A, would with
ease sacrifice the fle[et]³ and Army of G. B, at this
And
time chiefly collected about N. York —₍ the inevitable
consequence would be the quick reduction of the
W. India
British Islands, already bared of all defence by the
removal of their troops to this Continent.
~~These reasons view we have now given you~~ For the
reasons here assigned Gentlemen, you will readily dis-
to
the security of American independence ₍ & with ~~Spain~~
cern ~~the~~ how all important it is to ₍ urge France or
Spain⁵ into the War   As soon as may be, and if it be possible, ~~to~~ speedily to procure from the former the number
of line of battle ships you were desired in your instruction to obtain for us, the speedy arrival of of which
here, in the present state of things, might decide the
contest at one stroke.

We shall pay ~~a~~ proper attention to what Mr. Deane
writes about Dr. Williamson & Mr. Hopkins, and we
think the ill treatment this Country and Mr. Deane have
received from these men, strongly suggest the necessity

---

¹ Ms. torn.   ² Written over "now."
³ Ms. torn.   ⁴ Erased and illegible.
⁵ Wharton has no reference to Spain.

of invincible reserve with persons coming to France as Americans and friends to America whom the most irref- ragable proofs have not removed all doubt about. The British recall of their Mediterranean Passes is an Object of ~~much~~ great consequence, and may require much interces- sion with the Court of France to get ~~this matter~~ settled on the best footing for the security of American Commerce. But this subject has been already touched in your instruc- tions on the 6th Articticle of the Treaty proposed to be made with France. As ~~every~~ all affairs relative to Commerce ~~and importation~~ & ~~and~~ remittan[ce][1] ˄ pass thro another department, we beg leave to refer you to the Secret Committee and Mr Thomas Morris their Agent in France for every informa- tion on these subjects. As the neighborhood of Phila- delphia had by the enemies movements become the seat of war, it was judged ~~necessary~~ proper that Congress should ad- journ to this Town where the public business may be attended to with ~~that~~ the undisturbed deliberation that its importance demands. The Congress was accordingly opened here on the 20th instant. As it is more than probable that the conference with Lord Howe on Staten Island may be misrepresented to the injury of these States, we do ourselves the pleasure to inclose you an authenticated account of that whole business, which the possibility of Doc^{tr} Franklins not arriving renders proper. This step was taken to unmask his Lordship, and evince to the world that he did not possess powers, which for the purposes of delusion and division had been suggested. Mr Deanes proposition of Loan is accepted by Congress and they have desired 2 millions sterling

[1] End of line, effaced.

to be obtained if possible. The necessity of keeping up the credit of our paper currency, and the variety of important uses that[1] may be made of this money have induced congress to go so far as [6 per][2] cent, but this interest is heavy, and it is hoped you may be [able][2] to do the business on much easier terms. The resolves of Congress [on thi][2]s subject are enclosed, and your earliest attention to them is [desire][2]d that we may know soon as possible of this application. Another resolve inclosed will shew you that Congress approve of armed Vessels being fitted out by you on Continental account provided the Court of France dislike not the measure, and blank commissions for this purpose will be sent you by the next opportunity. Private Ships of War, or Privateers, cannot be admitted where you are, because the Securities necessary in such cases, to prevent irregular practices, cannot be given by the Owners & Commanders of such Privateers. Another resolve of Congress which we have the honor to inclose you, directs the conduct to be pursued with regard to Portugal. We have nothing further to add at present, but to request that you will omit no good opportunity of informing us how you ~~proceed~~ ^{succ} in your mission, what events take place in Europe by which these States may be affected, and that you contrive us in regular succession some of the best London, French, & Dutch newspapers, with any valuable political publications that may concern North America

We have the honor to be with great respect and esteem &c.

P.S. The American captures of British Vessels at Sea have not been less numerous or less valuable than

---

[1] Ms. torn.
[2] Ms. torn. Supplied from the text in Wharton.,

before Doctor Franklin left us. The value of these Captures has been estimated at two millions.

[CIRCULAR LETTER TO THE STATES][1]

SIR,
[Dec 29 1776]

Ever attentive to the ~~preservation and safety~~ of ~~Social~~
security   civil

Congress w

liberty ~~we should~~ not have consented to the resting of
such powers in the military department ~~of~~ as those
which the inclosed resolves convey to the ᴧ Continental
~~trust~~ * * * [?]

Commander in Chief, if the situation of ~~our~~ ᴧ affairs
public

did not ᴧ require ~~that decision & vigor~~ which distance
at this Crisis   a decision & vigor

and numbers deny to ~~numerous~~ Assemblies far removed from each other and from the immediate seat
of war. The strength & progress of the enemy joined
to prospects of considerable reenforcement have rendered it not only necessary that the American force
should be augmented beyond what Congress had be-
designed

fore contemplated, but that it should be brought into
the field with ~~all~~ all possible expedition. These considerations therefore ~~influence that Body~~ to request in
induce Congress

the most earnest manner that the fullest influence of
your State may be exerted to aid such levies as the General ~~may~~ direct in consequence of the powers now given
shall

[1] A. dr. L. American Philosophical Society, Lee Papers, I. 241,
No. 69. Lee, Wilson, and Adams were the committee appointed by
Congress, December 28, to prepare a letter to the States explaining the
reasons why Congress enlarged Washington's powers. The draft is in
the autograph of Richard Henry Lee.

and
him, ~~but~~ that your quota of Batallions formerly fixt
may be^ completed and ordered to head quarters with
all the dispatch that ~~the preservation of American in-~~
                                              secure
~~dependence can dictate~~ an ardent desire to ~~promote~~ the
public ~~good~~ happiness can dictate.

[COMMITTEE OF SECRET CORRESPONDENCE TO
COMMISSIONERS IN FRANCE][1]

BALTIMORE   December the 30th 1776

HONORABLE GENTL[EM][2]EN —

                    herewith
You will be pleased to receive ~~inclosed~~ copies of our last
letter of the 21st instant, and of its inc[los][2]ures, which
we recommend to your attention.   Since that letter was
written, Gen. Wash^n having been reenforced ~~with~~ by the
troops lately commanded by Gen. Lee, and by some
Corps of Militia, ~~and oth[ers.]~~[2] crossed the Delaware
with 2500 men and attacked a body of the enemy stationed at Trenton, and with the success that you will see
related in the inclosed hand bill.   We hope this blow
will   by
~~may~~ be followed ᴧ ~~with~~ others, that may leave the enemy
not so much to boast of as they some days ago expected,
and we had reason to apprehend —
    Upon mature deliberation of all circumstances, Con-
gress deem the speedy declaration of France, and Euro-

[1] A. dr. L. by Richard Henry Lee. American Philosophical Society, Lee Papers, I. 259, No. 75. A text in Wharton, *Diplomatic
Correspondence*, II 240, from the clerical draft in the Department of
State, has variations and additional matter and is signed by B. Harrison, R. H. Lee, J. Witherspoon, and W. Hooper.
[2] Ms. torn.

pean assistance so indispensably necessary to secure the independence of these States, that they have authorized you to make such tenders to France and Spain as they hope will prevent any longer ~~of~~ delay of an event that ~~they~~ is judged [1] so essential to the well being of N. America. Your wisdom we know will direct you to make such use of these powers as will procure the thing ~~so much~~ desired on terms as much short of the concessions now offered as possible, but [* * *][2] no advantages of this kind are

proposed   ~~and~~ contemplated
~~desired~~ to be ~~contemplated~~ at the risk of a delay that

may
∧ prove dangerous to the end in view. It must be very obvious to the Court of France, that if G. B. should succeed in her design of subjugating these States, that their inhabitants now well trained to the use of Arms, might be compelled ~~aga~~ to become instruments for making an conquest of the French possessions in the West Indies;

and
which would be a sad reverse of that security, ∧ commercial benefit that would result to France from the Independen of N. America. ~~We observe that Mr Deane In the~~ By some accident, in removing the papers from Phil.ª to this place, the Secretary of Congress has mislaid the additional instruction formerly given you, by which you were

Courts
empowered to negotiate with others ~~powers~~ than France, We think it necessary to mention this to you, least the paper should get into wrong hands, and because we wish to have a copy sent us by the first good opportunity. We observe that Mr Deane sent his dispatches for this committee open to Mr ~~Deane~~ Bingham, but we have a good opinion of that Gentleman, yet we think him rather too young to be made acquainted with the business passing between you and us, and therefore wish this may not

[1] Substituted for an illegible word erased.   [2] Erased, illegible.

be done in cases of much importance. The next opportunity will bring you the determination of Congress concerning the persons that are to be sent to the Courts of Vienna, Prussia, Spain & the Grand Duke of Tuscany. In the mean time it is hoped that thro the medium of the Ambassadors from those Courts to that of France, you may be able to procure their friendly mediation for the purposes proposed by Congress. One of our Continental ˄ Vessels of 14 Guns lately met with a Kings

Armed

Sloop of War of 12 guns and after a smart engagement the Sloop was brought into the Delaware — In our last we say the ~~number of~~ prisoners made by the Enemy at Fort Washington were near 3000, but the number is fixt at 2600, and the number of West Indiamen taken by our Cruisers ~~from that~~ [army ?] amounts to 256 — Wishing you health & success, we remain Honorable Gentlemen &c.

[COMMITTEE OF SECRET CORRESPONDENCE TO COMMISSIONERS IN FRANCE] [1]

BENJ HARRISON
RICHARD HENRY LEE

[B. FRANKLIN
'S. DEANE
A. LEE]

GENTLEMEN   BALTIMORE 9ᵗʰ January 1777

Captain Hammond [2] having been detained longer than we expected, furnishes us with an opportunity of giving you ˄ the information we have since ˄ received from the Army, — thro a Committee of Congress left at Phila-

our last

---

[1] A. L. S. by Richard Henry Lee. American Philosophical Society, Franklin Papers, Letters to Franklin. Benj. Harrison also signs in autograph. The letter is printed in Hale, *Franklin in France*, I. 97.

[2] Captain Hammond was ordered, January 2, to carry dispatches to France in the *Jenifer*.

delphia; for we have yet had no regular accounts from General Washington.

On the 2ᵈ instant, General Washington having received information that the enemy were on their march to attack him at Trenton, ordered two brigades of militia to advance and annoy them on the road leading from Princeton to Trenton, who falling in with the enemy about 3 miles from the latter place, engaged them, but being overpowered by numbers, made a retreating fight until they joined the main body who were drawn up on the heights west of a bridge that divides the village of Trenton nearly in two parts. The enemy attempting to force the bridge were repulsed with loss by a body of men with artillery placed there to receive them. In the mean time some batteries being opened on the heights soon drove the enemy from that part of the Town possessed by them. Thus the affair ended for that evening. But General Washington having received intelligence that Gen. Howe was in person coming up to join his army with a strong reenforcement, directing fires to be made ˄ on the heights to deceive the enemy, decampt at midnight and made a forced march in order to meet Mʳ Howe and give him battle before he joined his main body. About 3 miles short of Prince Town, the Van of our Army fell in with 600 British Infantry strongly posted behind a fence, and upon a hill, with artillery. They were attacked, & after a smart engagement, routed, having lost 280 killed and taken prisoners; among whom, were one Colonel, one Major, several Captains and Subalterns were slain, and about 20 Officers made prison[ers.] The fugitives were pursued thro Princeton where our Army halted a whi[le.] In this affair 6 pieces of Artillery with abundance of baggage fell into our hands. At Princeton, it was learnt that Gen. Howe was not with this party, but that he remained at Brunswick with 3 or 4 thousand men. There being a considerable force in the rear, and our men greatly fatigued with their march, and their baggage chiefly behind (it having been sent to Burlington) the General proceeded to Sommerset Court house that evening, a little to the Westward of the road leading to Brunswick, and about 7 or 9 miles from that place. Here we understand he expected to be joined by a body of 1500 or 2000 fresh troops, and that his intention was to attack M! Howe in Brunswick. On friday morning, when the enemy at Trenton missed our army they returned toward Princeton, but it seems, they left 3000 Hessians behind them, who following afterwards, were so fatigued with travel and want of food, that numbers were left on the road, and were straggling about the country in threes and fours. Many were taken by the Country people and brought in prisoners, many came to Trenton and surrendered themselves. The militia of Jersey [scouring?] generally, and it was thought few of these Hessians would get back again. This is the present state of our information, and we hourly expect a well authenticated account of the whole, and of much greater successes. We shall endeavor to give you the speediest account of what shall further come with to our knowledge from good authority. The above relation is taken from a Gentleman who was in the action, and who the Committee write us, is a person of sense and honor. The General has been too much engaged to write, & we suppose waits the final issue.

We most earnestly wish you success in your negotiation, and are with perfect esteem, honorable Gentlemen, your most obedient and very humble Servants.

P.S. In the engagement near Princeton we lost 15 privates one Colonel and Brigadier Gen Mercer a very good Officer and a worthy Gentleman — In secret Committee.

THE LETTERS OF RICHARD HENRY LEE

TO THE GOVERNOR OF VIRGINIA [1]
(PATRICK HENRY)

DEAR SIR, BALTIMORE, 9th January, 1777.

I have no doubt but that M! President inclosed you with his last dispatches the printed account of General Washington's success at Trenton. The number of Hessian prisoners there made do not fall much short of 1100. Since that event we have had no regular account from the army, but from a committee of Congress at Philadelphia we have the accounts brought into Philadelphia by a number of persons, and believed there, in substance as follows: The British forces stationed at Brunswick, Trenton, and other places in New Jersey, hearing of the success at Trenton, collected and marched towards that place to attack our army, now strengthened by the junction of all its detachments, and by several corps of Militia. Gen. Washington ordered two Brigades to advance on the Princeton road and interrupt the enemies march. About 3 miles from Trenton they met the enemy, and being attacked by a much superior force, were compelled to retreat, which they did slowly, keeping up a retreating engagement until they joined the main body, drawn up on a high ground on this side of a bridge that divides the village of Trenton nearly in two parts. The enemy attempting to force the bridge were received by Gen. Mifflin with the Philadelphia malitia and a number of Field pieces, which drove them back with great loss, and some batteries being now opened on the heights commanding the enemies' part of the town, they were soon obliged to quit it with loss. The armies still continued posted opposite each other until

---

[1] From the text printed in William Wirt Henry, *Patrick Henry*, III. 36.

midnight, when Gen. Washington (having reced. certain intelligence that Gen. Howe was on his march in person with a large reinforcement to join his army) having previously directed large fires to be made to deceive the enemy, decampt, made a forced march that night

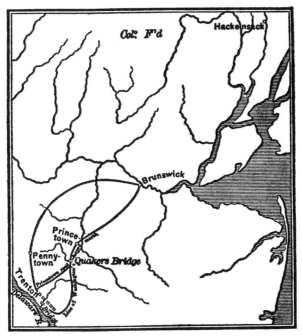

"Note. — For the sake of clearness Lee's diagram has been supplemented by a map of the surrounding country." See William Wirt Henry, *Patrick Henry*, III. 38.

to meet Gen. Howe, met with him at a place called Quakers bridge, gave him battle, and routed his troops, taking from 6 to 800 prisoners. Pursuing the fugitives he entered Princeton, where a number of officers, 6 or 7 field pieces, and the 40th regiment were taken. The British army that remained at Trenton knew nothing of General Washington's designs until they heard the firing next morning, and then, having possessed themselves of the heights for some time, they retreated toward Brunswick along the Pennytown road, a circuitous western way, leaving the place of engagement on the right hand a good distance. This extraordinary motion, denotes panic, because their direct route to the scene of action was along the road to Princetown, as thus [1]

The account goes on that our army was pursuing from Princeton to Brunswick, where the enemy had some large stores kept. We know that Gen. Heath with above 3000 men is about Hackingsack, and Col. Ford with 1500 Jersey militia is before him in the way to Trenton. This is the posture we understand things to be in, and we wait in hourly expectation of receiving authentic intelligence of the total rout of the enemies' army in Jersey, and their disgraceful evacuation of that state. Thus we bid fair to derive great advantage from what we once apprehended would injure us extremely, the dispersion of our army. The enemy knowing we had no army, and trusting to their Tory intelligence that no forces could be collected, had divided their troops in such a manner as to expose them to ruin from militia only, or chiefly so; for excepting about 1500 Eastern troops, the same number of Virginians, about 200 of Smallwood's Marylanders and a broken Pennsylvania regiment, the rest of Gen. Washington's army is militia. Another valuable consequence will result from this success, it will prove to our enemies that America, without an army, is formidable in its militia. For sudden exertions the militia certainly do well, but they cannot bear the continued discipline of Camps and campaigns. This certainly makes it of the last importance that our regular army should be assembled with all possible dispatch,

[1] Lee's diagram is here inserted, see map given on the preceding page.

and such you will find to be the sense of congress by their requests to the several states for this purpose. Our wicked enemy to freedom and all its friends are actually preparing to try Gen. Lee by a special court martial. For it seems that in order to be aided by a court martial that gentleman's resignation of his commission was not accepted. We have sent to remonstrate with Mr. Howe on this subject, to demand Gen. Lee's enlargement on his parole, and to assure that the same infliction exactly that is applied to Gen. Lee shall directly be applied to 5 Hessian Field officers and Col. Campbell, their favorite engineer, who shall be reserved for the special purpose. We have offered 6 Hessian field officers in exchange for Gen. Lee.

I heartily wish you the compliments of the season, and am with great esteem, dear Sir, your most affectionate and obedient servant.

His Excellency PATRICK HENRY, Esq. *Governor of Virginia.*

Be pleased to let the scheme of lottery be published in our papers, that people may be prepared against the Tickets are sent.

[MARINE COMMITTEE TO MARINE AGENTS IN MARYLAND][1]

JOHN HANCOCK	SAMUEL PURVIANCE
RICHARD HENRY LEE	[STEPHEN STEWART]
W.* WHIPPLE	

IN MARINE COMMITTEE 15ᵗʰ January 1777

Ordered that Messʳˢ Purveyance & Stewart the Continental Marine Agents in the State of Maryland be directed to proceed immediately to provide Timbe[r] for building the two thirty six gun Frigates ordered to

[1] A. L. S. by Richard Henry Lee with autograph signatures of Hancock and Whipple. Lenox Library, Emmet, 5763. Addressed by John Hancock to Samuel Purviance at Baltimore.

be built in the said State, and to proceed in other respects to provide materials for the completion of said Frigates. —

The particular Dimensions shall be deliver'd you.

TO PATRICK HENRY.[1]

DEAR SIR,   BALTIMORE, 17th Jany, 1777.

I am favored with yours by Maj. Johnston, and I should certainly have served him to the utmost of my power in Congress, if the appointment you proposed for Maj. Johnston had not now been in another channel. You know Sir, that by resolve of Congress the General is to fill up all vacancies in the Continental troops that shall happen for six months from the date of the resolve. I have recommended it to the Major to get a letter from you and the council, with one from Colonel Harrison, to the General in his favour, and if he is very intent on success, to carry them himself. I think this will not fail to procure him the commission he desires, and in the mean time, the Liutenants and Ensign may be recruiting the company. We have not heard from Gen. Washington since the 5th instant, when he was at Morris Town in West Jersey, about 20 miles from Brunswick where the enemy keep their head quarters. But a Gentleman who arrived here yesterday, and who passed through our army at Morris Town on the 8th, says, the men were in high spirits, that he thinks they were 12,000 strong, that they were under marching orders, and they were supposed to be going towards Elizabeth Town, which is between the main body of the enemy and New York. That Gen. Heath was to join

[1] From the text printed in William Wirt Henry, *Patrick Henry,* III. 40.

them on the 9th with between 2 and 5 thousand men. That the Jersey militia had many skirmishes with the British troops and always beat them. That he met large bodies of militia on march to the Jersies, whence he concluded that the enemy must either quit that state soon, or be exposed to great danger by remaining there. Unluckily our army consists almost entirely of Militia, whose stay is very uncertain, and renders the speedy coming of regular troops absolutely necessary.

I am with very particular regard and esteem dear Sir,
> Your most obedient and most humble Servant.

His Excellency PATRICK HENRY.

TO PATRICK HENRY [1]

DEAR SIR,   BALTIMORE, Jan'y 30, 1777.

'Tis with much pleasure I inform you, that our affairs in the Jersies wear as favorable an aspect as we could possibly expect. And if the militia remain with the General until the recruits get up, I verily believe the business of the campaign will be nearly finished for the winter. Wonderful as it may seem, yet it is a fact, that our great success in Jersey since the 24th of Decr has been obtained by an army chiefly irregular, and much inferiour in number to the regular force of the enemy. And the Army that now so greatly and so ignominiously distress the British force at Brunswick, is inferior in numbers to the one it now confines to the Brunswick hills. The committee of Congress at Philadelphia tell us, a report has come there of an engagement between Gen. Sullivan's detachment of the Army near Brunswick, and a strong detachment of the enemy. The issue

---

[1] From the text printed in William Wirt Henry, *Patrick Henry*, III. 41.

not certainly known, but they say a person immediately from Brunswick relates, that the British light horse came in much confusion from the field of battle to that Town, calling for a reinforcement. We therefore hope hourly for good news from that quarter, nor are we without hopes of a good account from N. York. We know they were in a very defenceless situation lately, and if the motions of Gen. Heath are not too slow, so that reenforcements may come from Rhode Island, or be sent from Jersey for the defence of New York, he will go near to free that city from the Tyrant's Troops. We have no late news from Europe except byway of Hallifax, where the report is, that a war between France and G. Britain is inevitable, and the B. officers there say, "The damn'd Rebels would keep America yet." I hope the rightful owners will keep America, and in despite of all the efforts of Tyranny & its tools.

Farewell dear sir, affectionately yours.

His Excellency PATRICK HENRY.

TO ROBERT MORRIS [1]

BALTIMORE, February 3. 1777.

DEAR SIR,

The impossibility of getting intelligence at present thro' this Bay, has obliged us to send an Express to the Council of Massachusetts, requesting they will immediately dispatch a quick Sailing Vessel with letters to the Commissioners. The only vessel we had sent from hence for this purpose, is now shut up in a small Creek below by the Men of War four of five of which are now in this Bay, as we are informed, & some of them as

[1] South Carolina Historical Society, Laurens Papers, Misc. Docs. 1776–1783. Copy in the autograph of Moses Young, secretary to Henry Laurens.

high as Smiths Point, mouth of Potowmack, they have taken Buchanans ship as she went down. We have reason to suppose that these are the ships that lately block'd up the Delaware, and that they are brought here by the fugitive Guthridge's and the Tories on the Eastern shore of Maryland. The latter are numerous, and we apprehend have informed of a quantity of Provisions preparing these for the Troops which they mean to assist in getting to the Enemy.

We are doing all we can in this slow place to get armed vessels down to obstruct this wicked design. In the mean time would it not be highly proper to send out immediately the Sachem or Race Horse, or both to the Capes of Virginia to notify coming in vessells of their danger, and also to suppress any Tenders that they may have out to intercept Vessels coming in, whilst they think themselves secure from interruption from hence by the large ships covering the passage of the Bay opposite Potowmack.

Captain Isaiah Robinson is as perfectly well acquainted with our Bay that he could in a swift sailing vessel not only give notice to Vessels bound in, but come in himself, suppress their Tenders, and, regardless of the bigger Ships run into a thousand places of protection and security where they cannot molest him, taking care of the Counties of Somerset, Worster and an adjoining Maryland Eastern shore. — If you approve this Plan can it not be immediately executed ? I am inclined to think your Bay is open now, and that it is a good opportunity to push Biddle and the other Vessels out on the business you mention. We shall keep the letters you sent us for France until we can get an opportunity here, when we propose sending out the Lexington

Bradford's Journal of the 29th of January contains a verry accurate account of the late Military Manouvers in the Jersies, it will be well to send three or four copies to the Commissioners and by all means let some go by this Express in the Packets for France.

I am dear Sir with particular Esteem
Your Affectionate & Obedient Serv!

Hon'ble Robert Morris Esquire Member of Congress at Philadelphia.

TO JOHN PAGE [1]

Baltimore—February 4 1777

Dear Sir,

Nothing material having occured since I wrote last in the military way this serves chiefly to inclose you the Tyrants speech, which is a curious craftey piece of business. Curious it is to find a man on so public a situation announcing to the world his utter disregard to the truth. Crafty it may be called, because of the mode taken to prove our good usage. He would have the world conclude that this good usage has been of his shewing & therefore our gratitude great in proceeding as we have done. The Court Logic seems clearly this — The American improvement in Arts & Arms shows they have been well used, it shews I have used them well, and therefore they are wicked in deposing me. Or, in other words, George the second used the Americans well. George the 3ᵈ has abused them extremely. Therefore they are criminal in opposing George 3? The visit paid us by the British ships, and as we hear the number of small craft they have seized in our narrow waters, prove incontestibly the disadvantage we shall forever be exposed to while we are in want of marine force. Had our Gallies been in good order and fit for business, the barges and small craft of the enemy would

[1] A. L. S. Library of Congress, Delaware Mss., II. 1. Copied through the kindness of Mr. W. V. Johnson. The letter is addressed, "To the Honorable John Page esquire at Williamsburg, Va."

never have dared attempt the capture of vessels in our narrow, shallow waters. And I will venture to affirm that if we had 8 or 10 such Gallies as Congress have built in the Delaware to carry 4. 32pounders each, with 10. 6pounders and 100 men. not less than a squadron of line-of-battle ships would venture up our bay.

Yours affectionately.

TO PATRICK HENRY[1]

DEAR SIR,   BALTIMORE, 6ᵗʰ Feby, 1777.

The events of war having not been considerable lately, this is chiefly intended to inclose you the British king's speech to his Parliament, which you will see in the News paper. Skirmishes are daily happening between our troops and the foraging parties of the enemy, in which we seldom fail to beat them and take their forage. Their numbers are this way daily decreasing, and the survivors in great distress for food and feed. The many horses we have taken from them are emaciated extremely. If our new army can be got up in good time I hope we shall deal effectually with these Tyrant Tools. Mr. Page writes us that a Vessel has arrived with you that brings continental soldier's cloaths. I hope that these being put on the backs of your new recruits, will greatly forward the new inlistments. That the troops should expeditiously join the General is a point so clearly necessary, that I am sure you will promote it with all your power.

I am, very affectionately yours.

His Excellency PATRICK HENRY.

[1] From the text printed in William Wirt Henry, *Patrick Henry*, III. 42.

THE LETTERS OF RICHARD HENRY LEE

TO [GENERAL CHARLES LEE] [1]

[Feb. 11, 1777.]

My DEAR FRIEND.

My feelings are not to be described. I would go to every extremity to serve my friend, and the able friend of liberty and Mankind. — But here, my power fails.[2] I have not the smallest idea of personal danger, nor does this affect the present question. Farewell my dear friend, may you be happy as you deserve, and then, the cause of humanity will have nothing to fear for you.

TO [ARTHUR LEE] [3]

BALTIMORE IN MARYL? 17ᵗʰ Feb? 1777

My DEAR SIR,

The papers that go with this, to yourself and the other Commissioners, are so full on the subject of news that it is not very necessary for me to say much on that subject here. There scarcely comes a post but brings us an account of some skirmish in which the enemy get beaten, and driven back (without their forage) within their lines on the hills near Brunswick, where their distress we know is very great. This has been a most fatal winter Campaign to our enemies, and unless some change

[1] A. L. S. American Philosophical Society, Lee Papers, I. 187, No. 55. A date "1776," given in pencil on the Ms., is an error. Endorsed, "Answer to Gen. /Lee's letter/ Feb? 1777." Charles Lee, then a prisoner in New York, had written to Richard Henry Lee urging that Congress send "two or three gentlemen" to communicate with him, under General Howe's promise of safe conduct; but Congress rejected the request and R. H. Lee's friends induced him not to go, as he desired, in his private character. See R. H. Lee, *Memoir of Richard Henry Lee*, I. 180.

[2] "The most distant apprehention to personal danger " is here erased.

[3] A. L. University of Virginia, Lee Papers, No. 36. Endorsed, "R? Henry Lee/Ag? the English/ & for french Connec?/N° 3."

happens in their favor, which cannot be seen at present, it bids fair to be abundantly more so yet. Upon the whole, notwithstanding the contemptible Ministerial boasts in their Gazettes, and in Parliament, the great force they sent here has cut a most pitiful figure indeed. In humanity they figure still worse than they do in arms. Their ravages in the Jersies, until they were checked and driven back, beggars all descriptions. Rapes, murders, and devastation mark their steps in such a manner as would have disgraced the Savages of the Wilderness. The old English esteem for valor seems quite done away, and in several instances where young Americans displaid heroic spirit, and happened to fall into their power, they have butchered them in cold blood in a most cruel and barbarous manner. They have been so frequently shamless in this way after remonstrance has been in vain made to Gen. Howe, that the patience of our Soldiery is exhausted, and it appears as if no more prisoners will be taken, until M: Howe & his people learn the practice of humanity. I have received two letters from [* * * * * * * *]¹. But he thinks strongly in favor of Great Britain.— Was it not the most unrelenting and cruel persecution of us that forced us from her, and are we not compelled upon the clearest principles of self preservation to seek from Strangers what our kindred denied us? Must a great Continent be buried in ruin because the people of England cannot rouse from a lethargy which suffers the most abandoned of Men to trample upon the rights of human nature? It is decreed above, and we are parted forever. Every friendly American Nerve will now be strained to procure the active interference of France, by which, under God, the liberty of North America must be secured. Mr. Lee's Stewart at Green Spring (Fauntleroy) has behaved so ill during our absence, that

¹ Two lines are here erased and illegible.

I have removed him, and got a manager from Hanover (,a John Ellis) who I believe will do well. I purchased a quantity of Oznaburgs from Philadelphia for the people this winter, and they make their own Woolen and Cotton Stuffs. I hope the time will shortly come, when we may correspond more openly, fully, and freely; in the meantime, cannot you send me by return of Captain Johnson two pounds of the best Jesuit Bark prepared? You know how necessary that medicine is for me, and I know that it is not to be had here on any terms at present. Let Mr. Lee know as much of this letter as imports him — The Congress have determined to return to Philadelphia in eight days from this time. We shall have a number of exceeding fine Frigates at Sea very soon, from 24 to 36 guns

Farewell & send me a long letter by return of this Vessel —

I am exceedingly uneasy about my poor Boys, & beg of you to get them to me in the quickest and safest manner.

[COMMITTEE OF SECRET CORRESPONDENCE TO COMMISSIONERS IN FRANCE][1]

BALTIMORE. [February 17, 1777.]

HONORABLE GENTLEMEN —

We have the honor to enclose you a resolve of Congress that is of great importance to the public service, which has suffered considerably the last fall, and during this winter, by the insufficient manner in which our Soldiers were clothed. Having found much delay heretofore in getting cloth made up hath induced Congress to

[1] A. dr. L. S. by Richard Henry Lee. Harvard University Library, Lee Mss. III. 13. The following letter (signed in autograph by Richard Henry Lee, Fra. Lewis, Wm. Whipple, and drafted by a hand

desire that forty thousand compleat suits of Soldiers cloaths may be sent — In giving directions for this business Gentlemen. it may be necessary to inform that both the Coats & Waistcoats must be short skirted, according to the dress of our Soldiery, and that they should be generaly for Men of stouter make than those of France. Variety of Sizes will of course be ordered. The Eastern Ports are generally entered with so much more safety than the Southern, that we recommend the former for these goods to be sent to, with orders for the Captain to give Congress immediate notice of his arrival by Express or by personal attendence. We expect this letter will be delivered you by Capt. Johnston Commander of the Lexington Armed Vessel, and as the Congress is very anxious to hear from you, it is probable Capt. Johnston will not remain long enough in France to get either cloth or cloaths in any quantity, but since it is necessary for the health of the Soldiers to cover them from the dews of summer, it will be of

similar to Lee's), referring to the above, is among the Lee Papers (No. 37) at the University of Virginia: —

"IN SECRET COMMITTEE OF CONGRESS.

"HONORABLE GENTLEMEN.

You will receive herewith a Copy of our Letter of Yesterday by the Lexington with its enclosures. This goes to Boston for a Passage from thence. And armed Vessel belonging to that State will carry the dispatches, & will be governed by your directions respecting her Load back, & the Time of her return. Should you have failed in obtaining the Loan, or of getting the Cloth, Cloaths, &c mentioned in the Resolve of Congress, you will please turn the Vessel over to Mess.rs Thomas Morris & William Lee, or either of them to receive such Continental Cargo as they may be enabled to send in her. Unless you should be of Opinion that the public Service requires that she should return immediately from North America with your dispatches, in which case you will direct what you judge best for the public good.

We are with perfect esteem, honorable Gentlemen, your most obedient and most humble servants.

BALTIMORE Feb.y 18.th 1777 "

great advantage to send a considerable quantity of blankets and Tent cloth by her, with Stockings, flints & small arms. The Soldiers cloaths and the Cloth should be so contrived as to reach North America by the month of September at furthest.

We are with esteem honorable Gentlemen
Your most obedient & very humble Servants.

80,000 blankets, 40,000 Compleat Suits Cloaths, green, blue & brown with suitable facings & Cloth of the same colors with facings proper for 40,000 suits more. 100,000 pr. yarn Stockings. 1 million Gun flints 200 Ton Lead —

[CERTIFICATE TO EDWARD WRIGHT FROM VIRGINIA DELEGATES IN CONGRESS] [1]

RICHARD HENRY LEE, FRANCIS LIGHTFOOT LEE, MANN PAGE, JUN.

[BALTIMORE, February 18, 1777.]

We the Subscribers Delegates in Congress from the State Virginia do certify that the Bearer Edward Wright is an Inhabitant of Westmoreland County in Virginia, a Man of good character, and employed by his industrious Neighbors to collect Cotton Cards for carrying on their domestic Manufactures And therefore that it may be suffered to pursue his business without molestation or interruption. Given under our hands at Baltimore this 18th day of February 1777.

To all whom it may concern.

[1] A. L. S. by Richard Henry Lee. Virginia State Library. Signed also by Francis Lightfoot Lee and Mann Page, Jun. This certificate is in the nature of a letter to the public.

THE LETTERS OF RICHARD HENRY LEE

[COMMITTEE OF SECRET CORRESPONDENCE] TO
COMMISSIONERS IN FRANCE[1]

[B. FRANKLIN, S. DEANE, ARTHUR LEE]

BALTIMORE IN MARYLAND Feb.ʸ 19ᵗʰ 1777

HONORABLE GENTLEMEN.

The events of War have not since our last furnished anything decisive. The enemies Army still remains encampt upon the hills near Brunswick, and still our Troops continue to beat back and destroy their Convoys, insomuch that we understand their Horses dye in numbers, and ∧ that the difficulty of removing their Stores, Cannon &.ᶜ will be insuperably great, until the opening of the Rareton furnishes a passage by water, for their return to N. York. The American Army is not numerous at present, but the new Levies are collecting fast as possible, and we hope to have a sufficient force early in the field. We see by the speech of the King of Great Britain to his Parliament, that much money will be called for, no doubt, to prosecute the War with unrelenting vigor. That we shall oppose with all our power. is certain, ~~will~~ be ~~uncertain,~~ until France shall take a ~~decisive~~ decided part in the war. ~~and then~~ When that happens, our ~~Independence~~ Liberties will be secured, and the glory and greatness of France be placed on the most solid foundation. . What may be the consequence of her delay, must be a painful consideration to every friend ~~to~~ of that Country

we have reason to believe (interlineation above "and ∧ that")

but the event must doubtful (interlineation above "is certain, will be uncertain")

---

[1] A. dr. L. by Lee. American Philosophical Society, Lee Papers, I. 283. A text with changes and signed by Harrison and Lee is in Wharton, *Diplomatic Correspondence*, II. 273. A text, also with changes, is in R. H. Lee, *Memoir of Richard Henry Lee*, I. 291.

and of[1] this. ~~This consideration~~ _{Thus viewing our Situation,} we are sure _A will occasion your strongest exertions to procure an event _{it} of such momentous consequence to your Country. It is in vain for us to have on hand a great abundance of Tobacco, Rice, Indigo, flour and other valuable articles of Merchandise, if prevented from exporting them[2] by having the whole Naval power of Great Britain to contend against — It is not only for our interest, but clearly so for the benefit of Europe in General, that we should not be hindered from freely transmitting our products, that abound here, and are so much wanted there — Why should the avarice & ambition of G. B be gratified, to the excessive injury of ~~all~~ other nations ?

We _A feel _A the disagreeable situation. Mr Deane must have been in from early in june to the date of his letter in October, but this ~~has~~ _{was} ~~been~~ occasioned by accident not neglect of writing, since letters were sent _A in all the intervening months which must have unluckily fallen into the enemies hands — or been destroyed —

Mr Bingham informs us from Martinique, that he learned from a Spanish General there, on his way to South America, ~~that~~ the King of Spain was willing to do the United States Offices of friendship, and that a loan of money might be obtained from the Court — As the power sent you for borrowing is not confined to place we mention this intelligence that you may avail yourselves of his Catholic Majesties friendly desings.[3] Perhaps a loan can be obtained there on better terms than elsewhere. Mr Deane recommends sending Frigates to France, and to convoy our Merchandise —

---

[1] Written over "to." [2] Written over "it." [3] Illegible erasure.

But it should be considered that we̶ ̶w̶e̶r̶e̶ are young in the
business of fitting Ships of War — That Founderies for
Cannon were all to m̶a̶k̶e̶, be e̶s̶t̶a̶b̶l̶i̶s̶h̶e̶d̶ ̶b̶u̶i̶l̶t̶ erected,
and the difficulty of getting Seamen quickly when Privateers abound as they do in from the States where Sailors are
chiefly to be met with. And lastly that our Frigates are
much restrained by the heavy Ships of the enemy which
are placed at the entrance of our Bays,.̶a̶n̶d̶ In short, the
attention of G. B. must ᴧin part be drawn s̶o̶m̶e̶t̶h̶i̶n̶g̶ ̶a̶w̶a̶y̶
from hence, before France can benefit largely by our com-
merc̶e̶i̶a̶l̶ ̶f̶r̶e̶e̶d̶o̶m̶ — We expect it will not be long before
Congress will appoint Commissioners to the Courts formerly mentioned, and in the mean time you will serve the
cause of your Country in the best manner possible with
the Ministers from those Courts to that of Versailles.
Earnestly wishing for good new and quickly from you,
we remain with friendship and esteem Honorable
Gentlemen your most obedient humble Servants.

P.S.   Congress adjourns this week back to Philadelphia —

TO JOHN PAGE [1]

Dear Sir,   Baltimore Feb.ʸ 19. 1777
   I am extremely obliged to you for your last favor, and
much pleased with the spirit of your letter. I am as
sure as of my existence that if our large Gallies were

---

[1] A. L. S. Lenox Library, Emmet, 3767. Addressed to "Honorable John Page esquire" at Williamsburg, Virginia. John, son of
the second Mann Page of Rosewell, was successively Burgess, member of the Virginia Council, member of the Virginia Convention of
1776, and Governor of Virginia, 1802.

manned, gunned, and fitted, that the navigation of our Bay would receive no interruption. I wish our Government would consult their Sister Maryland about this business, and with joint council and united strength, immediately equip such a number of strong Gallies as to free our Bay from these piratical incursions. Experience has proved the efficacy of these Vessels in small waters, and in the way of surprise against the largest Ships.[1] They are cheaper than Ships, and rigged Ship fashion will be well understood by our Navigators. They are the best batteries, because they are movable ones, and the circumstance of drawing little water, peculiarly fits them for the shallow waters on our coasts. I pray you Sir to exert your influence to obtain the speedy use of the valuable Vessels, the surest defence, and the cheapest we can employ. The events of war are at a stand until our new Army can assemble. The enemies horses are nearly all dead for want of forage, and this is withheld from them by our feeble force, which is wisely and bravely employed to watch and defeat every foraging party that descends the hills of Brunswick. How unhappy it is, and how disgraceful to America, that a Continent of Freemen should suffer 6000 Men determined upon their ruin, to winter upon a hill in their Country? But yet it is so, and every exertion of Congress, the most urgent calls from them on every part has been ineffectual to procure the destruction of these foes to human freedom! For heavens sake Sir press forward our Quota, that we may early in the Spring, or before the Winter is over, do something effectual with these our determined enemies. That a war in Europe is not far off, is very clear to me — The Tyrants speech strongly suggests it amidst his fears of alarming his deluded people — We every day expect the Vessel

---

[1] "Vess" written before this word is erased.

that carried D.ʳ Franklin, to return, & by her we hope for the most agreable accounts. However, on these I would not ¹ place our Reliance —

We have means enough, if wisely improved, to secure us against every wicked attempt to destroy our liberties — Procul a Jove, procul a fulmine.

Your brother & Sister were inoculated three days ago, and must of course remain here until their recovery — Congress have determined to return Philadelphia next Wednesday — In the recess, I shall carry M.ʳˢ Lee to Virginia that she may be indulged with the sight of her children, whom she longs to see after 6 months absence —

Farewell dear Sir.

Remember me to all friends — M.ʳ Wythe is amongst my chosen few.

P.S. A number of Seamen lately put on shore from Cam. Notham ² say that the Men of War are greatly afraid of our Gallies. Let us cultivate this passion by ordering our best appointed Gallies to lurk about them, & in Calms or thick weather to annoy them with all imaginable spirit & address.

TO [GEORGE WASHINGTON] ³

My DEAR SIR,   BALTIMORE Feb.ʸ 27ᵗʰ 1777

"My brother Delegates are of opinion that the in-closed papers may avail you something in settling some disputes" about rank that may come before you, and therefore it is sent. Congress never did any thing in

---

¹ The word "have" following here is erased.
² "Hotham"?
³ A. L. S. Library of Congress, Letters to Washington, XIV. 30.

this matter, as the business was put into other hands. I realy think that when the history of this winters Campaign comes to be understood, the world will wonder at its success on our part. With a force rather inferior to the enemy in point of numbers, and chiefly militia too, opposed to the best disciplined troops of Europe; to keep these latter pent up, harrassed, and distressed — But more surprising still, to lessen their numbers some thousands by the sword and captivity! All this Sir must redound to your glory, and to the reputation of the few brave men under your command. But whilst I wonder at your success, I am really astonished at the supineness of the people, to suffer your army to be so thin, whilst a cruel, implacable enemy is in the Country, and have providentially put themselves in the way of destruction, if the numbers of people that are not far off, would turn out for the purpose! We have done every thing in our power to hasten up the new Levies, and strengthen your hands, but the want of arms and cloaths, with the small pox, obstructs and delays us prodigiously. Industry and patience, will I hope surmount all obstacles, and at length collect an army together that will bid defiance to despotism, and secure the liberties of North America. About a fortnight ago, I received a letter from London, written by a well informed friend, which contains this paragraph and is dated, Oct.ʳ 9ᵗʰ last — "The War is likely to go on another year, in which case Cheasapeak Bay will be the seat; a plan for that purpose has been laid before Lᵈ Geo. Germaine & it is said is approved. The Eastern Shore is the first object, or place of landing"— This letter reached me just as three or 4 large Ships came lately into our Bay, and the Tory rising on the Marylᵈ Eastern Shore seemed to denote the beginning of this plan — But since, we learn that the Ships are gone & the Tories dispersed. My Informant is however so good, that I cannot help thinking [1] something like a diversion, at least, will be attempted there next Campaign. I cannot think they mean to relinquish their grand plan of joining their Canadian with Howes army. This consideration, has ever made me wish that Ticonderoga, and the avenues leading to Canada, were attended to, that the vigilance and Military talents of Gen. Carleton may be disappointed.

We are informed by our Agent in Martinique 7th of Jan? that a Spanish General, in a Frigate bound to S. America, called at that place in distress, sought opportunities of assuring him of the King of Spains good will to assist these States, and that a loan of money might be obtained from that Court — He further said, that a land and Sea force was gone to South America, where hostilities were before that time commenced with Portugal. The French finances are low, but the Spanish are not so, and the opportunity is so tempting that I think a general war in Europe unavoidable. At least, I hope so. I have sent you inclosed, the translation of a letter from Doct? De Bourg to Doct? Franklin which lately came to the Committee of Secret Correspondence. It furnishes much useful information, and evidences the old Gentlemans strong attachments to our cause. He is a Philosopher, a Physician, and a friend to America — And his interest at Court very considerable.

I have now to ask your pardon for this long letter, it is against my plan of not disturbing you, but perhaps it may be excused as I do it but Seldom

I am at all times, and places, and upon every occasion; dear Sir Your most affectionate friend and obedient Servant.

[1] The word "that" is here erased.

THE LETTERS OF RICHARD HENRY LEE

TO ROBERT MORRIS[1]

DEAR SIR,   BALTIMORE March 1ˢᵗ 1777

As far as I am able to judge, the plan suggested in the inclosed memoir, is admirably fitted to give a decided superiority to our Frigates above those of the Enemy. If you should think so, I know you will push into execution with the same zeal that animates you in every thing that affects the public. Will not the churches furnish their bells to make 24 pounders for the Randolph & the Delaware, when they are to be employed against an enemy who mean to exterpa[te their ?][2] religion and everything else valuable here? Shou[ld the ?][2] enemy get possession of Philadelphia, they will so [* * *][2] strip the churches of their bells, as perquisite for [* * *][2] chief Engineer, whereas, if they are lent to us, we s[hould][2] repay in kind. I hope you will not suffer the [* * *][2] enemy to have the honor of getting Philadel[phia].[2]

I am with truth & esteem affectionately yours.

TO THE GOVERNOR OF VIRGINIA[3]

(PATRICK HENRY)

DEAR SIR,   PHILADELPHIA, April 7, 1777.

I thank you for your favor, which I found here on my return from Virginia.

Weak, and exposed as our enemies are in the Jersies

[1] A. L. S. Library of Congress, Papers of the Continental Congress, L. 78, vol. 14, p. 159. Addressed, "Honorable Robert Morris Esquire / Member of Congress / Philadelphia // favored by the / hon. Mʳ President Hancock."

[2] Ms. torn.

[3] From the text printed in William Wirt Henry, *Patrick Henry,* III. 58.

to a stroke that would be decisive, we cannot avail ourselves of it for want of men, although we have arms,
tents, cloaths, and every necessary ready for 20,000
soldiers. The levies come up very slow, and these are
obliged to undergo inoculation before they join the army;
so that the General has not more than 4,000 with him
now, and the enemy have about 17,000. Yet they continue narrowed in their quarters and greatly distressed
for forage. O for 10, or 12 thousand Americans to
sweep these vermin from our land! We have received
very agreable intelligence from the commissioners (Dr.
Franklin, Mr. Deane and Dr. Lee,) of the United States
to the Court of France. They have been received with
great cordiality, promised protection, and an answer to
their proposals as soon as Spain has been consulted, with
which country France means to act in close concert.
The French had in January 25 sail of the line ready, &
Spain had 17. And both were certainly to have 30 by
April. Ten thousand French troops were marched to
Brest where the fleet lay, and opposite the English coast,
which will no doubt occasion alarm, and prevent the
sending more troops from G. Britain. The court of
London had solicited the guarantee of its continental
possessions in Europe, and was refused by the allies of
France in Germany. The commissioners had nego-
tiated a loan of two million of Livres, to be paid when
America was in peace and prosperity, without even the
mention of interest, and the ports of France, Spain &
Leghorn are open to our prizes as well as our trade.
These things look well, and if we are not wanting to
ourselves, must in time fix the freedom and happiness of
America. We have 12,000 stand of arms arrived at
Portsmouth in N. Hampshire, with other military stores,
and 3,000 stand come in here. The enemy lately made
an attack by surprise on our posts upon the highlands of
Hudson river, but they were repulsed, and driven on

board their ships with precipitation and disgrace, by an inferior number of American troops. They have lately embarked troops at N. York, the tories say for this city, themselves say they are going to Chesapeake Bay. Some think they mean nothing but to amuse, whilst others imagine they mean to renew their attack on the heights of Hudson river. Either of the two last opinions I prefer to the former. I hope to have the pleasure of seeing you in May at Williamsburg, and remain in the meantime with great friendship and affection, dear Sir,
Yours.

His Excellency PATRICK HENRY, Esq., *Governor of Virginia.*

[COMMITTEE OF CONGRESS TO GENERAL GEORGE WASHINGTON] [1]

SIR,   PHILADELPHIA April 10. 1777
    In obedience to an order of Congress we inform your Excellency ~~that~~ of the reasons and principles that have goverened Congress in their resolution for forming a Camp on the West side of Delaware. The repeated information that hath been received of the Enemies movements & it being the opinion of your Excellency as well as of many other General Officers that this City was the
                                           ~~prop~~ proper
Object of such Movements, rendered it,   that means should be fallen upon to prevent the success of
      a   guard against
such ᴀ designs, as well to ~~prevent~~ the bad impression that it would certainly have on the affairs of America in general, as to give security to the valuable Stores here collected, and which cannot speedily be removed. It

[1] A. dr L. by Lee. American Philosophical Society, Lee Papers, I. 293, No. 85.

has been considered, that if the real Object of the enemy
should be[1] this City, the Troops are here well ~~placed~~ fixed, and
will be an encouraging place of resort to the Militia of
this State, in their present unfixt condition, being between their old plan of Association, and their new but
yet unexecuted Law. On the other other hand, should
the design of the enemy be ~~th~~ upon Hudsons river or
more Eastward, the Troops here may with ease ~~be~~ reach
that ~~the North~~ ₍Hudsons₎ river before those, now at Head Quarters, can have all crossed ~~that water,~~ it But another
consideration ~~object,~~ remains ~~to be considered,~~ and that is,
should the enemy propose to remain in Jersey to attack
your Army, or should your Excellency mean to make
a dicisive impression on them ₍when your numbers are sufficient₎, in either of these suppositions, the Troops
ought not to be here — ~~With either of these Congress m~~
In the whole of this business, Congress mean not ~~to~~ in
any manner to interfere with the designs, or to counter
act the judgment of your Excellency, but wish you freely
to call up to Head Quarters, all, or any part of these
Troops encampt here as you shall please. It is not
supposed that this will occasion any delay, and will cer-
tainly prevent the injuries ₍that would be derived to the Troops, as well in health as discipline₎ ~~derived to the~~
from their entering and
remaining any time in this City —
We have the honor to be &c.

[1] The words "Hudsons river or a more Eastern one, that in such
case the Troops" are erased here.

THE LETTERS OF RICHARD HENRY LEE

TO GENERAL [GEORGE] WASHINGTON [1]

My DEAR GENERAL   PHILADELPHIA 10 April 1777

"The resolves of Congress" that you will receive by this Messenger, you may be assured, are not intended, by any means, to obstruct your views a single moment. If your judgement should incline you to think that the Troops had better march on to Head Quarters quick as possible, you have only so to order it, and it will give pleasure to every good man here. The business of speedily reenforcing you will not be obstructed, but accelilated, because they now enter the City, where every days stay is 30 days injury to the great purpose of strengthening your hands. And should the enemy destine here, something like a Military collection, may produce a greater resort — If you will indulge my conjecture, I think they cannot purpose coming here, because the water securities ag[a]inst such a plan are realy formidable, and the situation of the land, where the water obstructions are fixed, is such, that great delay, and probable ruin forbids the enterprize, as they cannot so fix land Batteries as to remove the strong Vessels that protect the Cheveaux de Frise, added to the numerous fire Rafts & Fire Ships that in a narrow water with strong current may destroy their Fleet.

Your Army Sir feeble as it is, and the North River, are more tempting Objects, because they are not strong, and because the defeat of the one, or the acquisition of the other, would avail our enemies greatly.

My wishes are Sir, and I think they correspond with the true interest of America, that you should quickly be possessed of a strong Army, that your powers might

---

[1] A. L. S. Library of Congress, Letters to Washington, XIV. 236. Addressed to Washington " at Head Quarters in / Maryland."

be such as to gratify your wishes of crushing of our enemies before an addition of strength to them may render the business more difficult & uncertain. I think[1] I[1] well know your situation, and from your excellent disposition, I know your feelings, and I do most ardently wish to make the former good, and to render the latter agreable, and therefore, whenever I can know either from[2] yourself,[2] all the powers I possess shall be exerted to accomplish both — The Troops of Maryland are now under inoculation, and so are, about 1000 Virginians from Baltimore to Wilmington inclusive — Here, we suppose, may be near a thousand of all kinds, who by the now plan of encampment, will be in Tents as quickly as the Physicians can discharge them, or the Officers collect them from this attractive Scene of debauch and amusement

With every hearty wish for your health and prosperity I remain dear Sir Most affectionately yours.

TO PATRICK HENRY[3]

My Dear Sir,   PHILADELPHIA, April 15, 1777.

The express who delivered me your favor of March 28th last, and who went on to Jersey, has either forgotten his promise, or not returned, because he has never since called on me. No person living detests more than I do the pernicious practise of engrossing, especially the necessaries of life. Tis begotten by avarice on inhumanity, and deserves every kind of discouragement. I have spoken to Mr. Morris, and he declares, that so far as he has been concerned, his agent was directed to

---

[1] Inserted above the line.   [2] Inserted above the line.
[3] From the text printed in William Wirt Henry, *Patrick Henry*, III. 62.

purchase for him with view of foreign commerce solely. It must deeply concern every good man to see our army collected so slowly, by which, instead of crushing the enemy before reenforcements arrived to them, we are still obliged to be on the defensive, having but 3000 to oppose to near 8000. And now they threaten to attack this City, 9 ships of war being already in the Delaware. The citizens however are in good spirits, & say they shall not have the Town. In the meantime their land force remains in its old situation at Brunswick. Two, or three days ago, they made two sorties nearly at the same time, one party attacking our Post at Bon Brook, and another, that at Quibble Town. The latter attack was immediately repulsed, but the former succeeded at first, so as to repel our men and get away 3 field pieces. But a small reenforcement coming up, they were beaten in turn and driven off, leaving 7 dead on the Field. We lost 5 men. I strongly incline to think that they mean only to amuse us and divert our attention from forming an army, until their succors enable them to take the field, and pursue to advantage their original plan of possessing the North river, and joining with Gen. Carleton. Be their designs what they may, it is evidently the business of every state to exert itself for furnishing its Quota of troops, that an army formidable may be collected, and sufficient to oppose every attempt. We have now arms and every other equipment ready for 20,000 men, and the Hospital department is put on the most liberal and judicious plan. Some of the best medical men on the continent are called to act in it, so that we hope this business will now be managed in the best manner, and the sick will be taken care of. A fine ship from Nantes, with powder, arms, & Woolens, was the other day chased on shore by two or three Frigates near the capes of Delaware. The Captain, after bravely defending himself for some time in vain, blowed up his ship rather than let her fall into the enemies hands. He lost his life, the rest of the crew were saved, and what is remarkable, a considerable part of the cargo was driven safely on shore by the exploding effort of the powder, and persons are now employed in securing it. We have intelligence from London, via France, late in Jan^y, by which we learn that Bankruptcies go on well, two West India merchants having failed for more than a million, and that general distress was great. The merchants tell the Ministry that they lost one million eight hundred thousand pounds sterling by the capture of their Vessels last year. The same accounts tell us that the practices at New York since the enemy got it, exceed everything described in history, unless it be the proceedings of the second triumvirate, and give dreadful specimen of what is to be expected when the power prevails. It is certain that the refusal of the India Company on account of difficulty and delay, alone prevented the Villains from sending American prisoners to the East Indies for slaves. And that being refused, they were on the verge of sending such of them to Africa as were in England. Yet these are the men, or Devils rather, that some among us would persuade submission to! For Heaven's sake let every nerve be strained to expel them far from North America. They contaminate the air they breathe. Excuse the length of this letter, and believe me to be, with affectionate respect yours.

His Excellency, PATRICK HENRY.

THE LETTERS OF RICHARD HENRY LEE

TO GENERAL [GEORGE] WASHINGTON[1]

[April 16,(?) 1777]

Your letter to the Committee was immediately laid before Congress, and in consequence thereof, Gen. Schuyler was ordered to carry your ideas into execution with all possible dispatch. The Troops are therefore ordered to Bristol without delay, and thither will go all such as come from the Southward. You have only to order them from Bristol to Head Quarters at your pleasure. The inclosures now sent are from France by the last Ship. The Memoire is written by one of the first Generals in France, or in Europe, purely from views of serving the American cause, which the Mareshal appears to love. The accounts from Nantes, are taken from a letter of Doct. Lee to the Secret Committee in his way from Paris to the Court of Madrid. I thought it might avail you to have the general idea therein given of the enemies views and designs the ensuing Campaign. In the letter signed by all the Commissioners, we learn that the capital operations will certainly be against New England; the exterpation of which is proposed, whilst military government & slavery is (as they think the milder punishment) intended for the middle and southern States. Conversing lately with M.r James Hunter of Fredericksburg, whose labors have benefitted the public greatly, I find that the

[1] A. L. S. Library of Congress, Letters to Washington, XX. 328. Addressed to him "at Head Quarters in / New Jersey," and enclosing an extract in R. H. Lee's autograph of a letter of Arthur Lee to the Committee of Secret Correspondence written from Nantes on February 11, 1777. The extract begins with the words, "By the information I have from London, which I think," and ends with "it is of itself a sufficient evidence of their merciless and tyrannical disposition towards us." For the entire letter, from which the extract is taken, see Wharton, *Diplomatic Correspondence*, II. 266.

indispensable article of iron has been greatly affected, and its production injured, by the constant practise of inlisting the Laborers in those works, and pressing the Teams belonging to them. There are few things more capable of throwing distress among the people, and injuring the public affairs, than such a proceedure. I would therefore submit it to your consideration Sir, whether (until the Legislatures can provide compitent laws) it will not greatly remedy the evil, if you were, by order published in all the papers, forbid all Continental Officers from enlisting persons engaged with, and actually serving in any iron works within the United States, or from pressing any horses, teams, or Carriages of any kind belonging to such works. I believe that this would in great degree remedy the evil, if not totally remove it.

I am with great affection and esteem, dear Sir your most obedient and very humble Servant.

TO [ARTHUR LEE] [1]

PHILADELPHIA April 20ᵗʰ 1777

MY DEAR BROTHER,

It gave me inexpressible pleasure to find by your joint letter from Paris to Congress that you were safely arrived in France. As well on your own account I was rejoiced, as on that of my Country, well knowing with what zeal and ability the cause of America and of mankind will be served by you. |[2] Heaven grant you may be as successful in your negotiations as you wish to be and as the greatest and most virtuous cause that the sun ever shone on deserves. That the exertions of

[1] A. L. S. University of Virginia, Lee Papers, No. 46.
[2] Vertical lines here and on p. 278, probably made by Arthur Lee, are in the Ms. to call attention to this portion of the letter.

America will be firm, and great as are in her power, you may rely upon with absolute confidence, but then, it ought not to be forgotten by those who wish our eternal separation from Great Britain, that the single strength of North America opposed to the united force of Great Britain and her Allies may prove an unequal contest, and should not be trusted too far. The difficulty of finding funds whilst our Trade is shut up by a superior marine strength, is very distressing, and would find present relief, if the United Fleets of Spain and France were to fall on that of G. B. in its present state of inferiority. It amazes me that the Politicians of these two Kingdoms do not see with what certainty they may, in conjunction with N. America humble the pride and power of Britain, as well as that if the latter accomplish their plan of subjugating America, the force of both must and will be applied to attach the American possessions of the House of Bourbon. | It is now in the power of Spain, with ease to get the Harbor of Pensacola for her homeward bound Ships, and surely the power of Great Britain & N America divided can never be so dangerous to her as when united, abstracted from the consideration of gratitude that must bind to her the affection of virtuous young Republics for timely and effectual aid afforded them in the day of their distress. It will be very long before such kindness will be forgotten. Since the 24$\underline{\text{th}}$ of december, we have been in a constant train of success against the enemy, and from that time, during the whole winters Campaign, for it has never stopt, we have reduced the enemies force at least 4000 men. They have been confined to the Hills of Brunswick in New Jersey the whole winter, and there they remain now, their foraging parties have been so beaten and driven back that their distress has been great, & their horses have died in numbers. And this has been done chiefly by Militia, our regular Army having

been dispersed last fall in consequence of short enlistments which had taken place in Spring 1776 in the
uncertain State that our affairs were then under.   The
Levies for forming a new Regular Army for duration
are now moving up to Head Quarters in Jersey from
all the States, and an Army is forming at Ticonderoga
ready to meet Gen Carleton as soon as the ice permits
him to cross Lake Champlain.   But we are greatly
retarded by the necessity we are under of passing all our
Troops thro inoculation before they join the Army.
And this I fear will prevent us from taking advantage
of the enemies weakness and presumption in remaining
where they are before they get reenforced.   Brunswick
(on the hills near which the enemy are fortified) is in
New Jersey upon the River Rareton which communi-
cates with the Sea at Amboy near New York.   The
Rareton is not navigable for Ships, but for small Craft,
and it is about 12 miles from Brunswick to Amboy, so
that you find they keep pretty nigh to their Ships.
What a fine Stroke it would be for a Spanish Fleet to
remove their small Ships of War, which would effectually deliver their Army into our hands.   And it would
not quickly be in the power of England to recover this
blow.   Except two, the other States have fixed, and are
exercising their new Governments, which you may well
suppose must add greatly to our force, safety, and
success.   We have 13 Frigates nearly finished and some
of them at Sea.   Our Privateers you know have been
very successful and still continue to be so.   You cannot imagine what universal joy and spirit it would
give to North America if Spain and France were now to
Attack Great Britain.   The success w^d be infallible,
and the independence of America immoveably fixed.

Before this reaches you, the former dispatches will
be arrived, by which you will see that Congress had
proposed Doctor Franklin to attend the Court of Spain

whilst you remained at Paris, but I suppose you have jointly considered that it may do as well for you to be at Madrid, and perhaps the Doctors age might render it inconvenient for him to travel so far — However, proper powers have long since been sent to Doctor Franklin appointing him to the Court of Spain, altho he is not deprived of right still to represent these States at the Court of France.

My obligations to you will never cease for taking care of my dear boys. But heaven knows what I shall do about making remittance whilst our Trade continues so obstructed by British Cruisers. Almost all the Frigates and Sloops of England are now employed against us — I have written to our[1] brother, who I expect will be in France by the time this reaches there, proposing if possible, that Thom should be employed as his Clerk or Secretary whilst he remains in France, and that Ludwell be instructed in Military matters, but more especially eloquence, and the principles of Natural law, that he may here turn either to[2] War or to the Law. But if this cannot be done, that they both be sent to me by the first of our Vessels of War that come to this Country. My wish, and my earnest wish, is, to put them both in a situation to be of service to their Country, and beneficial to themselves, but since the times admit not of remittances being made, that one of them, or both, as the case may be, that cannot be somehow employed in France so as to get a subsistence, I would have sent to me by the first of our Vessels that is most likely to bring him safely. By ours, I do not mean Virginia Vessels, for you know our trade used to be carried on, almost entirely, in British Bottoms, so that few if any Ships from Virg^a will for some time be sent to France; which renders it of great importance

[1] Word erased illegible.
[2] The word " the " was here written and erased.

indeed to both Countries, that the latter should force her Trade with the former thro the British Cruizers. It would benefit both amazingly, and every assistance will be given on our part. May 31st Since the above, the events of war have not been considerable — The Enemy, with about 2000 Men, from N. York pushed up the Sound by water, and made a forced March thro a small part of Connecticut to surprise & destroy a Magazine of provisions laid up there for our Army. They succeeded in destroying about 1700 barrels of Salted Meat and some grain, with about 1000 barrels of flour. However, the Militia assembled quickly as possible under command of Generals Wooster and Arnold to the number of about 1500 and attacked the enemy as they were retreating to their Ships where with great difficulty, and much loss they at length arrived. We learn that this trip has lessened their numbers at least 500, among the wounded and since dead we are told they count Majr General Goverr Tryon and a Colonel Wolcot. The loss of provisions has been amply made up to us by the Privateers who have taken 5000 barrels of Salted provisions coming to N. York from Europe. In a variety of squirmishes lately we have beaten them, and in some of these their best Troops have been foiled. | [1] By this opportunity Congress sends you a particular Commission as their Representative at the Court of Spain. In my judgment, and it is an opinion founded on the most accurate information,[2] the Independence, and security of N. America cannot be said to be certain until an Alliance with Spain & France is procured, and in consequence, the British Arms, and Arts not solely employed for our ruin. You may be assured *that* this is of infinite consequence to your Country and therefore you will conduct yourself accordingly. And for

[1] Mark probably made by Arthur Lee.
[2] Substituted above the line for " inquiry " erased.

the assistance of our finance, and extensive loan is indespensable.| [1]

If any untoward accident, should have befallen our brother the Alderman in which case I have desired my letters to him to be sent you for your perusal, the management of my boys must rest entirely with you, and in that case, at all events, *you* will see the necessity of sending them both immediately to me.

Farewell my dear Brother.

P.S. It will of be great consequence that I hear from you frequently & fully — If your letters come any where to the Northward of Virginia, or if they go by the West Indies, let them be directed to the care of [our] brother Dr. Shippen in Philadelphia.[2]

I believe Tryon is not dead & we have not heard more of Col? Wolcot.[3]

TO THE GOVERNOR OF VIRGINIA[4]

(PATRICK HENRY)

My Dear Sir, Philadelphia, 22nd April, 1777.

The enclosed resolve is now sent, principally with a view of rectifying some Typhographic errors that the copy formerly sent you contained. I am again in the

---

[1] Mark probably made by Arthur Lee.

[2] Lee's signature in initials here follows.

[3] This sentence is added by Richard Henry Lee in three short lines under his signature to the postscript, and on the other side of the manuscript is the following memorandum written in five lines: " 1 Let to Committee March 8ᵗʰ |2ᵈ March 16ᵗʰ |3. March 29ᵗʰ| 4. April 8. |5. April, 19."

[4] From the text printed in William Wirt Henry, *Patrick Henry*, III. 66.

name of Congress to desire your Excellency will detain the flour in Virginia, until further directions, that Mͬ Commissary Trumbul had sent Vessels from the eastward to remove. The reason you assign of danger from the enemy's cruisers, is conclusive with Congress for staying this provision awhile.

Since I wrote you last, few occurrences have happened worth noticing. Skirmishes often happen, in which we generally succeed. The enemy with 4000 men & 4 Genˡ officers surprised our post at Bound Brook, and carried off a few prisoners with 2 pieces of Cannon. But they quickly retired and not without loss. To revenge this insult, Gen. Stephen attacked one of their picket guards and drove it in, killing 7 and making 16 prisoners. It seems to be the opinion of all men, that 10 or 12000 men in the Jersies might quickly decide the fate of our enemies before reinforcements arrive to them. The Eastern Troops are all to undergo inoculation before they join the Army. Our Southern Troops that arrived here are all recovered and recovering from the Small pox, having had the distemper very favorably, and as far as I have heard, without loss. We have accounts just now that 2 of our privateers have taken and sent into Statia and Martinique, nine sail of Transports on their way to N. York — and two Guinea men bound to the West Indies. These transports were to call at the West Indies for rum for the Army, & to avoid as much as possible the Eastern Privateers. Deserters come out in numbers, and say the enemy's army is very sickly, and that the men die fast.

I am with great esteem, dear sir, your most affectionate & obedient.

His Excellency PATRICK HENRY, Esq., *Governor of Virginia.*

THE LETTERS OF RICHARD HENRY LEE

TO GENERAL [GEORGE] WASHINGTON[1]

My dear Sir,   Philadelphia 29$\underline{th}$ April 1777

Being often obliged to write in great haste, is the reason that I sometimes omit to date my letters. But I am now to acknowledge the favor of yours of the 24$\underline{th}$,[2] and I readily acquiesce with your reasons concerning the Iron Works — I was indeed not apprized of so great a number of these being in Jersey. I shall certainly exert myself to have your views for Gen. Arnold and Col? Huntington carried into execution. This day the Committee of Secret Correspondence received a letter from Doctor Lee of later date as you will see than the former of which I sent you an extract. From the letter now received is taken what I have now the honor to inclose you. I realy believe it contains the true design of the enemy, and it may serve to explain the late Apparatus of Boats with Gen Howe, and the continuance of the Troops at Rhode Island. It may be

---

[1] A. L. S. Library of Congress, Letters to Washington, XV. 76. Addressed to Washington " At Head Quarters in/New Jersey." Encloses, in R. H. Lee's autograph, this extract from A. Lee's letter, of February 20, 1777, to him: —

"Bordeau. Feby 20$\underline{th}$ 1777.

" Upon my arrival here in my way to Madrid, I found a letter dated Feby the 2^d from a confidential Correspondent, which contains the following passage.

"'Ten thousand Germans are already engaged, and Ships sent to convey them; the number of British cannot exceed three thousand, & those very indifferent. But much is expected from their being sent early. Boston is certainly to be attacked in the Spring. Burgoyne is to command. Howe will probably turn against Philadelphia. The Government expects great advantages from dissentions in Pennsylvania.'" See Wharton, *Diplomatic Correspondence* II. 272, and note, and *Ibid* I. § 150 as to this information.

[2] For this see R. H. Lee, *Memoir of Richard Henry Lee*, II. 12.

284

some advantage to us to be apprized of their intentions. Doctor Lee is of opinion that the state of Europe was so critical, that it seemed impossible a war could hold off three months. However this may be, you are certainly right Sir, that our utmost vigor and vigilance should be exerted.

I am, with most unfeigned esteem, dear Sir Your most obedient and most humble Servant.

P.S. I think this plan of dividing their force, highly advantageous for us. Be pleased to accept my thanks for Mͬ Swans appointment.

TO [THOMAS JEFFERSON]¹

DEAR SIR,   PHILADELPHIA April 29ᵗʰ 1777

If I were to consider punctilio more than the suggestions of friendship, I should expect an answer to some of the letters I have written you, before I dispatched another. But I ever hated ceremonies, and shall not commence ceremony with you. I wish it were in my power to give you any very interesting news, but alas, the slow assembling of an Army prevents any attempt from us upon the enemy, and will furnish them an opportunity of collecting reinforcements from all quarters. The french Ministry assure our Commissioners that few succors can be drawn from Germany, but we find they are endeavoring to supply deficiencies from among the Tories in the States of Connecticut, New York, and New Jersey, where they have secret [e]missaries in abundance. For these purposes of corruption, it seems that Lord Howe is furnished with a Secretary, who is

¹ A. L. S. Library of Congress, Jefferson Correspondence, Letters to Jefferson, Ser. 2, Vol. 51, No. 14.

the greatest Adept in the art of bribing that now lives. I am afraid this Country furnishes too good materials for him to work upon. The plan of the British Court, if they can find Men & money and should not be disturbed by other wars, as it was settled in January last, was to reenforce Carleton & Howe, the latter to enter New England with his whole force for their *extermination*, whilst the former kept the middle Colonies in awe by invading N. York thro the Lakes. Burgoyne with 10,000 men, chiefly Germans, to attack Virginia and Maryland — The Southern & Middle Colonies to be put under *Military Government*. This may be relied on a[s] fact, and shews, if it wanted shewing, the just & merciful spi[rit] that animates the Leaders of our Enemies in Council — and I assure you, those that execute in the field are faithful representatives. It is on all hands agreed, that our own Tories are more formidable to us than the British force. And that a few Leaders among these, are the Authors of all the mischief. Quere then, if it becomes not every Legislature to secure against their machinations by the most vigorous and discouraging laws? I realy believe that the numbers of our lazy, worthless young Men, will not be induced to come forth into the service of their Country unless the States adopt the mode recommended by Congress of ordering Drafts from the Militia. This may induce the young & lazy to take the Continental bounty, rather than serve for nothing of that sort. If the 88 Batallions were once complete, adieu to British Tyranny and every chance for its succeeding.

Howes Army still remains on the Heights near Brunswick, and Gen. Washington to occupy the Country round him

Farewell dear Sir — Regard me as your affectionate friend.

THE LETTERS OF RICHARD HENRY LEE

TO PATRICK HENRY [1]

Dear Sir,   Philadelphia, May 6th, 1777.

Having written to you so lately by Express, this chiefly serves to convey my wishes that another Delegate might be hastened here, for the reasons you will see in the inclosed note this moment put in my hands. By a late letter from France, we understand that our enemies have given up their plan of attacking Virginia for the present, in order to gratify their stronger resentment against New England. However, I greatly question their being able to do much against either, as a French and Spanish war seems inevitable. A curious Act of Parliament has passed, to make our opposition on the land high Treason, and on the sea Piracy. And directing a place of imprisonment in England, until it is convenient to try the offenders. It is an acrimonious and foolish display of Tyranny.

I am, with great respect, dear Sir, your most obedient and very humble servant.

His Excellency, Patrick Henry, Esq.

TO [HIS SONS, THOMAS AND LUDWELL] [2]

Philadelphia May 10th 1777.

I heared with great pleasure that my dear children, were safely arrived in France — Before this intelligence reached me, I had suffered much from apprehensions both for them, and their worthy Uncles, in a Country

[1] From the text printed in William Wirt Henry, *Patrick Henry*, III. 67. For a text with variations see the *Virginia Historical Register*, I. 173.

[2] A. copy L. University of Virginia, Lee Papers, No. 156. A transcript with slight variations is among the Lee Transcripts, Virginia Historical Society, and a text printed from this is in the *Southern Literary Messenger*, May, 1860, p. 349.

(England) where every consideration of virtue and justice, is sacrificed to wicked resentment and views of Tyranny. The risk and danger of correspondence to Great Britain, prevented me from writing to you whilst you remained in that Country, and not a want of affection, for whilst you continue to behave as well as you have done, my tenderest affection shall always be placed on you. The views I formerly entertained for my eldest Son must now be changed, with the great alterations that have taken place in the System of North America. Instead of the Church, I would now have him as knowing as possible in Commerce, as well the theory as the practical part. For this purpose, if his good Uncle William should reside in France, my son will be employed by him as Clerk, or Agent in some capacity; by which a temporary support may be gained, and a lasting knowledge of business at the same time. But whether he is under the immediate care of his Uncle, or any other gentleman in France, I hope and insist that he pay the closest attention to business, and the greatest respect and obedience to him under whose care and patronage he lives. Every present, and future good consequence will flow from such a conduct, and every evil from the contrary. Let my dear Son therefore, grave upon his Mind, and faithfully practise this advice of his affectionate father. It will be of great importance to learn well the French Language and be able to speak, read, and write it, with correctness and fluency. Our future commerce with France will be so extensive, as to render this indispensible, and I desire it may not be neglected. If Gentlemen in France observe your attention to business, and capacity for the discharge of it, there is no doubt but on your return to your own Country, you will be so trusted to conduct the business of foreign Merchants, as to be very useful to them, and profitable to yourself. Your.

THE LETTERS OF RICHARD HENRY LEE

TO PATRICK HENRY[1]

DEAR SIR,   PHILADELPHIA, 13th May, 1777.

The inclosed infamous Act of Parliament is taken
from the New York Gazette, and its authenticity therefore not to be doubted. The question upon this is,
whether every State will not pass acts appointing places
of security, where the prisoners they may take may
be safely kept as pledges for the good usage of our
people, or as objects of punishment in the way of retalia-
tion.

In proportion as our enemies lose the hope of sub-
duing us by open force, they endeavor more strenuously
to sap us by corrupt influence, and by the wicked machinations of their Tory friends. To put an effectual
stop to the proceedings of the latter, will it not be necessary so to provide by law, as that every Tory may be
precisely in the same situation if we succeed in this war,
that we undoubtedly shall be if the enemy prevail.
And what this latter will be, the inclosed Act of Parliament very plainly declares. The point is how to
distinguish previously the Whigs from the Tories. I
believe by a strict test, and by appointing a General
and County board of Commissioners, with small but
competent funds to carry on quick correspondence with
each other, and to search into the conduct of suspicious
residents, and of all unknown passengers or travellers.
As you may rely upon it, that Tory machinations are
now more wicked than ever, and their correspondence
with each other, and their injurious communications
not to be doubted, I wish some of the most sensible
Whigs in our Assembly would take under consideration

[1] From the text printed in William Wirt Henry, *Patrick Henry*,
III. 68.

289

what I have here suggested the propriety of. The necessity of completing our Batallion is so obvious, that I suppose the assembly will adopt the plan of drafting recommended by Congress, and if they do, will it not be highly proper to have discreet recruting officers at every place where the Militia is assembled for the draft, who by clearly pointing out to the young men the advantages of bounty, annual clothes, and land for those that voluntary engage, may procure a sufficiency on the willing plan. Nor is it a bad argument with them, to shew how safely and easily they are carried thro' the small pox at the public expence, by the present plan of inoculation. Above all things, my dear sir, let us secure the credit of our money by a vigorous taxation. Maryland has done so and so have the Eastern States, and all must do it to procure public confidence in our funds and the stability of our currency.

Our army is approaching the enemies' lines and promises soon to be active. We have no late intelligence from France, tho' we have reason every day to expect it. Capt Weeks in the Continental ship Reprisal, of 16 guns and 100 & odd men, has taken & sent into Port L'Orient, a Lisbon Packet of equal force to himself with three ships that were under her Convoy; and the provisions we have taken at sea, more than compensates for the Danbury loss, since the latter was only 1700 barrels of meat with some flouer & grain, and we have brought in 5000 barrels of meat bound to N. York.

Col. Nelson is gone home ill, so that we three are fixed here to hard service; we deserve compassion and relief. I have no objection to a service however irksome, if it is so contrived that a reasonable relief may now and then be interposed, so as to ease the individual without injury to the public. We learn lately, that the account of General Carleton's approach to Ticonderoga was

premature, and in the mean time a considerable reinforcement has arrived from the Eastward, so that we
are no longer in pain for that post.

I am with much esteem, dear sir Yours sincerely.

His Excellency, PATRICK HENRY, Esq.

[VIRGINIA DELEGATES IN CONGRESS] TO GEORGE
WYTHE [1]

[RICHARD HENRY LEE, FR. LIGHTFOOT LEE, MANN PAGE, JR.]

SIR,   PHILADELPHIA May 20th 1777

We are favored with yours covering a resolve of Assembly to which we shall pay due attention.   The first
Volume of the last edition of the Journal of Congress,
is now published, and shall be forwarded to Williamsburg by the first opportunity.   This Volume reaches
no further than the 30th of december 1775.   As our
duty directs, so our inclinations lead to an immediate
compliance with the desires of the House of Delegates,
but we apprehend insurmountable difficulty in getting
the manuscript journal, because the many secret articles
cannot be exposed to a Copier, and neither the Secretary or ourselves have time to do it.   The Printer has
hitherto been delayed for want of paper, but now that
is obtained, we shall urge the publication of the remaining Journal, and send it to you Sir, with all the dispatch
in our power.

We have the honor to be with esteem and respect
                    Sir Your most obedient servants.

[1] A. L. by Richard Henry Lee.   Virginia State Library.   Addressed
to Wythe at Williamsburg, Virginia, and franked by Lee.   The original signatures have been cut out and are supplied in the margin of
the Ms.

P.S. We shall endeavor to prevail with the Post
Rider to take the Vol of Journal with him this Trip.

TO [THOMAS JEFFERSON][1]

Dear Sir,   Phil.ᵃ May 20. 1777
   We are this moment informed here, that some evil
disposed people (no doubt hired for the purpose) have
industriously propagated among the N. Carolina Troops,
and among the Recruits of Virginia in the upper parts,
that the plague rages in our Army — In consequence
of which, it is said, the recruiting business stops, and
desertions are frequent. There never was a more
infamous and groundless falsehood —
   The Army is extremely healthy, and the wisest methods are pursued to keep them So — I mention this dear
Sir, that some adequate plan may be adopted to stop
the progress of such wicked lies as are now, with industry circulated thro the Country. Force having
failed, our enemies, fraud is substituted, and corruption is swiftly and silently pushed thro every
quarter.
   One plan[2] now in frequent use, is, to assassinate the
Characters of the friends of America in every place,
and by every means.
   At this moment they are now reading in Congress,
an audacious attempt of this kind against the brave
General Arnold.
   Farewell dear Sir, I wish you happy.

Nothing new in Jersey.

[1] A. L. S. Library of Congress, Jefferson Correspondence, Letters
to Jefferson, Ser. 2, Vol. 51, No. 15.
[2] The words "that is" are here erased.

THE LETTERS OF RICHARD HENRY LEE

TO [GENERAL GEORGE WASHINGTON][1]

PHILADELPHIA 22^d May 1777

DEAR GENERAL

The subject of your letter of the 27th is a very important one, and whilst it deserves the greatest attention, is certainly involved in great difficulty. Of one truth however, I beg you Sir to be[2] convinced — That no desire *to get rid of importunity* has occasioned these appointments, but motives military and political meerly.

These Adventurers may be divided into three Classes, some who came early and without any recommendation but apparent zeal, with Commissions shewing that they had been in service — Others that brought with them recommendations from our good friend the Count D'Argoud General of Martinique, and from Mr Bingham the Continental agent in that Island — A third Class includes those who come from France, generally under agreement with our Commissioners, or one of them at least — The strongest obligations rest upon us, (tho' the inconvenience is great) to make good engagements with the latter,[3] and if the second had been disregarded we might have offended[4] a good & powerful Friend in Martinique who has done many good offices there; or have brought our Agent into disrepute — Among the first Class, I realy believe there are many worthless Men, and I heartily wish we were rid of them. All this is true, and yet I feel the great force of your reasoning, and the many difficulties in the way of providing for them properly and that may be tolerably

---

[1] A. dr. L. American Philosophical Society, Lee Papers, I. 313, No. 90. For Washington's reply see R. H. Lee, *Memoir of Richard Henry Lee*, II. 18.

[2] A word erased here appears to be " ever."

[3] " We " is here erased.   [4] The word " our " is here erased.

[ag][1]reeable to them. It is of some consequence that we all, [in][1] our several departments, endeavor to smooth this rug[ge][1]d business as much as possible — When Gen. Con[way][1] was appointed, I did hope that as he knew most [of ?][1] them, and spoke both french & English well, tha[t][1] [h][1]e might relieve you from the greater part of this difficulty, for realy, the discontented importunit[y][1] of the greater part of those Gentle^m is too much to be borne un[der][1] [o][1]ur various & important attention [* *][1] I will prevail with the Committee for foreign applications to furnish you with the most explicit views of Congress in ev[ery][1] appointment, as well as with the recommendations under which each appointment was and is made. We have written both to France & to Martinique to stop the furthe[r][1] flow of these Gentlemen here, and after[2] the letters arrive I suppose we shall have no more — Many of the last Comers, are, I believe, Men of real merit, and if they will learn to express themselves tolerably in English, may be of service to the Army. — The desire to obtain Engineers, and Artillerists was the principal[3] cause of our being so overburthened — The first that came had sagacity enough quickly to discern our wants, and professing competency in these branches, — they were too quickly believed — And when our Commissioners abroad (,in consequence of directions for this purpose) enquired for those Artists, Military Speculation was immediately up, and recommendations were obtained from persons of so much consideration in France, that the success of our applications then made it quite necessary not to neglect them — And at this moment I am apprehensive that the discontent of many may injure our cause abroad when we would wish it to stand well. [4]As you express it Sir, the affair requires great deli-

[1] Ms. torn.   [2] Written above "when" erased.
[3] Inserted above the line.   [4] "The" is here erased.

cacy in its management, as well on the account of our own Officers as on that of these Foreigners.

TO JOHN PAGE[1]

My dear Sir,   Philadelphia 26 May 1777

Finding by your letter of this post to your brother that you suppose I have been negligent in my correspondence with you my chief purpose here, is to remove that charge —

I do not remember which of us is debtor on the letter score, but as far as I do recollect, I think I was the Writer, not the Receiver of the last letter. However this may be, it appeared the less necessary for me to write, as I knew M: Page furnished you with regular intelligence, of what passed in the war department, besides which, I had nothing worth troubling you with, or calling my attention from the busy scene around me.

I observe in the Gazette, your call upon our Countrymen to apply some of their attention to the business of philosophy. Your reasoning is just, and I hope will have its due weight. I am sure that some among us have abundant [necess]²ity both for the study and the practise of the Moral part of that noble science. If this had been better learned, such an industrious attempt to injure my reputation in the opinion of my Countrymen would not have taken place — It has been a wicked industry, the most false, and the most malicious that the deceitful heart of Man ever produced. I am not on my own account affected with this malice of my enemies, because I have long panted for retirement

[1] A. L. S. Lenox Library, Myers Collection. Addressed to Page at Williamsburg, Virginia.
[2] Supplied in ink, Ms. torn.

from the most distressing pressure of business that I ever had conception of. But my principal concern arises from the dreadful example my case presents to cool the ardor of patriotism, and prevent the sacrifice of private ease to public service. I ought at least to have been heared in my defence — But Sir I will not trouble you with my feelings.

The enemies expected reenforcements from Europe have not yet arrived, in consequence of which, our army in Jersey outnumbers theirs considerably, but since they do expect 8 or 10,000 Men from beyond the Atlantic, and may bring the greatest part of their force round from Canada in order to make one last dying effort, it behooves us to be prepared to meet the desperate designs of desperate men. If no disappointment takes place, when their whole force is collected, I do not think they will be so strong as when the field was taken last year, and the American Army promises to be much more formidable. Skirmishing, still continues, and still we keep the superiority; insomuch that by the late manœuvres of the enemy, it seems not improbable that they intend to quit Jersey soon [.][1] They paid severely for their [p][1]rovision destroying excursion to Danbury, where besides their disgraceful flight, they did not loose less than 450 or 500 men killed & wounded — Governor Tryon, late a Major General; and Col? Wolcot, are both dead of the wounds they received in that chace — The last account from York tell us, that the British Officers look grave, and say, all hope of conquering America but by disuniting it is now lost. Great efforts will be made this year for that purpose, and no art or expence omitted to obtain by fraud what force has failed procure, the Court favorite "Subduction of America."

We hear that in the West Indies French Privateers abound under Continental Commissions, which I

[1] Ms. torn.

think cannot fail to procure war if Great Britain is not dead to every feeling except resentment for the Virtue of their once affectionate brethren and fellow subjects. The inclosed pamphlet is well written, and will I hope amuse you — Be pleased to give my brother Thom the reading of it when you have finished it —

Adieu my dear Sir, I am your affectionate Kinsman.

I hope to see you e'er long in Williamsburg —

TO [PATRICK HENRY][1]

My Dear Sir,   [May 26, 1777.]

If I have contributed in any degree to your satisfaction, or enabled you to combat false news intended to injure the cause of America, I am happy. I love that cause & I have faithfully exerted myself to serve it well. Provided America be free and happy, I am not solicitous about the Agents that accomplish it. For this reason Sir, I look with indifference on the malice of my enemies trusting that the wisdom of my Country will employ[2] in its great concerns such Men only as are of known, uniform attachment to the cause of America, and who

---

[1] A. dr. L. S. American Philosophical Society, Lee Papers, I. 211. A printed text with variations is in W. W. Henry, *Patrick Henry*, III. 73, and a Ms. text in the Virginia Historical Society. Lee's laborious work in congressional committees had at this time undermined his health, and his enemies in Virginia had attacked him in his absence and prevented his reëlection as a delegate to Congress by the Assembly in May. For the attack and Lee's complete vindication by the Virginia Assembly, see R. H. Lee, *Memoir of Richard Henry Lee*, I. 191–194. The attack called out a spirited letter from Richard Parker, dated April 24, 1777, defending him, in his absence, from the accusations. See Ms., Virginia State Library. Compare note to Lee's letter of June 25, 1777 to Landon Carter.

[2] With the four words following substituted above the line for "trust with their great concerns" erased.

possess wisdom, integrity and industry. But it has ever been my wish to deserve the esteem of virtuous men, and to stand well in their opinion.

Upon this principle I hope for your pardon when I trouble you with a detail of the Lease business. From motives of private ease, and as I thought, of public good, if the same plan were generally adopted in Virginia, I determined some years ago to break my Quarters up and rent out all my lands to a number of industrious Men who might benefit themselves, and ease me of trouble at the same time. As the support of a numerous family depended entirely upon these rents I was[1] brought to the alarming situation of seeing that family infinitely distressed when the Associatio[n][2] took place, by the Tenants not paying me, and assigning for reason that they could not sell their produce.[3] The present evil was then great and pressing, and well know^g the determination of G. B. to push her ruinous System, which w^d of course drive America into a long and expensive war that could only be supported by immense imissions of paper Money, which falling in value with its excessive quantity would render my small income (but barely sufficient with the greatest œconomy to maintain my family in the best times) totally insufficient, I did propose to Col^o Marshall, (who was one of my Tenants & Collector in Fauquier) so early as August 1775 to propose, by himself & Mr Blackwell, to [m]y tenants such a change of Rent as might enable them to pay, prevent my total ruin, and at the same time be not injurious to them; since the plenty of money which might lessen *its* value, would at the same time increase the

---

[1] These words are here erased: " induced to receive money rents knowing that I was secured from the fluctuating nature of a paper currency by the laws which did not oblige me to take it."

[2] Ms. torn.

[3] The words "Thus I was at that time" are here erased.

value of all their produce —This proposition you will observe Sir, was made in August 1775, at a time when emissions of money for this War were scarcely begun, and when of course the malignant insinuation of my enemies could not have existed with me, that of depreciating a Currency not yet in being. And it is worthy of remark, that in August 1776 the tenants of Loudon County did themselves petition the Convention (if I forget not) to have their money Rents changed to Produce — Col? Marshall very much approved the reasonableness of my proposal and promised to offer the matter to the consideration of the Tenant — I returned to this place and Col? Marsha[ll] soon after went into the Military line, so that nothing, that I know of, was done in this business, until March 1776, when yet very little money had been issued, and when of course this alteration could possibly have had not the least effect upon the credit of the paper money — At that time for the reasons already mentioned, I had for more than a year rec? little or no support from my estate to the great injury of my family; and being obliged to return here, I engaged M? Parker of Westmoreland to go up to Fauquier and propose to the Tenants to alter the Rents to Tobacco at a price mutually to be agreed on — This he did, and returned to me the alterations agreed on by all the Tenants except two or three — It was evidently better for me to get something than nothing Produce the Tenants could pay, and that Produce might be conveyed (at expence indeed, to some place where it could be sold for something,[1] whereby to maintain 2 children in Europe & many here [2] — Upon this perfectly in-

[1] Substituted for " a pittance " erased.
[2] These words are here erased: " As soon as I heard that the tongue of Slander was at work to misrepresent this transaction, I wrote to Desire Col? Marshall (who was then returned to Fauquier, and was still proposing the change from Money to Produce to a sett of Tenants under

nocent business, have my enemies, a pitiful sett of corrupt,[1] evil disposed men, endeavored to remove me from the Councils of my Country,[2] it['s] . . . ., presumably because I have served that Country with unremitting zeal and industry, and in concert with other generous friends to human liberty and the rights of America, have gone far towards defeating our enemies and raising American triumphant over its cruel, vindictive and determined foes. — But it seems there are two other charges equally futile & false, the one that I have favored New England to the injury of Virginia — The other, that as a Member of the secret Committee I objected to their proceedings being laid before Congress meaning to insinuate that [I wish]ed to conceal embezlement of the public money! — The wretch who carried or sent this[3] last[3] account to Virginia, knowg perfectly well that my total abstraction from every Commercial concern renders it impossible that I can propose any kind of good to myself from Trading concerns — But I have strong belief that a charge is wished, in order to remove obstruction apprehended from me,[4] and to prepare the way[5] for the execution of private plans[6] in which the public will not be gainer The affair alluded to is this, — The charge of favoring N. En. is so contemptibly wicked, that I can scarce

his care and different from those M[r] Parker had treated with), to desist, determining rather to meet the greatest injury than to have it even supposed that any conduct of mine was calculated to injure the public."

[1] "Tory" is here erased.

[2] The words "for no other reason" are here erased, and the word "presumably" in this line is written above an illegible word following "it['s]," and is substituted for the word "that" erased.

[3] Substituted for "that" erased.

[4] The three words preceding are substituted for "on my part" erased.

[5] The words "for public plunder" are here erased.

[6] Five words are here erased and illegible.

bring myself to the trouble of refuting it, or trespass on
your time to read my observations on it — Our enemies, & our friends too know that America can only be
conquered by disunion — The former, with unremitting
art had endeavored to fix immoveable Discord between
the Southern & Eastern[1] Colonies, and in truth Sir
they had so far prevailed, that it required constant
attention and a firmness not to be shaken, to prevent
the malicious art of our enemies from succeeding — I
am persuaded as I am of my existence, that had it not
been for Virg.[a] & N. Jersey, with Georgia some times,
that our Union would [e]er now have been, by this
means, broken like a Potters Vessel dashed against a
Rock — And I heartily wish that this greatest of all
evils may not yet take place before a safe and honorable
peace is established — I am sure it will not be the fault
of many men that I know if this is[2] does not happen —
I defy the poisonous tongue of Slander to produce a single instance in which I have prefered
the interest of N. E. to that of Virg.[a] — Indeed I am
at a loss to know wherein their interests clash — The
guilt of N. E. is that of a fixt determination against
British Tyranny, and such I believe is the crime of
Virginia in the eye of their common enemies — Most
of the rest have entitled themselves to some hopes of
pardon from the Tyrant, by weak, dividing, irresolute
and pernicious conduct — One thing is certain, that
among the Middle & Southern States, Virginia has
many enemies arising from Jealousy and envy of her
wisdom, vigor, and extent of Territory — But I have
ever discovered, upon every question, respect and love
for Virginia among the Eastern Delegates — Folly and
ingratitude would have marked the Representatives
of Virginia had they shewn disesteem for the latter

[1] " States " is here erased.
[2] The words " not the case event " are here erased.

and attachment to the former — I have serve[d] [1] my Country Sir, to the best of my knowledge and with fidelity & industry, to the injury of my health and fortune, and a sequestration from domestic happiness — I shall rejoice to find that others are employed who will do the business better than I have done, and I shall be ever happy in the reflection, that those Malignants who would represent me as an enemy to my Country cannot make me so — The business of War remains as when I wrote you last — The American Army increases but not so that of our enemies I believe our numbers are now 16000, and the best account of our enemies force is, that it does not in Jersey amount to 5000. From some late Manœuvres, it is not improbable that they design to quit Jersey for the present — It seems likely that they may be reenforced from Europe with 8 or 10,000 Men, but with these, they will not be so strong as they were the last Campaign, whilst our Army will be much more formidable — We have pretty good Accounts from N. York that Gov⸢r⸣ Tryon is dead of his wounds in the Danb[ury] [2] affair, with Col⸢o⸣ Woolcot, the writer of the insolent answer to Gen. Washingtons plan of exchange of prisoners — The Danbury business has turned out a Very unhappy business for our enemies — Pardon the trouble I have given you, and believe me to be dear Sir Affectionately yours.

[1] Ms. damaged.
[2] Margin covered.

THE LETTERS OF RICHARD HENRY LEE

TO —— ——[1]

DEAR GENERAL.   PHILADELPHIA   May 26. 1777

I well know your attachment to men of worth, and I am sure it will not be esteemed the less because it comes recommended by me.   I therefore, with pleasure introduce to your acquaintance and civilities the Bearer Mͬ Demmere a Gentleman of Georgia, who comes to the Army with a strong desire of becoming a part of it.   Bregadier Gen. Howe of Carolina recommends this gentleman to me as a person of great spirit and zeal in the American cause, and one whose activity and influence has served it much.   Your pamphlets are ready and I will contrive them by the first safe conveyance.

I am, with great regard, dear Sir your most affectionate and obedient.

TO [LANDON CARTER ?][2]

DEAR SIR,   WILLIAMSBURG   25ᵗʰ June 1777

I have but a moment to return you my thanks for your friendly and obliging letter.   It was impossible for me to avoid feeling the unmerited ill treatment[3] that I had received, but I have now the pleasure to

[1] A. L. S.   Maine Historical Society, Fogg Collection.   The leaf with address is torn off.

[2] A. L. S.   Virginia Historical Society, Ms. among Arthur Lee Papers.

[3] For the subject of these charges see Col. Banister's letter in *The Bland Papers*, I. 57, and see also Lee's letter to Patrick Henry, May 26, 1777, herein.   From Ms. letters in the Virginia Historical Society it appears that on June 10, 1777, Mann Page Jr. and Francis

303

inform you that the two houses have removed all bad impressions by their favorable approbation of my conduct; and they have directed me to return to Congress as one of their Delegates. This letter is a most oppressive business, and therefore unsought by me, but having put my hand to the plough I am bound to go through. Not much important business has yet been done, but they propose to crowd a good deal into this week, at the end of which they talk of rising.

I am affectionately yours.

Lightfoot Lee wrote George Wythe, Speaker of the House of Delegates of Virginia, from Philadelphia, asking leave of the House to "return home immediately and that other gentlemen may be sent to fill our places," on account of what had passed in the House and the attack on R. H. Lee, as they said they feared when absent and engaged in a painful service they might be deprived "in an instant" of their reputations by "envy, hatred & malice." The attack on Lee was repeated, for Mann Page Jr. wrote October 27, 1777, to R. H. Lee that he hears another attack is to be made by his enemies, "their Catspaw" having carried to Williamsburg "an attested copy of your letter to Scott," and he asks if he cannot spare time to come and silence "such a set of miscreants." William Booth wrote R. H. Lee as follows: —

"DEAR SIR.   CAMDEN, Oct. 7th 1777

I take the opportunity by Mr Harvey to acquaint you that there is to be a severe attack made on you, at the meeting of the Assembly. I understand they have got your letter to Capt. Scott: I flatter myself you will be able to clear up the point to your satisfaction and all your friends' and that you may get the better of all your Enemies I shall be glad to hear from you by the first opportunity. I beg you will write me all the news you have, as we can hear nothing that can be depended on.

Your most affe^c, hble Servt

WILL. BOOTH."

THE LETTERS OF RICHARD HENRY LEE

TO ARTHUR LEE[1]

GREEN SPRING IN VIRGᴬ 30ᵗʰ June 1777

MY DEAR BROTHER,

Ten days ago I arrived at Williamsburg to attend our General Assembly on business. I left Philadelphia the 15ᵗʰ instant, and shall return again to Congress the 1ˢᵗ of August, after a months rest at home. From Philadelphia I wrote you a pretty exact detail of our Affairs from Gen. Howes retreat from the White Plains in the N. York Government up to the 15ᵗʰ instant. Since I came here, the last Post informs us that Gen Howe had arrived in Person at Brunswick in the Jersies with a strong reenforcement, and having thus collected his force from every quarter, his Army was rather superior in number to that of Gen. Washington — Say the former about 12,000 men & the latter about 10,000 — Gen Howe advanced with 7000 to Sommerset Court House going towards Delaware — Where about 6000 Militia were collected under the Generals Sullivan, Mifflin & Arnold — Gen. Washington had ordered 4000 Eastern Troops to join him from the East side of North river, where about 7 or 8000 were stationed to prevent by sudden Manœuvre the enemy from possessing themselves of the Highlands on Hudsons river and so opening the communication with Canada as they formerly proposed. The regular Army therefore joined to the Corps of Militia in Jersey it was expected in a few days would amount to 20,000 men, with which Howe would certainly be attacked, if he did not return quickly to his Strong Camp on the Brunswick hills, and it is not certain that he will long avoid the attack

---

[1] A. L. S. University of Virginia, Lee Papers, No. 60. Addressed, "Honorable Arthur Lee esquire / Commissioner from the American / Congress to the Court of Spain / at / Madrid."

305

even there. The American Troops are in high spirits and eager for action. Things are all well in the North about Lake Champlain, where a sufficient force will be in time collected to prevent any apprehention from Gen. Carleton. The necessity of passing all our Troops thro inoculation in this Spring hath retarded the making up our Army both in Jersey & at Ticonderoga, but this Herculean work is now pretty well over and we shall presently have a very formidable Army in the former and 10,000 men at the latter.[1] Great Britain may therefore bid adieu to N. America, which the most wanton folly has forever seperated from her. Nothing can prevent this if our funds do not fail us, but you may judge how precarious things must be that depend upon continued emissions of paper money, if no extensive Loan can be procured in Europe, or if a War in Europe does not so employ the British attention as to enable us to send our produce to European Markets. Both these points demand the deepest consideration of those who mean to secure the seperation of this Country from Britain.[1] Our Privaters & Armed Vessels continue to be very successful against the British Trade & Transports.

I have written by this opportunity to our brother William supposing him to be in France — I have told him that the times prevent me from making remittance, and therefore that my Sons must be sent to me by the first good opportunity if he cannot continue to advance for their frugal maintenance in France a small time longer — I wish Ludwell to go deep into the study of Natural and Civil law, and Eloquence; as well as to obtain the military improvement you put him on. My desire being that he may be able to turn either to the law or the Sword here, as his genius or his interest, and the service of his Country might point out. I want

[1] Marked with a line, by Arthur Lee probably, for emphasis.

Thom to possess himself of the knowledge of business either in M:̲ Sweighausers Counting House, or under his Uncle if he sh:̲ᵈ go into business in France, and learn the French language, so that when he returned to his own Country he might be qualified to undertake any foreign business that may be trusted to his care. But all or any part of this plan depends I apprehend entirely on their Uncle William —

Should any unhappy accident have befallen him and thereby prevented him from coming to France, I must rely on you to direct them to be sent over to me by the first safest opportunity — This M:̲ Schweighauser can contrive for me as you desire. This letter goes by a M:̲ John King of Hampton Merchant, a Gent:̲ of reputation here, and who goes to France on commercial motives, he sails in a swift going Vessel that probably cannot be taken, & I believe he will accommodate my boys with a passage if they are now to return.

God bless you and give your success in your Mission— Much very much depends u[pon it]

Farewell.

TO SAMUEL ADAMS [1]

July the 12ᵗʰ 1777. CHANTILLY.

MY DEAR SIR,

I thank you for your obliging favor of the 26ᵗʰ of June, it brought me the most circumstantial and satisfactory account of the enemies movements that I have received. As far as distance will allow us to judge of such things, it seems to me as if Gen. Howe designed, by his last sortie from Amboy, to remove our Army to such convenient distance, as to avoid the danger arising

[1] A. L. S. Lenox Library, Samuel Adams Papers. Franked, and addressed to Adams, "Member of Congress at/Philadelphia."

from embarkation in the face of a strong force. A proper attentention being paid to the means of rendering this Campaign successful, the next great object is certainly the *Confederation.* This great bond of Union, will more effectually than anything else, produce present strength, credit, and success; and secure future peace and safety: Nor can any human plan more conclusively establish American Independence. I incline to think that this last effect of Confederation is clearly discerned by the friends of Dependence, because it is obvious, that those generally, who were marked foes to . the declaration of independence, are the men that now thwart and delay Confederation, altho they are obliged to act with more reserve and cautious concealment of their true motives. These considerations should urge the friends of America to a firm and persevering union, to finish this all important business quickly as possible. Let the days appointed for this purpose be *devoted* to that alone, and let the Green mountain, and its Boys too; be sunk in the red Sea, rather than be the occasion of calling you off from the accomplishment of this momentous, and greatest of all earthly considerations. But what occasion can there be my friend, for such an infinity of criticism and care, about that, which is to undergo revision by our Masters before it becomes authentic ?

I grant it should be well considered, and digested with judgement; but such excessive refinement, and pedantic affectation of discerning future ills in necessary, innocent, and indeed proper establishments, I cannot hear with patience.

Hitherto Congress has been greatly wanting in not giving quick intelligence to their Commissioners in Europe of events here. You know how heavily they, and our other friends, have complained of this neglect. If the proper Committee does it not, I think Congress should take measures therein. The late movements of Gen. Howe, and their consequences, appear to me sufficiently important to be notified immediately. Slow moving France may have its pace quickned by shewing the weakness of G. B., and removing from her yet smarting apprehension, the dread of British power. If Howe has been obliged to change his situation from Continental to Insular, it will be a striking proof of this weakness. My friend Mʳ Lovell informs me that these words are to be inserted in the latter Commissions, "agreable to instructions now *and hereafter to be* sent" — I am utterly at a loss to know what good can result from this insertion. Are the instructions to be publickly produced, or is any business to be done? The former is without example, and the latter is fraught with most pernicious consequences. Indicision, doubt, and perhaps fraudulent intentions, may be charged upon such a mode of procedure; nor can I think that any sensible Man will be found to undertake a business, that must necessarily expose him to contempt, if not to worse consequences. I incline to think that if you wish to have this business done with propriety and effect, it will be better to agree on a P—n Agent, and one for Vi—n. a — less exposed to the envy & hatred of a certain sett than your friend the Al—d—n — I hope to be with you early in August, until which time, I wish your leisure may permit you to continue a correspondence so much valued by your affectionate friend.

THE LETTERS OF RICHARD HENRY LEE

TO THOMAS PAINE [1]

DEAR SIR,   CHANTILLY   July 13ᵗʰ 1777

Your obliging favor of the fourth I have received and thank you for it. Your conjecture concerning the principle on which Gen. Howes first movement to Somerset Court House was made, is I believe very just. And if it be true that he has crossed with his Army to Staten Island, I think it is pretty plain that his sortie from Amboy was calculated to remove our Army to a convenient distance, and there avoid the danger of embarking in the face of a powerful enemy. Upon the whole, these manœuvres evidently shew the weakness of our enemies, and the improbability of their quickly doing anything effectual to the accomplishment of their views against this Continent. In this light, it appears to me of much consequence that an early transmission of Gen. Howes motions, thus far, should be made to our Commissioners [2] in France & Spain — The procrastinating genius [3] of the Committee will, I fear, greatly injure our affairs in Europe, and produces a wish that you would, [4] officially, transmit the papers containing the Congress publications of these wants to Dᵣ Franklin & Dᵣ Lee. By sending them to a trusty hand in Massachusetts or N. Hampshire concerning which you may be advised by

<hr>

[1] A. L. S. American Philosophical Society, Lee Papers, I. 331, No. 95. Addressed to Paine as "Secretary to the / Committee of Congress / for Foreign Affairs." Lee's frank and direction are as follows: "Free 3 A / Col: Richᵈ Henry Lee Esqᵣ / of Chantilly / Westmoreland County / To be left with James Hunter Esqᵣ Mercht./ Near Fredericksburg/Virginia."

[2] The word "both" is here erased.

[3] Substituted for the words "mischief" and "spirit" written here first and erased.

[4] The words "ex officio" are here erased.

M⸱ Adams or Col⸱ Whipple, the frequent opportunities
from the Eastward will¹ furnish speedy & safe conveyances. I know that some adventurous Politicians think,
or affect to think, that it were better for America, Foreign interference should not take place until we had
evidenced our ability to work out our own salvation —
Whether a state of obligation be the best, I will not undertake to destmine, [determine?], but I incline to
think, that the reception of favors when they can be returned, serve to bind Men more strongly together in
friendly union — But whilst I feel myself compelled to
consider American Independence as the greatest good,
and a return to the domination of G. B after what has
happened, as the greatest evil, I am willing to embrace
every measure that tends to secure the one, and guard
against the other. I am alarmed for our funds, and² I
am not quite free from apprehension, whilst our enemies
whole force, both of Arms and Arts, is employed against
us. I wish therefore that France & Spain may come
forward without much longer delay, and by so doing,
render secure our best and surest good. Both France
& Spain doubt our strength, and fear our return to the
former connection — The unremitting care³ of⁴ the
Court of London hath been to cherish and support this
way of thinking — It is our business to counteract their
plan, by the most frequent & most authentic transmissions of our State & of events here — The first of
August I hope to see you in Philadelphia and remain
in the meantime
　　　　Sir &

¹ Substituted for "may" erased.
² "I have some under" is here erased.
³ Substituted for "power" erased.
⁴ "G. B" is here erased.

THE LETTERS OF RICHARD HENRY LEE

TO LANDON CARTER[1]

DEAR SIR,

CHANTILLY 22ᵈ July 1777

I shall take care of your letter for my brother, and of the parcel for Dᵣ Shippen.

It would give me pleasure to furnish you with better news than this post has brought us, however, it is what

[1] Ms. copy. Virginia Historical Society, Lee Papers, IV. 130. Mr. Cassius F. Lee added to the transcript this note: —

"Note: the foregoing letter was written on a half sheet of foolscap & Col. Carter writes thus on the back, taking up ⅔ds of the same.

'F. Lee writes July 14. to his brother R. H. Lee that Genˡ Schuyler on the 9ᵗʰ tells the Congress that Lieut. Hay, a deputy quarter Master at Ticonderoga informed him that on the 5ᵗʰ St Clair and the officers determined to evacuate Ticonderoga but he knows not why, and knew not the situation of the enemy. Accordingly St Clair and the Army marched out of the lines of Independence on the 6ᵗʰ, but with what design or whither gone nobody could tell, & St Clair has not been since heard of.

'Schuyler apprehends they may have surrendered to the enemy. Except 600 men who when St Clair left independence, came off with Vessells & batteus down with Ammunition &c, which all but the men fell into the hands of the enemy.

'Schuyler is at Fort Edward with 1500 men but without a necessary, as he had sent every thing to Ticonderoga. A Brigade from Peekskill was on the road from Albany to Join him (Schuyler). As the pursuing enemy was spreading an Universal Panic over all that part of the Country.

'Burgoyne dispersing most terrific Proclamations, threatening fire and sword to all who resisted: but mercy and Solid coin to all who submitted with their Provisions. Howe still at N.Y. expected every day to begin some operation. Who that ever heard of this Suspected Scotchman St Clair could have expected anything else but treachery. As soon as I heard Gates would not serve under him, I asked his Country? was told he was a Scotchman, and a Suspected one. Immediately I said farewell Ticonderoga. Thus are we every now & then paying for our imprudence by Seniority truly. We lost Quebec in the same way —

'Old Wooster was as ill suited to that long March, as I am: and had

312

we might expect after the intelligence of last week. I have enclosed my brother's letter to Col° Tayloe and desired him to send it [to] you.

My opinion is, that this success will only serve to bring Burgoyne into the Country, so far, as to produce his ruin — Which God of his infinite mercy grant. I thank you much for your very friendly wishes and assure you that I am with sincere regard your affectionate friend and obedient servant.

LANDON CARTER esquire of Sabine Hall.

TO SAMUEL ADAMS[1]

CHANTILLY IN VIRGINIA   July 27ᵗʰ 1777

I am extremely obliged to my worthy friend for his last favor of the 15ᵗʰ nor did the former one need any apology, it being by much the most satisfactory account of the enemies movements in Jersey that I have seen. I wish with all my heart we had given them a stroke before they got away. But a philosophic Poet tells us that "Whatever *is*, is right.'['] Let us comfort ourselves therefore with the hope that more complete vengeance is yet in store for these Hostes humani generis. The success of Burgoyne thus far, I own I did expect, if he made the attempt — But I am also inclined to think

he recovered the fatigue, tho' brave enough to die in the bed of honour: he knew as little of a Soldier as I do. No doubt St Clair has taken the advantage of the latter part of Burgoyne's Proclamation and I wish he may not persuaded the remaining of his 2000 men to do the same; for when such rascals command so snug at a distance they generally convey the same Poison in plentiful portions. It is this General Gray of N. Britain, Call a Scotchman a rebell and he is ready to swallow it, but yet say his for the Laird of his clan, & then you are his *****. And yet who so great enemies to this Present Tyrant?'"

[1] A. L. S. Lenox Library, Samuel Adams Papers. Addressed to Adams, "Member of Congress at / Philadelphia."

that if our Cards are well plaid, it may prove his ruin. There is nothing so delusive as prosperity, and I take Burgoynes mind to be one of those most likely to be injured by its impressions; he may therefore be hurried into some fatal mistake, provided we are ready to profit from his errors. Our friend Gen. Gates is devoted to the virtuous cause of America, and therefore above being too much moved by ill treatment, and so affected thereby as to withdraw his aid from the cause of Mankind —

Suppose He, & Gen. Arnold were sent Eastward to collect quickly, for a short service, an army equal to the purpose of catching Burgoyne at a distance from the water? Might not his return be for ever prevented, and a glorious issue given to this Campaign? I must confess that I should not hesitate about this proceedure, because, tho Burgoyne came not forward, the force so collected would be ready to assist in crushing Howe, should Heaven deliver him once more on the White Plains to the possibility of destruction. It will give me much pleasure to find on my return to Congress, that the Confederation has been duly attended to. That once concluded, and firmly ratified, will throw despair into our enemies politics, and their Tory Abbettor[s.] Our funds too demand most close & wise attention. A fine Battalion raised by this State, for its own use, was last Wednesday inoculated at Alexandria in its way to Head Quarters, and our Assembly have directed a draft, if the six last Regiments are not filled before the 25 of next month —

I hope to be with you on or before the 11th of August till when I remain as usual your affectionate friend.

THE LETTERS OF RICHARD HENRY LEE

TO JOHN PAGE[1]

PHILADELPHIA, 17th Aug. 1777.

MY DEAR SIR,

Were it not for the very disgraceful evacuation of Ticonderoga and the loss of our Stores there, we should have little but good to relate of this Campaign as far as it has gone. The Generals Schuyler and St. Clair are ordered down to Head Quarters, where an enquiry will be instituted, and the public fully acquainted with the whole of that business. Gen. Gates is reappointed to the command of the Northern Army and by this time has joined it. The Militia is turning out to join that army, and now that they have the General they love and can confide in, I hope our affairs in that quarter will soon wear a better countenance. Already Gen. Hackerman of the N. York Militia has beaten a part of the enemies forces and slain 50 Indians. Gen. Howes fleet was seen off the Eastern Shore of Maryland on the 7th instant, stearing southward, but it is somewhat doubtful whether his troops are on board now or not, and if they are, it is surely the strangest Manœuvre that was ever before put in practice — For, is it not wonderful, that whilst Burgoyne is pushing into the Country on one quarter, Howe should quit it on another? Time will explain this, at present, inexplicable movement. In the meantime Gen. Washingtons forces are so placed as to be ready to meet Mr. Howes visitation if it happens any where but on the two extremes of the United States. Our information from Europe does not promise us immediate war, but we are sure of very substantial aid from thence, whilst the powerful Armaments quickly preparing by France and Spain denote approaching war

[1] From a printed text in a New York Collector's Catalogue from an A. L. S. by Lee, presented by Dr. J. F. Jameson.

315

and certainly will check the British violence against or[1] by the necessity it creates of watching their powerful and dangerous Neighbors. The spirit of France rises with the increase of its Fleet, since we learn that when the British Ambassador lately told the Ministry that if N. America continued to be supplied from France, that the Peace could not long continue — He was answered 'Nous ne desiron pas la guérre, et nous ne le craignon pas.' Dr. Lee is returned from Spain, and set out in May for the Court of Prussia. Gen. Lee is removed on board the Centurion, but we are not certain whether the ship remains at York or is gone with the Fleet. We hear that a Speech of Lord Chathams in the house of Lords lately has come to N. York, but they will not publish it, in which his Lordship advises them to make peace with America immediately on *Any terms*, assuring them they have no more chance to conquer this Country with the force they have or can get, than he to conquer Britain with his Crutch, and that the longer they contend the more certain will be their ruin and disgrace. The good old Man, instead of being dead as was reported, is, it seems, recovered to better health and revived powers.

Pray my dear Sir urge on our Works near the Falls of James River, we want heavy cannon extremely — And it would be greatly to our advantage if Copper and Calamine could be found in·quantity sufficient to furnish us with Brass. My compliment to Mrs. Page.

Farewell dear Sir Affectionately yours.

P.S. If Government was now and then to stimulate the Managers of the Salt Works, might we not hope for a supyly[2] of that necessary. I fear Howe is gone to Charles Town in South Carolina. If so, against such

[1] Probably an error for " us."
[2] Probably a misprint for " supply."

a Land and Sea force no effectual resistance can be
made —   curse on his Canvas Wings.

Honourable JOHN PAGE esquire at Williamsburg in Virginia.

TO THOMAS JEFFERSON[1]

DEAR SIR,   PHIL.ᵃ August 25. 1777

It will not perhaps be disagreeable to you in your retirement, sometimes to hear the events of war, and how
in other respects we proceed in the arduous business we
are engaged in. Since the loss of Ticonderoga (into the
cause of which, and the conduct of the commanding
Officers, Congress have ordered enquiry to be made) and
Gen. Burgoynes speedy march to Fort Edward, our
affairs in that quarter begin to wear a favorable appearance. In addition to Burgoynes force, another Body
of Men came down the Mohawk river, by way of Os-
wego, and laid siege to Fort Stanwix, or Schuyler, as it
is now called. At this place, a battle ensued with the
Tryon County Militia, in which the enemy were driven
from the ground with a loss of more than 200 Indians
and several regulars. Col.º Willet making a Sally from
the Fort did great injury to the enemy, and took from
them a great quantity of baggage with 2 or 3 field pieces.
However, the Militia having lost many men in this
Action and their best officers having been killed or
wounded, they retired and left the enemy to return and
lay Siege to Fort Schuyler, which the garrison was
bravely defending, when Gen. Arnold was detached
with a body of men to relieve the place — We expect
every day to hear of his success — To the northward

[1] A. L. S. Library of Congress, Jefferson Correspondence, Letters
to Jefferson, Ser. 2, Vol. 51 No. 16. Addressed to him in Albemarle
County, Virginia.

of this, in the N. Hampshire grants, Gen. Stark with 2000 Militia attacked Col? Baum and 1500 Regular Troops behind works, and with Cannon — The consequence you will find in the enclosed Hand bill — This was an important victory, well timed, and will probably occasion M! Burgoyne to retire very quickly. If he does not, I can venture to *Augur* his distruction. He is at Saratoga & Fort Edward, our main Army a few miles in front of the mouth of Mohock river. I expect Generals Lincoln & Arnold will presently be in his rear, after which, his chance of returning will be very small. Gen. Gates has joined the Northern Army & now commands in that quarter — Putnam with 5000 men commands on the heights of Hudsons river above N. York, in which place Gen. Clinton is left with about 3000 men — After Gen. Howe had long raised the curiosity of this part of the world, to know what could be his view in embarking his Army and coasting it for 5 weeks in a most oppressively hot season; at length, he appears at the very head of Chesapeak Bay where he remains with more than 200 sail of Vessels — His troops not yet landed that we know of, but imagine they were put on shore yesterday. We are left yet to guess his object. It may be supposed either for this City, or to conduct a line from Chesapeak to Newcastle and thereby inclose a large tract of Country between that Bay, Delaware, and the Sea. Let his plan be what it may, Gen. Washington, with a gallant Army passed is gone to enter a Caveat. The General with his Army passed thro this City yesterday, and they made a fine appearance — To aid the Army, and make the business secur[e] Congress has called for Militia from this State, Delawar[e,] Maryland, & the Northern Counties of Virginia. Should Gen. Ho[we] venture to enter the Country against this force, I think his ruin will be sure, notwithstanding we are told his Master depends on the "desperate efforts that Generals Howe & Cornwalls must make to redeem their Bankrupt honor" So we learn from France the King of England hath said. We have no reason to suppose, from our foreign intelligence that a war in Europe will immediately take place, but that every preparation for it is making, remains without doubt; and in the mean time we shall surely receive most substantial Aid from our friends there. The fleet of France grows stronger daily, and with it, the spirit of the Court rises, as appears by the answer made to Lord Stormont when he told the french Minister that "the peace cannot continue long if N. America continues to draw supplies From France" "Nous ne desirons pas la gueer et nous ne le craignons pas" In truth, every art of falsehood and fraud has been practised to prevent a war there, but it seems clear that this will not *long* prevail — D̲r̲ Lee is returned from Spain, and is gone to the Prussian Court. That Monarck is fond of commerce and is desirous of being acquainted with the whole nature of ours. He is offended with the Court of London, and has no reason to fear its resentment. We have good reason to expect considerable advantage from his friendship — If our funds fail us not, and our Union continues, no cause was ever safer than ours — To prevent the former, most extensive and vigorous taxes should immediately take place. The sum in circulation is immense and no corrective can be applied but Taxation, nor was there ever a time when the vast plenty of money rendered that business more easy. The Loan Office, with that, will I believe answer, and upon the success of our funds will probably depend the Unity of our exertions. The Confederation goes on but slowly, occasioned by the immensity of business created by the war — But I find our right to our Charter bounds, as stated by our Act of Government will be strongly contested. The Charter of 1609 it is said has been vacated, and that no transfer of that Charter right can be shewn from the Company to the people of Virginia. That therefore the ungranted lands were the property of the Crown, & being taken from it, by common exertions, must become common Stock — Will you be so kind as favor me with your reasons & authorities in support of our right ?

I am, with great regard & esteem, dear Sir Your most affectionate and obedient Se[v.]

TO PATRICK HENRY[1]

DEAR SIR,   PHILADELPHIA 8th Sept.r. 1777.

Nothing new hath happened that we know of since my last. But it seems extremely probable that a general engagement will take place in a day or two between the American Army and Gen. Howe. The Quaker motto ought to be "Nos turba sumus," for if you attack one the whole society is roused. You will see by the inclosed testimonies a uniform, fixed enmity to American measures, which, with the universal ill fame of some capital persons, has occasioned the arrest of old Pemberton and several others, to prevent their mischievous interposition in favor of the enemy at this critical moment, when the enemies' army is on its way here, with professed design to give this city up to the pillage of the soldiery. They have taken infinite pains, according to custom, to move heaven and earth in their favor, and have transmitted copies of their indecent remonstrances over the country. Congress have, to prevent ill impressions, ordered their several inimical testimonies to be published in one Hand-bill. Altho' noth-

[1] From the text printed in William Wirt Henry, *Patrick Henry*, III. 92.

ing can be more certain than that allegiance & protection are reciprocal duties, yet these men have the assurance to call for the protection of those laws and that Government which they expressly disclaim, and refuse to give any evidence of their allegience to. There is no doubt but that they will endeavor by means of the "Friends" in Virginia, to make disturbance and raise discontent there, but this may serve to put you on your guard. We understand that Gen. Howe has put all his heavy baggage, and even his tents, on board ship, and that all his fleet, except a few ships of war, have fallen down to the mouth of Sassafrass, and many of them gone down the bay—The army has three or four days victuals cooked, and by all their maneuvres it seems clear that they mean to urge their way to this place. Genl. Washington is within 6 miles of their main body, and determined not to remove without a battle. By your letter of the 30th last, it would seem that you have not received many letters from me that I have written, not one post since my arrival here on the 12. of August having gone without a letter to you with all the national news, besides one by express. It is really discouraging to write so much as I do, having so little time, and yet my friends not receive my letters. This day Congress has proposed that the Quaker Tories should be sent forthwith to Staunton in Augusta. I hope you will have them well secured there, for they are mischievous people. Should Howe be disappointed here, as it seems very likely that he will, it is more than probable that he will endeavor to do us all the injury in his power as he returns, and therefore it will be wise to be as well prepared for him as possible — I am dear sir, most affectionately yours.

His Excellency, Patrick Henry, Esq.

P.S. — The worthy Baron Kalb desires me to ask your good offices in procuring his baggage to be forwarded, by sending you the enclosed, which shows the route travelled, and where his trunks were left — at Wright's ordinary.

TO PATRICK HENRY[1]

My dear Sir,   Philadelphia, Sep 13ᵗʰ 1777.

On the 11ᵗʰ instant at Chadsford on the Brandywine, about ten miles from Wilmington, we had a most bloody battle with Gen. Howe's whole army, which ended, after 4 hours engagement, in the enemies keeping the field and our army retiring. But Gen. Howe may say with Pyrrhus, such another victory will ruin me. Every account of officers and country people, who have been in the field since the action, say the Enemy's loss in killed and wounded must be between 2 & 3000. Nothing proves this more strongly than their remaining yet upon the field of battle, when every interest calls upon them to push on. Our loss in killed & wounded scarcely comes up to 500. The Militia were never engaged, nor was a strong division of our Army much in battle. The Virginia troops have gained immortal honor. No capital offices are lost, and none wounded, except the Marquis Fayette in the leg, & Gen Woodford in the hand, but neither badly. Our army is now, the greatest part, between Darby & Schuylkill, two brigades on this side — all in high spirits & wishing for another trial with the enemy. We are collecting reinforcements with all diligence, & hope yet to give a good account of Gen. Howe. Gen. Smallwood

---

[1] From the text printed in William Wirt Henry, *Patrick Henry*, III. 96.

THE LETTERS OF RICHARD HENRY LEE

FACSIMILE OF LETTER IN LEE'S AUTOGRAPH FROM DELEGATES TO CONGRESS
TO THE MORAVIANS OF BETHLEHEM, PENNSYLVANIA.

with 1500 Maryland militia is coming fast upon the enemy's rear.

Farewell dear Sir.

His Excellency, PATRICK HENRY, Esq.

DELEGATES TO CONGRESS TO [THE MORAVIANS OF BETHLEHEM, PENNSYLVANIA][1]

BETHLEHEM September the 22^d 1777

Having here observed a humane and diligent attention to the sick and wounded, and a benevolent desire to make the necessary provision for the relief of the distressed, as far as the powers of the Bretheren enable them. We desire that all Continental Officers may refrain from disturbing the persons or property of the Moravians in Bethlehem, and particularly that they do not disturb or molest the Houses where the women are assembled. Given under our hands at the time and place above mentioned.

[1] A. L. S. by Richard Henry Lee. Signed also in autograph by "Nathan Brownson, Nath!! Folsom, Richard Law, John Hancock, Samuel Adams, Elepht Dyer, Ja^s: Duane, W^m: Duer, Cour^d Harnett Henry Laurens, Benj Harrison, Jos: Jones, John Adams, Henry Marchant, Wm Williams; Delegates to Congress." Bethlehem, Pa. Facsimile given by the courtesy of the Proprietor of the Sun Inn and of the Sesqui-Centennial Memorial Committee of the Moravian Church; on this is written the following note: "The letter, of which the above is a Photographic Copy, was *written and signed* in *this the* 'Sun Inn'* September the 22nd 1777, as proven by the Moravian Church Records of that date. The Original is in the handwriting of Richard Henry Lee, & is yet in the possession of the Moravian Church, Charles Brodhead."

THE LETTERS OF RICHARD HENRY LEE

TO PATRICK HENRY[1]

My dear Sir,   York 8th Oct. 1777.

I must make one general apology for the matter and manner of my letters — the want of time to discharge with propriety an hundredth part of the business with which I am crowded. My eyes fail me fast, and I believe my understanding must soon follow this incessant toil. We have had another general engagement with the enemy at and near German Town — With ours, we attacked their army — The plan was well concerted, and the execution was so bravely conducted, that a most brilliant victory was on the moment of being obtained, when accident alone removed it from us. The morning was so foggy, which with the state of the air keeping down the smoke of the cannon &c, effectually prevented our people from knowing their success, occasioned delay, and gave the enemy time to rally and return to the charge, which they did five several times. But this was not the worst, our right & left columns mistook each other for enemies, and apprehending a fresh reinforcement, gave way too soon to a last effort of the enemy, and quitted a glorious victory absolutely in their power. However, they retired in order, and had so severely handled the enemy that they dared not pursue, and our wounded with everything valuable was brought off. Our army is now upon the ground they left before the battle, in high spirits, and satisfied they can beat the enemy. I hope they will quickly have an opportunity, as the reinforcements from our country have reached the army since the engagement. Our loss is pretty well fixed to 700, killed, wounded and

[1] From the text printed in William Wirt Henry, *Patrick Henry*, III. 100.

325

missing. That of the enemy not certainly known but surely very great, as you may judge by the following intelligence brought this evening by Gen. Green's aid, and which he says may be relied on. Genl Agnew, Colonels Woolcot, Abercrombie & Thos. Byrd (from Virginia) with General De Heister's son killed. Gen Knephausen wounded in the hand, and between 2 and 300 Waggons loaded with wounded sent into Philadelphia. That Gen Howe had sent about 2000 Hessians over Schuylkill (denoting a retreat,) and that he refused to let any of the inhabitants of Philadelphia go to see the field of battle. Gen. Schyler writes us the 29th of september, that if superior numbers, health, and spirits can give success, our army in the Northern department will have it this campaign. For my part, I do not despair of success in this quarter also. Another such battle as the last, will totally unfit Gen. Howe for pursuing further hostilities this campaign, and again possess us of Philadelphia.

Suffer me now, Sir, to recommend to your interest the appointment of the French Artillerists mentioned in our public letter by this express. You may depend upon it that these are masters of the art they profess, and are people of character. They are part, and the better part of General Coudray's Corps, who were returning to France upon the death of that general, but prevailed on to remain until our Country could be consulted about employing them. The terms seem high, but the knowledge they possess, and we want, is to us above price. Some Gentlemen from other States have been applying to them, but on inquiry they like the accounts they have received from Virginia better than any other. Now that we have got from under the protection of G. Britain, it is indispensably necessary that we understand well the use of cannon, and be strongly provided with them. Capt. Loyeaute, whom we propose for colonel of our Battalion of Artillery, is really a man of sience, and not unacquainted with practise, and if he can prevail on the Veteran Sergeants to go with him, we shall gain a competency in that art so necessary, and which we are so unacquainted with. The inclosed is the substance of the account brought by Gen¹ Green's aid. Be so good as to present my respects to Mr. Page, and excuse me for not writing to him as I really have not time.

I have a very good opinion of Col Carrington, and would willingly serve him, but I much doubt whether the erasure of the Journal you propose can be obtained, but I will try.

I am very sincerely and affectionately yours.

His Excellency PATRICK HENRY, Esq.

TO ARTHUR LEE [1]

YORK TOWN IN PENNSYLV^ 13ᵗʰ Oct! 1777

MY DEAR BROTHER,

I heard with much pleasure that you were destined to the Court of Berlin, because I think you may be able to do your Country essential service there. The power and the maginimity of the Prussian Monarch puts him above apprehensions from the Court of London for pursuing measures dictated by true generosity and the interest of his people. A Port in the North for our Privateers, Prizes, and for the conduct of Commerce, will much benefit both Countries. It is indisputably certain that a most extensive and mutually beneficial commerce may be carried on between the dominions of Prussia and these United States; But it is unfortu-

[1] A. L. S. University of Virginia, Lee Papers, No. 81. Addressed to him as "one of the Commissioners from the United States / of America to the Court of France, Paris."

nate for us, that whilst we are left singly to oppose the whole force of G. Britain (young as we are in war) we are prevented from giving experimental proofs of the benefits of our commerce, by the impossibility of sending our products or getting those of other Countries. His Prussian Majesty has power, by a variety of ways, to call away much of the British attention from us and thereby facilitating commercial intercourse. Add to this, that the public acknowledgement of the Independency of these States, by his Prussian Majesty would give dignity, and advantage to our cause, and procure the same acknowledgement from other Powers. The Committee have written so fully of the events of war in their public letter that I need not add here to what they have said; unless it be to say that our continued accounts confirm the great loss sustained by the enemy on the 4th instant, in the battle of German Town. We understand that Generals Agnew, and Grant are dead, and that Sr Wm Erskine is mortally wounded. Some reports place Gen. Kephausen among the slain, and Lord Cornwallis with the wounded. Our Army is, by reenforcements, stronger now than before the last battle, in high spirits, and we expect will give Gen. Howe further amusement in a short time — Suffer me here to observe a little upon the enemies possession of Philadelphia — In Europe, where our affairs are ill understood, perhaps it may make some noise, with us, it is really of little importance. When first we entered into this war, we not only considered, but absolutely declared that we considered our great Towns, as not defensible — But that the possession of these would avail little towards the accomplishment of the views of our enemy. In truth they are but spots in the great Map of North America — But it is far from being certain that Gen. Howe will retain Philadelphia two months. We know that during the late battle he had given orders for his

THE LETTERS OF RICHARD HENRY LEE

baggage to cross Schuylkil, and the friends of government as he calls the detestable enemies of their Country
to quit the Town — Boston was once theirs, but now
no longer so. It will be worth while to counteract[1]

[1] Arthur Lee in pursuance of this object sent a note to Count de
Vergennes, December 6, 1777, inclosing the following extract from this
letter, with verbal changes, together with an extract from a letter from
Washington.   [See archives at Paris, Affaires Étrangères, Correspondences Politiques, Angleterre, 1777, Vol. 526: fo. 185, 186.]
   " Extract of a letter from Richard Henry Lee, member of Congress
for the state of Virginia; dated York town in Pennsylvania Oct! 13th
1777
   'The Committee have written so fully of the events of war in their
public Letter, that I can only add that our continued accounts confirm
the great loss sustained by the Enemy on the 4th instant in the battle
of German-town.   We understand that Generals Grant & Agnew
are dead & Sir Will[m] Erskine mortally wounded.   Some reports
place Gen. Kephausen among the slain & Lord Cornwallis with the
wounded.
   'Our Army is now by re-inforcements, stronger than before the last
battle, in high spirits, and we expect will give Gen[l] Howe battle soon.
   'Suffer me here to observe a little upon the Enemy's possession of
Philadelphia.   In Europe where our affairs are not so well understood perhaps it may make some noise.   When first we enterd into
this war we not only considerd but openly declard, that we regarded
our great towns as indefensible, but that the possession of them wou'd
avail little towards the accomplishment of the views of our Enemies.
With us therefore the Enemy's possession of Philadelphia is really of
little importance.   In truth our towns are only as spots upon the
great map of our strength.   But it is far from being certain that Gen.
Howe will retain Philadelphia two months.   We know that during
the late battle he had given orders for his Baggage to cross the
Schuylkill, & the friends of government as he calls the detestable
Enemies of their Country, to quit the town.   Boston was once theirs.
They have no reason to triumph on that.' "

   " Extrait of the letter from G[l] Washington to the same, dated Oct!
the 5th
   'The event turned out contrary to the promising appearences at
the beginning.   But we are in as good a condition as before the battle,
except the loss of some officers & men   But our men have gained
what is always valuable to yung troops some experience.   I have

329

the magnified falsehood of our enemies concerning this subject. — What is become of our brother, we hear nothing of him. I have never received the Bark from Mr. Gardogue, but you may be assured it is extremely wanted by myself and my family. I make no doubt but you will do the best for my boys in conjunction with their Uncle — But if they cannot remain to be tolerably finished in France, let them be sent by the first good opportunity to me.

I am, with the most tender affection, and faithful friendship Yours.

TO PATRICK HENRY[1]

Dear Sir,   York Town 16ᵗʰ Oct 1777.

I congratulate you most sincerely on the very important intelligence that I have now the pleasure to inclose you, which came express this morning to the President in a letter from Col Trumbull, the deputy Paymaster General. We every moment expect an Express from Gen Gates with a more full account of this glorious victory — Gen Clinton having received a reinforcement, and knowing Burgoyne's critical situation, was urging his way up Hudson's river to relieve him, and had actually taken Fort Montgomery on the Highlands, after a severe conflict and much loss. Genls. Putnam and Parsons were between Clinton & Albany, with some continental troops & a large body of militia.

this moment seen Gˡ Green, whose column had also drove the Enemy & were about closing with ours when unhappily, for I can no otherwise account for it, each took the other for fresh troops of the Enemy & retreated. The fog & clouds of smoke contributed to this as we coud scarce distinguish objects at fifty yards distance.' "

[1] From the text printed in William Wirt Henry, *Patrick Henry*, III. 102.

This last general will now be compelled to return to his hiding place in the Island of York. The enemy have been foiled in various attempts to possess themselves of Fort Mifflin in Delaware, and were lately driven from Province Island by the Galleymen, with the loss of 53 men & 2 officers taken, & a 32 pounder brought there to annoy our Fort. Since the battle of German Town they have evacuated Billingsport, and it is now in our possession, where we have placed some large cannon to stop their ships. The General has sent a party to secure Red Bank, almost opposite the Fort, so that we have great expectations of preventing the enemy from getting to Philadelphia, in which case, Gen. Howe's situation must be a dangerous one. Our troops are now in possession of the country all round Philadelphia and the enemy, so that their distress for provisions must soon be very great. What the people in Town will do, God knows. Sour flour sells already for 30/ hard money a hundred. In a short time I hope to send you more important news both from this quarter & the north. Our army is in high spirits, and advancing upon the Enemy who are entrenching themselves.

I am with great regard, dear Sir, sincerely,

His Excellency PATRICK HENRY, Esq.

[VIRGINIA DELEGATES IN CONGRESS] TO GEORGE
PYNCHEON AND JOHN BRADFORD[1]

YORK IN PENNSYLV^A 16. Octr 1777

GENTLEMEN

The Bearer   whom we have employed to prevail, if he can, with eight Sergeants belonging to the late Gen. Coudrays corps of Artillery, to return, and enter into the service of the Commonwealth of Virginia;

[1] A. copy L. by Richard Henry Lee. American Philosophical Society, Lee Papers, I. 351, No. 102.

hopes to overtake this Corps at Springfield, but if not, he will proceed to Boston after them. If Monsr should succeed in his mission, it may be necessary that he should be furnished with the means of getting a waggon, or two, to convey these people and their baggage to this place. We have to request Gentlemen that you will do us the favor to assist this Gentleman in procuring the carriages that may be necessary for the above purpose, and your draught on the Virginia Delegates in Congress for the expence incurred in this [bus]¹iness shall be punctually and honorably paid.² We have [tak]³en the liberty, on the recommendation of M.ʳ [Presid]³ent [H]³ancock, to entreat your good offices in this affair, and remain with esteem Gentlemen &c.

To GEO. PYNCHEON & JOHN BRADFORD esq.ʳˢ

¹ Ms. damaged.
² This copy in Lee's autograph of an order is appended to the letter: —

"YORK TOWN, IN PENN.ᴬ 16 Oct.ʳ 1777
" Please pay to
the sum of eighty dollars & charge the same to the account of the Virg.ᵃ. Delegates.
We are &c.
To MICH. HILLEGAS, Esq. ⎫
Cont. Treasurer. ⎬
80 dollars." ⎭

The following interesting note regarding Richard Henry Lee is given in another's handwriting in the lower right hand corner of the manuscript page: "Mr. Lee's fortune not being very ample & having a large family to support, he was obliged to live on the pay ᵗˢ from the State of V.ᵃ — The States paid their respective Delegates — To be of as little expence as possible, to His Constituents, at a time when every Dollar was needed for their preservation, he Marketed for himself For two months during Nov & Dec.ʳ '77 which were unusually cold, he lived upon wild pigeons — Vast numbers of these birds were brought from the country which being very poor, were sold for a few cents p.ʳ Dozen & afforded but a scanty fare —"
³ Ms. damaged.

THE LETTERS OF RICHARD HENRY LEE

[COMMITTEE OF INTELLIGENCE] TO [DAVID] HALL
AND [WILLIAM] SELLEN[1]

Mess.ᴿˢ Hall & Sellen   [York, Pa.,   Oct. 17, 1777.]
      Gentle[men][2]
Congress having authorised their Committee of intelligence to get a Press fixed in this Town. I am as
Chairman of that Committee, to propose to yo[u that][2]
your Press be immediately brought here & set up that
the expence of bringing the Press shall be defrayed by
Congress, that you shall be employed in publishing for
Congress and paid a liberal price for so doing. The
Committee hope this will be a sufficient inducement,
when you consider that a Newspaper published by you
here, containing Congress intelligence, will be of extensive sale and very profitable, at all events, you will
be pleased to give me an immediate answer, and deliver
your Letter to General Mifflin, or the Quarter Master
who may be in Reading, in order that an express may
bring it without delay to this place,
I am Gentlemen Your Most Obedient Servant.

TO [DR. WILLIAM SHIPPEN, JR.][3]

My Dear Sir,   York Town, October 18ᵗʰ 1777
I feel too sensibly the number and weight of the
obligations under which your goodness has laid me, not
to entreat earnestly, that you will excuse me from this

---

[1] A. copy L. S. by Lee. University of Virginia, Lee Papers, No. 184.
David Hall of Philadelphia dissolved his partnership with Franklin
as a printer in 1766 and formed one with William Sellen. They were
the printers of the paper money of Congress, and of the *Pennsylvania
Gazette.*
[2] Ms. torn.
[3] Ms. copy. Virginia Historical Society, Lee Transcripts, III.

last effort of your friendship, and that you will suffer me to pay for the wine that I had of you. The friendship that bears alltogether on one side may be oppressive, and the excellence, if not the existence, of this virtue depends on reciprocal communications of benefits. I think the quantity of wine I applied to you for, was 25 gallons, which at 30/- p⁚ gal. comes exactly to One hundred Dollars, which you will please receive enclosed. If this is not right please to let me know, and the Error shall be rectified. I wish you health and happiness, being very sincerely you[r] affectionate friend and Bro.[ther][1]

25 gallons wine at 30/ = ... £37.10
100 dolls at 7/6 = ... £37.10

TO [GEORGE WYTHE][2]

DEAR SIR   YORK IN PENNSLV⁚ Oct⁚ 19. 1777

I have once before, since our Session here, given you an account of the progress of war in these parts and further North, but the irregularity of the Post gives reason to doubt whether you have received my letter. The boasting Burgoyne having been beaten in two pitched battles is on his return, with his shattered army, but whether he will be able to get back or not, time must discover. The want of a Press here obliges us to furnish manuscript accounts of military events, and this is attended with great difficulty amidst the pressure of much business. You will for this reason excuse my referring you to the inclosures sent M⁚ President Page, for a full account of the last action with Gen. Burgoyne

[1] Supplied in pencil.
[2] A. copy L. S. American Philosophical Society, Lee Papers, II. 3, No. 2. Endorsed by Richard Henry Lee, " Copy of Letter to M⁚ Wythe."

& an entertaining correspondence between him & Gates subsequent to the battle. Danger appears now to be thickening about Gen. Howe, so that I hope to be able e'er long to give you favorable accounts from the neighborhood of Philadelphia.

Permit me now Sir to trespass a little on your time and friendship with my private concerns. — I am sure to be indulged by the latter. and therefore more confidently complain of the malicious perseverance of my enemies, who, I am informed, propose to bring my letter to Mr Scot before the approaching Session of Assembly.[1] It is realy difficult to say whether the folly or the malice of these people is greatest, but it is certainly very insultive & degrading to the Great Council of the Commonwealth, to make it a Court of Scandal, and a Vehicle for conveying Slander against the reputation of innocent men; when the great and important affairs of Defense, Finance, and Courts of Justice, call so loudly for quick and wise determination. Let the date of my letter to Scott be attended to, the State of paper money at the time, the reasons and principles upon which my proposal was founded[2]; and my conduct will appear not only innocent but laudable. For it is certainly praiseworthy to prevent ones family from ruin by means that are just and fair.[3] The question then is,

---

[1] The preceding five words are substituted for " this assembly " erased.

[2] The words " be considered " are here erased.

[3] The following is here written and erased by cross marks: " If by a proper reflection upon Men and things, It was clear to me that my Rents established under different laws from the present, and upon principles that then appeared proper and permanent, would most probably, by the change that was working in our political system, be rendered of little value, where was the harm in proposing a change, by which I might be saved from ruin, and the Tenant not injured? Nor could this have operation upon a currency that then scarcely began to exist, and which from its then scarcity, was as good as any

was I obliged by law when these contracts were made, to receive any thing like the present currency in discharge of the rent reserved. You Sir will say no. When therefore the exigince of public affairs rendered it necessary to issue [1] such quantities of paper money as to lessen its value some hundred per Cents, and that a law should be made to establish its currency, this being subsequent to, and destructive of private contracts made under the faith of former laws, should not Individuals be saved from the retrospective destruction wrought by the change — And the more especially in instances where this can be done without injury to the other contracting party. For in this case the Tenants produce rises in value in proportion to the superabundance of circulating [2] money. Reasoning upon [3] the probility [sic] of the change, and as a good Citizen, willing to procur a just alteration before events took place that might render such an attempt liable to misconstruction, I long since endeavored to procure that which [4] would only in good faith obtain the original design of both the contracting parties[5]. And this point of reason and justice would long ago have taken place without murmur or noise had it not been for some Malicious enemies, Pseudo Patriots, and a few knavish

money whatever. In truth it was so scarce, that my Tenants either could not, or would not get it to pay me my rents, but offered me produce in lieu of money. In fact my plan was rather to affect futurity that [than] the present time, and a bargain made before the existence of the currency could not be intended to injure it."

[1] The preceding eleven words are substituted above the line for " then it became necessary for the public good to issue " erased.

[2] The word " paper " is here erased.

[3] Substituted above the line for " Foreseeing " erased.

[4] The preceding three words are substituted above the line for "obtain [illegible words] in the my rents, which " erased.

[5] The words " and no more " are here inserted above the line and erased.

336

Tenants, who under the cloak of public spirit have raised this clamor. Perhaps I may be considered as standing in the way of some private views — My wish is only to lend my helping hand to fix the independence of America on wise and permanent foundations, and then, with infinite pleasure I will return to my farm and eat the bread of industry in freedom and ease. I have no doubt Sir, but that you will on all proper occasions, as well upon principles of justice to injured character, as on account of the long friendship that has subsisted between us, place this matter in the clear light that your abilities enable you to do. It is long since my letter to M⸳ Scott was written, and having mislaid the copy, I do not perfectly remember its contents, but conscious of the purest intentions, I am sure that no sentiment can be found therein, inconsistent with virtuous patriotism. And after all it will be a ridiculous gratification of private malice for the Assembly to take up the consideration of such an affair as this. I have inclosed you a letter from Col⸳ Marshall to me on the subject, and one [1] to yourself from me, which I leave to your discretion and friendship to produce to the House or not, if any attempt sh⸳ be made there to my prejudice

I am, with particular esteem — dear Sir your affectionate friend and obliged humble Servant.

TO [GEORGE WASHINGTON] [2]

DEAR SIR,   YORK   the 20ᵗʰ October 1777

Your favor of the 16ᵗʰ I received yesterday, and was a good deal surprised to find you had been told that Congress had appointed Gen. Conway a Major General.

---

[1] An illegible erasure occurs here.
[2] A. L. S. Library of Congress, Letters to Washington, XIX. 21.

No such appointment has been made, nor do I believe it will, whilst it is likely to produce the evil consequences you suggest. It is very true, that both within and without doors, their have been Advocates for the measure, and it has been affirmed that it would be very agreeable to the army, whose favorite Mr Conway was asserted to be. My judgement on this business was not formed until I received your letter. I am very sure Congress would not take any step that might injure the Army, or even have a tendency that way; and I verily believe they wish to lessen your difficulties by every means in their power, from an entire conviction that the purest motives of public good direct your actions.

The business of a Board of War is so extensive, so important, and demanding such constant attention, that Congress see clearly the necessity of constituting a new Board, out of Congress, whose time shall be entirely devoted to that essential department.

It is by some warmly proposed that this board shall be filled by the three following gentlemen, Col^o Read, Col^o Pickering the present Adjutant General, and Col^o Harrison your Secretary. And that Gen. Conway be appointed A. G. in the room of Col^o Pickering. It is my wish, and I am sure it is so of many others, to know your full and candid sentiments on this subject. For my own part, I cannot be satisfied with giving any opinion on the point until I am favored with your sentiments, which I shall be much obliged to you for Sir as soon as your time will permit. It has been affirmed that Gen. Conway would quit the service if he were not made a M. General. But I have been told, in confidence, that he would leave it at the end of this Campaign if he *was* appointed, unless his word of honor were taken to continue for any fixed time. And it is a question with me whether the Advocates for Gen. Conway will not miss their aim if he should be appointed

A. General, unless he has the rank of Maj. General also. My reason for thinking so, is, that I have been informed Gen. Conway desires to retire to his family, provided he can carry from this Country home with him, a Rank that will raise him in France.

It is very certain that the public good demands a speedy erecting, and judicious filling of the new Board of War; and I sincerely wish it may be done in the most proper manner. I do not imagine Congress would appoint Col? Harrison without first knowing whether you could spare him, nor do I think that so important an office as that of A. G. should be touched without maturest consideration.

We every moment expect the Express with an account that will enable us to congratulate you on the surrender of Gen. Burgoyne and the remains of his shattered army. This will be one of the Prussian sixes, and I *augur* that the other will soon cast up upon the Delaware.

I am, with sincerest wishes for your health and success, dear Sir your most affectionate and obedient Servant.

TO [DR. WILLIAM SHIPPEN, JR][1]

YORK 22ᵈ Oct.ʳ 1777. 2 oClock

DEAR SIR,

The slow, but sure moving Gates has not yet sent in his Inventory,[2] but an Officer who saw Burgoyne with Gates tells a Gentleman that passed this Town as follows — 1 Lieutenant General, 2 Major Generals, 7 Brigadiers, 5000 men, 15,000 Stand of Arms, 40 pieces of Cannon and a considerable quantity of cloathing —

---

[1] A. dr. L. University of Virginia, Lee Papers, No. 186. Scratched hastily on a half sheet of paper, and endorsed as to "Dʳ Shippen."

[2] Inventory of Burgoyne's surrender, *cf.* letter of October 25, 1777.

THE LETTERS OF RICHARD HENRY LEE

DEAR SIR,

YORK 22ᵈ Octᵣ 1777.

The slow but sure moving Gates has not yet sent us his glorious Inventory, but an Officer who saw Burgery with Gates gives the following list to a Gentleman who is arrived at Reading —

[COMMITTEE OF CONGRESS] TO GENERAL [EDWARD] HAND [1]

YORK TOWN Octᵣ 24ᵗʰ 1777

SIR/

We enclose you herewith a resolve of Congress appointing us a Committee for the purpose described in the resolution, and we apply to you Sir as a Friend to the cause of America, and as an Officer high in rank in the United States, to give us the most full and perticular assistance in your power, for the better accomplishing the end of our appointment. — We understand that Col! Morgan has lately been confined on suspicion of disaffection to the interest of the United States — We wish to know the truth of this, and if true, the cause of it. — Whether any and what inquiry was made into the affair, and on what principles an acquittal was founded. — We rely upon your best aid in all things, that may contribute to the right discharge of our duty in this business, as it must be obvious of how great consiquence it is, that the Agents for Indian Affairs should be of unquestioned attachment to the United States, and your residence for some time in that part of the Country, which has been Colonel Morgan's Scene of action, may furnish you with knowledge on this Subject, that distance denies to us. — We have the pleasure to inform

[1] A. L. S. by Lee. Lenox Library, Emmet, 892. Addressed to him at Pittsburg, and signed by Richard Henry Lee, Rich. Law, and Daniel Roberdeau. Col. Hand was made Brigadier-General in 1777.

you that the friendship & alliance of the Northern and Southern Indians comes well authenticated to Congress — It will be very hard and unaccountable that those in the middle district should alone be our Enemies. — We are

Sir
Y.ʳ most ob.ᵗ & most hum.ᵉ Serv.ᵗˢ.
Gen.ˡ Hand.

COMMITTEE OF CONGRESS TO —— ——[1]

York Town in Pen.ᴬ 24ᵗʰ Oct.ʳ 1777.

Sir,

The inclosed resolve will explain to you the design of our appointment, and the reason of our present application. As a friend to the cause of America, and as a Gentleman living on the spot which has been Col.º Morgans scene of action since his appointment under the United States, we are to request of you Sir your candid sentiments [2] on the subject of charge against Col.º Morgan and you will further oblige us by obtaining the fair and uninfluenced testimony of disinterested persons on the same point — We wish to be well informed touching the political character of M.ʳ M.ᶜGee, whether he is considered as an Agent, or Friend, of G. B. and whether he does not profess himself a Subject of the British King — Whether Col.º Morgan has much intimacy with M.ʳ M.ᶜ Gee and [3] whether the latter was not carried by the former along with him on a visit to some of the Indian nations, and whether it was by Col.º Morgans influence that the Indians were induced to

---

[1] A. copy L. S. by Lee for the Committee. American Philosophical Society, Lee Papers, II. 7, No. 3. To some one at Fort Pitt.

[2] T e words " and information " are here erased.

[3] The words " if he was taken by Col.º M & " are here erased.

insist on M.: M.ᶜGees continuing to reside where he now does — Whether any letter has been seen from M.: Hamilton the Governor of Detroit to Col? Morgan, & what were the Contents of such letter — We are satisfied that you will excuse the trouble we have here given you, when you reflect how important a thing it is that the department of Agent for Indian Affairs should be filled by a person of clear and unquestioned attachments to the United States, and the impossi[bility fro]¹m our remoteness, of rightly answering the end of our [appointment?]¹ unless by the mediation of American friends in [that part?]¹ of the Country. We are Sir your most obedient
Servants.

TO PATRICK HENRY ²

DEAR SIR,   YORK, PENN. 25 Oct? 1777.

The *slow* but *sure* moving Gates has not yet sent us his glorious Inventory. However, the intelligence of Burgoyne's surrender comes to us through such good channels that we do not doubt its truth, but impute Gen! Gates' silence to his necessary attention to the great business of disposing properly of so many prisoners &c., &c. I lately wrote Mr. Page that the enemy had quitted Philadelphia. This came to us from the D. Quartermaster General, Col. Lutterlock, but it seems the motion of the enemies army was only

¹ Ms. torn. On the back of the sheet is the following: —

" SIR,   YORK the 14ᵗʰ of October 1777
I had the honor of your ticket yesterday whilst I was sitting in Congress, and I "

² From the text printed in William Wirt Henry, *Patrick Henry*, III. 107.

from German Town, within their lines that cross the common of Philadelphia from Delaware to Schuylkill. The body that crossed Schuylkill when Howe was supposed to be retreating, was 1,500 as convoy to 150 Waggons sent to Chester for provisions. The narrowing their lines, and sending for their provisions, evidences a design to keep Philadelphia if they can. But how they can, the inclosed letter from an Aid of Gen. Green will best satisfy you, for if they cannot get their ships up, it is not possible for them to remain at Philadelphia. I am just now well informed that Gen. Washington intended to move his army to the Chester side of Schylkill, in order to cut off the enemies' intercourse with their Ships, and the better to aid the Fort on Delaware. That a strong body of Militia will be left above German Town to prevent evil disposed persons from sending provisions to the enemy. I hope Burgoyne's surrender will be followed by that of Howe.

I am dear Sir affectionately yours.

His Excellency PATRICK HENRY.

TO [PATRICK HENRY][1]

DEAR SIR.   YORK IN PENNSYLV⁴ Oct⁴ 28. 1777

The anxiety at Williamsburg cannot be greater than it is here to have a particular account of our late glorious success in the North. For nine days past, we have hourly expected the arrival of a Messenger with Gates's magnificent Inventory, and in order to a quick transmission of it, we have detained, and still keep Col⁰ Masons Express. We now learn that Col⁰ Wilkinson

[1] A. L. S. Maine Historical Society, Fogg Collection. A printed text with minor variations is in William Wirt Henry, *Patrick Henry*, III. 109.

D. Adjutant Gen. is on his way with this long wisht for
Capitulation by which Gen. Burgoyne and his army
have surrendered themselves prisoners of war. Until
I can furnish you the authentic detail I will entertain
you with the relation of our late success on the Delaware below Philadelphia. It must be obvious to you
how important to the enemy it is, that they sh⁰ get their
fleet up to the City, for this purpose they have made
many efforts which have been repulsed with considerable
injury to their Ships, and loss of Men. The last attempt was the most powerful¹ and was as follows —
With 1200 Hessian Grenadiers led by Col⁰ Count
Donop they attack'd Red Bank, a post held by a party
of Troops under Col⁰ Green of Rhode Island nearly
opposite to Fort Island on the Jersey shore. The attack
was made by Storm, and they had passed the Abbatis,
gained the Ditch, and some of them, with Donop &
his Aid Major at their head, had passed the Pickets,
when they met so warm a reception as to be driven back
and forced to retire with great precipitation, leaving
the Count and his Aid with 70 wounded in our hands,
and upwards of 70 dead on the spot. 300 muskets with
swords &c &c are taken, one Lieut Col⁰ & some inferior Officers of the enemy are among the slain — The
routed party returned to Philadelphia, crossing Delaware opposite the City. An attack was likewise made
on Fort Mifflin by several Ships of War and by the
Batteries on Province Island, which was continued long
and with great violence,² at length the Ships retired and
two of them getting a ground (a 64 & a 20) were quitted
by the people after having set fire to them. They blew
up with a terrible explosion. Thus the enemy were
defeated and disapointed in this general attack.
Whether they will renew their attempts I cannot tell,

¹ Substituted for " considerable " erased.
² The word " until " is here erased.

but it is probable they will. That you may have a better idea of this important passage I have enclosed you a draught made by Capt. Loyeauté of Gen. Coudrays Corps of Artillerists, the same Gentleman whom we have recommended for the Command of our Bat? of Artillery — He is an Artist in the business of Artillery and not unacquainted with the Art of the Engineer, and will most assuredly benefit our Country much in this necessary department. I pray you Sir to interest yourself in procuring the appointment of this Gentleman — At all events it is proper that an answer be speedily sent here, that the Gentleman may not be unnecessarily delayed as There has been pains taken to get this Officer in other States, but we have prevailed with him to give Virginia the preference. The United States have a very considerable quantity of field Artillery at present, 30 pieces of which are laying idle at Charles Town in S. Carolina — Suppose Virginia was to direct their Delegates to apply to Congress for 6 or 8 of these pieces & if they are granted to us, let them be brot to our Country, where for the present they may serve to instruct the Men with, and be ready for use next Campaign if we should be visited, which I very much incline to think will be the case, since the enemy have been so baffled in the North as must, I think, discourage future efforts in that quarter. Capt. Loyeauté is of opinion that it would be quite proper to have that number of Field pieces at the least, for the purpose of instruction, as well as for use in war. There are so many places in our Country that requires to be fortified, and the use of Artillery is become so very important in war,[1] that I think we cannot be too well and too soon acquainted with this branch of the Art of War. These Officers of Gen Coudrays Corps have only leave of absence from the Court of France for 2 years, and I

[1] The words " among the modern " are here erased.

think it will be very unwise in America not to profit from this circumstance so as to acquire Knowledge of a necessary art which they understand so well, and which we are quite ignorant of. Mons! Loyeautè speaks english pretty well, and improves daily. The impatience of the Express will not suffer him to remain here any longer, and therefore we are not able to confirm the Northern News — This is the first moment of fair weather since Sunday morning, it having been constant and heavy rain for 4 days and nights past, which has prevented all intercourse with the Army or from the North — We shall send an Express to you immediately on receiving an authentic account from Gen Gates, which I hope will be the case in a short time. I am dear Sir most affectionately yours.

Oct! 30ᵗʰ 1777   10 °clock in the morning.

COMMITTEE [OF CONGRESS] TO COLONEL GEORGE MORGAN¹

YORK TOWN   Oct! 30 1777

SIR,/

*** We have it in Charge from Congress to inform you of the inclosed Resolution ² which we transmit you for that Purpose. You'll therefore, we trust, take due Notice thereof — and give your Attendance agreeable to the Requisition contained therein — that a proper Enquiery may be made in the Premisses — from yours &ᶜ.

COL? GEORGE MORGAN.

¹ L. S. Pennsylvania Historical Society, Dreer Collection, II. 5. Clerical draft signed, in the autograph of each, by Richard Henry Lee, Daniel Roberdeau, Richard Law as committee. Addressed to Morgan at Lancaster, care of Mr. Marcoe. Compare letter, of October 24, 1777, to General Edward Hand.
² The Resolution of Congress of October 22 relating to Morgan.

THE LETTERS OF RICHARD HENRY LEE

TO [GENERAL THOMAS MIFFLIN][1]

YORK Nov[r] 2. 1777

MY DEAR GENERAL

I thank you you for your obliging favor of the 28th past, and the inclosures accompanying it. I assure you sir that having received such original impressions of your firm attachment to the cause of America, I have ever placed you among the first, and most valuable friends.[2] Trusting therefore to your patriotism, and my hopes of your returning health, I had ventured to mention your name for one of the three Commissioners of the new board of war — A most important department, on which our righteous warfare eminently depends. Some Gentlemen supposed y[r] health would hinder,[3] others observed that the Continental policy forbid the union of two Offices in the same person, supposing that you might be prevailed on to retain your Commission of M. General would your health permitted action. The spirit of the Continental policy does forbid double salaries, but the Generalship might be continued with the Board of war Salary. Indeed, the

---

[1] A. dr. L. S. University of Virginia, Lee Papers, No. 191. Major-General Thomas Mifflin. Endorsed in autograph on the reverse, "Ans[r] to Gen. Mifflins/letter of Oct[r] 28, 1777/Tuesday 30 Sept[r]/Congress met in York 2 mil[s] of Livres 500/paid & 500 more on the first of April, July &/Oct[r]

12th March mention/of an Officer employed/to build 2 Ships of/War equal to 64'/what is to become of those/4000 hhds Tob? Contrac/ted for wth Farmers /2 mil[s] Livres first ad/vance for this Tob? to be paid in April — Dictionnaire/Francois & Anglois Par Louis Chambau/et/M[r] J. B. Robinet."

For Mifflin's reply see R. H. Lee, *Memoir of Richard Henry Lee*, II. 174.

[2] "You may judge then how un happy I am made by your resignation" is here erased.

[3] Substituted for "forbid" erased.

nature of the latter business renders rank and knowledge in War necessary. I love America and venerate its faithful friends, which must render it painful to be deprived, from whatever cause, of the assistance of its surest Supports in this crisis of its fate. I still hope however, that returning health, will enable you yet to continue your Aid for establishing the glory of North America on the most lasting foundation.

I am yours dear Sir with sincere affection.

TO [SAMUEL ADAMS][1]

York the 15th of Nov. 1777.

Dear Sir,

The Bearer of this, Capt. Romané is a Gentleman of Mons. Coudrays corps who arrived here lately from Charles Town and is now returning by the way of Boston to France with his companions. This young Gentleman is Nephew to General Grebouval Commander of the french Artillery, and he is a modest well behaved youth. At his request, I willingly introduce him to you, and I am sure that from personal, as well as political considerations, you will render Capt. Romanés stay in Boston as agreeable to him as possible. this gentleman had once determined to pass the winter at Annapolis in order to learn the English language, but his Countrymen, it seems, have persuaded him to return with them to France. Their design, we understand, for so doing, is to fortify themselves with interest and numbers, in order to give greater weight to their representations of ill usage in America. I am much dissatisfied my dear friend, with this whole business, because I apprehend pernicious consequences will result to our Country and its cause from the complaints

[1] A. L. S. Lenox Library, Samuel Adams Papers.

of these Gentlemen, who are of consideration in France and well supported there. I have endeavored to avert this mischief by every means in my power, and I think it will conduce to this end if the Gentlemen of Boston were to treat these Officers with attention and make their stay in Boston agreeable as possible. Our affairs about Philadelphia are in Statu quo, but how long they will continue so I do not know, because we learn that a fleet from New York has arrived in the Delaware with reenforcements to Howe. We have at length finished the Confederation and shall send it to the different States in a few days with strong exortation to give it quick consideration and speedy return. Taxation, Finance, and recruiting the Army will also be strongly recommended. Your utmost aid will no doubt be cordially applied to the expediting these important points

My health groes worse and will, I fear, compel me soon to return home.

My compliments to M⁻ J. Adams

Affectionately yours.

TO GENERAL [GEORGE] WASHINGTON [1]

DEAR SIR,   YORK 20ᵗʰ November 1777

I have no doubt of being excused by you for not sooner answering your favor of the 24ᵗʰ last, when you are informed that my ill state of health has prevented me from attending as I ought, to the important matter it contains. I gave M⁻ Jones the letter, that he might inform Congress of such parts as it imported the public they should be acquainted with. As it appeared by the letters of Gen. Mifflin that he objected only to serve in the

[1] A. L. S. Library of Congress, Letters to Washington, XX. 6. Addressed to him as "Commander in Chief of the/American Army." An A. dr. of this letter is in University of Virginia, Lee Papers, No. 196.

Quartermasters department, that his health was returning, and that he was willing to continue his aid to the
public cause, Congress appointed him one of the Commissioners of the new Board, because he is competent
to the right discharge of its duties, because that would
best suit his valetudinary state, and as shewing a just
sense of his uniform, vigorous, and well founded patriotism. I have strong hopes, that by the skill and industry
of this new Board, and from the right execution of business in that important department, you will in future
find great relief. Gen. Conway has not lately been
mentioned in Congress, nor has there been much talk
of an Adjutant General, since it is not certainly known
whether Col? Pickering will accept his new appointment. M: Flemmings character stands very fair,
and so far as I am able to judge, would answer well in
this commission. You will see in the inclosed what
M: Sergeant says of him. General Mifflin has proposed a plan for the Quartermasters department that
appears judicious, and well fitted to answer the purpose
of good service and œconomy at the same time. He
would divide this department into its military and civil
branches, the former to be filled by a person well qualified to discharge its duties, and the latter, again to be
divided into Commissaries of Teams, of Forage, of
Tents &c &c to be governed in their purchases by esti-
mates from the Quarter Master general who is to touch
no money but a moderate tho sufficient salary.

It unfortunately too true, that our enemies pay
little regard to good faith, or any obligation of justice
and humanity; which renders the convention of Saratoga a matter of great moment and it is also, as you
justly observe, an affair of infinite delicacy. The undoubted advantage they will take, even of the appearance of infraction on our part, and the American Character, which is concerned in preserving its faith inviolate,

cover this affair with difficulties, and proves the disadvantage we are under in conducting war against an old, corrupt, and powerful people, who having much credit and influence in the world will venture on things that would totally ruin the reputation of young and rising communities like ours. The English however, were not to blame in the business of Closter Seven. That convention was left incomplete by the Commanders who made it. 'Twas stipulated particularly that the Court of Versailles must ratify, and that within a certain time, which was not done until long after the time was elapsed, and before which ratification the Troops of Hanover had returned to arms. Upon this occasion the good faith of England is not impeached. It is greatly to be regretted that the situation of your Army unfits it for vigorous action, because it is very obvious that the enemies possession of Philadelphia this winter and the ensuing spring may produce consequences extensively injurious. You well know Sir, how weak and divided the people of this State are from various causes. Those of Delaware are still worse. In this condition, with the infinite arts of our enemies, pushed up almost to the center of the above governments, and aided by the powerful means of supplying the wants fanciful and real of the people with all kinds of European goods and Salt, it will be no great matter of surprize if we were to find a total revolution in Pennsylvania and Delaware. Add to this the ill condition of our finances which totter upon every seeming success of the enemy.

It is not to be supposed, that where so much is at stake, G. Britain will fail to make most potent efforts to recover her honor and prevent her ruin. Upon this ground we may expect considerable reinforcements, and early as possible in the spring. With an Army much strengthened, Gen. Howe may effect purposes dangerous to America. It happens too, unluckily for us, that in order to support the credit of our money, the several States must of necessity impose large and immediate Taxes. This is the most delicate and difficult of all government operations even in old and undisturbed States. Yet it is unavoidable, and Congress have pressingly requested that it may be quickly and extensively entered upon.

It was most evident to discerning men that the change in the Commissariat, at the time it was adopted would produce most mischievous consequences, yet such was the rage of reformation that no endeavors to prevent the evil could avail, and now I feel the most anxious solicitude for fear the consequences may disperse our army even in face of the enemy. A Committee is appointed to confer with the Commisary general and to try what can be done to avert the evil. I wish they may be fortunate enough to hit upon a remedy. That there should be a want of flour amazes me and proves great want of attention in the Comissary Gen. because I well know that any quantity might have been got in Virginia at a reasonable price. By our last dispatches from the West Indies, it would seem as if a war between France & England was inevitable, unless the meanness of the latter should restore all her Captures made from the former without the limits prescribed by treaty, and which have been made under authority of an Act of Parliament. But the royal spleen against America is such, that every consideration falls before the wish to Subjugate this free country. Yet Mꝛ Bingham mentions that the ministerial writings are calculated to rouse the national resentment against France If so, tis evident they want to set Europe on fire that the smoke may cover them from the eyes of their injured country. Mꝛ Carmichael writes that Dꝛ Lee was returning to Paris from Berlin, having finished his business successfully at the Prussian Court, & M.ʳ Bingham says 'tis certain that the King of Prussia has opened his Ports to the United States, and that Portugal has deserted the interest of England, and acceeded to the family compact. This is all good news, and will I hope furnish employment quickly for our unprincipled enemies.

My ill state of health will compel me to return home in a few days, where I shall continue ardently to pray for your health and success.

I am dear Sir affectionately yours.

TO SAMUEL ADAMS[1]

YORK the 23.ᵈ Nov.ʳ 1777.
MY DEAR SIR,

I need not make an apology for my paper because you know our choice of things here is confined within narrow bounds, as little occasion is there to excuse the slovenly manner in which this letter may be written, since you well know how seldom it is that we can command time in this busy scene. I had the pleasure of writing you lately by Capt. Romané, a young gentleman of worth who passes thro Boston in his return to his own Country. Since that letter was written we have lost Fort Mifflin, which our brave garrison was obliged to abandon after a most gallant defence, in which all their guns were dismounted but two, and all the works beaten away to about a rod and an half. The enemy brought up their cul down Indiaman between Province & Mud Islands and lay within musket shot of the Fort upon which they discharged a most furious cannonade with 24 & 32 pounders, and from Cohorns and Musketry in their Tops, drove the men from their guns.

[1] A. L. S. Lenox Library, Samuel Adams Papers.

Tis said the Gallies did not do their duty. Notwithstanding this, it is the opinion of many that the enemy will not be able to get their fleet up to the City, unless they can get red bank, which, with the Gallies may yet prevent their raising the Cheveaux de Frize. To remove this obstruction, we hear they have passed 3000 men over at Coopers ferry, and Cornwallis has crossed from Chester with 1500 more. Our force to oppose him is Brigadier Varnum's brigade of 1200, 4 Regiments in Red Bank fort with the Garrison of Fort Mifflin, and Huntingtons Brigade lately sent over. We understand that the Army has moved down upon the enemies lines in consequence of their weakness by these powerful detachments. Thus we daily expect some interesting event. The confederation is not yet returned from press but we expect it will in a day or two when it will be sent forward, and with it will come this letter. We have strongly pressed the speedy consideration and return of the Confederation, and we have urged the necessity of immediate and extensive Taxation, regulation of prices, and other Measures of finance, œconomy, and effectual recruiting the army. I know my friend M͏ͬ John Adams will say the regulation of prices wont do — I agree it will not singly answer, and I know that Taxation with Œconomy are the radical cures. But I also know that the best Physicians sometimes attend to Symptoms, apply palliatives and under favor of the Truce thus obtained, introduce cause removing medicines.[1] Let us for a moment check the enormity of the evil by this method, whilst the other more sure, but more slow methods secure us against a return of the mischief. The middle & southern States (particularly the insatiable avarice of Pennsylvania) having refused to join in the plan formerly, rendered the experiment on your part

[1] The three words preceding are substituted for " radical cures " and an illegible word erased.

inconclusive and partial; therefore I do not think Mr Adams's argument drawn from that trial quite decisive against the Measure. I incline to think that the necessity of the case will now procure its adoption universally, and then we shall see what great things may be effected by common consent. The American conduct has already shattered and overset the conclusions of the best Theorists, and I hope this will be another instance. Two days ago I moved the immediate recall of Mr Deane, which was agreed without dissent, and tomorrow is appointed for choosing a Commissioner in his place. Our friends Mr John Adams & Mr Denny are in Nomination, with some others — This appointment was strongly pressed on me in Congress, but my dear friend, rigid as you are in these matters, I am sure you would have admitted my apology. I feel the obligations of public duty very powerfully, but when these duties can be better discharged by others, why may not the *private* ones be suffered to prevail? Why may not chari liberi have their weight, when such a sacrifice is not *necessary* for the public service.

I remember that in some points our opinion differed respecting Mr Deane, but I feel myself obliged to think that he has pursued his best judgement for the good of his Country when he made.those distressing contracts, and perhaps his peculiar situation compelled him to carry them further than he might otherwise have done. Be this as it may, after Congress had so strongly determined concering these, it would have been out of all character to have continued him. Yet this is a matter of great delicacy and I am not well satisfied with the whole of it. If our friend Mr Adams should be chosen, I have earnest hopes that he will accept. The loss of time that will attend his refusal, independant of other considerations, renders it of much consequence that he should not refuse. Yesterday evening brought

us a letter from Mr Bingham covering one from M͗
Carmichael dated Paris June the 25 which contains the
following passages. " M͗ Lee writes me he is on his
return from Berlin having finished his business successfully. — If our enemies are not successful they mean to
close with us on the best terms they can, sensible that
if this great effort does not succeed, they have little to
hope in future — This is an animating reason for us to
persevere in the glorious contest. — The English have
compleated their loan amongst themselves — No foreigners have assisted them, altho the terms to the Lender
are better than any ever yet offered by that Nation except once — Foreigners know that they have yet several
millions to fund for which they must offer still better
terms — The Spaniards have refused the mediation of
France & England in their dispute with Portugal, being
determined to prosecute the war until Portugal makes
reparation and demands peace. They have taken the
important Island of S͗ Catherine on the coast of Brazil
without loss & mean vigorously to prosecute their
operations on the Brazils. This I have from *undoubted*
authority, one of the *family Ministers*. An account
prevails that the Indians of the east have fallen on their
Oppressors & have taken Madrass. India Stock has
fallen in consequence of this — Both France & Spain
continue their Armaments, as if preparing for some
great event. This obliges England to do the Same. Of
course all their Naval & Army Contracts are for 5
years. And they employ as many Work men in the
Dockyards as they did in the last War.[1] From this circumstance you may judge, however different their
declarations may be in Parliament, they have real apprehensions from this Court & that of Spain. — It would
render our negotiations with Prussia more successful,
if a Tobacco Ship could by any means be pushed into

[1] This sentence is inserted above the line.

356

Embden, which Ship might make her returns in manufactures necessary for us at 15 or 20 p! cent cheaper
than we can have them here. Capt? Weeks, Johnson, &
Nicholson have just destroyed 16 Vessels on the
English & Irish coasts — I am dispatching Conynghame
from hence on the same business — I begin to thing
War unavoidable"

Signed CARMICHAEL

M! Binghams letter covering the above is dated Oct!
13ᵗʰ and contains the following important intelligence —
"The General received a few days ago by a packet
from Rochelle 4ᵗʰ Sept! the following intelligence —
That a Courier had been dispatched with instructions
to the French Ambassador in London to claim all French
Vessels captured (without the limits settled by treaty
to bound the approach of french Vessels to the coast of
British America) by the English, which have been regularly cleared out for any french Ports. Which requisition if not complied with, is to be the signal for leaving
the British Court. The General has reviewed orders
to put everything in readiness for war and to lay an
Embargo on all Ships destined for Europe to prevent
their falling into the enemies hands. The Minister
informs the General that Transports are already engaged at Havre, Nants, & Bourdeaux for the transportation of 5000 additional troops to Martinique and
Guadaloupe. — At Brest, Rochford, and Toulon, they
work night and day, & the greatest preparations are
making for the immediate commencement of hostilities.
The Generals plan is immediately to attack the English
Islands, as his success depends on conducting his operations with such rapidity as to hinder any relief from
being thrown in. — The restitution of the Ship Seine &
her Cargo is loudly demanded by the Court of Versailles.
I mentioned in a former letter that Portugal had de-

tached herself from the interests of Great Britain & had entered into the family Compact — Authentic advices mention that the King of Prussia has opened his Ports to the Americans."

W⁼ BINGHAM

The union of Portugal with the Bourbon compact is a most injurious affair for England, to which, that wealthy Kingdom was a kind of Colony. This event has, I presume, been brought about by the success of the Spanish Arms in South America, by the death of the King of Portugal, and by the incapacity of England to assist her Ally. The above intelligence makes immediate war extremely probable in Europe — But the meanness of the Court of London will stoop to every thing rather than endanger success in trampling upon the liberties of North America. Perhaps the British Ministry begin to see the necessity of setting Europe on fire, that the Smoke may conceal them from the eyes of their injured Country. Gen. Mifflin has been here, and he urges strongly the necessity of having Gen. Gates to be President of the New Board of War — He thinks the Military knowledge and the Authority of Gates necessary to procure the indispensable changes in our Army — I believe he is right — The capital business of Congress for this winter is now over, and my ill state of health calls loudly for rest — I shall therefore withdraw in 8 or 10 days until the last of winter — I hope you will not forget to favor me frequently with the intelligence of your place — Where I am going is in absolute retirement, and will render more agreeable the news of the world — Your situation is one of the best, and most frequent information.

I have written you a long letter, one that might perhaps be construed trespass by any but a friend, I shall therefore conclude with assurances of my affectionate regard.

P.S. I formerly desired you might direct for me to the care of James Hunter, Esqr near Fredericksburg, but for the future the following will answer better

R. H. Lee of Chantilly, to the care of the Post Master at Leeds Town Kings George County

Virginia

My best respects to Mr J. Adams. [Will?] be extremely glad to hear from him.

TO [PATRICK HENRY?] [1]

Dear Sir,   York the 24th of November 1777

I am much obliged to you for your favor of the 3d, which I should have answered sooner if I had not been prevented by ill health and much business. The surrender of Burgoyne is no doubt of great consequence to our righteous cause, and I could wish it were in my power to entertain hopes of a similar event at Philadelphia. Howe has made his situation very strong by double lines and these strongly fortified. They do also contrive to get provisions up from the fleet in small Vessels by means of a channel between Province Island & Fort Island. The latter of these places having lately fallen into their hands will facilitate this business exceedingly. Yet the better opinion is that the fleet cannot get up so long as we hold Red Bank and the Cheveaux de Frize remain covered by the gallies. To reduce the former, we hear that Cornwallis lately crossed the Delaware with 3000 men. We are very strong at that place, fully so I hope to give his Lordship a sound drubbing. We every day expect important news from thence. We have just just received a letter

[1] A. L. S. Massachusetts Historical Society, Letters and Papers, 1777–1780, C. 81. A. 14.

THE LETTERS OF RICHARD HENRY LEE

from Mr. Bingham at Martinique, covering one from Mr. Carmichael at Paris dated June 25 & July 6. Mr. Binghams letter is dated the 13th of October. Mr. Carmichael tells us that D.ʳ Lee is returning from Berlin having finished his business successfully at the Court of Prussia. That the English could get no foreigners to assist in making up their last Loan although the terms were higher than usual. That twas reported Madrass had been taken by the Natives, which had fallen India Stock. That France, Spain, & England were preparing with all possible dispatch for War, and that he thought it was enevitable. Mr. Binghame says the General of Martinique had just received information from the french Ministry Septr. 4. that demand was made upon England for a delivery of all the French Vessels captured by the English without the limits prescribed by treaty for bounding the approach of foreign Vessels to the Shores of British America, and if this demand was not complied with the Ambassador was to leave the Court of London. That the General had orders to put the Islands in a posture for immediate war, and to prevent the sailing of all ships bound to Europe by embargo, least they should fall into the enemies hands. Five thousand troops were immediately to be sent to Martinique & Guadaloupe additional to those already there. Mr. Bingham further informs that the Ministerial Writers in England were endeavoring to raise the National Cry for a war with France, meaning to secure personal safety at the risk of National ruin. Thus these desperately wicked men are for setting Europe on fire that the Smoke may cover them from the vengeance of their injured Country. These are good presages for us, but yet I cannot help being astonished at the horrid iniquity of these Wretches. We have finished the confederation and it will go forward to the States in a few days, with strong exortation to consider and return it quickly. In this great business dear Sir we must yield a little to each other, and not rigidly insist on having everything correspondent to the partial views of every State. On such terms we can never confederate. If we take a view of the World, we shall find that numbers are by no means a just criterion to fix the relative riches of States. Of old times take Tyre and Scythia — Germany & Carthage — In Modern look at Holland & Poland — England & Germany — But the truth is, that let wealth flow into a Country from whatever cause, it will forever reflect value upon the lands of that Country, & they rise in value in proportion to the influx of wealth. Thus the value of lands in England has doubled & trepled as commerce has brought wealth into the Island. For my own part, I doubt extremely whether Virginia will not pay more by the presnt Mode than if it had been determined by numbers. But I am satisfied that the mode now fixt is the most just, and so fiat justicia, ruat Coelum. We have recommended extensive taxation, sinking the provincial currencies, and regulating prices. I think that if the States will vigorously execute the recommendations of Congress, we shall, under providence, be a safe and happy people.

My ill state of health will compel me soon to return home for the winter season. I shall be particularly happy to hear from you, as well before as after you get to Congress, and for this purpose you will please direct to me at Chantilly Westmoreland County, to the care of the Post Master at Leeds Town in King George County Virginia. I live at some distance from the line of Post, and therefore propose to send weekly to the Office for such letters as my friends may favor me with.

I am with sentiments of esteem and regard, Sir, your most obedient Servant.

P.S. I am sorry that my predictions about Red Bank have not been fulfilled. Cornwallis got up before our reenforcements arrived, which has occasioned the evacuation of that Post, and the Continental Vessels that were there have been destroyed to prevent their falling into the enemies hands. We understand the Stores at the [Fort] were saved and the Cannon spiked. Gen. Green is in the Jersies and he is very strong in Men, but whether there will be any fighting nevertheless is to be determined by events. It does not seem clear that the enemy will get their Ships up, because it is not certain that they can remove the Cheveaux de Frise at this inclement Season.

TO THE GOVERNOR OF VIRGINIA[1]
(PATRICK HENRY)

MY DEAR SIR   YORK, the 24th Nov^r, 1777.

I am just favored with yours of the 14th, and thank you for it — Every attempt to clothe the army is commendable, upon principles, both of humanity and policy. As there is great Trade at Charles Town, you have some chance for the woolens you want, altho' this is the worst season for application, on account of the many negroes they have to clothe in that Country — Either the Havannah or New Orleans are places where you may get Woolens and Military stores. Doctor

[1] The first two paragraphs of the text are from the *Calendar of Virginia State Papers*, I. 294, and the remainder of the body of the letter is from a transcript made by the Carnegie Institution of Washington and loaned by Dr. J. F. Jameson. A text of the entire letter, with slight varations, is printed in William Wirt Henry, *Patrick Henry*, III. 124, and from this the place and date and the superscription are taken, as these do not appear in the *Calendar of Virginia State Papers*, which gives only the body of the letter.

Lees' letters have repeatedly assured us that at these places would be lodg'd the above articles for N. America in general, and Virginia in particular. Small swift sailing Vessels sent to the former of these places from Virginia or North Carolina, freighted with fine flour or Tobacco would not fail to return loaded with necessaries, and by pushing into some of the Inlets in the Sea-Cost of North Carolina, might avoid the British Cruisers that infest our Bay, and the goods be safely brought over land. This appears to me the most expeditious and the most certain way. By this method the blankets & cloaths might yet be in Season to help the Soldiers before the winter is over. With respect to the loan of money, at the Havannah or N. Orleans, I am not able to form a judgment, whether it can be effected or not: the latter most probably, because Dr Lee was able to get but a small sum immediately from Spain for Congress, although he expected a larger Credit from Holland thro' the mediation and security of Spain — Add to this, the great probability of immediate war in Europe from which Spain will not be detached. I remember Dr Lee in many of his letters to me, previous to his visit to Spain said he should endeavor to negotiate a loan from that Court for Virginia & South Carolina, to support (as he said) the credit of our paper money. Since his return from Spain, he only mentions cloathes & military stores, that w^d be lodged at Havannah & Orleans for our use.

For the purpose of securing the credit of our money in a great emergence, it were to be wished a credit could be obtained as you propose, and therefore I think it will not be amiss to make the experiment. As for the goods, they may be had, in the way of Barter. Indeed, I understood Dr Lee, that the military stores and cloathing would be delivered with^t immediate pay of any kind — We formerly sent you the extract of a letter to Congress, which is all that has been received, unless it be a Spanish letter from the Governor of N. Orleans which Mr Morris took away to get translated, and it has not yet been returned. You shall have it when we get it.

Mons. Loyeaute declines the Rectorship of the Academy. He is a young Gentleman of high family, of fortune, and ardent in pursuit of military Glory. His father, who is a General in the Artillery of France, has taken pains to instruct this his son from his earliest youth and he is you may be assured, a Proficient — He is sober, temperate as a soldier should be, and seems to have none of the fashionable vices. He says he came not here for money, but to search for military honor, to assist America in establishing her freedom, but since he cannot be employed in that way, he shall return to his own Country, the business of an Academician better suiting Age and infirmity, with views of distant good, than youth, strength, and prospect of present action; and immediate benefit to the public.

I am concerned we have lost this Gentleman, on many accounts. I am sure my Country will suffer, for want of the knowledge he possesses — And the rejection of him happened at our unlucky crisis. All the rest of his Corps had just set out on their return to France, because Congress would not comply with the contract Mr Deane had firmly made with them in France, and which had disgusted them greatly. This Gentleman remained at our request, and although an engagement was not absolute, it was very strong, kept him from returning with his companions, and will, I fear, impress on all their minds, bad ideas of the Americans, and do us no service in France — This is well known here and the Delegates look rather small in the eyes of their brethren. I am sure we acted for the best, well knowing the utter deficiency of knowledge in this branch with us, its necessity, and having the best grounds for believing this Gentleman an Adept — It is certain we went rather too far. I am sorry for it, but we shall be less forward in future. Since I last wrote, the Enemy have taken Fort Island, After a most gallant defence on the part of the Garrison, which retreated from the Island in the night after all but two of their Guns were dismounted : and not more than a rod and an half of the works left. The Enemy brought their Culdown Indiaman between Province Island and them, from which they poured a most dreadful cannonade from 24 and 32 pounders, and from their Tops the fire of Coherns and musketry drove the men from their guns in the Fort — The better opinion yet is, that the Enemy cannot get their fleet up to the City, until they first remove the Gallies, the Chevaux de Frise and reduce Red Bank. To effect this latter purpose, we hear that Cornwallis with ———[1] men has crossed into the Jersies, and that our Army is gone down to attack their lines now weakened by such a powerful reinforcement sent away — If so, we may expect important news in a day or two — One Brigade from the Eastern Army with Morgan's Corps have lately joined Gen: Washington — 20 Regiments are ordered from Gates' Army. The Rhode Island expedition went no further than Providence, by the misconduct 'tis said, of old Spencer — There will be an enquiry — Our last intelligence from the West Indies, which covers news from France the 4th Sept[r] gives us abundant reason to think that a War between France and G. Britain is on the verge of taking place, if it has not already done so. The F. Amb[r] is ordered to demand all F. Vessels taken by England with[t] the limits prescribed by the Treaty, and to retire from the Court, if the demand was not

---

[1] Blank in the texts of the transcript and the *Calendar of Virginia State Papers*, but in the text given in W. W. Henry, *Patrick Henry*, I. 126, the word "his" is here supplied.

complied with. The Governors in the F. Islands are ordered to be in readiness for war, and to lay an Embargo on all vessels bound to Europe, to prevent their falling into the enemies hands — 5000 additional Troops are to be immediately sent to Martinique and Guadalupe — Portugal has acceeded to the Family compact. Dr Lee is returning from Prussia, hav^g finished his business successfully at that Court — The King of Prussia has opened his Ports to the Vessels of the United States, and Mr Carmichael writes that a Ship loaded with Tobacco to Embden would be attended with ———¹ consequences. The Cargo would be returned in manufactures very useful to us, and 15 or 20 pr: cent cheaper than from France — Can't we try this experiment at the proper season, which may be known by the Commercial Dictionaries — We expect daily to receive important news from Europe. My ill state of health produced by bad water, bad air, and excessive business, will compel me to return home for a few days for the severity of the winter season.

I am with sentiments of affectionate esteem & respect, dear Sir, yours.

His Excellency PATRICK HENRY, *Govr of Virginia.*

¹ This blank in the texts of the transcript and the *Calendar* is replaced by the word "satisfactory" in the printed text given in W. W. Henry, *Patrick Henry,* I. 126.

THE LETTERS OF RICHARD HENRY LEE

[VIRGINIA DELEGATES IN CONGRESS] TO THE GOVERNOR OF VIRGINIA[1]

(RICHARD HENRY LEE
JOS: JONES
FRANCIS LIGHTFOOT LEE)

(PATRICK HENRY)

SIR, YORK IN PENNSYLVA. Nov' 27th 1777.

Conversing with Mons' Loyeaute, on the subject of what you are pleased to say the assembly have in contemplation for him, we find the plan quite the reverse of his wishes, and inconsistent with his ideas of being personally and quickly useful in the field. Of good family, and early trained to war by his father, who is a general in the Artillery of France, he wants to be in action, and hopes to acquire glory by the good services of himself and the Corps he shall instruct. The probability of the war going south next Campaign, and the character he had learnt of Virginia, made him readily agree with the views of the Delegates to remain behind his Companions who are returning to France, in expectation of serving our country by introducing the knowledge of Artillery, in a manner consistent with his ideas of military character. We may yet avail ourselves of this Gentleman's abilities as you will see by the enclosed proposition,[2] which we pray you, Sir, to lay before the

[1] From the text printed in William Wirt Henry, *Patrick Henry*, III. 128. The letter is signed by the delegates whose names appear above.

[2] This was as follows: "Monsieur Loyeauté being desirous of proving by real service his zeal and ability to promote the cause of America, conceives that the view of the Assembly in appointing him to the Directorship of a Military Academy, may be effectually answered by adopting the following method, and which will better correspond with his wishes of being quickly serviceable in war should the enemy turn their attention to Virginia the next Campaign.

honorable Houses. We have many reasons for wishing this plan may meet with approbation. Because we are well convinced of its public utility. Because of the generous cordiality with which this gentleman accorded with our proposals, contrary to earnest solicitations of his countrymen to the contrary, and of others who wanted him to go to other States, and whom he has offended by giving ours the preference. And because, lastly, he is here left behind the rest of his Corps, who were departed before your answer arrived here. As Monsr Loyeauté has been informed that the number of British Cruisers in the Bay of Boston renders it difficult to get safely out of that Harbour, he has agreed to accept the invitation of R. H. Lee to pass some time with him at Chantilly this winter, so that if the Houses accept his proffered service, a letter sent to him there, will occasion his immediate attendance in Williamsburg. He is of opinion that for the business of instruction it will be quite proper that we should be provided with

" Monsieur Loyeauté would propose that one hundred men, in two Companies, each commanded by one Captain & two Lieutenants, be put under his command and direction to be instructed in the knowledge of Artillery. The men to be pickt, and chosen for this particular business, it requiring persons of nimbleness and address to manage Artillery. The Officers of this Corps, Monsr Loyeauté would wish to be industrious men, and cordially disposed to learn the art. By this method Capt. Loyeauté hopes to convince the honorable Assembly of Virginia, that in a reasonable time he will furnish them with a useful and a respectable Corps of Artillery.

" Capt. Loyeauté is very willing to submit to the Assembly the future increase of this Corps and of his Command, after they shall have had an opportunity of judging concerning his merits by what he has actually performed. Well earned military fame, and being of real use to America being the sole motives that brought him here, and which alone can induce him to continue in this Country." *

* For original see Virginia State Library, Executive Communications. Copy in the Carnegie Institution of Washington endorsed, " Letter from R. H. Lee/Nov: 27th 1777./respecting Capt Loyeauté."

six field pieces, and as there are many belonging to the Continent now laying idle at Charles Town, we have no doubt but that Congress will indulge our Commonwealth with six or eight pieces on application being made by desire of our Assembly.

We have the honor to be sir, your Excellency's most obedient and most humble servants.

His Excellency Patrick Henry Esq. *Governor of Virginia at Williamsburg.*

TO [GOVERNOR THOMAS JOHNSON][1]

SIR, STAFFORD COUNTY IN VIRG^A. 13 Decr 1777.

Passing thro this Country in my way home from Congress, I find it the common talk here, that many avaricious, inconsiderate, and illdesigning people, have practised largely the carrying live stock and other provisions to the enemies ships of war, now in Potomac river opposite our Boyds Hole. In particular, I am told of many boats loaded with provisions going to these ships from your shore, somewhere, I think, about halfway between Cedar point and Wicomico. I have already written to the Governor of Virginia on this subject, and I hope your goodness will pardon me for giving you the same information. It appears to me of much consequence to the common cause, as well as to the reputation of our respective governments, that this pernicious traffic should be prevented in future; and

[1] A. L. S. Lenox Library, Myers Collection, "Prominent Civilians and Members of the Continental Congress," p. 142, No. 276. Endorsed as received Dec. "21st." An autograph draft of this letter with erasures and endorsed "Copy of letter to Govr ~~Henry~~ Johnson" is in the American Philosophical Society, Lee Papers, II. 35. The letter is to Thomas Johnson, Governor of Maryland.

that those who have now offended against the laws of their country by supplying its enemies, should be punished for so doing. The artful enemy pretend they want to injure no body, desiring only to get fresh water, purchase provisions & that they would, if permitted, land Salt for the use of the poor &ᶜ — Many are taken in by this plausibility, and tempted by Salt, Rum, Sugar &ᶜ &c, which are first taken from us, or from our friends coming to trade with us, and made the means of procuring provisions that enable them to remain here distressing and destroying our commerce. When provisions come slowly, they encourage the Slaves to runaway, and keep them, as they say, to be redeemed by provisions. It is easy to see, besides the ill consequence above pointed out, how this kind of Trade may in time debauch the minds of the people, and produce extensive mischief. It appears to me, that if some of your Gallies, joined by some of ours, were constantly to attend upon the Men of War when they come up this river, and by keeping near the shore and abreast of the Ships, out of reach of harm from them; they might effectually obstruct this evil working trade.

I have proposed this to Governor Henry, who I am sure will, with pleasure, cooperate with you in this salutary work.

I have the honor to be, with great esteem, Sir Your excellencies most obedient humble Servant.

THE LETTERS OF RICHARD HENRY LEE

TO [GENERAL GEORGE WASHINGTON][1]

DEAR SIR,   CHANTILLY IN VIRG^A^ Jany 2, 1778

The inclosed come to my hand only a few days past
altho from its date it appears to have been written long
since. There are some useful suggestions in it, and
therefore I send it to you — I do not know the Writers
reason for dating it in April 1776 when from some parts
in the body of the writing it must [have] been written in
the cours of the year 1777. The arts of the enemies of
America are endless, but all wicked as they are various.
Among other tricks they have forged a pamphlet of
Letters entitled 'Letters from Gen. Washington to several of his friends in 1776.' The design of the Forger is
evident, and no doubt it gained him a good Beef Steak
from his Masters — I would send you this pamphlet
if it were not too bulky for the Post, as it might serve
to amuse your leisure hours during the inaction of Winter — We hear, that Lord Cornwallis is gone to England, probably[2] to encourage the hopes of Administration upon their sending out strong reenforcements in
the Spring. I am just informed from Williamsburg
that the Assembly have passed[3] the Confederation
Nem Con. and have Voted 2000 men to be drafted from
the Single Men to fill up the Regiments, also 10 Regiments of Volunteers to be quickly raised & Marched
to the Army for 6 Months — They have adopted a very
extensive Taxation which will produce a large sum of

[1] A. dr. L. S. American Philosophical Society, Lee Papers, II. 45,
No. 14. A text with variations is printed in R. H. Lee, *Memoir of
Richard Henry Lee*, II. 19.
[2] Substituted for an illegible erasure.
[3] This word is difficult to read and may possibly be "ratified,"
though it looks something like "possessed."

money, and thereby produce the most salutary consequences —

The injury my health received at York is not yet removed but I hope to be in Williamsburg to assist in Assembly by the 12 or 14 of this month — I wish you the compliments of the Season, and remain with true affection dear Sir Yours Sincerely.

TO GENERAL [GEORGE] WEEDON[1]

Dear Sir,   Chantilly January the 2ᵈ 1778

I thank you for your favor of the 16ᵗʰ last, which I received here a few days ago. We had heared of Gen. Howes sortie, which I think has been attended with as little honor as advantage to him. It proves however the propriety of your last adopted measure, to winter together. Safety to the American army, and distress to the enemy must result from this measure. I mean Safety from the mischief of sudden surprizes, and being cut off in detail. Less hardship to be sure would have been sustained by warmer quarters, but yet I hope such care will be taken to build good & well covered huts as will prevent much injury from the inclemency of weather. I consider that either Mʳ Howes army must winter in their lines, which will expose them to as much hardship as we endure, or they will winter in the City of Philadelphia, which if we may judge from all former experience will render them a much less formidable enemy in the Spring than if they had possessed colder quarters in the winter. To Hanibals wintering in Capua is ascribed his loss of Rome, and reason as well

[1] A. L. S. Haverford College, Charles Roberts Autograph Collection. Addressed, "Bregadier General Weedon/at the American Camp on/Schuylkill near the Sweeds/Ford in/Pennsylvania," and franked by Lee.

THE LETTERS OF RICHARD HENRY LEE

as experience proves that Cities enfeeble armies more than battles. Rest, with gentle exercise in the way of discipline, will I hope restore our brave soldiers to health, and fitness for an early expulsion of their detestible enemy from this Country, before reenforcements can arrive to assist them in their infernal projects of slavery, rapine & destruction. My letters from Williamsburg inform me that the confederation has passed Nem. Con. That 2000 men are to be drafted from among the unmarried to fill the Regiments, and that 10 Regiments of Volunteers for six months are to be immediately raised to join the General. A very vigorous and extensive taxation is adopted, which will call from circulation a large sum of money and of course appretiate the rest. I wish all the States may pursue measures of equal wisdom & vigor.

My health has not yet been such as to permit my going to Williamsburg, but I think of doing so about the 10ᵗʰ or 12ᵗʰ of this month — Remember me if you please to all friends in the Army.

I am dear sir Your most obedient and very humble servant.

TO [FRANCIS LIGHTFOOT LEE][1]

My DEAR BROTHER,   CHANTILLY January 3ᵈ 1778

The last Post day brought no letters from you or any of my friends, occasioned I suppose by the severity of the weather, which prevented the rider from travelling and crossing Rivers. I shall be well pleased to know the effect produced by 'Common Sense' and my Narrative upon Deanes execrable libel. If it is not the fate of mankind that they shall cherish vice in opposition

[1] A. L. S. University of Virginia, Lee Papers, No. 204. Printed in part in the *Southern Literary Messenger*, Jan. 1860, p. 11.

to truth and public good, no doubt will remain but that this impudent attempt will at length meet the censure it merits. I hope every Wretch whose crimes deserve it, will find the assertion of D: Cudworth to be just, "That truth is the most unbending and uncompliable, the most necessary, firm, immutable and adamantine thing in the world." But then some care and pains must be taken to produce and state this truth to public view and to general understanding. For this reason it seems to me of indispensable propriety that all the letters and Documents both of Congress and in private possession relative to Deane's misconduct should be laid before the public. A very few pertinent comments will do. I wish only that the world may perfectly understand M: Deane, and I shall be quite at my ease about any effect that his libels, and his low art of in-uendo can do, to produce either public or private injury and injustice. The employment he has been in, and the events that have taken place during that period, open the minds of people who know him not, to credit his talk of great sufferings and great doings. This again disposes to believe what this great sufferer and great Doer even insinuates by supposition or inuendo, Now the truth is, that these events would have indubitably happened if Deane had been all the time in the Hottentot Country — He was bound to France on his own private speculations, and surely the application of public money to support him in affluence and grandeur unknown to him before cannot be called *suffering*. And as far as his agency affected our affairs it was evidently to their injury, witness the illtimed, indecent fitting out of priva-teers, against the sense of Congress and the earnest repeated desires of the Court of France — Witness his conduct with the Cutters which was in direct opposition to the instructions of the Secret Committee. I suppose that I am within bounds when I say, that eight tenths of the Stores which have come, and come so late, are to be, and have been accounted for to others, altho these are ostensibly alluded to as the produce of three millions, which he has not accounted for. The early communication to London of the Treaty (before it was executed) by D: Bancroft, and the great intimacy of this last with Deane, are striking things. He says D: Lee's Secretary went to London — Let him be asked if no Clerk or Secretary of his went there — D: Lee might have private, very licit business, having lived there, but this was not the case with M: Deane. These speculations that D: Bancroft talks of deserve enquiring about — Was it gaming in the Funds or what! Lord North told M: Hartley that the American Commissioners were gaming in the funds of England — This may explain Bancroft. Now, since the papers which M: Adams, yourself, and Congress possess will state these matters very clearly, it must be of great utility to give them to the Public — It is happy for Mankind that depraved hearts are commonly joined with weak heads and therefore in the present libel Congress is as much traduced as Individuals. Their honor and the public good makes it necessary, that M: Deane should be rightly understood and that he should be called upon immediately to settle his accounts with Vouchers before intelligent, honest, and spirited Commissioners, to be appointed for the purpose. It must be of great importance to summon M: Stephenson, S: James Jay, and M: Diggs: to give evidence concerning M: Deane — M: Stephenson did certainly declare in the lobby of our House of Delegates, that M: Deane was concerned in trade, which the latter publicly denied to Congress.

My health is much better, but I have not got my cloaths made — We are miserably off here for Taylors, and my winter Apparatus very bad. My friend Col? Geo. Mason has been a week here and keeps me from going into some necessary preparatives for my return to Philadelphia — I hope however to sett out in 15 or 16 days hence — The old Squire of Maryland has lost his eldest Son Phil Lee. our love to M͞r͞s Lee and the Shippens, and cordial respects to our friends

Most affectionately Yours.

P.S. Infinite pains are taking to spread about Deane's libel here —

TO PATRICK HENRY[1]

My Dear Sir,   Chantilly the 7ᵗʰ of Janʸ, 1778.

The state of my health has hitherto by no means permitted me to leave home any distance, or I should certainly have obeyed your summons —I hope however, in a few days to be able to pay my respect to the general assembly. It seems the determination of Providence, whose superintending care of Virginia has been evident from the origin of our country, that we shall not want the great and necessary security which is derived from a well formed Artillery. The Bearer of this is one of those Veteran Sergeants of Artillery, whom you see made mention of in the Delegates' engagement with Monsʳ Loyeauté. This Gentleman, pursuing his point with that zeal and industry that distinguishes his character, took immediate and effectual measures to procure the return of these old and skilful soldiers, whose abilities he knew to be so necessary for the right forming of a useful and serviceable corps of this kind. Notwithstanding therefore the great pains taken to prevent these people from coming, as well by their dis-

[1] From the text printed in William Wirt Henry, *Patrick Henry*, III. 140.

contented Countrymen who were returning to France, as by some who wanted them elsewhere; by the care of a colonel of Artillery to whom Monsr Loyeauté had written, and of Monsr Pierre, who is likewise mentioned in the Delegates' agreement, the Sergeants, five in number, with Monsr Pierre, Monsr Bigarre, & Monsr Coyette are on their way to Williamsburg. This sergeant has travelled before the rest, and was sent on to Williamsburg from York, and called here having been informed that Capt. Loyeauté was at this place. The knowledge of artillery is so indispensible to the public security according to the modern mode of making war, that I cannot help rejoicing at the opportunity we now have, if it be rightly improved, of possessing the best artillery of any state in the Union. Beneficial indeed will be the change to that, from being almost the worst provided! When I know that most of the other States are cautiously providing in this way, and wisely strengthening themselves in this branch, I own, I am alarmed at our great deficiency, and small prospects of being better off without the aid of imported knowledge. These officers and men, being among the best in the french army, their leave of absence is limited to a year from this time, but in that space, aided by a little longer indulgence, which may be procured by the influence of Capt. Loyeauté's father, who is a General in the Artillery of France, they may be able to place us in a situation such as to complete effectually what they begin. Neither this sergeant, nor any of the absent corps yet know that Mons' Loyeauté has missed command of our regiment, and probably discontent & desire to return, may arise from that knowledge, so that it will be well to have the determination of the Assembly on Captain Loyeauté's last proposition before they are made acquainted with this gentleman's disappointment. In a few days we shall be in Town, and in the mean time be pleased to give directions how the Bearer is to be supported. When President Hancock returned to Boston, the Delegates obtained his promise to give every facility in his power to the return of these Veterans, and to furnish what might be necessary for them. In consequence of which, this Sergeant tells us, Mr. Hancock advanced them 600 dollars to bear the expense of the corps to Virginia.

I am with sincere esteem & regard, dear sir, your most obedient and very humble servant.

P.S. By the late arrival of a store ship at Portsmouth in N. Hampshire, The United States are now, in the whole, possessed of about 200 field pieces of Brass — These are many more than they want, and in consequence, if application were made to Congress for six of those now at Charles Town in South Carolina, there is no doubt but they will be lent to our State, and on light travelling carriages may soon be transported hither — Capt Loyeauté thinks this quite necessary to conduct properly the b——— of instructions. I wish the affair was immediately taken up in the Assembly.

His Excellency, Patrick Henry.

TO —— ——[1]

Dear Sir, Williamsburg 15th Jany 1778

I am exceedingly obliged to you for your favor of the 28 Ult°., by the contents of which I have reason to think you have written me a letter that has never come to hand — Indeed I strongly suspect infidelity in the Post-office — It may be possible to discover the certainty of

[1] A. L. S. Massachusetts Historical Society, Waterston Collection. Endorsed, "From Col. R. H. Lee 15th Jan^{ry} 1778./Answer'd 5th Feb."

this — I have received since my arrival in Virgᵃ two letters from you, the first came by Post to me three weeks ago, and the last I received today, directed to the care of the Post Master at Leedstown, but mentioned to be by *Express* — If more than these have been written & sent by Post, the miscarriage is in the Post office — The first of your favors I answered by return of Post, and this acknowledges the last — Profitable as is the game that France now plays, she may probably not wish to change it quickly — Yet I think the greater interest, or necessity, will work a change in our favor e'er long — But my wish is, that we rely not at all upon the aid of others, but trust to our own wise and manly exertions — Wise, in the instant and total discarding of every Tory or suspected Tory from every department, and by securing a vigorous Army and its thorough supply with every necessary — Nothing can prove infamous misconduct more conclusively, than there not being plenty of provisions in a Country abounding extremely in this Article. But we must not only drive the Tories from the State, the Army, and from every office of our appointment; but we must also render it inconvenient as possible for them to find existence in this land of freedom, which they wish to poison with the bane of Tyranny. It is of infinite consequence to the success of our virtuous cause that its friends should have the surest & quickest intelligence, yet these are much worse informed than our enemies are — The latter not only have private riders, but they certainly contrive to corrupt the Post in some places, and make it an instrument of our injury instead of being a useful channel of conveyance — Our Assembly have gone largely into the business of Taxation, and they have shewn much zeal in their plan for strengthening the Army — Their wish for Union is evident from the expedition with which they have unanimously and

quickly assented to the Confederation — I pray you Sir
to continue your obliging correspondences which shall
be carefully returned by dear Sir your most obedient
& very humble Servant

TO PATRICK HENRY [1]

My Dear Sir,   Greenspring, 25th Jan'y, 1778.
I find Mr. Ellis desirous of superintending the estate
of Mr. Paridise and this at the same time, and I am
very willing to second his views in this matter, because
I am satisfied it will redound to the benefit of both
estates.   Heretofore (until lately) they have always been
under the same management, and from their situation,
and other circumstances, capable of co-operating and
assisting each other.   Mr. Ellis's fitness to manage both,
is I believe equal to any mans.   The act of assembly
lately passed for sequestering British property, evidently
designs nothing at present unfriendly to the Owners
of such property, and therefore I should suppose, that
in appointing a Commissioner for the estate of Mr.
Paradise, regard may properly be had to the choice of a
person who is at once friendly to the public and to the
Proprietor of the estate.   Such a person, in this instance
is Col'o Henry Lee.   He is willing to undertake it, and
he is uncle by marriage to the Lady of Mr. Paradise.
Should these things appear to you in the light they do to
me, I shall be obliged to you, sir, for having the business
so managed as that Mr. Ellis may succeed in his desire.
    I have the honor to be with great esteem and respect,
dear Sir, your most affectionate and obedient.

His Excellency, Patrick Henry.

[1] From the text printed in William Wirt Henry, *Patrick Henry*, III.
142.

THE LETTERS OF RICHARD HENRY LEE

TO [WILLIAM LEE][1]

My dear Brother   Greenspring   Jan.[y] 25th 1778

Referring you to the many letters I have lately written several of which have I hope reached you, this shall be chiefly confined to private business. My ill state of health obliging me to leave Congress the 6th of last december, I returned to Chantilly where I found yours from Nantes with the pamphlets, for which I thank you. Your packet for our brother Frank I have opened and delivered the various Accounts of Sale, as Loudon was absent at Congress — I have already paid Col.[o] Geo Lee's estate 900 dollars, or £200 Sterling on your account, and the ballance of my debt to you on that account shall be soon applied as you desire. Col.[o] Mason has delivered me the orders you gave him on Triplet & Thornton & M.[r] Mills, as he says he would rather choose the money should rest in your hands until he has occasion to draw for it. The Col.[o] says that his only reason for drawing on you formerly in favor of Pliarne Gruel & C.[o] was because he apprehended you still continued in London and fearing that our enemies might proceed to confiscation of American property in their power, but since you are in France he is Well satisfied that you did not pay the draught, as he is better pleased with the money being in your hands — The bill was not remitted to that house in payment, but for Col.[o] Masons own use, in order to remove his money from England — So that matter stands right. Our Assembly having just risen, I am now here on my way home, and I have directed Ellis to make out his accounts and write you fully concerning your affairs under his

[1] A. L. Virginia Historical Society, Lee Papers, IV. 117–120. See *Ibid.*, II. 8.

381

direction   Considering the most infamous condition in which Fauntleroy left everything here, I think Ellis has done well, and he is going on to do much better — I assure you, that as far as I am able to judge, you have got a prize in him, and I hope soon to see your affairs here in a flourishing way.   To the things Ellis has written for I think you should add a small box of well assorted medicines for the Use of your people — This is certainly a very sickly place, and medicine here is now so scarce and so excessive dear, that in this way they are without remedy.

Once more I must propose to you the plan of selling all your property in this Country, & for the following reasons, which are now abundantly more powerful than ever the reasons for this measure were formerly — In the first place you may rely upon it that the Western people will soon force a removal of the Seat of Government, in which case, the quality of these lands being but very indifferent, your interest here will be depreciated some hundred per cent — But this is not all, we have now began from the necessity of the case to impose extensive Taxes — And the mode adopted is an assessment of Lands, Slaves of all Ages, Cattle, Horses &c &c &c — The excessive quantity of paper currency in circulation has raised the value of everything 4 or 5 hundred per Cent above its natural Standard — In this unnatural tumid State of things, & the contiguity of this Estate to the Seat of government, the Assessed value of your estate will be exceeding great & the ½ per cent Tax upon the whole will call for an annual large sum.   Should the Seat of government be removed, I verily believe there would with good management, not be much more made than would discharge the Annual Tax.   My plan then is, to take advantage of the present inordinate value of things, sell the whole & as it will produce a very large sum put it immediately into the Continental Loan Office where it will draw six per Cent paid in draughts on France at 5 livres money of france for every dollar of interest. You will have $\frac{1}{2}$ per Cent tax to pay on this, & when the Taxes by lessening the quantity of money shall have restored its value, you will then remained possessed of the large sum at interest which the present advanced rates would produce — Nor would any injury be risked from the removal of the Seat of Government. If the American cause succeeds this Bank will be infallibly secure, if the cause fails, neither Bank nor Land will avail you — But then this plan if adopted, should be quickly put in practice, & proper powers signed by M.ͬˢ Lee & yourself sent over. I think the act passed for this purpose under the new Government makes three witnesses necessary and that the Feme be privily examined by a Magistrate of the place & the whole authenticated by the Seal of the Corporation where the parties reside. — Against this I think the only objection is the parting with the Negroes, upon principles of humanity, but a few of the oldest & best Servants may be kept & placed in good families until they may be wanted — Hereafter money will rise in value & land fall, so that if it be necessary, other & better lands may be purchased for less than what these will now fetch.[1]

[1] Arthur Lee made an extract of the portion of the letter between the *'s, and sent it to William Lee with the following addition: —

"The Letter is long. Approves of y.ͬ manager. Encloses a letter Invoice from the Squire & a Bill to him on you by Dolman for £200. J.ⁿ Ellis y.ͬ Manager writes you that he has been on the Estate 16 months — shall clear £400 after clothing the negroes whom he found naked, has made but 8 or 9 hhds tob.º Desires you will send him 2 doz p.ͬ good Cards one of each kind & Blankets for the People, it will do. Salt also is wanted. On his own Acct. he desires 1 p.ᶜᵉ Linnen at 2/6y.ᵈ, 21 y.ᵈˢ Com.ⁿ Cambric Strong Cloth to make a great Coat. 10 papers of pins & 500 needles. List of negroes old & young 151 —"

I have written you so frequently about my Sons that I think you must fully possess my ideas respecting them. I wish Ludwell to study eloquence and lay the foundation for practising law in this Country which is the ready way to honor & to fortune — Military exercises may be his amusement — Thom I wish to be expert in business — But it is impossible to make remittances now, and at any rate, I fear the expence — Perhaps it might be the best way, if the eldest cannot be employed so as to prevent the whole expence of his stay in France from falling on me, and if any consignments come here which with proper assistance he might manage, it would be better to send him over, and let Ludwell finish his Studies. I wish you would pursue that plan respecting them which your judgment shall approve as most fit for all parties joining together œconomy & solid good for them —

I have orders on you from Col? Hulls estate, from Capt. John Hull & Mr Charles Bell amounting in the whole to £22 or 3 pounds sterling which from the necessity of the case I must assign to Miss Panton for her wages as Tutoress to my children — She is going to Europe & there is neither Specie nor bills to be had here, and our paper money will do her no good. The Squire desires the inclosed bill may be put to his credit if you can receive the money, and he requests that the small inclosed invoice may be complied with by the first opportunity. For the greatest part of my life I have been used to Wine & to Jesuits Bark & now I

Arthur Lee also adds an extract from a "Letter from J. Mills, 'Will^b Mar. 28. has received y^r Acct. Sales, Ballance in his hand Col. Mason refus^d to receive it, as he had drawn on you But R. H. L. letter says that is sett^{ld} w^h ye Col. who desire his balance may remain in y^r hand. Desires y^r advice about gett^g property to France. Thinks he ordered the proceeds of Tobc? shipt to Griffith Eden & Co to be p^d to you, asks if you rec^d it.(?)' " [These extracts in the autograph of Arthur Lee are in the Virginia Historical Society, Lee Papers, II. 8.]

have neither — It goes hard with me — But the establishment of public liberty smooths all ways however
rugged—I shall return shortly to Congress and shall
continue there longer than I expected when last I
wrote you on this subject — I hope e'er now. [*The remainder of the Ms. is missing.*]

TO [LANDON CARTER] [1]

DEAR SIR,   CHANTILLY 6ᵗʰ Febʸ 1778
    Your boy overtook me yesterday on my way to the
General Muster where I was detained until after Sunset. This morning I take the boy with me to Court
where I expect to receive letters from the North that if
there should be any news you may have it.
    The best method that had appeared for making Syrup
from the Corn Stalk was sent here by me whilst at Congress, and from hence some person has unfortunately
removed it. The method of granulating I was never
possessed of. My brother Frank had it and I proposed
to take a copy of the paper but came away and forgot it.
However all this need not be any interruption to you,
since the first thing is, to cultivate the Corn, and before
the Stalk is fit for use, which I think will be best in September, you may rely on my best endeavors to furnish
you with the whole process from the best practise. I
do not know but it may be necessary to prepare proper
wood and have it well seasoned for making the Mill,
which is nothing more than the common Apple Mill,
except that three Cylinders are used instead of two in
the Apple Mill. As they generally cultivate what is
called the Rare ripe Corn in New England perhaps there
may be difference between that and our common Corn

[1] A. L. S. Virginia Historical Society, Lee Papers, IV. 125.

— I am inclined to think that the small Negro Corn will answer better than any other, the Stalk being perceptibly more heavy for its size than any other, which may be imputed to the greater abundance of saccharine juice — I suppose the best way will be to make experiments with all three kinds of Corn —

Two posts have now passed since I received a letter from Congress, and therefore I am without news, except the prevailing report of the Canadians having revolted from the English, taken S͂t Johns, Quebec &c — This account comes so directly and thro such good channels that I begin to give credit to it. * * * *

P.S. My Servant is returned from Leed['s ?] without any letter from Congress. Inspector General Loyaute informs me that a Gentleman just from Charles Town tells him that a french Man of War of 74 guns had engaged and beaten an English Frigate that had taken a French Merchantman bound to Charles Town and that the M. of War afterwards convoyed the Merchant Ship into Charles Town and that she immediately sailed to drive away another English Frigate that lay in the Roads of Charlestown — Mons͂r Loyauté further says that he has information that the French put war down for certain in the month of March — I see in a late paper that D͂r Franklin was stabbed[1] at Paris in December but likely to recover —

Please let our friend Col° Tayloe have this news —

[1] Endorsed on the back of the Ms., " The Stabbing our agent Shows the dread our enemies have of a French war, as well as the presumptive Certainty they know they can do but little more within; or why the endeavor to kill an old man 77."

THE LETTERS OF RICHARD HENRY LEE

TO JOHN PAGE[1]

DEAR SIR,   CHANTILLY Feb⁷ 14. 1778.

I have written very largely to the Governor on several subjects that appear to me of the greatest consequence to our success, if the Governor is not in Town, the letters are directed to you — I earnestly pray your attention to these subjects — It was with much regret that I had not an oportunity of passing some time with you when I was last in Williamsburg — I wished extremely to have bespoke your patronage of Mons⁴ Loyeaute. As well because I am convinced this Gentlemans abilities are great in the way he has engaged to serve this country, as because his zeal in our cause is fully equal to his abilities; and the Commonwealth will be benefitted in proportion to the support and the countenance he shall receive from the Government in all his Operations. Satisfied of this, I am very sure you will aid to the utmost of your power this Gentleman in his plans for the strength and security of our Country. Mons⁴ Loyeauté has sense, industry, and great temperance in every thing — I am sure he will truly exert his abilities for our benefit. How infamously do our enemies conduct their opposition ? — Assassinations, corruption, robbery, and every vileness is their practice — If the cause of virtue be the care of Heaven, and vice its detestation, these people can never succeed —

Farewell dear Sir affectionately yours.

[1] A. L. S. John Carter Brown Library, Ms. Collections. Addressed to him at Williamsburg, and franked by Lee as "On the public service."

THE LETTERS OF RICHARD HENRY LEE

TO [ARTHUR LEE][1]

My dear Brother,   Chantilly Feb.ʸ 23.ᵈ 1778

It is now something more than two months since my ill state of health compelled me to leave Congress for a time. Being pretty well recovered, I shall return to Congress in a fortnight. Since my being in Virginia I have interested myself so effectually in behalf of Mons.ʳ de Loyeauté that he is appointed Inspector General of the Artillery and Fortifications of this State. He is an able young Officer and very capable of doing Virginia great service and himself much honor. To answer these purposes effectually, something that we have not is necessary. Various kinds of military Stores are indispensable — A good Founder is wanted, and an expert Armorer. To obtain these, Mons.ʳ Loyeauté and myself did here contrive the following plan, which is sent to the Governor and Council for their adoption if they approve it. A proper fund for the payment of what these things shall cost is to be lodged in France, Mons.ʳ Le Maire an intelligence french Officer is to be sent immediately to France with letters from the Governor & myself to you, and from General Loyeauté to his Father who is a Lieutenant General in the French Army and an Inspector General of the Artillery — The design of this is to be able to obtain leave to purchase from the royal Arsenals such Stores as we want and such as are really good in their kind. Having obtained these Mons.ʳ Le Maire is with secrecy and celerity to transport them hither in an armed Cutter. That he may be able to land in our Eastern Shore or in North Carolina he is to take a good Coast Pilot out with him. * You will I am sure give this plan all the

[1] A. L. S.   University of Virginia, Lee Papers, No. 145.
* Ms. marked with a vertical line, probably by A. Lee, for emphasis.

388

success in your power if it should be adopted, because I assure you it is quite necessary for our proper defense. Mons? Loyeauté recommends Mons? Le Maire strongly to me and I can rely on the judgment and integrity of the former. So I hesitate not to recommend Mons? Le Maire and his business strongly to you. The sooner he returns the better. since we cannot tell how soon the war may be transported to this Commonwealth It may be very well to get acquainted with Mons? Loyeauté's father in France, because cooperation may benefit us.* Since I left Congress they have received abundant reason to suppose that General Burgoyne does not intend to observe the Convention of Saratoga, in consequence of which, Congress has ordered that Gen! Burgoyne & all his Army shall be detained prisoners of War until the Court of London shall ratify the Convention of Saratoga. Our enemies no doubt will endeavor to persuade the world that this is a act of perfidy, but the propriety of the measure will be evident to all who are acquainted with the reasons that our enemies themselves have furnished. We receive at this place but imperfect intelligence, being removed from the Post Road, and out of the way of much company — But the last time I heard from the Army, Gen. Washington was placed about 17 miles from Philadelphia in which the enemy were, and where they suffered a good deal for most kinds of provisions and forage, the American Army being so placed as to prevent them from getting supplies of this kind.* We are preparing for an early and vigorous Campaign. I hope this year the Cort of London will have other force to contend with besides North America.

My love to the Alderman his Lady & my Boys farewell.

Let me hear often from you.

* Ms. marked with a vertical line, probably by A. Lee, for emphasis.

THE LETTERS OF RICHARD HENRY LEE

TO [SAMUEL ADAMS][1]

My dear Sir,   Chantilly March 1ˢᵗ 1778

Your favor of January the 5ᵗʰ came to hand 10 days
ago, and gave the same pleasure that I always receive
when attending to your sentiments. The important
objects you animadvert upon deserve the closest attention
of every American, but those more especially to whom
the public councils are intrusted. God grant them
fortitude, wisdom and perseverance to guide us safely
thro the storm that surrounds us. I came here for
repose, but I have not be able to find it. Our Assembly
being sitting called me to Williamsburg where I became
busied in the public councils, and since that, much engaged in the country with the execution of a very important Act, for making drafts from the single men to
recruit our regiments in service of the Continent. From
this draft, added to one of our State regiments ordered
to be made complete, we shall furnish very certainly,
and pretty speedily about 2500 recruits. We have also
proposed to raise 5000 Volunteers for six months, and an
Act passed to encourage the project; but I am not able
to say that many men will be produced by this plan.
The design was, to make early and vigorous impression
upon the enemy before reinforcements can arrive.
Let this latter plan succeed or not, the former will, and
if the other States reenforce the Army in proportion to
our 2500 men, we shall be strong enough to undertake
the most decisive measures. I make no doubt but the
virtue and vigor of our eastern brethren will fully equal
Virginia on this all important occassion. We certainly
may be able to finish the war on land if we so manage
as to be in condition to take the field with a strong
army by the middle of April. As things are now cir-

[1] A. L. S. Lenox Library, Samuel Adams Papers.

cumstanced, our enemies must either give up the contest by land armies and have recourse to arts, or they will make one last and vigorous effort to subdue. Amidst a thousand artful designs, this latter intention is obvious in a lately arrived Speech. We ought always to be ready my friend to oppose Art with wisdom and to repel force by force. From the first moment, I have been opposed to the new Commissari[es] plan, and wish things were restored to their first simple and effective State, but in the meantime every State whe[re] provisions are must exert every nerve or our danger wil[l] be extreme. Ample magazines in safe place should wit[h] all speed be formed, and effectual modes fallen upon for speediest transportation. It must never be that the cause of human nature fall sacrifice to a few venal or vicious Commissaries. Our executive is with all its energ[y] engaged in this business, and the Legislature has enabled them by law to seize what shall be necessary for the Army from Engrossers & Forestallers. We have passed a law to prevent forestalling, and a very extensive taxation has taken place. Our courts of Justice are opened, and the best Judges we can find appointed to fill them. This Assembly has adopted exactly your sentiments respecting the Confederation, having passed it Nem. Con. altho many wished it were changed in some respects. But the great Object of Union overcame lesser considerations, and their Delegates are ordered to ratify it in Congress.

I shall be in Congress about the 15th instant, and I hope, because I see the greatest necessity for it, that we shall have a full congress. Your presence I am sure will greatly promote the public good — Farewe[ll] My dear Sir and be happy as you deserve most certainly to be.

P.S. I shall get my daughter to direct this letter to avert Tory curiosity

THE LETTERS OF RICHARD HENRY LEE

TO MRS. HANNAH CORBIN[1]

My Dear Sister,   Chantilly, March 17, 1778.

Distressed as my mind is and has been by a variety of attentions, I am illy able by letter to give you the satisfaction I could wish on the several subjects of your letter. Reasonable as you are and friendly to the freedom and happiness of your country, I should have no doubt giving you perfect content in a few hours' conversation. You complain that widows are not represented, and that being temporary possessors of their estates ought not to be liable to the tax. The doctrine of representation is a large subject, and it is certain that it ought to be extended as far as wisdom and policy can allow; nor do I see that either of these forbid widows having property from voting, notwithstanding it has never been the practice either here or in England. Perhaps 'twas thought rather out of character for women to press into those tumultuous assemblages of men where the business of choosing representatives is conducted. And it might also have been considered as not so necessary, seeing that the representatives themselves, as their immediate constituents, must suffer the tax imposed in exact proportion as does all other property taxed, and that, therefore, it could not be supposed that taxes would be laid where the public good did not demand it. This, then, is the widow's security as well as that of the never married women, who have lands in their own right, for both of whom I have the highest respect, and would at any time give my consent to establish their right of voting. I am persuaded that it would not give them greater se-

---

[1] Text derived from a clipping from the *Alexandria Gazette* of December, 1875, in the possession of Mr. Joseph Packard, of Baltimore, who kindly allowed it to be transcribed. The copy of the letter was furnished to the *Gazette* by Mr. Cassius F. Lee, of Alexandria, Virginia.

curity, nor alter the mode of taxation you complain of; because the tax idea does not go to the consideration of perpetual property, but is accommodated to the high prices given for the annual profits. Thus no more than $\frac{1}{2}$ per ct. is laid on the assessed value, although produce sells now 3 and 400 per cent above what it formerly did. Tobacco sold 5 or 6 years ago for 15s and 2d — now 'tis 50 and 55. A very considerable part of the property I hold is, like yours, temporary for my life only; yet I see the propriety of paying my proportion of the tax laid for the protection of property so long as that property remains in my possession and I derive use and profit from it. When we complained of British taxation we did so with much reason, and there is great difference between our case and that of the unrepresented in this country. The English Parliament nor their representatives would pay a farthing of the tax they imposed on us but quite otherwise. Their property would have been exonerated in exact proportion to the burthens they laid on ours. Oppressions, therefore, without end and taxes without reason or public necessity would have been our fate had we submitted to British usurpation. For my part I had much rather leave my children free than in possession of great nominal wealth, which would infallibly have been the case with all American possessions had our property been subject to the arbitrary taxation of a British Parliament. With respect to Mr. Fauntleroy, if he spoke as you say, it is a very good reason why he ought not to be assessor. But if he should be the law has wisely provided a remedy against the mistakes or the injustice of assessors by giving the injured party appeal to the commissioners of the tax, which commissioners are annually chosen by the freeholders and housekeepers, and in the choice of whom you have as legal a right to vote as any other person. I believe there is no instance in our new government of any unnecessary placemen, and I know the rule is to make their salaries moderate as possible, and even these moderate salaries are to pay tax. But should Great Britain gain her point, where we have one place-man we should have a thousand and pay pounds where we pay pence; nor should we dare to murmur under pain of military execution. This, with the other horrid concomitants of slavery, may well persuade the American to lose blood and pay taxes also rather than submit to them.

My extensive engagements have prevented me from adverting to yours and Dr. Hall's subscription for Lord Camden's pictures not having been refunded, as the rest have long since been, but the money is ready for your call.

> I am, My dear Sister,
>
> Most sincerely and affectionately yours,

MRS HANNAH CORBIN.

TO THOMAS JEFFERSON[1]

DEAR SIR,   YORK May 2ᵈ 1778

We are this moment made acquainted by the War Office that an Express was immediately to depart for Virginia, and I take the opportunity of enclosing by him the last papers, which contain all our news, except it be a report that seems not illy founded, that Gen! Amhers & Adm! Keppel are arrived at Philadelphia as commissioners from the King & Parliament of G. B. to carry into execution the very curious plan that

[1] A. L. S. Library of Congress, Jefferson Correspondence, Letters to Jefferson, Ser. 2, Vol. 51, No. 3. Addressed to "Thomas Jefferson esquire/or in his absence to the honorable/George Wythe esqʳ At Williamsburg/in/Virginia//R. H. Lee./By Express."

one of the inclosed papers contains — Tis happy for America that her enemies have not sufficient ability to give even a specious appearance to their wicked designs. In this case the Peasantry here develope the cheat. We have no news/not a scrip from our Com[mi]¹ssioners — The Gold and the Sea power of our enemi[es]¹ have [p]¹ revailed to deprive us of most important dispatch[es].¹
Adieu my dear Sir.

Gen. Lee is fully exchanged and is sent for from . . .² to attend the Army. For Gods sake, for the love of our Countr[y]¹ my dear friend, let more vigorous measures be quickly adop[ted]¹ for reinforcing the Army — The last draft will fall greatly short of the requisite number — Our enemies are sore pressed, wisdom & vigor now will presently compel G. B. proud as she is, to acknowledge our Independency —

TO [THOMAS JEFFERSON]³

DEAR SIR,   YORK 3ᵈ May 1778
Having detained the Express that he might carry you the news that we heared was on its way from france, I am furnished with an opportunity of congratulating you on the important event of a Treaty of Commerce, and one of Alliance & Amity, havᵉ been signed at Paris on the 6ᵗʰ of february last, between France and these United States.⁴ Having been as particular as we could on this subject in the Delegates letter to the Governor,

¹ Ms. damaged and marked by print, probably of inclosures.
² Illegible word or words.
³ A. L. S. Library of Congress, Jefferson Correspondence, Letters to Jefferson, Ser. 2, Vol. 51, No. 18.
⁴ See *Journals of Congress*, May 2, 1778. (Ford, XI. 417, 418.)

I must beg leave to refer you to that for further information, being compelled to shortness here as the Express waits. Great Britain has now two Cards to play but which she will choose we cannot tell, although we certainly [o]ught in wisdom to be prepared for the worst — She may then acknowledge the Independency of America and make [a] Treaty of Commerce with her and thus be at peace with us [a]nd with all the World; or she may submit to the [u]ninterrupted progress of french commerce to avoid a war with that Power and yet push her whole force against [u]s this Campaign and thereby injure us extremely if we [a]re not prepared with a strong force to prevent it. She has [n]ow at Philadelphia 12,000 Veteran Troops, and may [p]ossibly collect and send over 8000 more for a last [e]ffort — This consideration points out the necessity of having a having a strong Army immediately. I do sincerely hope that our Assembly will vigorously and early take up this consideration, because I am sure that their last plan will not procure our quota by a considerable number.

I am dear Sir most affectiona[tely].

[VIRGINIA DELEGATES IN CONGRESS] TO GOVERNOR OF VIRGINIA[1]

RICHARD HENRY LEE
FRANCIS LIGHTFOOT LEE
JOHN BANISTER   (PATRICK HENRY)
THOMAS ADAMS

SIR,   YORK 3ᵈ May, 1778.

Having heared that a Messenger from France was on his way to Congress with important dispatches, we detained the Express who otherwise would have set out

[1] A. L. S. by Richard Henry Lee. Virginia State Library, Executive Communications May 4–June 1, 1778, to October 5–December 19, 1778. Addressed to "His Excellency Patrick Henry esquire, Governor of Virginia, at Williamsburg."

yesterday that we might furnish your Excellency with the intelligence he brought. It is with singular pleasure we inform you Sir that his messenger has brought to Congress authenticated copies of a Treaty of Commerce, and a Treaty of Amity and Alliance signed at Paris on the 6th of february last between France and these United States, and we understand there is abundant reason to suppose that that the whole Bourbon family will immediately acceed thereto. The Treaty of commerce is exactly conformable to our own proposals, and it is upon the most generous and equal principals. The treaty of alliance &c. is professedly for the security of the Sovereignty and absolute Independence of these States both in Government and Trade, and it agrees that if G. B. declares war against France on this account, or causes a war, or attempts to hinder her Commerce, that we shall make a common cause, and join our Arms and Counsels against the common enemy. Each Country guarantees to the other the possessions that they do or may possess at the end of the war.[1] Having heared these Treaties read but once in Congress, we cannot be more particular now. In general we find that his most Christian Majesty has been governed by principles of Magnanimity and true generosity, taking no advantage of our circumstances, but acting as if we were in the plenitude of power and in the greatest security. We are shortly to receive considerable Stores from France that come under a Convoy of a fleet of Men of War. The King of Prussia has actually refused to permit the Hessian and Hannau Troops that England had engaged for America to pass through his Territories — We congratulate you Sir and our Country on this great and important event, but we beg leave further to observe that it is in our opinion of infinite consequence that the Army should

[1] These words are here erased, "France disclaiming Active use[?] & Possession."

be quickly and powerfully reenforced. Because, if Britain should meanly permit the trade of France to proceed without interruption, and push her whole force against us this Campaign, it might be attended with very pernicious consequences. But with a strong Army, we shall, under God, be perfectly secure, and it will probably compel G. B. to a speedy recognition of our Independence, and thus secure the peace of Europe, with the peace, happiness, and glory of America.

We have the honor to be, with much esteem, Sir your Excellencies most obedient and very humble servants.[1]

TO GENERAL [GEORGE] WASHINGTON[2]

DEAR SIR, York the 6th of May 1778

The unfortunate cause which hath prevented me from attending to your last favor sooner, will, I hope, be my excuse. The long sickness and death of my much loved brother of Belleview, has for some time past confined me in Virginia, and removed every other consideration from my mind. I now embrace the first good opportunity of sending you the pamphlet of forgeries that I formerly

---

[1] This postscript, written and signed by Francis Lightfoot Lee, and signed in autograph also by John Banister and Thomas Adams, is added below Richard Henry Lee's signature:
" P.S. It is very prudently wished by our Commissioners that those of the French nation in our States may be treated with kindness and cordiality."
The following was added below the postscript by Patrick Henry:
" P.S. The postscript not to be printed. P. H.[ENRY]"
" N.B. A pen was drawn across the postscript that the printer might not publish in his hand bill which was deemed improper.
P. HENRY."
[2] A. L. S. Library of Congress, Letters to Washington, XX. 108. Addressed to him at "Head Quarters/Valley ,Forge."

mentioned. Tis among the pitiful arts of our enemies to endeavor at sowing dissention among the friends of liberty and their country. With me, such tricks can never prevail. Give me leave dear Sir to congratulate you on the happy event of our Treaty with France being so effectually concluded — Congress has ratified on their part and ordered the ratification to be delivered in due form. This will be announced to the public immediately. The counsels of France have been governed in this affair by true magnanimity and sound policy. It was magnanimous in his most Christian Majesty not to avail himself of our situation to demand unequal and oppressive terms, and it was wise to leave the Commerce of America open to all the Maratime States; which will prevent their jealousy & enmity, and make them foes instead of friends to England. Great Britain has its choice now of madness, or meanness. She will not war with the house of Bourbon and N. America at the same time, so that I incline to think meanness will be her choice as best befitting her present State and the minds of her Rulers. It will probably happen that the Trade of France will not now be interrupted; and thus, by affording no pretext for war, the whole force of our enemies may be devoted to one last and vigorous Campaign against us. As wise men we ought to be prepared for such an event by collecting a strong army, and by every other means that can discourage and defeat such intentions of our inveterate enemies. Being disappointed this Campaign, must infallibly compel the acknowledgement of our independence and keep the world for some time longer in peace. England alone will pay for her wickedness and folly by the loss of North America.

Our information is good that very few Troops can come here from Germany, and private letters, as well as public papers say that the plan of getting Regiments by subscription; tho much boasted of at first, has fallen very low. From the Highlands of N. Britain some men will be obtained, and perhaps a few from England and Ireland, but there seems no reason to suppose that their every exertion can add more than four or five thousand to the present force in N. America. But this will require a very considerable strength on our part to make the event certain. An unsettled dispute between the Emperor and the King of Prussia (which England will undoubtedly foment) concerning the division of the estate of the late Elector of Bavaria has threatened a rupture in Europe not for our advantage, because the former of these Princes being with us, the latter might be disposed to favor the views of G. B. to our injury. Alderman Lee writes that there is some hope of this being negotiated happily. An intelligent Correspondent in England writes Alderman Lee that it was uncertain whether Lord Norths bills would be agreed to or not, but that they were industriously sent over here and circulated to prevent our Treaty with France from being concluded. Vain and unwise Men, their means are always destructive of their ends. Norths delusive and indecent propositions have accelerated an adoption of the agreement with France. — I am much concerned to find in Virginia such want of method and industry in collecting and bring⁹ forward the Drafts. When I came away there were all the Men (amounting to forty one or two) both of the former and the latter drafts remaining in King George — [1] Merely for want of an Officer to bring them away, and I am misinformed if it is not the case in other Counties. As far as I have been

[1] The corner of the Ms. is here torn off, but probably no words are missing. Jared Sparks gives a text of this letter, in his *Correspondence of the American Revolution*, II. 123, with many verbal and other changes, under the erroneous date of May 16. This passage is there printed as a continuous sentence.

able to learn, it is probable, that if dexterous recruiting Officers were properly furnished for the business, and sent out, almost all these Veterans that have been discharged from our 9 Regiments would reenlist in a short time.

I am, with sincere esteem, dear Sir your most affectionate and obedient Servant

P.S. Aldderman Lee says they talk of sending Lord Westcote and Hans Stanley here to treat with us, and that they are to bring half a million guineas to bribe the Congress — From their own corruption these men reason to the corruption of all others —

I had alm[os]t forgot to mention that four expresses have been sent fr[om] S! James's on the subject of Generals Howe and Clinton — The latter had leave to go home, the Court was disgusted With the former and had recalled him, but recollecting that Clinton might be come away, another Messenger was sent to stop Howe if that should be the case. I hope they are both gone —

TO [THOMAS JEFFERSON][1]

DEAR SIR,   YORK the 11th of May 1778

We have once more ventured into the field of composition as the inclosed Address will shew you. And I have the pleasure to acquaint you that Congress have unanimously ratified the Treaties with France, and directed the ratification to be presented for exchange in due season. The inclosed pamphlet I t[ake t]o be a production of D! Franklin, it is well written, and was published first in Holland — When it began to make a noise, the B. Minister procured its suppression, but

[1] A. L. S. Library of Congress, Jefferson Correspondence, Letters to Jefferson, Ser. 2, Vol. 51, No. 17.

this, as usual, raised the public curiosity and procured it additional Readers.

We have translated it here, and omitting one or two paragraphs that are not now true, it will be published next week in the Gazette of this place. The reasons are good and may be well used in these States to support public credit. Suppose you were to have a translation published by way of supplement to our Virginia Gazettes ? —

My heart is so bent upon the success of our Country that it grieves me extremely to hear a probability of measures being adopted that I am sure will injure us. I am told that application will be made to this Assembly to revoke Mons: Loyeautes Commissi[on] from the last — Is it possible that such an application can be attended to ? Thus to treat a Gentleman of unquestioned ability, of reputation in France, and after we have applied to that Court to obtain leave for his longer residence among us than his furlough permitted ! His character will not be hurt b[y] it, but how mutable shall we appear. And how totally wrong it will be thus to dismiss an able zealous, and most industrious Artist, whilst we remain utterly ignorant of the necessary knowledge that he is both able and willing to instruct us in ? I think the wise Men of our Assembly will suppress the spirit of vain ambition that prompts to this selfish application.

We are told that the enemies movements at Philadelphia denote their departure, but these perhaps may be designed to amuse us, and prevent the collection of a strong army.

I am dear Sir sincerely yours.

THE LETTERS OF RICHARD HENRY LEE

TO [ARTHUR LEE][1]

MY DEAR BROTHER, YORK, PENNSYLVANIA, 12th May, 1778.
Your favors of Oct., 24. Dec[r] 6, 8, & 19th by Capt
Young, and M[r] Deane came safe to hand and deserve
my thanks on many accounts, but on none more than
for the care you have taken, and propose to take of my
dear son Ludwell. Under your kind protecting hand
I hope he will be reared to much use both public and
private. I approve altogether of your designs respecting him. * * *
It is with infinite pain that I inform you, our dear
brother of Belleview[2] departed this life on the 13th of
April last, after sustaining a severe Rheumatic fever
for 6 weeks. D[r] Steptoe attended him the whole time,
and I was also with him. Both public and private
considerations render this loss most lamentable. He
had been just appointed one of our five Judges of the
General Court, in which station he was well qualified
to do his Country eminent service. He has left behind
him a numerous little family (7 children) & a very dis-
consolate widow. . . .[3]
Congress has now resolved the same for the support
of their Commissioners at Madrid, Vienna, Berlin and
Tuscany as for those at Paris, and they are authorized to draw bills of exchange on the Commissioner or
Commissioners that may be at Paris, for the money
they want to defray their expenses. This makes each
. . .[4] and will for a time at least render it unnecessary to send particular remittances to those places

[1] Virginia Historical Society, Lee Transcripts, III. 27. A printed
text is in the *Southern Literary Messenger*, Dec. 1859, Vol. 29, p. 431.
[2] Thomas Ludwell Lee.
[3] Some lines, written partly in cipher, are here omitted.
[4] Apparently several words, in untranslatable cipher.

in the way of Commodities. You may be assured that Congress are ready and willing to send powerful remittances to Europe in the way of Commodities, but the attempt now, would be only supplying the Enemy, whose cruizers are so numerous on our Coast, and in our bays that almost every vessel is taken. When a war with France or Spain shall take place, the numerous ships of England will find some other employment, than bending their whole force against us. Then it will be in our power to make the remittances we wish to make. Congress has not yet taken up the consideration of appointing another Commissioner; when they do I think there can be no objection to the Gentleman you recommend, or that he should be appointed to Spain. Gen. Burgoyne has leave to return to England upon parole. But his army is detained untill the Court of London shall notify to Congress their Ratification of the Convention of Saratoga. The detention of this Army was founded, partly on the reasons you assign, and for other powerful ones which Burgoyne himself furnished us with. In the enclosure which our public letter contains, you will see the reasons more at large. I am very happy to be able to observe to you that the unalterable attachment of Congress to Independence is clearly evinced by their Resolutions upon Lord North's insidious bills of Pacification, some days before they had any notice of the Treaty with France. I think you may make a good use of this with those who may doubt our firmness. . . .[1]

New Orleans is so removed from us, and so situated as to make the difficulty of getting any thing from thence very great, that the Havannah would answer much better. The English ships have taken and destroyed so many French and some Spanish vessels the last winter and Spring upon our coast, that it appears to me upon

[1] Some lines, written partly in cipher, are here omitted.

every principle of policy, unwise for these powers to keep their Marine force unemployed, whilst the whole active naval force of England is warring upon their Commerce, — that part of it at least which approaches our shores. I should be glad to know the particulars of Mons. Ellis's[1] theft of your papers. If you can contrive me any valuable new publications in England, I shall be glad to have them, [and I pray you will not forget an annual supply of Jesuits bark, for we have very little here. I have yet received only 8 pounds of what you formerly mentioned, but I thank you greatly for this].

God bless and preserve you.

The British Army have been closely confined in Pha, this winter. It is yet there; our army is daily growing stronger, both in numbers and discipline, and we expect soon to begin offensive operations against them. My Bro. Frank and myself are both of us eligible to Congress for three years to come; our Bro. appears inclinable to quit the service, but it shall depend upon my Country whether I do so or not, untill I see a proper peace upon proper principles.

TO [JOHN ADAMS][2]

My Dear Sir.　　York, in Pennsylv-a 13th May 1778

Our public letter does not leave me much to add, but friendship will not suffer me to let this opportunity to pass, without expressing my wishes to congratulate you on your safe arrival in France. You will find our affairs at your Court in a much more respectable Train than they have been heretofore, and therefore no doubt more agreeable to you. Finance seems now the only

[1] This should be " Elliot's." Elliot was the British envoy at Berlin.
[2] Adams Papers. Copy supplied through the courtesy of Mr. Charles Francis Adams.

rock on which we have any danger of splitting. How far European loans may help us you can judge, but I fear that the slow operation of Taxes, which indeed are pretty considerably pushed in many States, will not be adequate to the large emissions of paper money which the war compels us to make. The number and activity of the British Cruisers on the coast, and in the Bays of the Staple States, render it utterly impossible with any degree of safety, and therefore very unwise, to attempt making remittances to Europe at present. It is in fact furnishing the enemy with what they want extremely, and much to our injury. Surely the Court of France will now give protection to their Commerce to and from America, the clearest policy demands it. Sir you would be greatly surprised at the number and value of the French Vessels taken and destroyed by the English on our Coasts this last winter and spring — Thus the Marine force of G. B. is actively employed in ruining the Commerce of France, while her powerful Navy remains unemployed. Can this be wise? Gen Howe remains yet in Philadelphia, and our Army where it was, but daily growing stronger in discipline and in numbers. I am inclined to think that the enemy will this Campaign act chiefly on the defensive (carrying on the small war to plunder and distress) holding all they can in order to get the better bargain of us when a Treaty shall take place. I wish for the sake of future peace, that we could rush these people quite off this Northern Continent. Mons – r Beaumarchais by his Agent Mons – r Francis has demanded a prodigious sum from the Continent for the Stores &c furnished the States. His accounts are referred for settlement to the Commissioner at Paris, and[1] I hope they will scrutinise most carefully into this business, that the public may not pay a large sum wrongfully. We have been repeatedly

[1] The letter " a " is here written over " and " repeated and erased.

informed that the greater part of these Stores were gratuitously furnished by the Court of France — How then does it come to pass that a private person a mere Agent of the Ministry, should now demand pay for the whole? It will give me singular pleasure to hear from you by all convenient opportunity, for I am dear Sir, with great sincerity
your affectionate humble Servant

P.S. Be so kind as to take care of the letters for my brothers and get them conveyed.

[FOR COMMITTEE OF FOREIGN AFFAIRS] TO THE COUNCIL OF MASSACHUSETTS BAY[1]

GENTLEMEN, YORK TOWN May [15?] 1778
The Navy-board having been directed to keep two Packet-boats ready for your Orders, we now send to your Care very important Dispatches[2] for France, which you are requested to give in Charge to a trusty Captain, to deliver with his own Hand to our Commissioners at Paris. Your wisdom will dictate pointed Orders for conveying the Packets without Injury, with Secresy & with Despatch; but, for sinking them in Case the Vessel should be unfortunately taken.
We are respectfully Gentlemen Your most humble Servants.
HONBLE COUNCIL Massachusetts Bay

[1] A. L. S. by Richard Henry Lee, signed also only by James Lovell. Office of the Secretary of the Commonwealth, Boston, Massachusetts Archives, Vol. 199, p. 145.
[2] Apparently those of May 14 and 15 printed in Wharton, *Diplomatic Correspondence*, II. 574–581, 582.

THE LETTERS OF RICHARD HENRY LEE

TO [ARTHUR LEE] [1]

YORK IN PEN. 19 May 1778

MY DEAR BROTHER,

Your several favors by the Vessel from Spain with duplicates of the treaties with France are arrived and shall have my most particular attention. In Virginia we have determined to retain in our practical jurisprudence the Common law of England excepting such parts as relate to royalty and purogative. Also some of the Statutes that are of a nature most general. These, with our own Acts of Assembly constitute our Code of Laws. You see therefore that Ludwell may be fully employed with you in reading the Common law and the Statutes, leaving the Municipal law of Virginia until he comes home. But I wish him much to have the ground work of the law of Nature and Nations with the Civil law and Eloquence. I have not got the Virg.ª Acts of Assembly here, and it would be difficult to send them if I had. . . .[2] The Members of Congress are so perpetually changing that it is of little use to give you their Names — From Massachusetts now come Mess.ʳˢ Hancock, Sam Adams, Payne, Elbridge Guerry, M.ʳ Dana & M.ʳ James Lovell — Connecticut Mess.ʳˢ Roger Sherman, Huntington, Dyer Woolcot & Williams N. York Duane, Governeer Morris, Duer your acquaintance, Livingston, Francis Lewis. Rhode Island Mess.ʳˢ Merchant and Ellery. Pennsylv.ª R. Morris, Read, two Smiths & Roberdeau — Jersey D.ʳ Witherspoon &c. — Maryland Chase Col.º Plater, Carrol, Henry, Stone. Virg.ª R. H. Lee. F. L. Lee. Harvey Bannister, John Adams. S.º Carolina Mess.ʳˢ Laurens, W.ᵐ H. Drayton, Hayward & 2 new ones. Tis not

[1] A. L. S. University of Virginia, Lee Papers, No. 190.
[2] Some lines, written partly in cipher, are here omitted.

worthwhile to mention others, you know them not and they are new Men. The Express is going so God bless you & farewell

Campaign not begun — Love to the Alderman &c. & to my Son Ludwell.

TO JOHN PAGE [1]

My dear Sir,   York the 25ᵗʰ May 1778

I am much obliged to you for your kind letter by last Post, by which however I see you had not received any of the several letters I had written to you since my arrival here. The prevailing opinion both here and at Camp is, that the enemy are designed soon to embark their Army and quit Philadelphia, as they have, 'tis said, wooded and watered their Transports, and fixt up Stalls for the horses on board Ship. It is my opinion that this move will depend entirely upon the event of a French war taking place or not. And that this will happen soon seems doubtful at present, for it is very evident that those who direct the Councils of G. B. will submit to every insult rather than venture on a war which must remove for ever all hope of gratifying their revenge upon these States. France may force the war upon them, but they, I think, will not commence the war with France. Marquis Fayette went lately upon the enemies lines with 2500 men with design to act, as occasion should point out; but one of his men deserting and informing the enemy of his force and his situation, they marched almost their whole army quickly in the night to surround the noble Marquis — However, he made good his retreat with! any loss save a few Packs — Some Oneida Indians skirmished with the

[1] A. L. S. Lenox Library, Ford Collection, unbound Ms. Addressed, "Honorable John Page esquire/at Williamsburg in/Virginia," and franked by Lee.

enemy & killed a few of their light Horse. Gen. Gates is gone to command upon the North river where the Eastern Levies are ordered to halt until the design of the Enemy are more clearly fixed.

I am yours dear Sir with much affection.

TO [ARTHUR LEE][1]

MY DEAR BROTHER, YORK, PA 27th May, 1778.

Having written you fully and very lately it is not necessary, nor have I time now, to be long. All your letters covering Missives, Certificates &c. have safely arrived and will be maturely attended to. I hope the safe arrival of Mr Adams & the recall of Deane will benefit extremely the public business. The latter is in every respect the reverse of Mr Adams, and so you may form your judgment of the former. I have found ample cause to love and esteem Mr Adams in our joint labors for the public good. My eyes are so extremely injured by their constant application, that without the aid and support of Spectacles I fear I shall soon lose the use of them. I pray you then to procure me a pair of the best Temple Spectacles that can be had. In fitting these perhaps it may be proper to remember that my age is 46, that my eyes are light colored, and have been quick and strong, but now weakened by constant use. My head thin between the temples. The British Army yet remains at Pha., and ours at Valley Forge, about 18 miles from the City. The latter growing daily stronger in Numbers and discipline. The former lessening in numbers by various casualties, but chiefly by desertion. We have the best authority for believing they are about embarking soon from Philadelphia, so that my next letter may be from that City. If the

[1] Ms. copy. Virginia Historical Society, Lee Transcripts, III. 32.

Spectacles are sent to my son at Nantes, he can contrive them to your ever aff! Bro. & faithful friend.

[DRAFT OF AN ANSWER TO THE FIRST PEACE COM-
MISSION][1]

My Lord   [June 6, 1778.]

The unprovoked and cruel war that has been waged against these States, renders every idea inadmissable, that proposes a return to the domination of that Power which by its own Acts of devastation and slaughter, has forced a separation.   The Acts of the British Parliament lately transmitted by your Lordship having this domination principally in view require no further comment   But the good people of N. A. my Lord[2] not insensible of what belongs to humanity,[3] can forgive their enemies, and wish to stop the effusion of human blood.   When therefore the king of G. B. shall be seriously disposed to peace, Congress will readily attend to such terms as may[4] consist with the honor of Independent nations, with the interest of their Constituents, and with the sacred regard they mean to pay to Treaties.
By order of Congress.

[1] A. dr. L. by Richard Henry Lee.   University of Virginia, Lee Papers, No. 9.   Endorsed, "Draught of answer for the British Commission./June 6, 1778."   The signature "H. Laurens" is erased. Lee was a member of the committee of five appointed to answer Adm. Lord Howe's letter of May 27 and General Henry Clinton's letter of June 3.   Clinton was probably acting in the place of the other member of the first commission, Sir William Howe, who had returned to England on May 24.   See for the complete draft adopted, *Journals of Congress*, June 6, 1778 (Ford, XI. 574).
[2] The word " are " is here erased.
[3] The word " they " is here erased.
[4] Substituted for " shall " erased.

THE LETTERS OF RICHARD HENRY LEE

TO [THOMAS JEFFERSON][1]

DEAR SIR,   YORK IN PENNSYLV[A] 16 June 1778

I thank you for your favor of the 5th which I received yesterday, it is the only satisfactory account I have received of the proceedings of our Assembly. The enemy have made many insidious attempts upon us lately, not in the military way, they seem tired of that, but in the way of negotiation. Their first, was by industriously circulating the bills of *pacification* as they call them, before they had passed into Acts, in order to prevent our closing with France — These bills received a comment from Congress on the 22[d] of April, which no doubt you have seen. The inclosed paper will shew you the second attempt from Lord Howe & Gen. Clinton, with the answer of Congress. The third movement happened very lately, when Clinton desired a passport from Gen. Washington for D[r] Feruson[2] to come to Congress with a letter from the newly arrived Commissioners Lord Carlyle, W[m] Eden esq[r] & Governor Johnston. The General refused the passport until Congress should give leave. The letter from Clinton was transmitted here, but the impatience of the Commissioners did not suffer them to wait for an answer — Thro the medium of the General, leaving their Secretary D[r] Ferguson behind, the packet arrived containing a letter from the Commissioners with a copy of their Commission. Their letter is a combination of fraud, falsehood, insidious offers, and abuse of France. Concluding with a denial of Independence — The sine qua non being withheld, you may judge what will be

[1] A. L. S. Library of Congress, Jefferson Correspondence, Letters to Jefferson, Ser. 2, Vol. 51, No. 21. See letter following.
[2] Evidently written for " Ferguson."

the fate of the rest — An answer has not yet been sent — In due time you will have both the letter and its answer. I dont know whether to call Governor Johnston an Apostate or not. He has been in opposition to the Ministry & has spoken some speeches in our favor, but I believe he has never been a friend to American Independence. However, there seems no doubt but that he has on this occasion touched Ministerial gold — The others are notorious Ministerialists. It is amazing how the Court of London does mix pride, meaness, cunning, and folly, with Gasconade, and timidity. In short the strongest composition is there formed that ever disgraced and injured Mankind. The King of Prussia has declared in terms explicit, that he would follow France in acknowledging our Independence, and his hobby horse is, to become a maritime power. Yet he seems, by his movements, disposed to quarrel with the Emperor about the division of the Bavarian dominions, the Elector being dead without Heir of his body, the next Heir who is the Elector Palatine must loos[e] his right between the two great Spoilers — We have been long amused with accounts of the enemy abandoning Philadelphia — I believe they will do so when they can stay no longer, but not until then — They have certainly removed al[l] their heavy Cannon, Baggage &ᶜ — And fearing a french war every moment they keep in readiness to depart. We did latel[y] shatter extremely a 20 gun Ship belonging to the enemy in the North river, and sent her away to York, in no condition for service — I observe by our last delegation that my enemie[s] have been again at work, however, they shall not gain their point of withdrawing me from the public Councils.

I am dear Sir your affectionate friend and obedient Servant.

THE LETTERS OF RICHARD HENRY LEE

[DRAFT OF AN ANSWER TO THE SECOND PEACE COMMISSION] [1]

My Lords & Gentlemen   [June —, 1778.]
I have recei your letter of ——— and laid it
before Congress with its inclosures — In answer I
am instructed to inform you, that Congress ever ready
to stop the effusion of human blood — have been

---

[1] A. dr. L. by Richard Henry Lee. American Philosophical Society, Lee Papers, II. 128, No. 36. Endorsed, " Letter from Congress/to the kings commissi/oners." See *Journals of Congress*, June 17, 1778 (Ford, XI. 615), for a draft in the writing of Gouverneur Morris almost identical with the following letter from the Lee Papers, No. 309, University of Virginia, written in Richard Henry Lee's handwriting. Lee was chairman of the Committee appointed to prepare the letter. See Ford, *Journals of Congress*, XI. 610.

" To their Excellencies the right Hon : the Earl of Carlisle William Eden Esq : George Johnstone, Esq : Commissioners from his Britannic Majesty. Philadelphia. —

" I have received the letter from your Excellencies, of the 9th instant, with the enclosures, and laid them before Congress Nothing but an earnest desire to spare the farther effusion of human blood could have induced them to read a paper, containing expressions so disrespectful to his Most Christian Majesty the good and great ally of these States, or to consider propositions so derogatory to the honour of an Independent Nation.

" The acts of the British Parliament, the commission from your Sovereign, and your letter, suppose the people of these States to be Subjects of the Crown of Great-Britain, and are founded on the idea of dependence, which is utterly inadmissable.

" I am further directed to inform your Excellencies, that Congress are inclined to peace notwithstanding the unjust claims from which this war originated, and the savage manner in which it has been conducted. They will therefore be ready to enter upon the consideration of a treaty of peace and commerce, not inconsistent with treaties already subsisting when the King of Great-Britain shall demonstrate a sincere disposition for that purpose. The only solid proof of this disposition will be, an

induced to[1] hear your letter read, thro out and have Considered it with a coolness that that having to consider its inclosures and[2] notwithstanding the very inadmissible[3] and offensive things that are contained in the former. Tho[?] It is impossible Congress can fail to be affected with the highest resentment[4] at the indignity offered them by the indecent reflections you have thought proper to make upon[5] his most Ch. Majesty the Great[6] &[6] good ally of these States. The Commission from his Britannic Majesty under which you act, a copy of which you have inclosed, and the Acts of Parliament on which the Commission[7] is founded, being both formed upon the idea of the good people of these States being Subjects of the Crown of Great Britain, and proposing peace upon dependent principles and a return to the domination of a power that hath accumulated every injury and insult, on their unoffending State, Congress consider them both

explicit acknowledgment of the independence of these States, or the withdrawing his fleets and armies.

I have the honeur to be,
Your Excellencies most obedient humble servant.
Signed by order of the unanimous voice of Congress
HENRY LAURENS, *President.*

YORK TOWN, June 17 1778
" Resolved unanimously that Congress approve the conduct of General Washington in refusing a passport to Doctor Ferguson.
Published by order of Congress
CHARLES THOMSON, *Secretary.*"

[1] The word " read " is here erased.
[2] The preceding seven words are inserted between the lines.
[3] The word "injurious" as an alternative is written above this word.
[4] This word is written below an erasure of the same word on the line, while "indignation" written above the line is erased.
[5] The word " the " is erased.
[6] Substituted before the word " good " for "& faithful" after it, erased.
[7] The two preceding words are written above " it " erased.

as totally inadmissable, and cannot consent to any further communication on such grounds —[1] I am further instructed to inform your Excellency that Congress will be alvays ready to enter upon the Consideration of a [2] a Treaty of Peace, when a [3] sincere disposition thereto shall be evidenced on the part of G. B.[4] by an explicit acknowledgement of the Independence of their States, and by withdrawing his Fleets from our Coasts and his Armies from the 13 States —

TO [JOHN ADAMS][5]

My dear Sir.   York in Pennsyl-a. 20th June 1778

Our enemies in N. York had contrived to distress us a good deal by a publication that the Boston was taken & carried into England   We were at first greatly concerned for our Friend, until we reflected on the lying genius of our enemies, and the improbability that Heaven would permit such a triumph of Vice over Virtue.   Now we are made happy by an account from Boston that you are safely arrived in France.   The Treaty with France was soon ratified here, desiring only that the 11th & 12th Articles might be reconsidered and omitted.   Three Copies of ratification have been sent away from hence near a month and now 3 more are dispatching.   The former dispatches would inform you the determination of Congress upon the English Acts of pacification, before we knew of our new Alli-

[1] " Congress " is here erased.
[2] The preceding four words are written as an alternative above " a Treaty."
[3] Lee here wrote and erased " cordia."
[4] As an alternative expression " his B. M. " is written above the line.
[5] Adams Papers. Copy supplied through the courtesy of Mr. Charles Francis Adams.

ance, and these will acquaint you with the reception Messrs the Commissioners from London have met with. The figure they cut is truly ridiculous. If this were all it would be happy for England, but she seems now to be a setting star. Two days ago the B. Army abandoned Philadelphia and our troops are in possession of that City. The enemy are in the Jersies, but whether they mean to push for Amboy, or embark below Billingsport on the Delaware, is yet uncertain. The Jersey Militia are in readiness, & if our Army can cross Delaware in time, the gentry will yet get a parting blow. The friends to the future happines and glory of America are now urging the Confederation to a close, and I hope it will be sighned in a few days. All but a few delegates have powers, and those that have not come from Small States, that will undoubtedly fall in. Our next business is Finance, and this is a momentous point in deed. Every State exclaims We are overflown with our emissions of money yet all seem to be going on in the same beaten Track, and will I fear until invincible Necessity shall force a change. I wish to bring you, and my brother Dr Lee to be well acquainted. Republican Spirits who have so successfully labored for the liberty of their Country, and whose sole object is the security of public happiness, must esteem each other. The Continental Army is now on a much more respectable footing, both for numbers and discipline, and supplies of every kind, than it has been since the War began — It will give me singular pleasure to hear of your happiness at all times.

I am dear Sir most sincerely and affectionately yours.

P.S. Cannot Mons – Beaumarchais demand against us [be] as fully and fairly explained? There is mistery in this business that demands to be thoroughly developed. Be so kind as to contrive letters for my brothers safely to them.

THE LETTERS OF RICHARD HENRY LEE

TO [THOMAS JEFFERSON] [1]

My dear Sir, York the 23ᵈ June 1778

The inclosed Gazette will shew you the progress and perhaps the end for some time, of our negotiation with the British Commissioners. They, with their whole Army have abandoned Philadelphia, and our Troops are in possession of that City. The enemy are pushing thro Jersey for South Amboy, and in their front is Gen. Maxwell with a brigade of Continentals and the Jersey Militia — They have impeded the enemies progress by breaking up the roads & bridges; and we have just been told that Maxwell has attacked and gained an advantage over part of their army. Gen. Washington with 13,000 men, is in hot pursuit of the enemy — He was about crossing Delaware the day before yesterday. If our Army can come up with them before they embark, we may have a second edition of Burgoyne. Governor Johnsone tries every art to gain admission among us. He abuses his Masters, flatters America, and is willing to yield us every thing if we will be perfidious to our Ally & again submit to the domination of his King & Parliament. This Man possesses in abundance Scottish cunning and Scottish impudence. But it is too late in the day — The Sunshine of liberty & independence prevails over the dark arts of Turanny & its Tools —

We hope in 6 or 8 days to ratify the Confederation (all but two or 3 Small States, at the head of which is Maryland, and all of whom I have no doubt will soon fall in) witht amendments — After which Congress will adjourn to Philadelphia — I am dear Sir affectionately yours.

[1] A. L. S. Library of Congress, Jefferson Correspondence, Letters to Jefferson, Ser. 2, Vol. 51, No. 20.

THE LETTERS OF RICHARD HENRY LEE

TO [GENERAL GEORGE WASHINGTON][1]

DEAR SIR.   YORK   the 24ᵗʰ of June 1778

I should long since have answered your favor of the
25ᵗʰ of May had it been worth while for any thing I had
to communicate, to interrupt your attention from the
important affairs with which you are surrounded   It is
indeed more from motives of cOmplaisance than any
thing else that I now write — But I cannot help congratulating you Sir on the enemies abandoning Philadelphia, because, let their motives be what they may,
this step evidently proves their[2] prospect of conquest
here is vanished.[3]

I fancy Gen. Clintons future operations depend much
upon the Chapter of Accidents.   A french war being
avoided, their efforts will continue to be exerted for some
time against us, but a foreign War must of necessity
cary this Army to Secure the now defenceless Islands
of G. B. in the W. I.   A war with France, in the better
days of England, would instantly have followed the
Message of Marquis de Noailles, but the mean &
wicked determination to enslave America, removes all
thoughts of every thing but the accomplishment of their
favorite object.   The British Kings message to his Parliament, altho it shews mortified [p]ride, and strong sense
of insult, yet it clearly marks indicision, and doubt about
the propriety of resenting the affront.[4]   We see by a
publication of the enemy in the Newport paper that
there is a great probability of Spain having acknowledged

[1] A. dr. L. S.   American Philosophical Society, Lee Papers, II. 71,
No. 21.   Printed with minor changes in R. H. Lee, *Memoir of Richard
Henry Lee*, II. 21.
[2] Words erased, " cause of . . . to be in the descending scale."
[3] Words erased, " grows less is pretty well over."
[4] The following words are here erased, " I must confess that I
think it would."

the Independence of these States, & joined in our Alliance, The Ambassaders of Spain & of G. B. were on the point of returning each to his respective Country. Of this event taking place, I had no doubt, so soon as the plate fleet should have reached old Spain. Should G. B. be engaged in war with the Bourbon family it furnish us an opportunity of pushing the former quite off this Northern Continent, which will secure to us peace for a Century, instead of War in 7 years, which the British possession of Canada, N. Sco. & the Floridas, will inevitably produce. You have no doubt heard Sir that our last Assembly have voted 2000 Infantry to join the Army & a sum of money to forward Gen. Nelsons Cavalry — The latter may soon be expected at Head Quarters — I am with sincere esteem dear Sir your most affc: & obedient Servant

TO FRANCIS LIGHTFOOT LEE [1]

MY DEAR BROTHER,   PHILADELPHIA 5th July. 1778

I wrote you four days ago by M: Armstead who promised to send the letter to Mount Airy by his servant from Fredericksburg — Since that we have had a more accurate account of the battle in the Jerseys from General Washington — The number of the Enemy's dead buried by our people was 252, and several graves besides on the field in which they had buried their dead during the Action. Upon the whole the battle was fairly won by our Army, & the best troops of Britain beaten in an open field. The whole loss of the enemy,

[1] A. L. S. University of Virginia, Lee Papers, No. 236. An extract of this letter in M. D. Conway, *Edmund Randolph*, 40, is mistakenly described as written to "his brother Ludwell." The letter is addressed to Francis Lightfoot Lee of Manokin, Richmond County, care of the postmaster at Leeds Town, and to be sent by the "Chantilly Rider."

in killed, wounded, & deserters, is at least 3000 since they left this City. The American Army is now at Brunswick and will presently proceed to the North river, Gen. Conway came here the other day, and having been informed of some disrespectful words spoken of him by Gen. Cadwallder, the former challenged the latter, and they met on the Common yesterday morn — They threw up for the first fire and Cadwallder won it. At the distance of 12 paces he fired and Shot Conway thro the side of the face, on which he fell & was carried off the field. He is supposed not to be in danger unless an unforseen inflammation should produce it. We had a magnifincent celebration of the anniversary of Independen[ce][1] yesterday, when handsome fireworks were displayed — The whigs of the City dressed up a Woman of the Town with the Monstrous head-dress of the Tory Ladies, and escorted her thro the town with a great concourse of people — Her head was elegantly & expensively dressed. I suppose about three feet high and of proportionable width, with a profusion of curls, &ᶜ &ᶜ &ᶜ — The figure was droll and occasioned much mirth — It has lessened some heads already, and will probably bring the rest within the bounds of reason, for they are monstrous indeed.— The Tory wife of Dᵣ Smith has christened this figure Continella, or the Duchess of Independence, and prayed for a pin from her head by way of Relic —

The Tory women are very much mortified notwithstanding this — As we have left York, and Dunlap publishes a gazette here, I have entered your name with him instead of Hall & Sellen, and I shall pay him for your years papers — I have directed him to send me your paper weekly, whilst I stay, that I may enclose it to you — We have heard nothing from the English Commissioners since our answer from York, and I sup-

[1] Stain in the Ms.

pose they conclude us less liable to be amused since the late drubbing we have given their Army. I this day went round the Enemies' lines — They pass from Delaware to Schuylkill so as to include Gov.ʳ Hamilton's House about 200 yards within the line, and consist of very strong Redoubts at a quarter of a mile distant from each other, and the spaces between guarded by very thick Abbatces, made of Apple Trees fast staked down, and the ends of the twiggs sharpened — All the houses, except Bush Hill, for a considerable distance without & within the lines, are burnt down — My love to M.ʳˢ Lee and kind remembrance to all friends in Richmond — I am most affectionately yours.

TO FRANCIS LIGHTFOOT LEE[1]

PHILADELPHIA 12 July 1778.

MY DEAR BROTHER,

I had prepared a letter to you three days ago intending to have sent it to Chantilly by a Mr. Muse, but he slipt me without calling for my letter. Since that the Count D'Esteing, with a french Squadron under his command has arrived in Delaware Bay, and last thursday morning he proceeded to N. York with determination to loose no time in attacking the English in that Harbour. On the 19ᵗʰ of May he declared war against G. Britain on board his fleet then at Sea, and since that, he takes every English vessel that he meets with. The strength of this fleet is one 90, one 80, Six 74. Three 64 & one 50 with 4 frigates and between 10 and 12,000 men on board — In this fleet came the french Ambassador Mons.ʳ Gerard who is expected in Town evry hour Carriages being sent to Chester for him. Silas Deane

[1] A. L. S. University of Virginia, Lee Papers, No. 239. Addressed to him at Manokin, and to be sent by the "Chantilly Rider" from the postmaster at Leeds Town, Westmoreland County.

is also arrived in this fleet, and I expect that he & Carmichael will soon begin to intrigue. We have received a very polite Address from the Count D'Estaing enclosing us a copy of his powers from the King of France which are plenepotentiary to treat wth Congress. The King styles us his most dear friends and great Allies. The Count says that nothing but the necessity of immediately executing the duties of his office as Commander of the Fleet would have permitted him to delay paying his respects Men famous thro Europe for their wisdom and, firmness. We have been very busy in Marine Committee this morning, altho 'tis Sunday, directing fresh provisions and Water to be sent to this fleet. Gen. Washington is directed to Cooperate with Count D'Estaing in offensive operations against the common enemy. We may expect good events from this if Keppel with his 11 Sail of the Line do not interrupt us too soon. He was in St. Helens the 19th of May bound to N. America. But we expect he will be narrowly watched by the Brest fleet which consisted of 25 Sail of the Line ready for Sea. Thus the Ball begins to open, and the guilty Sons of G. Britain upon the eve of making severe retribution for the heavy crimes both in the east and the west. The Ambassador is arrived, and during the course of dinner I have had an opportunity of conversing largely with him. I find that the King of france considers the King of Englands message upon Marquis Noailles communication of our Alliance as announcing hostility and determines to act accordingly — With effective hostility indeed, but with^t formal declaration of war in Europe, for this he says, we must wait until Spain is ready — The flota was not arrived on the 10th April. Monsr Gerard seems rather above 50 years of age is as grave as a Frenchman can be, and he is a wise well bred Gentleman. We are told that many of the first Nobility of france solicited his missions in vain.

I am much grieved to hear that my honored friend Col? Tayloe grows worse — Is it it impracticable for him to visit the Springs — The Indian irruptions I expect will be presently quieted by the Army under M?Intosh going to Fort Detroit, and the expedition into the Seneca Country. These must wall and keep every Indian at home.

My love to Mrs. Lee and respects to all friends.

Most affectionately yours.

P.S. The post this day brings me no letter from N. Nec[k][1] except from my friend Mr. Page I have none from Rappahanock or Potomac — From Boston we learn of a quick arrival that brings account Lord Chatham died on the 1st of May, he was forming a party against the Independence of America, which he has lately thunder'd against in Parliam! and was opposed by the Duke of Richmond with great spirit & force of Reason — Stocks fallen greatly, and the Kingdom in much confusion — 40 frigates recalled from N. America — But Coun[t D'Estaing?] wont let them get out of the Harbour of N. York — [It is?] true that Capt. Jones carried a 20 gun Ship of the Tyrants into Brest with 3 other prizes — He had a severe conflict with the Ship of War and killed the Captain and first Lieutenant, killed and wounded 42 men, — Lost 8 — He landed at Whitehaven and fired the Shipping in the Harbour, and did them other damage, where he also spiked 30 or 40 pieces of Canon.

[1] Ms. damaged, hole.

THE LETTERS OF RICHARD HENRY LEE

MARINE COMMITTEE TO [COUNT D'ESTAING][1]

SIR   PHILADELPHIE,   July 16th 1778

The marine Committee of Congress have received information that the Squadron under your Excellencies command has occasion for a supply of water and fresh provisions and they have taken proper measures to furnish both with all possible expedition.

The frigate Chimere and the two vessels with her will be dispatched immediately with as much water as we can find casks for; the enemy lately here having destroyed every thing of this kind that they could discover. The same vessels will bring your Excellency some hundred barrels of bread and flour, with a small supply of fresh provisions. A commissary has orders quickly to collect near Shrewsbury and the Hook 50 bullocks, 700 sheep, with a quantity of vegetables and a number of poultry; and he will wait on your Excellency to know your pleasure concerning the particular place on the water where he must bring them to be shipped.

The same commissary has general orders to furnish your Excellency with such further supplies as you may please to direct

The accidents of wind and weather may possibly prevent the Chimere from arriving with water so soon as it shall be wanted, and therefore I am to inform your Excellency that at Little Egg harbor or Thoms river, neither of them far from the hook, fresh water can be conveniently obtained. The Pilots on board the fleet will conduct vessels sent for the purpose to either of these places.

[1] A. L. S. by Richard Henry Lee, "Chairman of the Marine Committee." Paris, Archives de la Marine, B. 4: 146: fo. 211. Copy secured through the courtesy of Dr. J. Franklin Jameson and Mr. W. G. Leland.

Your Excellency may be assured that Congress is disposed to supply your Excellency and the Squadron under your command with everything in their power that may conduce to the accomplishment of the valuable ends you have in view against the common enemy.

I have the honor to be, with the highest respect, your Excellencies most obedient and most humble servant.

TO [THOMAS JEFFERSON][1]

DEAR SIR,   PHILADELPHIA July 20th 1778

The condition of our affairs is much changed since last I had the pleasure of writing to you, as by the favor of his Most Christian Majesty we now are become Masters of the Sea, on our own Coast at least, Ten days ago arrived in the Delaware a french Squadron commanded by Count D'Esteing consisting of 12 sail of the Line & 4 frigates, having of Seamen & land Troops 11,000 Men on board. There is one Ship of 90 guns, one of 80, 6 of 74, three Of 64 & 4 frigates. Having missed the English here, they have proceeded to N. York in quest of them, and are now before that Harbour, the depth of water being unfortunately insufficient to admit such large Ships. The English, whose fleet is inferior, are well contented to remain within the Narrows, and suffer Mons.ʳ the Count to intercept every Vessel coming to N. York — He has already taken 15. Sail. But the french Admiral being an Officer of great activity and spirit, he seems not content with this small work, & therefore I believe he will go immediately to R. Island where he can easily destroy the Ships, and with the assistance of our force there, make prisoners

[1] A. L. S. Library of Congress, Jefferson Correspondence, Letters to Jefferson, Ser. 2, Vol. 51, No. 19. Printed with variations in R. H. Lee, *Memoir of Richard Henry Lee*, II. 42.

of 2000 British Troops on that Island. With this Squadron came Le Sieur Gerard Minister Plenepotentiary from his Most Christian Majesty — He is a sensible well bred Man, and perfectly well acquainted with the politics of Europe — From him I learn that the Court of France consider the Message of the King of England to his Parliament & their answer, upon the Count Noailles notification of our Alliance, as a denunciation of War on the part of G. Britain, and that they mean to Act accordingly, without an express declaration, leaving this last to England. We are busied now in settling the Ceremonials for the reception of foreign Ministers of every denomination — And I assure you it is a work of no small difficulty — When this is finished, Mons.[r] Gerard will have his audience in Congress — I suppose this week — Gen. Washingt[on][1] has crossed the N. River, and will cooperate with the Admiral in Measures to be concerted against the comm[on][1] enemy — The B. Commissioners have sent us a second letter, very silly, and equally insolent — The preliminaries insisted on by Congress (an acknowledgement of Independence or a withdrawing of their fleets & Armies) not having been either of them complied with, this letter is to receive no answer — We have detected and fully exposed Gov.[r] Johnstone, who under the plausible guise of friendship & Virtue, has endeavored to bribe Members of Congress — The whole body indeed, as well as individual Members — The Confederation is ratified by 10 States, there remains only Jersey, Delewa[re][1] & Maryland; but I suppose their obstinacy will e'er long submit to their interest, and a perfect coalition take place — I am, much hurried, tho with great esteem, dear Sir your most obedient Serv[ant].[1]

[1] The letters enclosed in square brackets are concealed by the binding.

THE LETTERS OF RICHARD HENRY LEE

TO [FRANCIS LIGHTFOOT LEE] [1]

My Dear Brother, Phil.ᴬ July 27ᵗʰ 1778.
Your letter of the 12ᵗʰ came only to hand this day by Post, amazing delay, but I have spoken to the Post Master on this business until I am tired — It astonishes me that neither you or my other friends receive my letters, altho I write so many. To you I have not missed above one post since we parted and then I wrote by Mᵣ Armstead — I trust that before this gets to hand you will have received my letters in which I have given you a full account of the transactions in the Jerseys, of the arrival & progress of the french Squadron, & of the coming of a Plenipotentiary from the Court of france to Congress. The Squadron is gone to Rhode Island to make a sweep there as the large ships of this fleet cannot find water enough, to enter the Harbor of N. York, wherein the English Ships keep themselves close. I understand measures will be taken to prevent egress from York or succors getting in. It is this day confidently reported that 27 sail of the provision fleet from Cork have fallen into the hands of Count D'Estaing, this is not yet certain, but we know such a fleet has been long & daily expected — We understand the enemy are greatly distressed for provisions in N. York, particulary of the bread kind. — Gen. Washington has sent two brigades to join 3000 Men under General Sullivan to assist in the business of Rh. Island — Where you are nothing better can be done, than to inform the people and prevent their being imposed on — The change in Affairs has occasioned Congress to desire that both supplies of Infantry & Cavalry from Virgᵃ voted by last Assembly, may be not sent forward, & the expedition

[1] A. L. S. University of Virginia, Lee Papers, No. 244.

428

against Detroit is changed to a Chastisement of the offending Indian Tribes to the West and North West. I will attend as you desire to the payment of Hillsymer & will keep the rest of y.ᵉ money for your further orders. There has been no time yet to procure an order for settlement of Accounts either here or abroad, but I hope it will be done soon — . . .[1]

I am really tired with the folly & the wickedness of Mankind, and wish most earnestly to be retired absolutely —

M.ʳ Holker has been, since the arrival of the Plenipotentiary, appointed by him agent for the marine of France in these States, but more of this hereafter — I will send y.ᵉ bark if a good opportunity offers, & I thank you for your offer to use what I wont, but I am pretty well supplied —

My love to M.ʳˢ Lee & regards to all friends — Much hurried — Yours sincerely.

Let me know how Col.º Tayloe does, I am greatly concerned for him.

MARINE COMMITTEE TO THE COUNCIL OF MAS-SACHUSETTS BAY[2]

MARINE COMMITTEE OF CONGRESS
PHILADELPHIA   August 4ᵗʰ 1778

GENTLEMEN

It is the request of this Committee that you will aid the Navy Board with the powers of Government in manning the Continental Ships of war that are at Boston, which have been ordered out to join the French Fleet under the command of Vice Admiral the Count

---

[1] A sentence, partly in cipher, is here omitted.

[2] L. S. by Richard Henry Lee as Chairman of the Marine Committee of Congress. Office of Secretary of the Commonwealth, Boston, Massachusetts Archives, Vol. 199, p. 396.

D'Estaing and which Congress most earnestly wish may
be speedily accomplished.

The Honorable   We have the honor to be
The COUNCIL   Gentlemen
OF MASSACHUSETTS BAY.   Your very obedient Servants.

TO [THOMAS JEFFERSON][1]

DEAR SIR,   PHILADELPHIA 10ᵗʰ Aug! 1778

I agree entirely with you concerning the importance
of the confederation, and have never failed to press it.
Ten States have ratified — Jersey, Delaware, & Maryland have not, and one of them, Maryland, has adjourned
until November, so that the new Congress under the
Confederation cannot meet this year at the time proposed by the Confederacy.   The inclosed paper contains all the news we have, except that it is well reported
that Lord Howe being reenforced by 4 Ships of the Line
sailed from N. York on thursday last with his whole
force to Attack the french Squadron now at Rhode
Island — Howe has a greater nu[mber][2] of Ships, but
Count D'Esteing has heavier Metal — The attack by
Sea and Land was to be made this day on the enemy at
R. Island, where they have 5500 men strongly posted
and 3 or 4 frigates — Our force will be about 14000 men
besides the Squadron.   Success seems certain if Lᵈ
Howe does not get up in time to prevent it.   The Count
D'Esteing is an Officer of approved merit, and his Ships
very strong in every respect, so that I think he will
check the British insolence on the Sea as we have already done on the land.   No war in Europe on the 10ᵗʰ

[1] A. L. S. Library of Congress, Jefferson Correspondence, Letters to Jefferson, Ser. 2, Vol. 51, No. 22. Printed with variations in
R. H. Lee, *Memoir of Richard Henry Lee*, II. 43.
[2] Ms. torn.

of June, nor do I believe G. Britain means to resent the proceedings of France It seems to be a contest between the two Nations which shall be last in declaring War — Some advantages to accrue from Treaties is the cause of this — To us it matters little since we so powerfully experience the aid of France. For it is certain this Squadron is to Act with and for us so long as the enemy by continuing here renders it necessary. There is great probabil[ity] that the Emperor of Germany & the King of Prussia will fall out about the Bavarian dominions — Theirs will be a battle of Giants each party having 300,000 men, the best disciplined Troops in the world — France, I fancy, has taken measures to avoid engaging in this quarrel, that her whole force may be employed against England —

[Th][1]e design against Detroit is abandoned for the present, and a for[ce] will be sent into the Indian Country to chastise their late insolence. I heartily wish that the wisdom of our Country may be early next Session employed to regulate our finance, restore public credit determine about our back lands, and if poss[ible] get rid of our public Commerce. If it succeeds with us, I believe it will be the first instance that has ever happened of the kind. But many there are of injury derived from such Trade. Whilst necessity impelled, it was unavoidable, but now that private Commerce will furnish abund[ance] of all things, I incline to think our interest will consist in withdrawing from governmental Tra[de]. Remember me to Mr. Mazzie — I am yours dear Sir very sincerely —

[1] Ms. torn. In all other cases in this letter, except the two noted, the square brackets enclose letters concealed by the binding.

THE LETTERS OF RICHARD HENRY LEE

TO GENERAL [WILLIAM] MAXWELL [1]

SIR, PHILADELPHIA August 29ᵗʰ 1778

I was yesterday favored with your letter of the 25ᵗʰ instant, for which be pleased to accept my thanks. I do recollect that when my brother practiced physick in Virginia about ten or eleven years ago, I then heard him sometimes mention a Doctor Berkenhout who had written a pharmacopea which he esteemed, and that he had an acquaintance with and regard for the Doctor — Beyond this my knowledge of Doctor Berkenhout or his concerns extends not; having never had a word concerning him from my brother, since that time nor did I ever see the Doctor that I remember —

I have laid your letter before Congress, and their sense seems to be, that you use your discretion in cases similar to that of Doctor Berkenhout, governing yourself by the nature of the circumstances.

I have the honor to be, with regards Sir your most obedient and very hble Servt.

GEN. MAXWELL.

TO GENERAL —— —— [2]

DEAR GENERAL, PHILA. Augt. 29th 177[8].

I am to entreat your pardon for not having sent you the enclosed letter before now, and I think I shall obtain my request when you know the reasons that have caused the detention. This letter arrived before we left York, and b[ef]ore my brother returned to Virginia from

[1] A. copy L. S. University of Virginia, Lee Papers, No. 256. William Maxwell was commissioned Brigadier General, October 23, 1776.

[2] A. L. S. Harvard University Library, Sparks Mss., XLIX. iii. 43. The letter is endorsed as from Lee, "Aug. 29, 1778."

Congress. Among many other foreign letters, this by mistake was carried to Virginia by my brother, and not until lately returned. I hope however that no ill consequence will have arrisen from its not reaching you sooner.

It grieves me that our flattering prospects at Rhode Island are so changed. This change of affairs will probably sustain the hopes of our enemies, and induce them to disturb our tranquility much longer than otherwise they would have done. I do not see how a war between France and G. Britain can now be avoided. Yet you may disover by admiral Keppels letter about the taking of two french frigates, that he considers his Ministry as acting with fear and trembling about things that may involve the necessity of rupture. I cannot help wishing that they may get heartily at it, because I think that during the progress of such a contest, we may find means of most effectually securing our independency.

The Dutch, according to custom, are for nieutrality and commerce, and commerce with these States — How the latter can be prosecuted without destroying the other, time will discover. But it would seem that G. Britain must, upon her own principles oppose such commerce; whilst the Dutch I presume will not acquiésce with the capture of their Ships coming here.

I wish you happiness and success being very sincerely dear Sir your most obedient and very humble Servant.

TO [ARTHUR LEE] [1]

PHILADELPHIA Sept. 6. 1778

MY DEAR BROTHER,

Having written you very lately from hence it would have been unnecessary to write so soon again if some military events had not taken place that you may be

[1] A. L. S. University of Virginia, Lee Papers, No. 232½.

desirous to know. The Count D'Esteing has no doubt informed his Court of his Manœuvres with the British fleet commanded by Lord Howe. We have here no actual knowledge of this affair, but what we do know is as follows, that the Count, in conjunction with Gen. Sullivan who commanded the Continental Army, was beseiging about 6000 English & foreign Troops that had retired within Lines around the Town of Newport on Rhode Island, when L.ᵈ Howe appeared in the offing — This suspended operation on the Island as the Count immediately reshipped his Troops and went out to fight the British fleet, which, tho consisting of many Vessels, was inferior in number of guns and weight of metal to the Counts fleet — The British fled & were pursued the first day, on the next day a furious Storm arose which saved L.ᵈ Howes fleet by dispersing both fleets — The Count lost all his Masts before he fired a Gun, and a ship of 74 lost her foremast and Bowsprit — A partial fighting between single ships took place but nothing of conseque[nce] happened in this way — The Count returned to R. Island missing the Cæsar of 74 guns and he carried in prizes the Senegal Sloop of war and a Bomb Ketch — We hear the Cæsar has since arrived at Boston — The french Admiral determined to go to Boston (and refit his Squadron) which he did immediately — By this time Gen. Sullivan had approached within Musket Shot of the enemies Lines — The departure of the fleet, exposing our Army to the arrival of the Succors from N. York quickly thro the Sound, and Ships also to cut off our retreat, determined a Council of War to raise the seige of Newport and return to the Main — The enemy, upon our retreat came out, and a battle ensued, the consequence of which was a victory on our Side as you will see by the enclosed Gazette — The Army was not off the Island when the last Express came away, but no doubt they would soon as possible return to the Continent. We hear that Succors were on their way from N. York thro the Sound for R. Island — Gen. Clinton Army is still shut up in N. York by the American Army which lays just above Kings bridge at White Plains. Congress has not yet taken up the consideration of foreign affairs, but they soon will, I expect in a few days, when I will write you more fully. We are very anxious here to know that Spain has acceded to our Alliance, and it would be very pleasing that Holland had determined to open Trade with us. We impatiently expect to hear from Europe I refer You to my last in which I request, with regard to Ludwell that you may either keep him with you or send him to me, as your judgement and perfect convenience shall direct — Remembering that I have a large family, and that I wish to do the equal justice — That I am very willing to assist Ludwells genius and application as far as I am able to render him useful to himself and beneficial to his Country — Send our brother Alderman this intelligence with his love

Farewell.

My love to my dear Ludwell — We do not know whether the British fleet has ever returned to N. York in the whole — Reports are various — Some say they are all returned — Others, that they have met with great loss.

TO [ARTHUR LEE][1]

My dear Brother,   PHILADEL⁴ 16ᵗʰ Septʳ 1778

This will be delivered you by the Baron Arand who has served sometime in our Army, and who now re-

---

[1] A. L. S. University of Virginia, Lee Papers, No. 235½. Endorsed in Richard Henry Lee's autograph: "Letter for Dʳ Lee Septʳ 1778. Returned the Officer leaving it behind. Some of this letter to be written yet."

turns to France, with leave, on account of his health —
Your two letters of July the 3ᵈ and March 2ᵈ came to my
hands two days ago — where the latter has so long been,
I do not know — I shall observe the caution contained
in the former, and give Loudon the same — I do not
know that we have erred in this way upon any occasions
of consequence — I must here repeat my former advice,
not to use the book cypher you have hitherto done, unless where you have reason to suppose the Bearer, of the
letter will deliver it himself — It may be good against his
curiosity, but not against that of many others who by
Carmichaels treachery have got possession of the key
to this mode of corresponding. You are mistaken
in the union you supposed would be formed here
between Carmichael & . . .[1] I wish our brother
may succeed in either of his missions — I fear he
will in neither until these Courts have taken decided parts with regard to their contemplated war —
The arrival of Byrons Squadron has given the enemy
superiority at Sea over our friends, but we hope it
will not long continue so. The Count is at present
refitting safely in Boston from his damage in the
Storm where he will soon be ready — The English
Fleet has been off that harbor but are now off Rhode
Island — The movements in New York denote an
intention soon to abandon that place, I suppose to
strengthen Canada, Halifax & the West Indies. Our
accounts are now very good that the enemy lost between 12 and 1500 killed and wounded in the late battle
where they were defeated on Rhode Island — I pray you
my dear brother not to keep Ludwell a moment longer
than it is convenient for you — A well grounded knowledge of eloquence, Civil, and natural law will fit him
for pursuing in Virginia the study of the laws of Engᵈ and

[1] A passage, equivalent to some forty printed lines, partly in unin-
telligible cipher, is here omitted.

his own Country — Besides, the justice I owe my other children will not allow very great partiality in expense on any one or two — Yet I would not withhold what may be necessary for good foundations — But my income is chiefly paper money, and that you know will not re-emburse you in Europe or serve my sons there — Can you contrive the contents of this letter to William, I know not whether to address him at Vienna or Berlin. The Bark you kindly sent me has been of great service to me, but I shall want more next year, therefore pray send me some if possible, directly to Virginia. I shall be glad of any valuable new publications whether in France or England —

Not being forewarned at the time, and it being so long since Sim. Deane's arrival that I cannot recollect all the letters you sent me a list of — I did receive several by him, but I do not remember those for Owen and Pringle — I believe the rest came.

I sincerely wish you health, happiness & success — Adieu.

My best love to my boys, brother and Sister — Remember me affectionately to M⁵ Adams.

TO THOMAS JEFFERSON[1]

DEAR SIR, PHILADELPHIA October 5. 1778

A few days past, since the last post left us, M⁵ Harvey presented me your favor of August the 30ᵗʰ, to which this is an answer; and which I shall direct to Williamsburg upon a [s]upposition that the Assembly has called you there by the time the letter can reach

---

[1] A. L. S. Library of Congress, Jefferson Correspondence, Letters to Jefferson, Ser. 2, Vol. 51, No. 24. Addressed to him at Williamsburg, Virginia. The bracketed letters are concealed in binding.

that place. The hand bill you have seen was certainly written by Manduit, and circulated under the auspices of [a]dministration. I was intended to feel the national pulse, and to prepare its mind for the reception of events, which are now become [u]navoidable. I agree with you Sir that the fishery is a most important [p]oint, nor will the limits of Canada be with less difficulty settled in [th]ose negotiations which precede a peace. The arrival of Adm. Byrons squadron has given to our enemies a temporary superiority[1] [on] these Seas — The sending him here was more necessary than it can be [ca]lled bold — But the fleet of Great Britain is, by this detachment, [re]ndered inferior to that of France in the Channel of England.

My brother informs me from Paris July 4 that an engagement [is] every day expected between the two fleets. Later accounts say it [h]as happened and that the English fleet was beaten. Our information [fr]om the West Indies says that Dominica is fallen, and that Jamaica and S⸱ Kitts are in Jeopardy. I believe our enemies would willingly change their war of conquest into a war of revenge, but revenge must be postponed to safety; and I think they will rather endeavor to save what remains, than endeavor to get back what they have lost, or to gratify their [m]alignity put Canada, Nova Scotia, the West Indies, and even G. Britain and Ireland in danger. But wisdom points to precaution, and they may attempt Boston, as some think; in order to destroy the french fleet. If they do, and fail in the attempt, they will be defenceless in every part of the world by the destruction of the only army on which they can hang their hopes. I have a very high opinion of the republican principles and of the ability of M⸱ Mazzie — And I think that if M⸱ Maddison were sent to Genoa with him for Secretary we might have a good chance to

---

[1] Substituted on the line for " security " erased.

438

succeed in borrowing there one of the millions, five of which are absolutely necessary to sustain, and restore our falling currency — To cultivate a good understanding with the nations in the south of Europe is undoubtedly wise policy, and may produce the most profitable consequences — These affairs will come present[ly] under the consideration of Congress, when I shall not forget the useful possessions of M? Mazzie. M? Izard is the Commissioner for Tuscany, my brother William is appointed both for Vienna and Berlin. He has been some time at the former Court, but the latt[er] refuses to receive a Minister from us or to acknowledge yet our Independence, altho he did by his Minister most unequivoca[bly] promise my brother he would do so, as soon as France should set the example. Since this he has quarreled with the Emperor about the Bavarian succession, and wanting the aid of Hanover Hesse, Brunswic &c he chooses to be well with England. The Emperor is not a little puzzled in the same way and for the same reasons. Tis a matter, not of the greatest moment to us at present, since the war between the two Giants will swallow up in their respective vortices the lesser Tyrants and thus prevent him of England from bringing German Auxiliaries to distress our Alliance. There is nothing that threatens so much injury to ou[r] cause at present as the evil operation of Engrossers. If something decisive is not quickly done by the Legislatures to stop the progress of Engrossing, and to make these Miscreants deliver up their ill gotten collections, the American Army must disband, and the fleet of our Allies remain in Boston Harbor. I know the root of this evil is in the redundance of money, but until the latter can be reduced some measures are indispensable to be taken with the Engrossers. You will see the expedients devised by us. A more radical cure will follow shortly, in a proposition of Finance now under consideration. I am so greatly pressed with business that I cannot now write to Mr. Mazzie and must beg the favor of you to make this apology for me. [Be ? so ? k]¹ ind as remember me affectionately to Mr. Wythe & Col? * * * [i]¹ f he is with you

I am affectionately yours.

P.S. Col? Baylor, with a Corps of 60 light Dragoons, was lately surprised in the Jerseys, between Hackinsack & the North River — Himself made prisoner, and his party chiefly put to the Bayonet, it is said, in cold blood —

TO [GEORGE WASHINGTON] ²

DEAR SIR,   PHILADELPHIA October the 5ᵗʰ 1778

I hope the measures you have taken will be effectual to the purpose of reenlisting the Army, because it is an object of great importance; and I readily admit the propriety of first trying those methods which promise fewest ill consequences. Danger will only arise from pressing such too far, and urging the experiment too long. I very much fear Sir, that the knowledge of depreciation has reached the most uninformed, and therefore, that every evil which can, will happen to us from this cause. But I am not without hope that such measures will be adopted as may, before it is too late, restore our currency to its proper value.

It is indeed no easy matter to judge of the designs of the enemy — They have created to themselves a great choice of difficulties. I believe they would willingly change their war of conquest to one of Revenge altogether, but revenge must be postponed to safety. Gen. Clintons Army is the only hope of Canada, Nova Scotia,

¹ Ms. cut or torn.
² A. L. S. Library of Congress, Letters to Washington, XXVII. 61.

Floridas, the West Indies, and I may safely add, much so of Great Britain and Ireland — Whilst this is the case, altho Boston in its present situation is a very tempting object, I cannot think they will undertake it. However what can be attempted may be attempted, and wisdom points to precaution. If it be true, and our information comes pretty direct, that Dominica has fallen, that Jamaica and S! Kitts are in jeopardy, and that Keppel has fled from the fleet of france, we may suppose that our enemies can make no long stay with us. Distance and Land carriage, distress us greatly in the article of bread provision, to which is added an artificial scarcity created in the midst of plenty, by an infamous act of Engrossers who have raised the price of flour from four dollars an hundred to five and six pounds. I hope the measures we are taking with these gentry will make them suffer in a way most hurtful to them.

M! Custis had quitted this City before your letter came to hand, and as he is gone to the Army, I have inclosed the letter in this.

I am, with much esteem and regard dear Sir your most obedient and very humble Servant.

TO [FRANCIS LIGHTFOOT LEE][1]

My dear Brother,   Philadelphia   Oct! 19. 1778.

Monsieur the Marquis De la Fayette having done me the honor to take a letter for you, I am happy in the opportunity of bringing two men acquainted with each other whom I greatly love. All good men in these United States esteem the Marquis for his brave and generous attachment to the cause of America, and for the services he has performed as a General in our Army.

[1] A. L. S. University of Virginia, Lee Papers, No. 263.

It is impossible that a person of such worth should not feel the obligation of returning to offer service to his Country when engaged in war. Yet the Marquis still continues a Major General in the Army of the United States, and we hope will be permitted by his Sovereign to come back more effectually to our aid, by adopting the plan proposed by Congress, for an account of which I refer you to the Marquis.

Be so kind as introduce my son Ludwell to the Marquis, and charge the Youth to respect Mons.͏ Fayette as the much esteemed friend of his father. I am my Dear brother most affectionately yours.

MARINE COMMITTEE TO MAJOR–GENERAL HEATH [1]

MARINE COMMITTEE OF CONGRESS

SIR   PHILADELPHIA   Octo.͏ 20.͏ͭͪ 1778

We have been informed that it has been the practice to the eastward to exchange the Prisoners taken by the French Fleet without the consent of the Admiral or Minister of France.

We request that you will give strict orders forbidding this practice unless when done by order of the Admiral or Minister aforesaid.

We are Sir
Your obed Serv.͏ͭˢ

The Honble Maj.͏ Gen.͏ HEATH.

[1] L. S. by Richard Henry Lee as Chairman. Massachusetts Historical Society, Heath Papers. Obtained through the courtesy of Dr. E. C. Burnett.

THE LETTERS OF RICHARD HENRY LEE

TO PATRICK HENRY[1]

My dear Sir,   PHILADELPHIA 21ˢᵗ Oct 1778.

This will be delivered to you by Major General Lincoln, a brave and able Officer, who goes to command the Troops that are to oppose any attempt of the enemy upon Charles Town in South Carolina. As the General can give you the news of this place I should not have troubled you with this letter, were it not for the following purpose. It was proposed to send 50,000 dollars to the paymaster in Virginia for the purpose of forwarding the thousand men designed to assist South Carolina — Whereupon I reminded the Congress of a motion long since laid upon their table, in consequence of letters from yourself & Mr. Page informing that arrears were due to the continental soldiers in Virginia & the militia that had been called into continental service — And I proposed making the 50, an hundred thousand dollars, and to word the resolve for the purposes "of paying the arrears due to the continental soldiers in Virginia, and to the militia of that state which had been the last year in continental service," as well as for forwarding the thousand men to S. Carolina — This was readily agreed to, and the money (100,000 dollars) is ordered forward — Now Sir, I presume that Gen. Lincoln will, on your application, and showing him the resolve, take measures, by ordering the payment himself if the accounts of arrear are ready, and if not, by authorizing you to call on the paymaster for the money when these accounts are prepared. I beg leave to refer you to the General for our news being in great haste. I subscribe myself with much esteem and affection yours.

His Excellency, PATRICK HENRY, Esq.

[1] From the text printed in William Wirt Henry, *Patrick Henry*, III. 196.

P.S. —Since I wrote the letter on the other side, I find upon conversation with Gen. Lincoln that if the pay rolls of the militia should not happen to be ready when he passed through Williamsburgh, that it would not be in his power to order payment, as he could not delegate his authority — Therefore, I proposed the inclosed resolve which I hope will remove all difficulty.
farewell.

His Excellency, PATRICK HENRY.

MARINE COMMITTEE TO WILLIAM SMITH [1]

MARINE COMMITTEE,
SIR   PHILADELPHIA October 24ᵗʰ 1778

We have received your Letter of the   insᵗ informing the arrival of the Schooner Swan at your Port. As you have already shipped the Flour that remained in your care on board a Vessel for Boston, and the Captain of the Swan does not relish proceeding to Sinepuxent to take in what flour & Iron remains there, we have directed the Commissary General of Purchases to give immediate orders for a lading of flour at your port or any other place in Cheseapeake Bay that may be more convenient to the Magazines — You will order the Captain to proceed where he may be directed to take in his Cargo.

In our last we wrote you to send your Accounts, and now request you will do so as soon as you can — please to particularize the quantities shipped in each Vessel and what remains at Sinepuxent. We must request you to take bills of lading and Invoice for the flour now to

[1] L. S. by Richard Henry Lee as Chairman, with a postscript in the autograph of Lee signed by him as Chairman. Pennsylvania Historical Society, Etting Collection. Smith was a Member of Congress and lived in Baltimore.

be Shipped in the Swan and send the same to the Navy
Board at Boston
 We are Sir

Your Obed^t Serv^{ts}.

P.S. We are just now well informed that a frigate
and two or three small armed Vessels of the Enemy are
cruising in Chesapeake Bay which have taken some
private Vessels with flour bound to the Eastward. This
renders it necessary that the Swan should not be dispatched until you know the Bay to be cleared of the
enemies Cruisers, but as quickly after as possible.

24th Octr 1778
WILLIAM SMITH Esqr.

TO [ARTHUR LEE][1]

MY DEAR BROTHER,   PHILADELPHIA, Oct. 27. 1778.

The Marquis Fayette left us today for Boston where
he is to embark — This letter will follow him with our
Dispatches. I wish that a true friendship may take
place between you and the Marquis, because I discern
in this young Nobleman those principles that I think
cannot fail to render him a great Man. And his virtue
is such as will make him superior to all those mean and
selfish considerations which mark too many. . . .[2]

Will it not be well, besides taking other wise precautions, to speak to the[3] with the candor, firmness,
and sincerity, on this subject, that becomes a Man
concerned in the welfare of his Country — The whole
tribe of wicked ones at Passy and all their Coad-
jutors will be employed in this nefarious business —

[1] Ms. copy. Virginia Historical Society, Transcripts from the
Leffingwell Collection.
[2] Two short paragraphs, partly in cipher, are here omitted.
[3] A word in cipher is here omitted.

But a sensible and virtuous Minister will esteem the integrity of a Man who faithfully discharges his trust by seeing and pursuing the interest of his Country, in the Station you have been in. The wickedness of Deane & his party exceeds all belief, and must in the end fail them notwithstanding the Art with which they clothe themselves — The wicked and some weak can alone support them — No Man knows better than Deane how to avail himself of the glare cast around him by the favor of the Great, which mere circumstances not his merit or his virtue have procured him. This Wretch would rise upon the ruin of the first, the finest, & most uniform friends of this Country and of France. But I trust all his Manœuvres will fail him. If you have time it may be well to give his papers to Congress, which are now sent you, a well considered and well established refutation — I can detect, as I read it, numerous falsehoods & sophistry —

Give my respects to Mr. Izard & tell him [I] greatly admire his spirit & good sense. Remember what I have written you about Ludwell, my bark, & spectacles. Let the Alderman know that his affairs at Green Spring are under the care of an able Stewart.

I am most sincerely & affectionately yours.

P.S. I hope our affairs in Spain have eer this taken so favorable a turn that you will be presently repairing to that Court. The affairs of finance have, with other adventitious business so engrossed us that we have not yet been able to take up our foreign Affairs, which will presently be done upon a large Scale. I am going to Virginia in a few days, and expect our brother Frank here to take my place.   farewell.

THE LETTERS OF RICHARD HENRY LEE

TO [JOHN ADAMS][1]

My dear Sir.   PHILADELPHIA Oct–29 1778

I am exceedingly happy to hear of your arrival, and I
hope agreeable accommodations at Paris. At first I
doubt not, the splendid gaity of a magnificent Court,
accorded not so well with the temperate manners of a
sober Republican. But use reconciles most things.
It may soon happen that you be desired to visit Holland,
where I believe they yet retain much of that simplicity
of manners which first raised that people to greatness.
Our finances want the support of a Loan in Europe.
81,500,000 of dollars with increasing demands as depreciation advances with emission, cannot be cured by the
slow working of Taxes. The latter is I believe deeply
gone into by all the States. I have seen your letter to
our common friend Mr S. Adams, and do most thor
oughly accord with you in sentiments. The battle of
Monmouth in June last, and the subsequent arrival of
Count d'Estaing has kept our enemies in pretty close
quarters this Campaign at N. York — The better opinion is that they mean shortly to abandon that City. But
where they intend next, we are at a loss to guess. Indeed
they have such a choice of difficulties, that it is not an
easy matter for themselves to determine what course
they shall steer. Never did Men cut a more ridiculous
figure than the British Commissioners have done here.
Their last effort is a formal application to each State,
and to all the people in each, by a Manifesto sent in
Flags of Truce. We consider this as a prostitution of
the Flag, and have recommended the seizure and imprisonment of the people, and the publication of their
Manifesto. In some instances the Sea has saved us

[1] Adams Papers. Copy from the original furnished through the
courtesy of Mr. Charles Francis Adams.

the trouble by previously swallowing up these silly Missives. I shall be at all times extremely glad to hear from you, being very sincerely dear Sir your affectionate friend.

TO GENERAL [WILLIAM] WHIPPLE [1]

DEAR SIR,   PHILADELPHIA Oc'r 31 1778

On principles of old acquaintance and much regard, I should have been well pleased to have had the pleasure of seeing you here before my return to Virginia.[2] It will give me much satisfaction in my retirement to hear from you when your leisure will permit. The long evenings that are coming on will present you with opportunities of informing a friend how things proceed here. Let me know how my friend Mr. Langdon does. As I hope you will be closely employed this winter in forming plans for the increase and regulation of our Navy, it will make me happy to hear that you are proceeding well, and harmoniously in that line. My direction is at Chantilly, to the care of the Post Master at Leeds Town in Westmoreland County, Virginia —
I am dear sir sincerely yours.

[1] Transcript. Pennsylvania Historical Society, Langdon Collection. Addressed to him as "of the New Hampshire Delegation/to Congress."
[2] Whipple did not appear in Congress till November the 4th. For his reply, see R. H. Lee, *Memoir of Richard Henry Lee*, I. 216. Lee had impaired his health by arduous committee service and left Congress on November 3 with leave of absence.

THE LETTERS OF RICHARD HENRY LEE

TO SIR JAMES JAY[1]

DEAR SIR,   PHILADELPHIA Nov! 3. 1778

Your favor of October the 20th is put into my hands just when I am upon the point of setting out for Virginia, and therefore you may suppose me not so well circumstanced for giving you such an answer as I could wish. I esteem Sir, a cooperation with you in bringing to detection and punishment the plunderers of the public as being honorable to myself and useful to the Community I believe upon the whole, that this Country has suffered more from its pretended friends, than from its open enimies.

Such has been the variety and importance of the business before Congress, that neither the affairs of Car—m—l[2] or D—e[3] are yet finished.

[4]The delay producing the powers of some men,[5] the destruction of time under pretext of order, and by long confident speeches, that I have never seen less business done in any Assembly than has been with us the last six or eight months. Mr. Izard has written to Congress complaining most heavily of D—e[3] and F——n[6] There appears to me to have been great misconduct, but I hope time and attention will discover and rectify all.[7] It is my sincere opinion that with your powers, and your knowledge of facts, you can cause such instructions to

[1] A. dr. L. University of Virginia, Lee Papers, No. 265. Jay, knighted in 1763, was a physician in New York and instrumental in the passage of the New York act of attainder, and in raising money for Kings College.
[2] [William] Carmichael.
[3] [Silas] Deane.
[4] The words "Such are" are here erased.
[5] The words " and such " are here erased.
[6] [Benjamin] Franklin.
[7] The words " To effect this " are here erased.

be given your Delegates to Congress as will more certainly and speedily effect this, than can by any other means be done —

You wish to know how your Delegates have acted in this affair and whether they were for the Viva Voce narrative. Amidst the variety of questions that are propounded in Congress it is not easy to remember what part particular Members take, nor do I recollect whether or not M.ʳ Lewis was present but as well as my memory serves me I think your State was against the written Narrative and for its being Viva Voce. That matter is a thing determined, and therefore I am at liberty to answer your questions as well as I am able on that point, but many other subjects of your enquiry I could answer to your satisfaction if I were not restrained by the rules of the house respecting unfinished affairs — That large sums of money have been expended in France is indubitable, that no adequate account is yet obtained is certain; and to me the reasons for its not being so are by no means satisfactory — He who undertakes public business without competency is culpable and a capable Man will at all times be able to shew satisfactorily how his business has been conducted even to the greatest minutiæ. It is an insult on common sense to produce a Bankers charge of money issued, to account for the expenditure of Millions, during the transactions of near a year and an half. We have a letter written by Cunninghame (who commanded the Cutters fitted at Dunkirk, and which have cost the public more than 100,000 Livres) complaining heavily for himself and his people of finding them [1] the Commander of a private Armed Vessel, when he & they conceived themselves in the service of the U. S.

---

[1] Substituted for " himself " erased.

THE LETTERS OF RICHARD HENRY LEE

TO [PATRICK HENRY][1]

MY DEAR SIR,   CHANTILLY Nov.[r] 15th 1778

I send you by this opportunity the trial of Gen. Lee,
which be pleased to let our friends Col.[o] Mason, M[r]
Wythe, and M[r] Jefferson see, after you have read it. I
will not anticipate your judgement, the thing speaks fully
for itself. In my public letter to you, I observe that the
enemy still continue at N. York. Their reason for so
doing is not obvious. Their exposure to almost certain
destruction destruction in the West Indies, their exceeding weakness in every part of the world where they have
possessions, seems to demand their quitting us for other
objects, and this I should suppose they would do if their
hopes were not sustained by other causes than the expectation of conquest by force of arms. Division among
ourselves, and the precipice on which we stand with our
paper money, are, I verily believe, the sources of their
hope. The former is bad, but the latter is most seriously dangerous! Already the continental emissions
exceed in a sevenfold proportion the sum necessary for
medium; the State emissions added, greatly increase the
evil. It would be well if this were all, but the forgeries
of our currency are still more mischievous. They
depricate not only by increasing the quantity, but by
creating universal diffidence concerning the whole paper
fabric. In my opinion these Miscreants who forge our
money are as much more criminal than most other
offenders, as parricide exceeds murder. The mildness
of our law will not deter from this tempting vice. Certain death on conviction seems the least punishment that
can be supposed to answer the purpose—I believe most
nations have agreed in considering and punishing the

[1] A. L. S. Lenox Library, Myers Collection, "Distinguished Americans," 658. A printed text is in W. W. Henry, *Patrick Henry*, II. 10.

contamination of money as the highest crimes against Society are considered and punished. Cannot the Assembly be prevailed on to amend the law on this point, and by means of light horse to secure the arrest, and punishment of these Offenders, with! giving them the opportunity to escape that now they flatter themselves with. I hope Sir you will pardon my saying so much on this subject, but my anxiety arises from the clear conviction I have that the loss of our liberty seems at present more likely to be derived from the state of our currency than from all other causes — Congress is fully sensible of this, and I do suppose, that in order to detect forgeries and reduce the quantity, it will be requested of all the States to call into the Loan Offices the Continental emissions previous to april last, by compulsory laws — This is a bold stroke in finance, but necessity, and experience in the Eastern States, sanctify the measure. The next cause that threatens our infant republics, is, division among ourselves. Three States yet refuse to Confederate, Maryland Delaware, & Jersey — Indeed N. York can scarcely be said to have confederated since that State has signed with this condition, to be bound in case all the States confederate. Maryland, I fear will never come in whilst our claim remains so unlimited to the westward. They affect to fear our power, and they are certainly envious of the wealth they suppose may flow from this source — It is not improbable that the secret machinations of our enemies are at the bottom of this — Some of the most heated Opponents of our claim, say that if we would fix a reasonable limit, and agree that a new State should be established to the Westward of those limits, they would be content to confederate. What do you think Sir of our proposing the Ohio as a boundary to the Westward, and agreeing that the Country beyond sh^d b[e]^1 settled for common good and make

^{1} This and the other bracketed letters are covered by a patch.

a new State on condition that compensation reasonable should be made us for Dunmores, Col? Christians, and our late expedition. This might perhaps be agreed to and be taken well as coming freely from us. When we consider the difficulty of republican laws and government piercing so far from the seat of Governmen[t] and the benefit in point of œconomy from having a frontier State to guard us from Indian wars and the expence they create, I cannot help thinking that upon the whole this would be our wisest course. We should then probably unmask those who found their objection to Confederacy upon the extensiveness of our claim, and by having that bond of Union fixt foreclose forever the hopes of our enemies[.] I have a prospect of paying my respects to you and the Assembly between this and Christmas, if the distracted state of my plantation affairs can soon be put in reasonable order. I am, with sincere affection and esteem, dear Sir your most obedient humble Servant.

TO GENERAL [WILLIAM] WHIPPLE [1]

My dear Sir,   Chantilly Nov'r 29ᵗʰ 1778

I thank you sincerely for your obliging favor of the 8ᵗʰ instant which I received a few days past Nothing can be more pleasing to me in my retirement than to hear from my friends, and the pleasure will be increased when they inform me that the Vessel of State is well steered and likely to be conveyed safely and happily into port. My clear opinion is that this good work must be chiefly done by the Eastern Pilots.

[1] Transcript. Pennsylvania Historical Society, Langdon Collection. Addressed to him as, "Member of Congress at Philadelphia." A transcript with omissions and variations is in Harvard University Library, Sparks Mss., LII. ii. 220.

They first taught us to dread the rock of despotism, and I rest with confidence on their skill in the future operations. I venerate Liberty Hall, and if I could envy its present inhabitants anything it would be the sensible sociable evenings they pass there. I have not yet been able to quit the entertainment of my prattling fireside, when I have heared every little story and settled all points, I shall pay a visit to Williamsburg where our Assembly is now sitting. Mrs. Lee remembers her friends from the East with great respect, and returns you thanks for the kind interest you are pleased to take of her. Before this reaches you, I hope your labors in the Hall will have put the finishing hand to our important business of finance — If our money matters were once in a good way, we should have the consent of our wise and cautious friend Mr. Sherman to the pushing forward with Zeal the Navy of the United States — An object in my opinion of great magnitude. I may be mistaken but I have thought our Sensible friend rather too cautious upon this head. A well managed force at Sea would not only make us very respectable, but presently repay its cost with interest. We shall surely err by reasoning from what has happened to what will happen because we have till now singly opposed our feeble force on the Sea to the overgrown power of Great Britain — But now, our Marine force, under the supporting wing of our great and good Ally will thrive I hope, and grow strong upon the spoils of our Common foe. I wish the Marine Committee may stoutly contend against all opposition, and vigorously increase the Navy. In favor of this System we may say that the wealth and glory of many States have been obtained by their Fleets, but none have immediately lost their liberty thereby. Let the Man be produced who can truly say as much of Standing Armies. I left my worthy Colleague of the Marine Committee

well disposed to relieve us this winter from the depre-
dations of Gutride's fleet of Pirates, which infests
the Coast extremely from New York to Cape Fear —
They not only injure our Commerce greatly in these
middle States, but they prevent in great measure the
water communication between us and our Eastern
friends. This fleet consists of one brig of 16 guns, a
Schooner of the same force a Sloop of 12 guns, and the
rest of little strength —. Whilst your Northern Seas are
too tempestuous for cruising, this Southern Coast supplied with such convenient Harbors, may be visited by
the Continental Frigates, making Chesapeak Bay
their place of Rendisvous, to the exterpation of these
Sea Banditti that disturb us so much at present. A
stroke * * * of this sort would do credit to our Committee, and serve the Common cause. If the Frigates
came 3 or 4 together, they would be ready for any small
British force that might accompany the Gutridges.
The fortifications of Portsmouth, Hampton & York,
will afford them a sure asylum against any Superior
force. Remember me with affection to the Society at
Liberty Hall, to my friends of Connecticut, R. Island,
Jersey, Pensyln'a & Delaware. I fancy this is as far
as I can Safely go, unless I were to admit the good old
President.

I sincerely wish you happy.

TO MONSIEUR GERARD [1]

SIR   CHANTILLY IN VIRGINIA 13 Dec.er 1778.

I have heard with great pleasure of the dispersion of
Admiral Byron's fleet, the loss of the Somerset and

[1] Paris, Ministère des Affaires Étrangères, Correspondences Politiques, États-Unis. Vol. 5, No. 119 (fols. 317–318). "Copie d'une
lettre de M. Richard Henry Lee, à M. Gérard datée de Chantilly en
Virginie le 13 X.b 1778." Minister of France to the United States.

the sailing of M. Le Count d'Estaing On all which happy events, I beg leave to have the honor of congratulating you.

These things present to my hopes two good consequences the future success of the Count and the reduction of that proud power which has so long and so injuriously triumphed at sea. I assure you, Sir, that I shall always revere his M. C. M? and esteem the french nation for the wise and generous aid we have received for the security of our independence and the happiness of my country.

France has now the honor Sir, to lead other nations in philosophy, and to be far above all in the best branch of it, the philosophy of humanity. Such wisdom and generosity cannot fail to be attended with correspondent effects, preeminent greatness.

The late last supply of provisions sent to Antigua denotes the enemies opinion that the West Indies will in future be the seat of war: I hope the aid of his. C. M. I. will be an additional means of frustrating every plan of defence that our enemies may form in that quarter.

As my wishes for your health are very sincere so it will give me pleasure to hear that you are perfectly recovered from the indisposition that afflicted you when I left Philadelphia

I have the honor to be with sentiments of the highest esteem and regard, Sir, your most obedient and humble servant.

THE LETTERS OF RICHARD HENRY LEE

TO THE PRINTER OF THE PENNSYLVANIA GENERAL ADVERTISER [1]

[December 16, 1778.]

I have just read in your paper of december the 5th a long libel signed Silas Deane, but I have read it with that composure that ever attends a good conscience, and that satisfaction which arises from an additional proof that I have well done my duty as a servant of the public. Had the latter not been the case, had I winked at all information of public abuse, I do not think that I should [have] [2] incurred Mr. Deanes censure. But whilst I am [honored] [2] with public trust it shall be my constant endeav[or to] prevent the community from being injured, and c[ertainly] [2] to insist that those who have fingered large sums [of the public] [2] money should be called upon for fair and honest settlement. From the first origin of Congress to the present day, I have been constantly a Member of that body, and I can safely appeal to every gentleman with whom I have served, and to all who know me in private life, whether I have yielded to any of my Colleagues in zeal for the American cause, and industry to promote its success. Whether thro the various stages of prosperity and adversity my sentiments and conduct have not been uniformly warm for the freedom happiness, and independence of my Country. That the Alliance with France has been my constant wish and hope no man who knows me will deny, and those gentlemen of that country with whom I have had business can bear me witness of of my attention and re-

---

[1] A. dr. L. S. University of Virginia, Lee Papers, No. 268. The address and text from the asterisk to the end are in autograph. A duplicate, with minor differences, wholly in autograph is in the same collection. A copy was printed in the *Virginia Gazette* of January 1, 1779.

[2] Ms. damaged.

457

gard to their affairs. With such unvarying conduct and sentiments when I had not a pulse but beat to independence, and with a mind filled with reverence and gratitude for France in consequence of her wisdom and goodness in allying with us, it seems hard to be attacked by an innuendo man for sinister designs in favor of a detested enemy against a good and able friend. But the case of Berkenhout is the foundation whereon this calumny rests. A worse foundation was never given to an abominable superstructure. It has already been related in a former paper, how I came to know that such a man was in America. The truth is that I was a total stranger to him. And when I received a letter from Gen. Maxwell informing me that such a person had been with him, it was some moments before I could recollect the name, having only heared Dr. Lee say ten years ago that he was the author of a good pharmacopea, a person with whom he [was]¹ acquainted, and who was a man of parts. I then immediately [read]¹ the letter to Congress and informed them what I knew of Dᴿ [Berk]¹ enhout, which is as above related. Soon after this he arrived in [town an]¹d sent me a ticket to know when he should wait on me. [Being]¹ at dinner, when we arose from Table, I asked an honorable [memb]¹er of Congress (Colᵒ Scudder of New Jersey) to walk with me to [see him]². We went and after some general conversation, he asked me if I had received any letter from Dᴿ Lee concerning him. I answerd no, he appeared concerned, and imputed it, as my memory serves me, to his having left England too soon after requesting such introductory letter. This is a strong circumstance against the supposition that he brought letters for me; for if he had, why not then produce them. He brought neither letter nor letters for me, nor carried any from

¹ Ms. damaged.
² Ms. damaged, but the reading is confirmed by the duplicate.

me, altho both are insinuated. The next day, I think, he came to my lodgings and informed me that his intention in coming to America was to provide a settlement for his family in a land of liberty, and to find a place where he could practice physick to advantage, on which subjects he asked my advice. I gave him the best in my power, and I promised to introduce him to the Delegate of Massachusetts that he might be informed whether Bos[ton affor][1] ded a good opening for a physician. I did so, as these gentlemen know and finished the afternoon by walking round a [square or two][1] of the Town and parted. After this I never [saw D! Berkenhout but][1] a few minutes in company [with other gentlemen in a public ro][1]om. I do declare upon the [honor of a Gentleman][1] and the [faith][1] of a Christian, that I had not the most distant cause to suppose that he had other views in coming to America than those already mentioned, which he related to me as the true ones. In all his conversation, which was sensible, he discovered strong attachments to America, and to confirm this opinion of him he gave me a pamphlet as written by himself and published in England in 1777 which strongly contended for the independence of North America. From once reading this pamphlet I thought it well written, and I believe it is now in the hands of a Member of Congress to whom I lent it — In this situation of things, it may be easily imagined that I was surprised at a publication in the Advertiser stating Dr. Berkenhout and Mr. Temple as Ministerial Agents from a newspaper publication in England. This I understood procured the arrest of the former. How long he remained in prison, when, and how he was discharged I am an utter stranger to. It is certain that his conduct and conversation had strongly impressed my mind with a belief of his attachment to our cause, and as a friendless stranger too, it is

[1] Ms. damaged, but the reading is confirmed by the duplicate.

not to be wondered at that I expressed favorable sentiments of him whenever he was m[enti]¹ oned in conversation. If I think a man innocent, and [believe]¹ him to be a friend of America, it appears to me both unjust [and]¹ ungenerous not to say so, when I see him oppressed. Give [me]¹ satisfactory proof that any man willingly injures, and is an enemy to the interest and independence of America I am from that moment his enemy. It is said by M: Deane that D: Berkenhout was sent back with the knowledge he had been able to collect — I am at a loss to discover what collection injurious to us he could have made in Jail, for I believe he was but a few days at large, and in a City where he was very little known. But it seems that D: Berkenhout has said that by the Alliance with France, America was at liberty to make peace *without consulting* her Ally unless England declared war, and it is as confidently asserted that I have constantly and pertinaceously maintained this doctrine. Innuendo, that D: Berkenhout got this² information from me. I absolutely deny having ever conversed with him on any such subject, and I do as positively deny having ever maintained that America had a right by the Alliance to make [p]³ eace *without consulting* her Ally if England did not [dec]³ lare war. I know that war may be made without [de]³ claring it, and I have both within and without doors said, that if England would acknowledge the independence of America and not resent the part that France had taken, America was at liberty to make a similar treaty with England or any other Nation. And I should be glad to know if the Ministers of France have not made like declarations to the Courts of London & the Hague? Was not the fact so? But there is no bound to disingen-

---

¹ Ms. torn, but the reading is confirmed by the duplicate.
² The word "doctrine" here written upon the line is erased.
³ Ms. damaged.

uous and malevolent interpretation, nor to the dark work of innuendo and evil insinuation. I am to ask pardon of the public and of you Mr Dunlap for having said so much on so frivolous an occasion. But I have such deep respect for the public opinion, and such desire not to be misunderstood or disesteemed by one worthy Man in the United States, that I shall not regard my trouble if I prevent a single honest, [frie][1]nd of America from being imposed on.

For the curious charges brought by Mr Deane against Wm Lee and Dr Lee, he will be called to answer at another time and in another place. For the present I can say, that from a very intimate acquaintance with those gentlemen, and from their uniform public conduct so far as the same has come to my knowledge, I know them to be devoted to the cause of America. That they have made great sacrifices to this cause, and that their hopes rest alone upon its success. That their present political appointments did not arise from the solicitation of themselves or their relations, but from their known public and private attachment to their native Country and its liberties. Mr Deane talks much about his great services and good conduct, but how happens it that of four Commissioners besides himself three are so clear and so strong in reprobating that [con]duct[2].

---

[1] Ms. damaged.

[2] In the other draft occurs the following: "conduct? Nor are these the only men that have done so, as I shall make appear hereafter. I cannot help concluding this hasty narrative with cautioning my Countrymen against the present industrious art of our enemies practiced in order to create doubts concerning the character of the firm invariable [fri]*ends to our glorious cause, and to throw the public councils of America into confusion and contempt. But I trust it will be as effectually baffled by the virtue of America as their other Arts have been whether of force or fraud.

RICHARD HENRY LEE."

* Damaged.

And these three known friends of America, and two of
them having good [1] ~~But more of this in due time.~~
Nor are these three Commissioners the only persons
that have done so in France. But more of this hereafter.
I [cannot help][2] concluding this Narrative with cautioning my Countrymen against falling in with the present
Arts of the Enemy who are endeavoring by every means
to traduce in every part the most uniform and firm
friends to our glorious cause, and to throw the Councils
of America into confusion and contempt. But I trust
this their last hope will, with their other arts be frustrated by the wisdom of America.

Virginia 16 dec.[r] 1778.

TO [HENRY LAURENS][3]

CHANTILLY IN VIRGINIA   December 26. 1778

DEAR SIR,

I returned from Williamsburg yesterday evening to
this place where I found myself honored with your favor
of the 15th instant, for which be pleased to accept my
thanks. I should much regret your quitting the Chair,
if I were not certain that your able services on the floor
will greatly avail the public. Pardon me Sir for expressing the honest dictates of a mind that has been
attentively observing men and things for some years
past. Since I had the honor of your acquaintance I
have expected great public advantages from your ability,
and virtuous attachment to the American cause, a cause
to which, sacrificing every consideration of private and
very dear interests, I have long since devoted myself.

[1] Omission. This partial sentence is inserted above the line in
the Ms.

[2] Ms. stained.

[3] Transcript. Long Island Historical Society, Laurens Correspondence, No. I. c. Endorsed, "Recd not till the 9th of febry —"

Of all the pervertions which the wicked heart of man is capable of, I never expected to be charged with that which more than any other my soul abhors. A coalescence with our enemies against our friends. You Sir, have rightly termed M.ʳ Deanes publication a "pernicious and und [*sic*] unproked libel" The Congress is possessed, on paper and in memory, of facts that absolutely disprove the greater part of it, and of course divests of credit the remainder, which rests solely on assertion, and calumnious innuendos. M.ʳ W.ᵐ Lee is charged with remaining inactive in France because he apprehended mischief to his private affairs. M.ʳ Deane knows perfectly well that the cause of this inactivity was the injurious and culpable detention from M.ʳ Lee of his appointment to the commercial Agency. Of this, M.ʳ Lee complained to Congress in a letter laid before them at York in Oct.ʳ or Nov.ʳ last, which produced the resolution that the Commissioners should have power to displace any Agent acting improperly &c. I think my brother Frank can shew you the copy of a letter from M.ʳ Ross to M.ʳ Deane at Paris, which confirms this fact and puts the matter in the clearest point of view. With respect to the delay in going to Vienna, M.ʳ Deane knows that he approved of M.ʳ Lee going first to Nantes after the death of M.ʳ Tho.ˢ Morris to arrange the public commercial affairs, and you know Sir that both M.ʳ Izard & M.ʳ Lee have complained that the money necessary to defray their expences was long witheld, and M.ʳ Deane was one of the Withholders. These, with other public reasons, detained M.ʳ Lee & M.ʳ Izard. When M.ʳ Lee left London, he left his family, and almost the whole of his European fortune in posseesion of the enemy, yet willing [1] to risk all for the good of his native country and the cause he had so uniformly and publicky espoused, he was greatly chagrined to

[1] Blotted.

find himself, on coming to France, deprived of power to rectify the abuses he saw, because his appointment to the agency was withheld from him. But M! Lee is continued in the list of Aldermen, so is every person else under the old arrangement. The foolish pride of our enemies will not suffer them to suppose that any-thing[1] we have or can do will work a change. Besides is M! Lee answerable for what our enemies do, or do not? God forbid. So much for this part of the Libel, which going on, represents, that D! Lee, by a wanton display of his errand, gave great and just cause of distrust to the Court of Madrid, & he returned, having gone no further than Burgos. The former part of this Sentence is assertion without proof, and the latter part Congress knows to have arisen from the Court of Spain being then not in condition to break with England. But Congress also know, that the same Court, in that negotiation, agreed to assist us with money and stores, which has been done — See D! Lees transmissions to Congress on this subject. All this M! Deane knows as well as Congress. No man can answer for his doors and locks being forced, which the British Envoy pro-cured to be done at Berlin, but which the speedy applica-tion of D! Lee prevented him from profiting by, and threw him into disgrace at[2] that Capital. The number of injurious and scandalous insinuations of suspicions having fastened on D! Lee for being in the British interest &c, being unsupported by evidence, will not be regarded by any person of sense, justice, or candor. We need not refer to a letter supposed to be written by D! Lee on the day the Treaty was signed, for the means by which M! Fox gained his knowledge. My brother Frank can shew you copy of a certificate by which a M! Livingstone declares he read a letter in [Lon][3] don from D! Bancroft (whose hand he knew, and who is

[1] Blotted.　　[2] Written over other letters.　　[3] Torn.

the friend and Counseller of M.̱ Deane) which advised his Correspondent to push his speculations, for the Teaty (he had it from the best authority) would be signed the 5.ᵗʰ or 6ᵗʰ of Feb.̱. This letter from D.̱ Bancroft is dated, I think, soon in January. The libel supposes that M.̱ Deanes recall was founded on D.̱ Lee's transmissions to America. Congress knows that it was founded on the contracts made by M.̱ Deane with foreign Officers, and many of its Members know that I advocated M.̱ Deanes cause on that occasion, and upon the very principles that he has since defended himself. The truth is Sir, that until I returned to Congress in May last, I never had received a suggestion of any varience among the Commissioners, and then I got copies of M.̱ Lloyds of So. Carolina (then at Nantes, his letter[1] to D.̱ Lee, M.̱ Stephensons and M.̱ Thorntons letters to D.̱ Lee, informing him of M.̱ Carmichaels charges against M.̱ Deane, when the former was at Nantes in his way to America. The substance of which I laid before Congress, and copies of which letters are now in my brother Franks possession. The injury I thought done to the public from the account contained in these gentlemens letters, and from a variety of other circumstances, induced me to press for a settlement of M.̱ Deanes accounts, and to take the part I did in Congress. And it is this that has drawn on me the most ill founded and most improbable of all calumnies. A calumny which every part of my public and private life most pointedly contradicts. As well might it have been attempted to persuade the world, that part of it which knows me, that a Miser had leagued with a third person to rob himself of his beloved gold! M.̱ Deane is too vain in supposing that Providence had unfolded to him in particular the transactions in that affair. His providential relations were many of them

[1] Blotted.

465

immediately known to several persons. In ten minutes after I received Gen. Maxwells letter informing me of Berkenhouts arrival, I read it openly in Congress. Told them the Man was a perfect stranger to me— He applied to me as the brother of a person he had formerly been acquainted with. He told me a very plain story, and seemingly a very honest one concerning the causes of his coming here; which I have sent to the Philadelphia and Virginia Presses, the former of which I beg leave to refer you to. By our own rules persons coming to settle in America are not to be obstructed. And from every thing Dᵣ Berkenhout said to me I firmly believed his design was realy to fix among us with his family as the friend of this Country, and a detester of British tyranny. These are the sentiments I love, and no [wo]¹nder I expressed my favorable opinion of him, when a newspaper publication onl[y]¹ represented him in another light. I could not penetrate his heart to know his secret designs if he had any. If Mᵣ Deane knew any ill of the man, he was unpardonable in not communicating it immediately to the executive council. But he was waiting for the inspirations of Providence — Rediculous idea! The morning of the day that Dunlaps paper came out, mentioning from an English paper that Mᵣ Temple and Berkenhout were in Ministerial employment, the latter came into a public breakfasting room where I was, and I never saw him since. I have a great deal more to say upon the subject of this Seditious libel, but I will not trespass further upon your patience. No person can credit it, except my particular enemies, (and even they I believe do not) the enemies of America, and some who are disposed to believe stories because they are altogether incredible. The public interest and the honor of Congress makes it necessary that Mᵣ Deanes conduct and accounts should be thoroughly investigated, and

¹ Torn.

these his charges properly exposed. Bad as the season is, I will return to Philadelphia as soon as I can here get a warm suit of cloaths made, and the pains both of gout and rheumatism in my foot and shoulder permit. Travelling from Williamsburg in the Snow and extreme cold weather has injured my health, but whilst I live I will strain every nerve to secure the independence, interest, and happiness of my country against all attempts to the contrary. Permit me to admire the generous, Roman resolution you have made and declared "at the hazard of life fortune, and domestic happiness, to contribute, by every means to the perfect establishment of our Independence." I hope you will have many generous Minds to assist you in the noble work. And that you may meet with complete success may Heaven in its goodness grant. I am, with the greatest respect and perfect esteem, dear Sir your most obliged and most obedient Servant.